Before God's Wrath

Books by H. L. Nigro

Before God's Wrath:
The Bible's Answer to the Timing of the Rapture

The Everyday Evangelist:
Real-Life Tales of Sharing God's Truth in Ordinary
Circumstances

Do You Really Want to Self-Publish Your Book?

Before God's Wrath

The Bible's Answer to the Timing of the Rapture

Revised and Expanded Edition

By H. L. Nigro

Strong Tower Publishing
Bellefonte, PA

Strong Tower Publishing

P. O. Box 973

Milesburg, PA 16853

www.strongtowerpublishing.com

ISBN 0-9704330-7-7

Cover design by Wade Thompson

H. L. Nigro combines the studious analysis of a researcher with the inquisitive instincts of a reporter. What's most refreshing is that she's not motivated by the desire to be "right" about doctrine, but by her Berean devotion to serve the Word of God.

Mark Daniels
WFIL Talk Show Host
Philadelphia, PA

The author asks the question, "What does the Bible really say about the rapture?" The operative word is "really." And the author does not disappoint us. With clarity, insight, boldness, and grace, H. L. Nigro supplies the answer. Within these pages, the readers will not find speculation or sensationalism. However, they will find a powerful and convincing presentation for the chronological sequence of the Lord's Second Coming and its practical implications for the believer.

Marvin J. Rosenthal
Author, *The Pre-Wrath Rapture of the Church*
President
Zion's Hope, Inc. &
The Holy Land Experience

Before God's Wrath examines the timing of the rapture from a purely biblical standpoint. The book compares parallel passages in both the Old and New Testament to arrive at the order of the events to form a biblically sound interpretation of end-times prophecy. I can enthusiastically recommend this book for anyone who wants to understand what the Bible really says about the timing of the rapture.

Richard Deem
Volunteer Apologist, Reasons to Believe
Founder, Evidence for God From Science

There are so many prophecy books in the market today. It's rare to find a writer who shows as much scriptural evidence, interesting thoughts, grace for the opposing views, and passion for the subject as H. L. Nigro. *Before God's Wrath* is an important read for every Christian.

Dave Bussard
Author
Who Will Be Left Behind and When?

———————————

Before God's Wrath provides a clear, biblical presentation of the timing of the rapture of the Church. H. L. Nigro writes in a straightforward style that is neither too lofty nor too simplistic. All relevant passages are examined and the author provides many biblical and logical arguments for the prewrath rapture position. Rather than being purely academic, this book also shows that a proper understanding of the return of Christ is a critical component in living a life of faith. As the end times rapidly approach, I pray that *Before God's Wrath* will get a wide reading since it brings a message that is vital for the Church today.

Gary Vaterlaus
Instructor, Biblical Research and Education
Sola Scriptura
(Formerly The Sign Ministries)

Table of Contents

Appendixes

Chart Index

Acknowledgements

To my Jesus, for whom this book was written and without whom I can do nothing. To my husband, Tom, who has borne my years of single-mindedness on this topic with patience, prayers, and good humor. To my friend Michelle Graham, whose prayers and unwavering belief in this project gave me hope that people might actually want to read it someday. To my parents, Gary and Carolyn Tolliver, who served as a sounding board, who edited my copy, and especially my father, whose library of resources was used by the Lord to provide me with inspiration. To my friend Molly Joss, for her encouragement, support, and help in preparing the original files for the printer. To Marvin Rosenthal of Zion's Hope, whose scholarship undergirded my early research. To my grandmothers, Madge Tolliver and Mary Helen Whaley, whose incessant prayers opened many doors for me. To my pretrib pastor friend (who asked not to be named) whose library was opened to me during my research in hopes of convincing me of prewrath's error but, in fact, further assured me of its truth. To Pastor Tom Keinath, my former pastor at New Life Assembly of God in Lancaster, PA, now a professor at Central Bible College, who was my first sounding board for this manuscript. To Charles Cooper at Sola Scriptura, whose comments on the nearly completed draft stimulated me to new thinking and helped me to tie up loose ends. And a very special "thank you" to Gary Vaterlaus, instructor of biblical research and education at Sola Scriptura, who took the time out of his busy schedule, even as he relocated his family across the country, to provide additional insights and invaluable content to this revised edition.

Foreword

by Gary Vaterlaus

There are many precious biblical doctrines that are foundational to our Christian faith: the Trinity, the inspiration of the scriptures, the deity of Christ, the virgin birth, and salvation by grace, to name just a few. These are teachings of the Bible that we are to embrace and defend. What one believes in regard to these doctrines determines one's orthodoxy.

During the last 50 years or so, we have seen much of evangelicalism add another teaching to this list of "untouchable" doctrines. I speak of the teaching of the pretribulational rapture of the Church. For many, this doctrine has become the primary test of one's orthodoxy. To question it is to invite ridicule and assertions of ignorance, or worse, apostasy. In many circles, the authority of man has replaced the Bible as the source of truth. Well-known prophecy teachers are never questioned, and to do so is tantamount to questioning the truth of the Bible itself. Fictional books and movies have been received as "gospel truth" while the Bible is placed on the shelf.

While I believe that the scriptures are clear as to the timing of end-times events, and while there are certainly practical implications to the position one takes, the timing of the rapture is by no means a salvific issue. Nor is it to be a test of one's orthodoxy. It is indeed sad that the timing of the rapture has become a defining issue for many believers, churches, and even denominations. Certainly, there is a place for charity in the discussion of the rapture. I would hope that there is room for re-examining our views on this issue, as well.

The pretribulation rapture is by no means the final word on the subject, and as you will read in this volume, the position has many problems. The book that you hold in your hands is an examination of what the scriptures teach about the coming of Christ and the timing of the rapture. I encourage the reader to have an open mind and a prepared heart as they read this thought-provoking work. There may be some new ideas that challenge what you believe. That is a good thing. Just be sure to go back to the scriptures for your answers, for the Bible alone is our standard of truth.

> And now I commend you to God and to the word of His grace, which is able to build you up and to give you the inheritance among all those who are sanctified. (Acts 20:32)

Gary Vaterlaus
Instructor, Biblical Research and Education
Sola Scriptura

"But...! But...!"
Questions and Answers About the Prewrath Rapture and About This Book

Q: What are the differences between all of the different rapture positions anyway?

A: The Bible teaches that the cup of man's iniquity will one day be full, and God will return to judge the earth. The preparation for His return and the execution of His judgment on the wicked and rebellious world will occur over a seven-year period broken into three waves: the seal judgments, the trumpet judgments, and the bowl judgments, each with increasing intensity. At the end of this period, Jesus will ride forth at the Battle of Armageddon and claim His rightful throne. Before God pours out His wrath, however, the Bible promises that Jesus will rapture His Bride, the true and faithful Church, by whisking believers away to heaven.

The pretribulation rapture position teaches that God's wrath will start at the beginning of this seven-year period, a time that is commonly called the "Tribulation period." Therefore, it teaches that the rapture must occur before the "Tribulation" begins. The midtribulation rapture position teaches that God's wrath will begin sometime midway through the "Tribulation period"; therefore, the rapture will occur midway through this period, as well. The posttribulation rapture position teaches that God's wrath, and therefore the rapture, will occur at the end.

Recently, there has surfaced a new position, the prewrath position, which is the position taken by this book. Like the midtribulation position, it teaches that the rapture will occur midway through the seven-year "Tribulation" period, but instead of placing it at a nebulous midway point, the prewrath position places the rapture in a specific, well-defined position in the timeline of events—before the Day of the Lord, which contains God's wrath. It is my belief that this is the most scripturally accurate teaching and is the position taught by Jesus and the New Testament writers.

Q: Why do you pick on pretribulationism and not the other rapture positions?

A: Unlike midtribulationism and posttribulationism, which teach that believers will undergo some or all of God's end-times judgments, pretribulationism teaches that believers will be raptured before the seven-year "Tribulation" begins, leaving believers vulnerable and spiritually unprepared for the most dangerous time in history. While I disagree with the timing espoused by midtribulationists and posttribulationists, I am not as concerned about their conclusions because it is the Church's preparedness, not splitting doctrinal hairs, that is of greatest concern to me.

Q: From a scriptural standpoint, what's so wrong with pretribulationism?

A: It cannot be found in scripture. Even pretrib scholars admit that there is no direct scriptural evidence for this position. The error introduced by this approach can be found as early as in its name, the pre-*tribulation* rapture. There is no period in the Bible called "the Tribulation period." This time period is more correctly called the 70th Week of Daniel, from Dan. 9:24. Ultimately, the pretrib position presents a timing for the rapture that is different from what would be determined by the most natural, common-sense reading of the text. For the generation entering the end times, which I believe we may be, the practical consequences of this error could be serious.

Q: How can you go against what scholars have been teaching for 2,000 years?

A: I am not in conflict with theologians for the last 2,000 years. I am in conflict only with *some* theologians for the last 180 years. The pretribulation rapture position was developed only in the early 1800s, and there are a great many classic Bible scholars who have rejected this position in favor of other views.

Q: Why not just let scholars figure it out?

A: I believe that most of today's prominent pretrib scholars are godly men who sincerely believe that the pretrib position is correct. However, the Bible commands believers to test everything and hold fast to what is good (1 Thess. 5:21). This doesn't mean letting pastors or theologians do the thinking for us. It is the responsibility of every believer to test the teachings of men against the Word of God.

Q: Isn't the Church exempt from "the Tribulation"?

A: No. Scripture tells us that the Church is exempt only from God's wrath. God's wrath is contained in the Day of the Lord, which occurs after the opening of the sixth seal. The Great Tribulation coincides with the fifth seal, which precedes the outpouring of God's wrath.

Q: Isn't the Great Tribulation only for the Jews?

A: In Matthew 24, Jesus' disciples asked the question, "What will be the sign of Your coming, and of the end of the age?" In response, Jesus gave a specific list of end-times signs, including the Great Tribulation, that will precede His return. Many have suggested that His answer applies only to Israel since this question was asked prior to the creation of the Church. However, the disciples who asked this question were the same disciples who were to experience Pentecost. Jesus was talking to believers.

Q: Does this mean you believe that God's programs for the Church and for Israel are the same?

A: No. God made a covenant with Israel and He will fulfill this covenant with Israel. However, as a graft into the olive tree (Romans 11:17), the Church is part of God's plan. While that plan may be different, the time periods overlap.

Q: Paul says that we are not destined for wrath. Aren't the seals God's wrath?

A: No. God's wrath is part of the Day of the Lord, which does not start until after the opening of the sixth seal.

Q: Why would God make the Church go through judgments designed for Israel?

A: When Jesus returns, He is coming back for a Bride "without spot or wrinkle" (Eph. 5:27). Can we truly say that if He returned today, the entire body of believers could be described as "without spot"? The seals are a time of refinement by fire so that the Bride may be presented blameless before Him. While the Church may be *positionally* righteous before God, this is a far cry from being without spot.

Q: During the seal judgments, up to one quarter of the earth's population will be killed through bloodshed, disease, famine, and natural disasters. That's more than a billion people! God wouldn't do that to His children.

A: Why not? He has in the past and He will again. Throughout the Old Testament, God sent war, famine, drought, and plagues upon Israel to break His people of idolatry. I encourage those who make the "God wouldn't do that" argument to read Deuteronomy 28.

Q: If the Church will go through some of God's judgments in Revelation, why isn't the Church mentioned after Chapter 4?

A: It is. John just doesn't use the word "church." John only uses the word "church" to describe Jesus' warnings to *specific* bodies of believers, not to the Body of Christ as a whole. Therefore, the lack of the word "church" in later chapters cannot be used to argue that the Body of Christ won't be here during this time. In fact, the letters to the seven churches in Revelation 2 and 3 are strong indicators that the Church *will* be here during the first six seals. Jesus tells five of these churches to repent and tells six of them to overcome. For the reader, this leads to the natural question, "Overcome what?" Jesus immediately answers this question by describing the seal judgments.

Q: When John is called into heaven in Revelation 4, isn't this the rapture?

A: No. The context of Jesus' calling John up to heaven is to view the things that are "soon to take place." To suggest that John's ascent is symbolic of the rapture requires the reader to switch from a literal reading of the Bible to an allegorical one. Even many pretrib scholars agree that this is not the appropriate reading of this passage.

Q: Doesn't the Bible teach that we will be "kept from the hour of trial?"

A: Once we understand the biblical meaning of the phrase, "kept from the hour of trial," it becomes clear that it cannot be used to support the teaching that the Church will be raptured to prevent believers from entering the "Tribulation period," or more accurately, Daniel's 70th Week. Rather, it strongly supports the idea that the Church will be present during this time, but in the midst of it, God will supernaturally protect one group of believers, the Church of Philadelphia, His true and faithful Bride.

Q: Don't the letters to the six churches represent one true Church that will be raptured prior to the Tribulation and five false churches that will be here during the Tribulation?

A: Jesus never said that these were false churches. In fact, several of these churches are praised for their works, their adherence to sound doctrine, and their faithfulness. Although four of the six are told to repent of their sins, to hold fast, and to overcome, this is the same admonition given to believers of all ages, including ours.

Q: These letters were written to first century churches. Why do they apply to us?

A: It is true that these churches were actual first century churches. This is not, however, a good argument for dismissing these passages for us today. If we are going to make this assertion, we should also throw out all of the New Testament except the gospels, since these were also letters written to specific individuals or churches at the time. Moreover, we know that the letters are relevant for end-times churches because they contain specific end-times references. For example, Jesus tells the loveless and compromising churches that He will "come quickly"; the corrupt church He tells to "hold fast till I come"; and the dead church He warns that He will "come as a thief," a reference to 1 Thess. 5:2.

Q: Couldn't the letters to the churches refer to church ages, not to the Church as a whole?

A: To accept the "church age" teaching, one must reject a straightforward, normative reading of the Bible and accept an allegorical one. In addition, one must be willing to accept that the entire Body of Christ is the Church of Philadelphia: loving, sanctified, and ready to be taken up into heaven. As nice as this picture is, a realistic look tells us that this isn't the case.

Q: Doesn't the Bible teach that the Holy Spirit must be removed from the earth before the Antichrist can arise?

A: No. This argument comes from 2 Thess. 2:7: "He who now restrains will do so until He is taken out of the way...." However, the Holy Spirit's job is to teach, comfort, intercede, convict, guide, strengthen, sanctify, and regenerate, not to restrain from sin. Furthermore, Jesus said that He would send us a Helper, the Holy Spirit, to be a comfort and teacher to *all* believers, which means that He must be available to those who are saved after the rapture, as well.

Q: If we are supposed to look for the Antichrist as a sign, why didn't any of the New Testament writers tell us to do so?

A: Three of them did: Matthew, recording the words of

Jesus in Matt. 24:15; Mark, recording the words of Jesus in Mark 13:14; and Paul, writing in 2 Thess. 2:3–8.

Q: If you place the rapture between the sixth and seventh seals, aren't you contradicting Jesus' teaching that no one knows the hour or the day?

A: No. Jesus said that when we see the signs, we will know that our redemption "draws near." He made a similar point in the parable of the fig tree in Matt. 24:32–34. There will be a period following these events when believers will anticipate, but not be able to calculate, the return of the Savior.

Q: Doesn't the Bible teach that the rapture will be a silent event, known only to believers?

A: Scripture teaches that Jesus will return to earth in the same way that He ascended: in bodily form. He will come with a shout and a blast of the heavenly trumpet that draws our attention to the sky, where He will be visible to all. The dead in Christ will burst from their tombs and they, along with the living believers "who remain," will be caught up in the sky to be with Him forever. The Church will be whisked away all right, but the entire world will watch.

Q: But isn't Jesus' return at the rapture only a "partial" or spiritual return? Isn't His bodily return at Armageddon?

A: Jesus returns only once—to rapture His Church and pour out His judgment on an unrepentant world. Hence *the* Second Coming and *the* return of Christ. There is only one. Furthermore, every scriptural reference to His coming indicates that it will be in bodily form. "For the Lord Himself will descend from heaven with a shout, with the voice of an archangel, and with the trumpet of God. And the dead in Christ will rise first. Then we who are alive and remain shall be caught up together with them in the clouds to meet the Lord in the air" (1 Thess. 4:16). And, "Now, brethren, concerning the coming of our Lord Jesus Christ and our gathering together to Him..." (2 Thess. 2:1). There are many others.

Q: Doesn't the Bible say that the rapture will be a surprise? That it will come as a thief in the night?

A: No. The Bible teaches that the rapture will be a surprise only for the unbelieving world. Although Paul writes: "For you yourselves know perfectly that the Day of the Lord so comes as a thief in the night" (1 Thess. 5:2), two verses later, he clarifies for believers: *"But you, brethren, are not in darkness, so that this Day should overtake you as a thief.*" Paul clearly taught that the return of the Lord should *not* be a surprise to the Body of Christ. Jesus also gave us very specific signs to look for, including the rise of the Antichrist, the Great Tribulation, and the cosmic signs in heaven (Matt. 24:15–31, Mark 13:14–27, Luke 21:20–28). When we see these signs, Jesus said, "know that it [His return] is near—at the doors!" (Matt. 24:33).

Q: Aren't there multiple raptures?

A: When you take all of the rapture verses together, you can see that they each contain a set of very specific and consistent characteristics. If we take the Bible literally and normatively, we must see these as all the same —singular—event.

Q: The Bible says that Jesus will come at a time of peace and prosperity. Doesn't this put the prewrath rapture in contradiction with the Bible?

A: No. Jesus refers to His coming as being like the times of Noah, when people were eating and drinking, marrying and giving in marriage. His point wasn't that this was a time of prosperity. His point was that, in spite of Noah's warnings, the people of the earth were oblivious to the wrath to come. The parable of the foolish virgins tells us even more about the timing of His coming: that the bridegroom comes *at midnight, the darkest hour*, after the virgins have given up all hope of His coming. This doesn't sound like a time of prosperity and light.

Q: If the rapture occurs midway through the Tribulation, why don't we see the it described in Revelation?

A: This question exists for the pretrib rapture, as well. Nowhere in Revelation do we see a description of the actual rapture event. Immediately following the seal judgments, however, John describes a great multitude from all tribes, tongues, and nations that "come out of the Great Tribulation" (Rev. 7:9). This is an indirect reference to the rapture that occurred just a few verses earlier. The pretribulation position, on the other hand, either requires there to be no mention of the rapture in Revelation at all, or relies on Jesus' command to John to "Come up here" in Rev. 4:1 to symbolize this event.

Q: Your arguments rely heavily on the judgments of Revelation as being consecutive. Revelation is a very confusing book. How can you be so sure?

A: There are textual indicators—not the least of which is the ordering of each set of judgments from one to seven—that clearly indicate that the judgments are in consecutive order. These include unambiguous time references, such as "then," "after," and "after all these things," that indicate the order in which events occur. The well-defined structure of Revelation also bears strongly upon the consecutive nature of the judgments, as does the symbolism within it. This does not mean that all of the events in Revelation are consecutive, but the judgments themselves are.

Q: Aren't the seals an overview of the 70th Week?

A: The overview interpretation creates many contradictions of scripture. One of the most glaring is its contradiction with Joel 2:31, which describes the sun turning dark and the moon turning to blood "before the great and terrible Day of the Lord," which is the Old Testament (and New Testament) term for the time that God judges the ungodly and unrepentant world. This description is a near word-for-word correlation with the sixth seal. How can the sixth seal be *part of* the Day of the Lord, as the overview position contends, if Joel 2:31 tells us that it must *precede* the Day of the Lord? It cannot do both.

Q: If Jesus comes in bodily form for the Church after the sixth seal, then appears in bodily form again at Armageddon, doesn't He come twice?

A: No. The Bible tells us that there is only one Second Coming of Christ. The New Testament writers frequently used the Greek word *parousia* to refer to this event. *Parousia*, or "coming," has the meaning "to come and to stay; a continuing presence." Thus, Jesus returns only once and remains on earth during the administration of the judgments of the Day of the Lord. When the armies see Him at the battle of Armageddon, He is simply manifesting Himself in His rightful role, which He assumed on arrival—as King of kings and Lord of lords.

Q: If there are events that must occur prior to the rapture, doesn't the prewrath rapture destroy the idea of imminence as described in scripture?

A: The word "imminence" is never used in scripture. The Bible records an attitude of expectation, which is quite different from the "any moment" event that pretribulationists teach. According to *Webster's Dictionary*, the word *imminence* means "ready to take place, especially hanging threateningly over one's head." Because of the days in which we live, the return of Jesus is doing just that. In fact, we can say that His return is hanging more threateningly now than 100 years ago.

Q: When Jesus comes in Matthew 24, isn't this the same as His coming at Armageddon?

A: This is a very different event, with a very different set of identifying characteristics. There is no blast of the trumpet, no rising of the dead, and no deliverance of God's people. Jesus' arrival at Armageddon is for one purpose only—to defeat the beast and his false prophet. His physical return occurred much earlier, after the opening of the sixth seal when He raptured His Church.

Q: What practical value does this have for me today?

A: Jesus repeatedly referred to the end times as being like the days of Noah. The certainty of God's impending judgment gave Noah a boldness he would not have otherwise had, a willingness to risk everything to be obedient to the Word of God. If Noah risked all for the gospel because he knew the end was near, how much more burdened for souls should the end-times Church be? The prewrath rapture is also an exhortation to personal holiness. Only one church will be "kept from the hour," the loving church, the Church of Philadelphia. When Jesus comes, I want to be in Philadelphia.

Q: Why does all this matter anyway? Shouldn't we just be prepared for Jesus, whenever He comes?

A: If pretribulational rapturism is true, I would agree. But if pretribulational rapturism is false, the consequences will be serious. The majority of Christendom, expecting to be taken before the most devastating period in history, will be completely unprepared. Many could stumble, even perish.

Q: What if you are wrong?

A: It will be the best mistake I ever made. But more importantly, what if I'm right? Millions of believers will not be prepared for the most devastating and spiritually dangerous time in history. If there is going to be an error, I would rather it be mine.

Introduction

For most of my life, I took the pretrib rapture for granted. Jesus was coming back at any moment. I, my family, and my friends would be swept into the clouds silently and without warning, leaving the world wondering where millions of those crazy Christians went. I heard this "any moment" theory from the pulpits, on the television and the radio, and in the books I was reading. From what I could tell, no one around me questioned whether it was true. Then one day as I was reading Matthew 24, commonly called the Olivet Discourse, I realized that what I had been taught didn't match what I saw in the Bible. How could this be? How could a teaching so fundamental to Christian living be so different from what I saw in the scriptures?

So I began to investigate. I re-read the gospels. I re-read 1 Corinthians and 1 and 2 Thessalonians. I re-read 1 Peter and Revelation. I saw the rapture, all right, but I didn't see it pretribulationally. And I certainly didn't see the "any moment" timing that my church was teaching. I began to ask around, probing the thoughts of friends and family who were also students of the Bible. I was surprised to discover that many of them didn't think that what they were being taught matched what they read in the Bible either. As a firm believer in *sola scriptura*, this alarmed me, and studying this issue became the driving factor in my life for the next three years.

During the early part of this period, I did very little studying as to *why* so many people believed in the pretrib rapture. I just wanted to know *what* the Bible actually taught. As a professional business writer, I had written thousands of articles, market research studies, and other business documents, so I attacked this question the same way I would any other project, researching

1

thoroughly and methodically, reserving judgment until all the facts had been collected. Because I was concerned only with the facts, I did not start with commentaries or other writings that might bias me toward one conclusion or another. I spent nearly all of my time studying the Bible itself, with *Strong's Exhaustive Concordance* and its dictionaries of Greek and Hebrew words at my side. To my surprise, no matter what premise or scripture I started from, I ended with the same conclusion. This conclusion arose clearly, repeatedly, and without contradiction. And it wasn't pretribulational.

At that point, I began reading Marvin Rosenthal's *The Pre-Wrath Rapture of the Church*. This excellent book, published in 1990, opened my eyes to the fact that there was already a base of scholarly support for my growing understanding of the scriptures. This led me to the writings of Robert Van Kampen, author of *The Sign* and *The Rapture Question Answered: Plain and Simple*. Although these authors' roads to the timing of the rapture differed from mine, their conclusions were the same. They also gave me a label for the timing I saw in the Bible: prewrath.

During my first two years of study, I kept my ears and eyes open for information on the pretrib teaching. I asked a lot of questions, learning what I could about this doctrine's scriptural foundations. In popular treatments of this subject, I continued to find little or none. It wasn't until my third year of study, after my conclusions had been finalized, that I began reading studies by academic pretrib scholars. This became an interesting challenge for me. Could my understanding of the scriptures stand in light of the scholarship of these great men of God? Could the scholarship of these respected theologians really be wrong?

Prewrath: Standing the Test

First, I discovered that the pretrib rapture is a newcomer on the scene. I had heard Marvin Rosenthal say it, but now I heard pretrib scholars say it, too. Contrary to the common belief that the early church believed in a pretribulation rapture, the pretrib doctrine, with its "two-stage" return of Christ (a spiritual or "partial" return at the rapture, and a physical, bodily return at Armageddon), was developed by John Darby around 1830. It was adopted as a mainstream teaching only after it appeared in the *Scofield Reference Bible* in 1909. Thus, prewrath is not a reading of scripture in conflict with theologians for the last 2,000 years. It

2

is in conflict only with *some* theologians for the last 180 years.

Nor is the prewrath teaching new. Dr. Renald Showers, who holds to the pretrib position, has written that prewrath is "a variation of the midtribulation rapture and therefore is not actually new but a revision of an already existing position."[1] I would actually argue that most of the proof texts for the prewrath position agree with an even older position, the posttribulation position. Although prewrath's conclusions about the timing are different (that the rapture will occur after the midpoint of the "Tribulation period" but before the outpouring of God's wrath, rather than at the end, as held by posttribulationism), the scholarship supporting the interpretations of many passages is similar. Thus, if the test of time is to be used as the standard by which credibility is judged, it is not the prewrath position but pretrib that has the burden of proof.[2]

I also discovered that my non-pretrib stance shares company with many classic Bible scholars, including John Wesley, Charles Spurgeon, Matthew Henry, John Knox, John Hus, John Calvin, Isaac Newton, John Wycliffe, John Bunyan, and, most importantly, the Apostle Paul. In fact, with the exception of one brief reference in the fifth century, pretrib's belief in a two-stage return of Christ did not surface until after the first 1,800 years of church history.[3]

---

[1] *Maranatha! Our Lord Come! A Definitive Study of the Rapture of the Church* (Friends of Israel Gospel Ministries, 1995), p. 13.

[2] John Walvoord has argued vehemently against this assertion, claiming that modern posttribulationism, which is both posttribulational and premillennial, is actually younger than pretrib. I would disagree on the basis that, while many of the modern proof texts for the posttrib position are new, the position itself is not. Even Walvoord admits that many of the church fathers were posttribulational, and while he would like to trace the roots of pretribulationism to the church fathers, too, he can do so only by tying the biblical concept of expectancy to an "any moment" event. The fact that many church fathers believed in both imminence and posttribulationism, as Walvoord concedes, is a strong argument against his own interpretation.

[3] The claim that Ephraem the Syrian's sermon supports a pretrib rapture is a claim made by pretribulationists, but upon examination of the sermon, it actually supports a posttribulational rapture position. URLs are always changing, but text of the full sermon can be located by doing an

3

The more I studied, the more amazed I became, first at the lack of evidence for the pretrib position; then, at pretrib scholars' admission of such. Even top scholars like John Walvoord admit that there are no direct scriptural references for this position. In fact, Walvoord calls any attempts to find them "strained."[4] In contrast, the prewrath timing *is* based on direct scriptural references—lots of them. No straining necessary.

Finally, I discovered that many of the "radical" ideas I had formed were neither radical nor new. Most have been presented and argued by scholars for years. There was nothing new, for example, in my discovery that the rapture is the trigger event that ushers in the Day of the Lord. This is a view held by John Walvoord. There is nothing new in my suggestion that the events described in the Olivet Discourse are the same as the seals in Revelation. This is a view held by Renald Showers. There is nothing new in my contention that the rapture can be found in Matt. 24:31. This is a view held by Robert Gundry. Many scholars, of course, do not agree with me or even with one another. Walvoord and Showers, for example, disagree with many fellow pretrib scholars; the two men often disagree with one another; and both disagree with Gundry.

There are three things about the prewrath position, however, that *are* relatively new. First is the formal coining of the term "prewrath."[5] Second is this position's systematic placement of the rapture in the order of end-times events (this is not date-setting, since the order of events is not the same as the time). Third, and most important, is that this systematic presentation allows the scriptures to be read in their straightforward common sense meanings. With other timings of the rapture, many scriptures have to be "tweaked" or allegorized to fit into an eschatological (end-

---

Internet search using terms like "Ephraem" or "Pseudo-Ephraem" and "sermon."

[4] John Walvoord, *The Rapture Question: Revised and Enlarged Edition* (Zondervan Publishing House, 1979), p. 182.

[5] In recent years, the popularity of the prewrath teaching has led some to mistakenly apply the term to the seventh trumpet rapture, which places the rapture at the seventh trumpet, just before the bowls of God's wrath. These are different positions, with different timing and exegesis. The seventh trumpet rapture, which is really a posttribulational position, should not be included as part of classic prewrath.

times) framework. This tweaking varies from author to author. If the entirety of scripture could be described as Cinderella's glass slipper, the pretrib doctrine is a foot that is just a little too small and the posttrib and midtrib doctrines are feet that are just a little too big. But the prewrath timing is the foot that fits the glass slipper just right.

Now *that* is something new.

Prewrath, however, is *not a new interpretation of scripture.* The truth has been there since the completion of the New Testament canon, and I am convinced that many Christians already know it, even if they have not taken the time to research it themselves. Writes Robert Van Kampen:

> The prewrath position is not a 20th Century position. It was the position of Christ. It was the position of Paul. It was the position of Peter. It was the position of John. Even our Lord's revelation to Daniel refers directly to it....It was also the position of the early church fathers, including the *Didache, The Teaching of the Lord Through the Twelve Apostles,* which is perhaps the oldest commentary on the Olivet Discourse in existence today."[6]

How Can So Many Be Wrong?

So if prewrath is right, how can so many people be wrong? There are many periods in church history in which the dominant teaching was later shown to be in error. In the fourth century, for example, the Greek Church threw out the book of Revelation as noncannonical, and it stayed out for several centuries, only later to be restored. In the 16th Century, Martin Luther rebelled against the Roman Catholic Church by asserting that the Bible should be the only source of doctrine. He was branded a heretic and started the Protestant Reformation. In the early 20th Century, the dominant millennial theology was postmillennialism (the idea that the Kingdom of God will not be ushered in by the Second Coming of Christ but by the hand of man through the Church), but this was largely shattered by the horrors of World War I and World War II. To suggest that the current fad of pretribulationism is wrong is not

---

[6] Robert Van Kampen, *The Rapture Question Answered: Plain and Simple* (Fleming H. Revell, 1997), p. 206.

heresy. If pretribulationism is wrong, it would not be the first time that a prominent church teaching was in error.

But with so little scriptural support, what is the foundation of pretribulationism that has caused it to sweep through 20th Century evangelical churches? At its core, I believe it is preference. This is because despite the intensity with which this position is defended and the confidence with which it is promoted, it is impossible to find in the Bible itself. In my experience talking with most Christians who hold the pretrib position, they do so because it is what they have been taught, and when asked why they continue to believe it, even when presented with scriptural evidence of its error, most defend their beliefs based on *why* God wouldn't put us through any part of the "Tribulation," not *when* scripture says the rapture ought to be.

Swimming Against the Tide

As I did the research for this book, I found myself swimming against the tide. Many took offense to the fact that I would question the teaching of some of today's most highly esteemed scholars, not to mention thousands of churches, book authors, and television personalities. For this reason, the question of whether the average believer can be expected to reach a reasonable conclusion about the rapture became extremely important to me.

From a pretrib perspective, the answer to this question is "no." Pretribulationism requires complex analyses of Greek and Hebrew grammar from the original texts linked to the use of dispensational theology, a method of biblical interpretation taught in seminaries. Therefore, defense of the pretrib doctrine requires a level of education not available to the average believer. This, in itself, is a strong argument against this position. The Bible says that, with diligent study, all believers *can* and *should* discern all of the truth of scripture, which includes the timing of the rapture. Addressing all believers, 1 John 2:27 says: "You do not need that anyone teach you, but as the same anointing [of the Holy Spirit] teaches you concerning all things." Also, in 2 Tim. 2:15, "Be diligent to present yourself approved to God, a worker that does not need to be ashamed, rightly dividing the word of truth." Paul isn't telling Timothy that the meaning of God's Word is hidden between the lines for only scholars to find. Rather, he is suggesting that with diligence, all believers can understand the

6

truths that God is communicating.

Many Christians, however, are frightened by in-depth Bible study, saying, "I don't have the education to discern the deep truths of scripture." To these I would ask, "To whom was the Bible written?" Jesus' followers were a motley crew of fishermen, prostitutes, and tax collectors. They were the lost, the hurting, the downcast of society. They are those the late singer and songwriter Rich Mullins described as "the ragamuffin band." In fact, to those of great education, Jesus offered this warning: "I thank you, Father, Lord of heaven and earth, that you have hidden these things from the wise and prudent and have revealed them to babes" (Matt. 11:25). I am a strong proponent of in-depth study of the Bible. However, when a biblical interpretation can *only* be derived from specialized academic studies, and results in a teaching that does not agree with the plain meaning of the text, I believe this warning is well taken.[7]

In contrast, the prewrath position is straightforward, biblically consistent, and readily available for study in hundreds of direct scriptural references. This evidence is so abundant, in fact, that when I began to share the results of my investigation with others, I did not find myself trying to convince them of some new concept. I heard many exclaim, "That's what I thought! I just didn't know who to ask." This reinforces my belief that the study of the rapture is not something that should intimidate Christians. The ability to evaluate truth from error is within the grasp of every true believer.

With these thoughts in mind, I ask readers to give the prewrath view a fair hearing. At the same time, I also ask readers to test everything against scripture. For Paul commands us, "Test all things; hold fast what is good" (1 Thess. 5:21). While this

---

[7] I am not suggesting that pretrib scholars are deliberately twisting the common sense meaning of the text. After doing an in-depth study of pretrib scholarship, I understand how, by reading the scriptures with a pre-existing bias, one might overlook even the plainest meaning. Specialized translations of Greek and Hebrew words can give entire passages new meanings, and while these meanings often conflict with other passages, after enough years of scholarship, these passages have been, in the words of John Walvoord, "harmonized" with the pretrib view.

scripture applies to all areas of our lives, Paul was specifically talking about the return of Christ and the rapture of the Church. In other words, it is the responsibility of every Christian to test all of the teachings of men, whether friends, family, pastors, or television preachers, even authors like me, against God's infallible Word. I believe that, if we allow the Holy Spirit to guide us, we will eventually come to knowledge of the truth.

For God promises,

> If any of you lacks wisdom, let him ask of God, who gives to all liberally and without reproach, and it will be given to him. (James 1:5)

May the grace of our Lord Jesus Christ be with you all. Amen.

1

Why the Timing Matters

And I saw in the right hand of Him who sat on the throne a scroll written inside and on the back, sealed with seven seals. Then I saw a strong angel proclaiming with a loud voice, 'Who is worthy to open the scroll and to loose its seals?' And no one in heaven or on the earth or under the earth was able to open the scroll, or to look at it. So I wept much, because no one was found worthy to open and read the scroll, or to look at it. But one of the elders said to me, 'Do not weep. Behold, the Lion of the tribe of Judah, the Root of David, has prevailed to open the scroll and to loose its seven seals.' And I looked, and behold, in the midst of the throne and of the four living creatures, and in the midst of the elders, stood a Lamb as though it had been slain, having seven horns and seven eyes, which are the seven Spirits of God sent out into all the earth. Then He came and took the scroll out of the right hand of Him who sat on the throne. (Rev. 5:1–7)

As we passed the turn of the Millennium, believers began turning their thoughts more frequently to end-times events. The popularity of books, videos, and movies on prophecy and end-times themes has exploded. But there is danger. That danger is that the Church isn't ready for the most cataclysmic event in the earth's history—the rise of the Antichrist and the outpouring of God's fierce, righteous judgment on an unrepentant world. This is because the mistaken belief in a "pretribulation" rapture has led believers to think that this deliverance will occur prior to Jesus' opening of the seven seals. If Jesus does not come pretribulationally, as this book contends, this would leave them

9

unprepared for Satan's attacks during that time. Many could stumble, even perish.

Why is the rapture so important?

After Jesus' resurrection, He walked among His disciples and talked with the people of Galilee for several days. Then, at the appointed time,

> He was taken up, and a cloud received Him out of their sight. And while they looked steadfastly toward heaven as He went up, behold, two men stood by them in white apparel, who also said, "Men of Galilee, why do you stand gazing up into heaven? This same Jesus, who was taken up from you into heaven, will so come in like manner as you saw Him go into heaven." (Acts 1:9–11)

Earlier, Jesus Himself made this same promise to the disciples, telling them that, while He must go away for awhile to prepare a place for them in His Father's house, He would return for them and take them to be with Him forever (John 14:1–3).

Is Today the Day?

Two thousand years later, people are still staring into heaven, wondering if today is the day that Jesus will come again. For believers, this promise is a joyous one, for we will be changed in an instant, "in the twinkling of an eye" (1 Cor. 15:51–52) into new, glorified bodies suited to living forever with Him.

Truly, this moment will be a glorious one. Paul writes of it in his first letter to the Thessalonians:

> For the Lord Himself will descend from heaven with a shout, with the voice of an archangel, and with the trumpet of God. And the dead in Christ will rise first. Then we who are alive and remain shall be caught up together with them in the clouds to meet the Lord in the air. And thus we shall always be with the Lord. (1 Thess. 4:16–17)

For the rebellious and unbelieving world, however, this promise is a terrifying one. For when Jesus comes, it will not be as the suffering servant as at His First Coming, but as the King of kings and Lord of lords to judge and rule the nations.

10

Now out of His mouth goes a sharp sword, that with it He should strike the nations. And He Himself will rule them with a rod of iron. He Himself treads the winepress of the fierceness and wrath of Almighty God. And He has on His robe and on His thigh a name written: King of kings and Lord of lords. (Rev. 19:15–16)

In the day of His coming, the name of Jesus Christ will be vindicated throughout all the earth. It will be a time when unrepentant hearts will drink the wine of the wrath of God, which is "poured out full strength into the cup of His indignation" (Rev. 14:10). It will be a time of darkness, of complete and utter devastation. In both the Old and New Testaments, this is called "the Day of the Lord."[8]

Because of this Day's ferocity and purpose, it is also called "the Day of God's Wrath":

The great day of the Lord is near, it is near and hastens quickly. The noise of the day of the Lord is bitter; there the mighty men shall cry out. That day is a day of wrath, a day of trouble and distress, a day of devastation and desolation, a day of darkness and gloominess, a day of clouds and thick darkness, a day of trumpet and alarm against the fortified cities and against the high towers. I will bring distress upon men, and they shall walk like blind men, because they have sinned against the Lord; their blood shall be poured out like dust, and their flesh like refuse. Neither their silver nor their gold shall be able to deliver them in the day of the Lord's wrath; but the whole land shall be devoured by the fire of His jealousy, for He will make speedy riddance of all those who dwell in the land. (Zeph. 1:14–18)

---

[8] Throughout this book, the phrase "the Day of the Lord" is used to refer to the period of time from the opening of the seventh seal through (but not necessarily ending with) Armageddon. Although some define this "Day" as ending prior to the Millennial Reign, I see no reason to do so. For centuries, Jewish scholars have interpreted the Day of the Lord as including the thousand-year reign of the Messiah and the creation of the new heavens and the new earth. The prewrath timing does not necessarily favor either of these views. Only the start of the Day of the Lord is important, since it is this period of time that is tied wit the return of Jesus and, therefore, the rapture.

The Day of the Lord will be a time when the proud are humbled and the Lord magnified. At a time when men have exalted themselves, they will be brought low. Neither their money, nor their status, nor their false gods will save them:

> Wail, for the day of the Lord is at hand! It will come as destruction from the Almighty. Therefore all hands will be limp, every man's heart will melt, and they will be afraid. Pangs and sorrows will take hold of them; they will be in pain as a woman in childbirth; they will be amazed at one another; their faces will be like flames. Behold, the day of the Lord comes, cruel, with both wrath and fierce anger, to lay the land desolate; and He will destroy its sinners from it. For the stars of heaven and their constellations will not give their light; the sun will be darkened in its going forth, and the moon will not cause its light to shine. I will punish the world for its evil, and the wicked for their iniquity; I will halt the arrogance of the proud, and will lay low the haughtiness of the terrible. I will make a mortal more rare than fine gold, a man more than the golden wedge of Ophir. Therefore I will shake the heavens, and the earth will move out of her place, in the wrath of the Lord of hosts and in the day of His fierce anger. (Isaiah 13:6–13)[9]

In the last book of the Bible, the Revelation of Jesus Christ, the Lord paints yet another graphic picture of what the last days will be like. Stars will fall from the sky, locusts will swarm from the bottomless pit, burning asteroids will collide with the earth, and men will suffer from plagues, boils, and terrible sores. Seas and rivers will turn to blood, and earthquakes will rend entire cities in two.

Where will believers be? According to scripture, "God did not appoint us to wrath but to obtain salvation through our Lord Jesus Christ" (1 Thess. 5:9). By His own promise, Jesus will return

---

[9] There are many mentions of the Day of the Lord in the prophetic writings of the Old Testament. Not all of them have an end-times context. Some have already been fulfilled; others have been partially fulfilled; others are still waiting for fulfillment. I am not suggesting that all mentions of the Day of the Lord should be used to determine the timing of the rapture. Those mentioned in this book are end-times references that are accepted as such by most eschatological scholars.

to rescue the Church before the Day of His Wrath, catching us in the air to be in His glorious presence forever.

> Behold, I tell you a mystery: We shall not all sleep, but we shall all be changed—in a moment, in the twinkling of an eye, at the last trumpet. For the trumpet will sound, and the dead will be raised incorruptible, and we shall be changed. (1 Cor. 15:51–52)

What an awesome moment that will be! No wonder it is called the blessed hope. Not only will we be with our Lord and Savior for eternity, where "there shall be no more death, nor sorrow, nor crying" (Rev. 21:4), but in His great mercy, Jesus will exempt us from His ferocious judgment of the earth.

Does the Timing Matter?

There are three distinct periods of judgment in Revelation: the seven seals, the seven trumpets, and the seven bowls. These judgments are consecutive, with each growing in intensity.

During the seal judgments, a world leader (the Antichrist) will rise to power with great guise and deceit. He will be empowered by Satan and be given authority over "every tribe, tongue, and nation" (Rev. 13:4, 7, 14). He will also be granted complete power over God's people, and in his burning hatred of all that is holy, will war against them (Rev. 12:17). This unparalleled slaughter will reach its apex during the fifth seal, when God's people will cry with a loud voice, "How long, O Lord, holy and true, until You judge and avenge our blood on those who dwell on the earth?" (Rev. 6:10). This period coincides with what is commonly called the Great Tribulation (Matt. 24:21) and is brought to conclusion with the great triple sign of the sun, moon, and stars that ushers in the Day of the Lord.

The Day of the Lord will include two devastating sets of judgments—the seven trumpets and the seven bowls—that will bring such horrors as waters turning to blood, the death of one-third of mankind, and earthquakes that shake the foundations of the world. This terrible time will conclude with the arrival of Jesus Christ and His armies at the Battle of Armageddon.

There is great debate as to when, during this series of events, the rapture will occur. Here in the United States, the most popular

13

position,[10] the pretribulation position, is that it will occur before all of them. This argument is based on the promise, "we are not destined for wrath" (1 Thess. 5:9). If we are not destined for wrath, the argument goes, we must be raptured before all of God's end-times judgments, which include the seals, trumpets, and bowls.

Just being in the majority, however, never made anyone right. There is a great deal of scripture that discusses the return of Christ and the rapture of His Bride. In a straightforward, literal reading of the text, scripture teaches that Jesus will come after the sixth seal, just prior to the Day of the Lord (and, therefore, prior to the trumpet and the bowl judgments). The Day of the Lord, or the Day of God's Wrath, which includes both the trumpet and the bowl judgments, starts more than halfway through the "Tribulation."

Pretrib Vs. Prewrath Timing of the Rapture

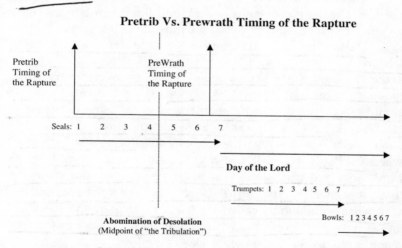

This distinction is important, because according to the pretrib position, God's wrath starts with the first seal, before the "Tribulation" and the rise of the Antichrist. The prewrath position places God's wrath during the Day of the Lord and several years

---

[10] With the exception of the countries of the affluent West, the posttrib position—the position held by the church fathers—is dominant among premillennialists worldwide. In many non-Western countries, believers are under no illusions of escaping the Great Tribulation because they have already endured, or are currently enduring, severe persecution.

political power

into the "Tribulation" and the reign of the Antichrist.[11] If the prewrath position is correct, and the Church will not be raptured until just prior to the Day of the Lord, Christians will have to endure at least three-and-one-half years of the Antichrist's reign.

What About Constant Vigil?

Some people say that the timing of the rapture doesn't matter. They say it is a divisive, nonessential doctrine that is best avoided. "What's important," they argue, "is that people are ready when Christ *does* come." This argument, that constant readiness is more important than the timing of the rapture, is called "constant vigil." If the rapture is pretribulational, I would agree. But if the rapture is not pretribulational, the consequences will be serious. The majority of the church population, expecting to be taken before the most devastating period in history, will be completely unprepared.

Consider the events that will occur during this time:

 The Seal Judgments

- First seal—the rise of false christs, including the ultimate false christ, the Antichrist.
- Second seal—the Antichrist gains further power through bloodshed.
- Third seal—worldwide famine.
- Fourth seal—widespread death takes the lives of up to one-quarter of the earth's population.
- Fifth seal—widespread persecution and martyring of Jews and Christians.
- Sixth seal—devastating earthquake and cosmic disturbances, with the sun turning black, the moon turning red as blood, and the stars falling from the sky.
- Seventh seal—silence in heaven for half an hour, which ushers in the Day of the Lord (seven trumpet and seven bowl judgments).

---

[11] The term "reign" here refers only to political power, starting with the Antichrist's confirming of the seven-year covenant at the beginning of the 70th Week of Daniel.

✳ The Trumpet Judgments

- First trumpet—hail and fire are mingled with blood, one-third of the earth's vegetation is burned.
- Second trumpet—a "burning mountain" falls into the sea, one-third of the sea turns to blood, and one-third of the sea creatures die.
- Third trumpet—a star called "Wormwood" falls from heaven, turning one-third of the earth's fresh water bitter.
- Fourth trumpet—one-third of the sun, moon, and stars are struck so that they do not shine.
- Fifth trumpet—locusts rise like smoke from the bottomless pit to torment those on the earth.
- Sixth trumpet—angels kill one-third of mankind.
- Seventh trumpet—ushers in the seven bowl judgments.

✳ The Bowl Judgments

- First bowl—foul and loathsome sores.
- Second bowl—the sea turns to blood and all sea creatures die.
- Third bowl—freshwater rivers and springs turn to blood.
- Fourth bowl—mankind is scorched with fire from the sun.
- Fifth bowl—widespread darkness and pain.
- Sixth bowl—Euphrates River dries up, allowing the armies of the Antichrist to gather for the battle of Armageddon.
- Seventh bowl—thunder, lightning, and a worldwide earthquake so great that "the islands flee away and the mountains will not be found."

Once these judgments are complete, God's full glory will be revealed. The heavens will open and Jesus will ride forth in glory to destroy the armies of the Antichrist and the rest of the armies who have gathered to fight. The Antichrist and his accomplice, the false prophet, will be cast alive into the lake of fire, and Satan will be bound in the bottomless pit for one thousand years. This will usher in Christ's thousand-year reign, called the Millennium, after which Satan will be released, conquered in God's final victory, and Jesus will prepare a glorious new heavens and new earth in which believers will live for eternity.

Getting "Battle Ready"

For those who do not believe the timing of the rapture to be important, consider the severity of the seal judgments. The doctrine of "constant vigil" makes sense in theory, but how ready

16

can the Church be if she is expecting to be raptured before these judgments occur? How well trained can soldiers be if they think that they will never have to fight? If the Church is expecting to be raptured any time, as the pretribulation position teaches, then unexpectedly finds herself facing world famine, war, natural disasters, and martyrdom, many Christians could stumble, disillusioned with their pastors and their churches, even questioning the truthfulness of the Word of God.

This is not to say that teachers of the pretribulation rapture believe that we will not go through hard times. They do, often pointing out that believers in other parts of the world are already enduring persecution, famine, and war. But what happens when *you* start losing the security of *your* food, *your* clothing, and *your* shelter? What happens when earthquakes are tearing *your* neighborhood asunder and just practicing your faith can, and will, get you killed? Spiritual preparation suddenly takes on new meaning.[12]

Jesus emphasized that, even for believers, the end times will be a period of *unparalleled* trouble, a time like the world has never seen. "For then there will be great tribulation, such as has not been since the beginning of the world until this time, no, nor ever shall be" (Matt. 24:21). It will be worse than the Crusades, worse than the Spanish Inquisition, worse than the Holocaust and the torturing and killing of believers in the modern day. The devastation will be worldwide, occurring on our doorsteps, not isolated in other parts

---

[12] Many prominent pretrib rapturists bristle at this position. Says Grant Jeffrey, a leading teacher on biblical prophecy, "Some critics have claimed that those who teach the hope of the pretribulation rapture are guilty of leaving Christians unprepared for the possibility that they might have to endure the persecution of the Tribulation period. However, in 30 years of teaching Bible prophecy, I have not witnessed anyone who believes in the pretribulation rapture who has taught that Christians are immune from all end-time persecution" (Grant Jeffrey, *Armageddon: Appointment With Destiny*, Frontier Research Publications Inc., July 1997, p. 170). With all respect to Jeffrey, I submit that, no matter what gets taught from the pulpit, by virtue of human nature, the pretrib teaching *does* lead to spiritual unpreparedness in the majority of Christians. Church leaders are not responsible for how their flocks respond to their messages, but they are responsible for accurately teaching them the Word of God.

of the globe. Christians must be ready spiritually, physically, and emotionally, and no manner of "constant vigil" will suffice. We need to go through spiritual boot camp. The timing of the rapture *matters*. (For those who believe that God does not allow His people to go through trials of this magnitude, I highly recommend reading *Foxe's Book of Martyrs*, along with the book of Job.)

The prophet Daniel emphasized that it is not just for our own sakes that we should seek understanding, but also for the sake of others. "Those who do wickedly against the covenant, he [the Antichrist] shall corrupt with flattery, but the people who know their God shall be strong, and carry out great exploits. *And those of the people who understand shall instruct many* [emphasis mine];[13] yet for many days they shall fall by sword and flame, by captivity and plundering" (Dan. 11:32–33). How can we provide hope and instruction to others unless we, ourselves, know what is afoot?

In Billy Graham's crusade in Ottawa, Ontario, he made a statement that astounded his audience. He pointed out that the Bible mentions the need to be born again, which is the foundation of the gospel, nine times. The need for repentance, which is the key to salvation, is mentioned 70 times. Baptism, without which we cannot fully identify with our Savior, is mentioned 20 times. But the return of Jesus Christ is mentioned 380 times, more than *ten times* the number of mentions of other critical church doctrines.[14] Was this some kind of mistake? Did God place the emphasis on the wrong place? I don't think so!

God has a plan. He gave us the signs of His coming and we are given careful instruction to watch for them so that we can be prepared. Unfortunately, we haven't heeded His warning. As we sit on the edge of the rise of the Antichrist, the greatest natural and spiritual disaster in history, the Church is an army asleep.

---

[13] While the Church was a mystery to the Old Testament prophets, this verse sets forth a general principle for the end times. The phrase "those of understanding" most likely refers to Jewish believers in Christ whose spiritual eyes have been opened and therefore have access to the full revelation of the New Testament scriptures. Thus, if this verse addresses Jewish believers, then, by association, it addresses the Church.

[14] Taken from a sermon by Billy Graham entitled, "The End of the World" ©1998 Billy Graham Evangelistic Association.

In the parable of the foolish virgins, Jesus warned us of such a sleep. He said,

> Then the kingdom of heaven shall be likened to ten virgins who took their lamps and went out to meet the bridegroom. Now five of them were wise and five were foolish. Those who were foolish took their lamps and took no oil with them, but the wise took oil in their vessels with their lamps. But while the bridegroom was delayed, they all slumbered and slept. And at midnight a cry was heard: "Behold, the bridegroom is coming; go out to meet him!" Then all those virgins arose and trimmed their lamps. And the foolish said to the wise, "Give us some of your oil, for our lamps are going out." But the wise answered, saying, "No, lest there should not be enough for us and you; but go rather to those who sell, and buy for yourselves." And while they went to buy, the bridegroom came, and those who were ready went in with him to the wedding; and the door was shut. (Matt. 25:1–10)

There are many morals to this parable, but the one I want to draw readers' attention to is this: The bridegroom comes at a time when the virgins least expect, *after they have given up hope of His coming*. Right now, the Church is expecting Jesus to come at any time, prior to the rise of the Antichrist. The time the Church least expects is after the rise of the Antichrist, well into what many erroneously call "the Tribulation period." If the Church does not awaken from its stupor, the parable of the foolish virgins may well reflect the state of the Church as she endures the reign of the Antichrist and the seal judgments of God. What a terrible tragedy it would be if, when Jesus returns to earth, it is after the Church has given up hope of His coming.

2

What the Bible Says
About the Rapture

Despite the popularity of the pretribulation rapture, this teaching cannot be found in the plain reading of scripture. It must be inferred from a handful of passages, and even then, it is a stretch. According to this position, Jesus will return to rapture His Bride, the true believers who make up the body of Christ, prior to the seven-year "Tribulation period" described in the book of Revelation. This period includes three series of judgments: the seals, the trumpets, and the bowls. Because the pretrib doctrine sees all three periods of judgment as God's wrath, it teaches that the Church must be raptured before these judgments begin. This teaching is based on the promise, "for God did not appoint us to wrath, but to obtain salvation through our Lord Jesus Christ" (1 Thess. 5:9).

It is at the earliest stage that the pretrib position falters. Nowhere does the Bible refer to the seals as God's wrath. It is true that they are a period of intense difficulty decreed by God, but this does not make them His wrath. To get a sense of just how different judgment and wrath are, let's take a look at the dictionary's definition of these two words. According to *Webster's Ninth Collegiate Dictionary*, judgment in this context is defined as "a divine sentence or decision; a calamity held to be sent by God." Wrath, on the other hand, is defined as "strong, vengeful anger or indignation; retributory punishment for an offense or a crime." There is a big difference.

Throughout history, God has decreed many judgments — upon individuals, upon nations, and upon mankind as a whole. In

20

the Garden of Eden, God pronounced judgments on Adam, on Eve, and on the serpent (Gen. 3:14–19). In the time of Noah, He pronounced a judgment on the whole world (Gen. 6:7). In the first century, Jesus pronounced judgments on the fig tree, on Jerusalem, and on cities that rejected the gospel (Matt. 21:18–19, Matt. 11:21–24, Luke 24:2). There are hundreds of judgments in the Bible, including the seal, trumpet, and bowl judgments described in Revelation.

Could all of the judgments described in Revelation also be God's wrath? Maybe. The question is: Are they? No. The Bible teaches that God's wrath will begin after the opening of the sixth seal, as part of the Day of the Lord (see Chapter 4, "When Does God's Wrath Begin?"). Thus, there is no scriptural reason to require the rapture to occur before then. In fact, this would create many contradictions of scripture, as we will discuss here.

So when will the rapture occur?

The Bible tells us that, as in the time of Noah, there will come a day when God will run out of patience with the wickedness of mankind. Although most people think of "the end of the world" as the battle of Armageddon, "the end of the age," as Jesus taught, will actually begin sometime earlier when He returns to earth to take His rightful place as conquering King (Matt. 24:3, 29–30). This will usher in the Day of the Lord, during which God will pour out His wrath on an unrepentant world.

When Will Judgment Come?

Once Jesus' disciples recognized Jesus as the Messiah, it was only natural that they would want to know when the Day of the Lord would begin. Jesus had already told them that He would go away for awhile, and while the disciples did not—nor could they—understand the full nature of His departure, they knew one thing: Jesus was coming back, and when He did, He would judge the earth as the prophets foretold. But when? This was exactly the question they were asking in Matthew 24: "What will be the sign of Your coming and of the end of the age?" (v. 3).

Jesus replied by giving a long list of events that would precede His return:

1. There would be a rise in false christs (v. 5).
2. There would be a rise in wars between nations (v. 6).

21

3. There would be famines, pestilence, and earthquakes in various places (v. 7).
4. The Antichrist would desecrate the temple of God (v. 15).
5. There would be a period of severe tribulation for God's people, more intense than any other in history (v. 21).

Then, after describing all of these events, Jesus said,

> Immediately after the tribulation of those days, the sun will be darkened, the moon will not give its light; the stars will fall from heaven, and the powers of the heavens will be shaken. Then the sign of the Son of Man will appear in heaven, and then all the tribes of the earth will mourn, and they will see the son of Man coming on the clouds of heaven with power and great glory. And He will send His angels with a great sound of a trumpet, and they will gather together His elect from the four winds, from one end of heaven to the other. (Matt. 24:29–31)

The timing couldn't be more clear. There will be specific signs—the rise of false christs; widespread war, famine, pestilence, and earthquakes; the desecration of the temple by the Antichrist; the Great Tribulation; and the triple sign in the sun, moon, and stars—that, one by one, will lead us closer and closer to His return. When we compare these signs to the seal judgments described in Revelation, we see that they are one and the same (the significance of this will be seen later).

Disciples Learn of the Rapture

Through the Apostle Paul, Jesus also revealed that the Church would not have to live through the period of destruction and wrath that would follow Christ's return. Rather, believers will be miraculously transformed into new, heavenly bodies and removed from the earth before Jesus takes vengeance on the ungodly during the Day of the Lord.

Paul described this wonder in 1 Cor. 15:51–52:

> Behold, I tell you a mystery: We shall not all sleep [die], but we shall all be changed—in a moment, in the twinkling of an eye, at the last trumpet. For the trumpet will sound, and the dead will be raised incorruptible, and we shall all be changed.

22

What a beautiful picture! Paul elaborated on this promise in his first letter to the Thessalonians:

> For the Lord Himself will descend from heaven with a shout, with the voice of an archangel, and with the trumpet of God. And the dead in Christ will rise first. Then we who are alive and remain shall be caught up together with them in the clouds to meet the Lord in the air. And thus we shall always be with the Lord. (1 Thess. 4:16–17)

And thus, the early church was introduced to the concept of the rapture. As we would expect, this description is the same as Jesus' description of His coming in Matthew 24:[15]

> ...and they will see the son of Man coming on the clouds of heaven with power and great glory. And He will send His angels with a great sound of a trumpet, and they will gather together His elect from the four winds, from one end of heaven to the other. (Matt. 24:29–31)

Therefore, when Jesus comes on the clouds after the Great Tribulation, He will also rapture the Church.

By the way, have you ever wondered where we get the word "rapture"? It doesn't occur in the Bible. For centuries, the scriptures were in Latin. The Latin word for "caught up"—as in "caught up together in the clouds"—is *rapere*. Although the word "rapture" does not appear in the Bible, this is why we say it.

Putting this all together, we see that Jesus' return, and therefore the rapture, will be preceded by a series of clearly identifiable events. First will be the rise in false christs, world war, famine, pestilence, and earthquakes that Jesus called "the Beginning of Sorrows" (Matt. 24:5–8). Then will come the Antichrist, who will defile the temple and initiate the Great

---

[15] Although the Church is not specifically in view here (since the Church was not founded until Pentecost), Jesus was speaking to Jews who would soon become the New Testament Church. Furthermore, one of the mysteries revealed by Paul is that the Second Coming would include not only the gathering of the elect but the translation of the living in the rapture (1 Cor. 15:51-52, 1 Thess. 4:16-17). Thus, we can legitimately read Matt. 24:31 as *applying to* the Church, even though it wasn't *spoken to* the Church.

23

Tribulation by persecuting the people of God (vv. 15-21). This will be followed by the great cosmic sign of the sun, moon, and stars, signaling that the Day of the Lord is about to begin (v. 29). At this time—just prior to the Day of the Lord—Jesus will appear in the clouds to rapture His Church.

Looking for the Sixth Seal

When, during the "Tribulation" period, will these signs, and therefore the rapture, occur? Let's take another look at the cosmic disturbances that will immediately precede the return of Christ:

> Immediately after the tribulation of those days, the sun will be darkened, the moon will not give its light; the stars will fall from heaven, and the powers of the heavens will be shaken (Matt. 24:29).

To students of Revelation, these signs should look familiar. They are the same as the signs described in Rev. 6:12–13 as part of the sixth seal:

> I looked when He opened the sixth seal, and behold, there was a great earthquake, and the sun became black as sackcloth of hair, and the moon became like blood. And the stars of heaven fell into the earth, as a fig tree drops its late figs when it is shaken by a mighty wind.

In other words, the clear, direct evidence from scripture places the rapture after the opening of the sixth seal. As I mentioned earlier, the events Jesus describes as part of the Beginning of Sorrows, the Great Tribulation, and the great triple sign in the heavens parallel the events of the six seals. This places the fifth seal during the Great Tribulation, which will occur a little more than three-and-one-half years into the "Tribulation period." Thus, the return of Christ and the rapture of the Church, which will occur after the opening of the _sixth_ seal, will occur sometime after the midpoint of the "Tribulation" as well.

But wouldn't this put the Church under God's wrath? Why would the Church have to endure a period of retribution designed for the world? First, the seals are not God's wrath. Second, they are not a time for punishing the world, but for evangelizing it. They are also a time of "refining fire" for the Church.

24

Straightforward Answer

At this point, the important thing to take from this discussion is the straightforward nature of Jesus' answer to His disciples. Essentially, they came to Him and asked, "When are You coming back?" and He gave them a straightforward answer. By comparing Jesus' description of His coming to Paul's descriptions of the rapture, we see that they are one and the same event. Then, when we compare the signs of the coming of Christ to the sixth seal, we also see that they are the same event.

Thus, the return of Christ and the rapture of the Church will immediately follow the opening of the sixth seal, sometime after the midpoint of the seven-year "Tribulation" period.

The Second Coming of Christ and the rapture of the Church are not mysteries. They can be found in the most plain, straightforward reading of the scriptures. If this is all you wanted to know, you can stop reading right here. The rest of this book is devoted to the many ways that this same conclusion can be reached over and over again. It also attempts to answer the many questions that will be raised by this timing—not because it is unclear or unscriptural, but simply because people have been taught something else.

Wrath and the Day of the Lord

What about God's wrath? How does this relate to the rapture? In Chapter 1, we looked at several verses describing God's judgment associated with the Day of the Lord.

Let's look again at one of the key verses:

> Wail, for the day of the Lord is at hand! It will come as destruction from the Almighty. Therefore all hands will be limp, every man's heart will melt, and they will be afraid. Pangs and sorrows will take hold of them; they will be in pain as a woman in childbirth; they will be amazed at one another; their faces will be like flames. Behold, the day of the Lord comes, cruel, with both wrath and fierce anger, to lay the land desolate; and He will destroy its sinners from it. For the stars of heaven and their constellations will not give their light; the sun will be darkened in its going forth, and the moon will not cause its light to shine. I will punish the world for its evil, and the wicked for their iniquity; I will halt the arrogance of the proud, and will lay low the haughtiness of the terrible. (Isaiah 13:6–12)

Isaiah makes it clear that God's wrath is contained in the Day of the Lord. As mentioned in the last chapter, the Day of the Lord is also called "the Day of God's Wrath."

Now, let's go back to the rapture verses in 1 Thess. 4:15–18:

> For this we say to you by the word of the Lord, that we who are alive and remain until the coming of the Lord will by no means precede those who are asleep. For the Lord Himself will descend from heaven with a shout, with the voice of an archangel, and with the trumpet of God. And the dead in Christ will rise first. Then we who are alive and remain shall be caught up together with them in the clouds to meet the Lord in the air. And thus we shall always be with the Lord.

A few verses later, Paul continues,

> But concerning the times and the seasons, brethren, you have no need that I should write to you. For you yourselves know perfectly that the day of the Lord so comes as a thief in the night. (1 Thess. 5:1–2)

Compare Paul's reference to the *coming of the Lord* in 1 Thess. 4:15 with the reference to *the Day of the Lord* in 1 Thess. 5:1–2. Notice the use of the two different phrases, *the coming of the Lord* and *the Day of the Lord*. Both here and in 2 Thess. 2:2, Paul makes it clear that the coming of the Lord and the rapture of the Church *precede* the Day of the Lord. Thus, if God's wrath is contained within the Day of the Lord, and the rapture occurs before that Day, then the rapture also precedes God's wrath.

Signs Preceding the Day of the Lord

When does the Day of the Lord begin? Scripture leaves no room for doubt. The Day of the Lord is one of the most often prophesied events in the Bible. It is described by more than half a dozen Old Testament writers, including Isaiah, Zephaniah, and Joel, as well as New Testament writers like Peter, Paul, and Luke.

Descriptions of this event are often accompanied by clear and unmistakable signs. The prophet Joel gives us one of the most vivid descriptions of those signs:

The sun shall be turned into darkness, and the moon into blood, before the coming of the great and awesome Day of the Lord. (Joel 2:31)

Peter reiterates these signs in the book of Acts:

The sun shall be turned into darkness, and the moon into blood, before the coming of the great and awesome Day of the Lord. (Acts 2:20)

When will these cosmic disturbances occur? Once again, the scriptures point to the sixth seal:

I looked when He opened the sixth seal, and behold, there was a great earthquake; and the sun became black as sackcloth of hair, and the moon became like blood. And the stars of heaven fell to the earth, as a fig tree drops its late figs when it is shaken by a mighty wind. (Rev. 6:12–13)

This provides additional confirmation to a question that was answered earlier: If the Church is raptured after the sixth seal, doesn't this mean that the Church undergoes God's wrath? No. God's wrath does not begin until the Day of the Lord, which begins *after the sixth seal*.[16] Jesus returns, raptures His Church, and with His Bride safely out of the way, begins His judgment of the rebellious world.

Four Events Coinciding

If this all sounds complicated, it's not. At the opening of the sixth seal, four things are essentially occurring at once: (1) the sixth seal is coming to a conclusion (2) Christ is returning to earth to (3) rapture the Church and (4) prepare to administer His

---

[16] There is yet additional confirmation that the Day of the Lord starts with the opening of the seventh seal. The Day of the Lord is described by the prophet Zephaniah, who writes: *"Be silent in the presence of the Lord God, for the day of the Lord is at hand"* (Zeph. 1:7). If the Day of the Lord starts with the seventh seal, we might expect to see silence described prior to seventh seal in Revelation. Indeed, this is exactly what we see. After describing the first six seals, John writes, "When He opened the seventh seal, there was silence in heaven for about half an hour" (Rev. 8:1-2). This agrees perfectly with the description given by Zephaniah.

judgment. Christ's return can be thought of as a "trigger event" that brings into effect these other two.[17]

To better understand the beautiful inter-relationship between these events, it helps to make a comparison to the marriage relationship. Think of Christ as the loving husband and believers as the loving wife, who on her birthday is anxiously awaiting her husband's return from work. For her, his return brings joy, the expectation of flowers and kisses, and perhaps a romantic evening together. For the children, who were extremely naughty that day, his return means something entirely different. It means that they will soon face the stern hand of discipline. The same event, the return of the father, initiates two different and completely separate series of events for different members of the family.

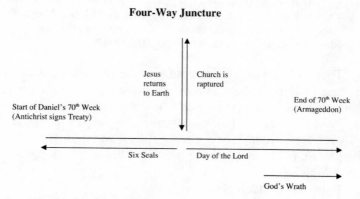

Four-Way Juncture

Putting It All Together

What does this mean? The events leading up to the Second Coming of Christ and the rapture of the Church will follow a pattern clearly set forth in scripture. First will come a series of devastating world events (the first five seals of Revelation), followed by the triple sign of sun, moon, and stars described in Joel, Matthew, and Revelation (the sixth seal). Then Christ will come to rapture the Church. Following this glorious event, the

---

[17] Although John Walvoord places the timing of the rapture at the beginning of the 70th Week rather than after the sixth seal, he also ties the rapture to the beginning of the Day of the Lord (*The Rapture Question*, pp. 175, 212).

seventh seal will unleash the Day of the Lord, which contains the trumpet and the bowl judgements of God's wrath.

This position—that Jesus will return after the sixth seal, prior to the outpouring of the Day of the Lord and God's wrath—is called "prewrath."[18] This phrase was coined by Marvin Rosenthal and Robert Van Kampen and was first published in Rosenthal's book, *The Pre-Wrath Rapture of the Church*.

Let's look again at the timing that Jesus Himself gave in Matthew 24, this time with the seals of Revelation in mind:

> Take heed that no one deceives you. You will hear of wars and rumors of wars **[the first seal]**...for nation will rise against nation, and kingdom against kingdom **[the second seal]**. And there will be famines, pestilences, and earthquakes in various places **[third and fourth seals]**.... Therefore when you see the abomination of desolation spoken of by Daniel the prophet [the Antichrist standing in the yet-to-be-rebuilt temple in Jerusalem, which will occur at the three-and-a-half year point into Daniel's 70th Week]...then let those who are in Judea flee to the mountains.... For then there will be great tribulation, such as has not been since the beginning of the world until this time, no, nor ever shall be **[the fifth seal]**. And unless those days were shortened, no flesh would be saved; but for the elect's sake, those days will be shortened.... Immediately after the tribulation of those days, the sun will be darkened and the moon will not give its light; the stars will fall from heaven, and the powers of the heavens will be shaken **[the sixth seal]**. Then the sign of the Son of Man will appear in heaven, and then all the tribes of the earth will mourn, and they will see the Son of Man coming on the clouds of heaven with power and great glory **[Christ's return]**. And He will send His angels with a great sound of a trumpet, and they will gather together His elect from the four winds, from one end of heaven to the other **[the rapture]**. (Matt. 24:6, 7, 15, 21–22, 29–31)

---

[18] The term "prewrath rapture" is a bit of a misnomer, since the pretrib, midtrib, and posttrib positions also see the rapture as occurring prior to the outpouring of God's wrath. The real differences lie in how much of the "Tribulation" (more properly, Daniel's 70th Week) each believes that the Church will have to endure and why.

This explains the importance of recognizing the events of Matthew 24 as being the same as the seal judgments in Revelation 6. When viewed this way—the way given to us by Jesus Himself—the timing of the rapture couldn't be more clear.

What About a Spiritual Return?

Proponents of the pretrib position would argue this timing, countering that when Christ returns to rapture the Church, He does not return in bodily form, but in spirit form. They contend that He does not return in bodily form until seven years later when He returns with the heavenly host at Armageddon. Not only does this contradict the clear timing outlined by Jesus Himself, but it also contradicts what the apostles were told by the angel in Acts 1:11: "'Men of Galilee, why do you stand gazing up into heaven? This same Jesus, who was taken up from you into heaven, will so come in like manner as you saw Him go into heaven'" (Acts 1:9–11).

Jesus was not taken up in spirit form; and the angel makes it clear that neither will He return for believers in spirit form, but in body. Paul reaffirms this truth, saying, "Now, brethren, concerning the coming of our Lord Jesus Christ and our gathering together to Him, we ask you not to be soon shaken in mind or troubled...as though the day of the Lord had come" (2 Thess. 2:1–2—NASB, NIV). Paul was very certain that the rapture will occur at the bodily return of Christ and that the bodily return of Christ will occur before the Day of the Lord.[19]

---

[19] Although he argues against the conclusion, Paul Feinberg points out that the Greek verb and noun forms of "gather together" used here occur only nine times in the New Testament. Of these nine references, only three have eschatological significance: 2 Thess. 2:1, Matt. 24:31 (which describes Jesus' coming on the clouds and the gathering of the elect), and its synoptic parallel, Mark 13:27. The other six are only general uses. I see all three of these as rapture references, allowing perfect consistency throughout scripture. In *Three Views on the Rapture*, Feinberg, however, argues that this parallel is not as conclusive as it may seem, saying, "It seems clear that any identification based on this word rests on the slightest of evidence" (p. 231). Needless to say, I believe that the opposite is true. I would agree with Alexander Reese, who writes, "The assertion...that there is no rapture at Matt. 24:31 is as bold as it is unfounded. Our Lord in that passage gave a perfect picture of the assembling of the saved of this dispensation by means of a rapture; St.

This same affirmation is made in 2 Thess. 1:5–7:

> ...we ourselves boast of you among the churches of God for your patience and faith in all your persecutions and tribulations that you endure, which is manifest evidence of the righteous judgment of God, that you may be counted worthy of the kingdom of God, for which you also suffer; since it is a righteous thing with God to repay with tribulation those who trouble you, and to give you who are troubled *rest with u s when the Lord Jesus is revealed from heaven with His mighty angels* [emphasis mine].

Throughout scripture, the term "rest" is used to symbolize a cease from labor—hence the Sabbath day "rest" for God's people, the Jubilee "rest" for the land, and the spiritual "rest" that God has for His people (Heb. 4:9–10). Considering that the context of the book of 2 Thessalonians is the end times, the return of Christ, and the rapture of the Church, this reference to the people of God being delivered from their enemies by being given rest with Christ when He comes with His mighty angels can only be the rapture.[20]

Mark even used for 'gathering' the verbal form of the same word used for 'gathering' in 2 Thess. 2:1, where Paul refers to the rapture. To unbiased minds, the gathering of the saved, or the elect, in Matt. 24:31, is the prototype of Paul's teaching in 1 Thess. 4:16-17 and 2 Thess. 2:1" (*The Approaching Advent of Christ*, p. 208). I believe this to be particularly true, considering that 1 Thess. 4:16-17 uses many of the same elements, and nearly identical language, to Matt. 24:29-31—"the Son of Man coming on the clouds, in glory, with the blast of a trumpet, and with the heavenly angels." I like Reese's language: "to the unbiased mind." Certainly, to the unbiased mind, the correlation is difficult to miss.

[20] Many pretrib proponents would argue this point, claiming that this is an example of "telescoping"—that this rest comes with Christ's spiritual return at the rapture, not at His bodily return at the Second Coming, which they see at Armageddon, and that it is only the habit of the prophets to telescope events that makes them appear to be one and the same. I see three problems with this argument: (1) telescoping occurred in the Old Testament, not the New Testament, where "mysteries" were revealed; (2) telescoping was done by prophets, and while Paul's writings were certainly prophetic, he was not a prophet in the Old Testament sense; and (3) the scriptural pattern is consistently to refer to

This is confirmed when Paul goes on to describe the angels as coming "in flaming fire, taking vengeance on those who do not know God and on those who do not obey the gospel of our Lord Jesus Christ" (v. 8). Scripture teaches that, after Jesus comes to rapture His Church, He will judge an ungodly and unrepentant world during the Day of the Lord. This is exactly what Paul describes here: "rest with Christ," followed by flaming fire and vengeance on those who do not know God and who do not obey the gospel.

Yet another linking of the rapture with Christ's bodily return can be seen in Titus 2:13, in which Paul exhorts believers to live soberly, "looking for the blessed hope and glorious appearing of our great God and Savior Jesus Christ." And again in James 5:7–9: "Therefore, be patient, brethren, until the coming of the Lord....You also be patient. Establish your hearts, for the coming of the Lord is at hand." Paul clearly believed that when Jesus appears to take His Bride, it will be in bodily form.

Glimpse of the Raptured Church

Although Revelation does not describe the rapture event itself, John does give us a glimpse of the first moments of the Church after she is taken into heaven. Immediately after John describes the six seals and before he describes the seven trumpets, he writes:

> After these things I looked, and behold, a great multitude, which no one could number, of all nations, tribes, peoples, and tongues, standing before the throne and before the Lamb, clothed with white robes, with palm branches in their hands and crying out with a loud voice, saying, "Salvation belongs to our God who sits on the throne and to the Lamb!" (Rev. 7:9–10)

What a beautiful sight this will be! The men and women of the Church, now in their new, heavenly bodies, worshipping and glorifying their God. The reference to salvation in this passage is appropriate, not simply because God has given them salvation of

---

deliverance of believers from tribulation at the bodily return of Christ. The scriptural pattern of tribulation, followed by deliverance and Christ's bodily return prior to the outpouring of God's wrath, is consistent only with the prewrath view.

their souls, but in this case because He has also given them salvation of their bodies from the first death. This is consistent with Paul's promise in 1 Thess. 5:9: "For God did not appoint us to wrath, *but to obtain salvation through our Lord Jesus Christ.*"

The multitude does not simply represent believers who died at some earlier time in history. We know this is the raptured Church because John tells us so. He continues:

> ... And one of the elders answered, saying unto me, "Who are these who are arrayed in white robes? And from where did they come?" And I said unto him, "Sir, you know." And he said to me, "These are they who come out of the great tribulation, and washed their robes and made them white in the blood of the Lamb. Therefore they are before the throne of God, and serve Him day and night in His temple. And He who sits on the throne will dwell among them. They shall neither hunger anymore nor thirst anymore; the sun shall not strike them, nor any heat; for the Lamb who is in the midst of the throne will shepherd them and lead them to living fountains of waters. And God will wipe away every tear from their eyes." (Rev. 7:13–17)

The fact that Christ will rapture the Church out of the Great Tribulation also answers one of the riddles posed by Jesus in the Olivet Discourse: "And unless those days were shortened, no flesh would be saved; but for the elect's sake those days will be shortened" (Matt. 24:22). What is this shortening of days? God will not *physically* shorten the Antichrist's reign, because this is set at 1,260 days. However, Jesus will cut the Great Tribulation short by catching His Bride into the sky to be with Him.[21]

The Antichrist will continue to persecute those who become believers after the rapture, but once Jesus raptures the Church, his burning desire to destroy God's people will likely be diminished as locusts swarm from the bottomless pit, burning mountains fall from the sky, rivers and oceans turn to blood, and other catastrophes pour onto the earth during the Day of the Lord. What was once single-minded, unholy passion will get swallowed up in damage control.

---

[21] For a more detailed look at this subject, see Appendix B.

The Four Winds

Further evidence that the rapture occurs after the opening of the sixth seal is the presence of the four winds. In Matthew 24, after describing the cosmic disturbances associated with the sixth seal, Jesus says, "And He will send His angels with a great sound of a trumpet, and they will gather together His elect *from the four winds, from one end of heaven to the other*." This phrase, "the four winds," once again ties the rapture to the events of the sixth seal: "After these things [the cosmic disturbances of the sixth seal], I saw four angels standing at the four corners of the earth, *holding the four winds of the earth*, that the wind should not blow on the earth, on the sea, or on any tree" (Rev. 7:1).[22]

Not only does John use the same phrase "the four winds," but he uses it in the same sequence of events:

Matthew 24
1. The persecution and martyrdom of God's people.
2. The sun turning dark, the moon not giving its light and the stars falling from the sky.
3. The four winds.
4. The gathering of the elect.

Revelation 6–7
1. The persecution and martyrdom of God's people.
2. The sun turning dark, the moon turning to blood, and the stars falling from the sky.
3. The four winds.
4. The raptured Church worshipping the Lord in heaven.

---

[22] There are some who would argue that this uses a definition of the four winds that is too restrictive. They would point out that this is a general phrase that may or may not have any relevance for tying together related passages. This point is well taken. However, God uses this phrase, "the four winds," only nine times in the Bible, all in a prophetic context (Matt. 24:31; Mark 13:27, Eze. 37:9, Rev. 7:1, Jer. 49:36, Dan. 7:2, Dan. 11:4, and Zech. 2:6). The power of this argument is that, in this case, the uses occur in the same context and in the identical order of prophetic events.

The timing of the bodily return of Christ and the rapture is not a mystery. Nor was it ever meant to be. The evidence for these events is clearly and liberally laid out in scripture. The evidence for the prewrath rapture, which occurs after the opening of the sixth seal, is by no means exhausted here.

3

Faulty Foundations of Pretrib

There are many reasons that the pretrib timing of the rapture doesn't work. The first is that the scriptures clearly tell us when the rapture occurs, and it cannot be pretribulational. Another reason is that the pretrib position, as taught by most churches today, is supported only by a handful of verses, and when we take a closer look at those verses, we see that they do not support the position that pretrib teachers are trying to prove.

The popular approach to the pretrib position boils down to three foundational pillars:

> 1. God's wrath is poured out during the seven seal judgments, the seven trumpet judgments, and the seven bowl judgments described in Revelation.
> 2. This period of time is called "the Great Tribulation."
> 3. Jesus will rapture His Church prior to the pouring out of God's wrath and therefore prior to the Great Tribulation.[23]

With the exception of the Church's exemption from wrath, there are no direct scriptural references to support these points. This is because they are built upon *inference*. This inference starts with the first point that, because the seal, trumpet, and bowl judgments bring such trouble upon the earth, they must all be part

---

[23] As mentioned, these points reflect the popular treatment of the rapture, not the scholarly treatment, which is less simplified but comes to the same conclusions. Short discussions of some of these approaches are covered in the footnotes and more in depth in the appendices of this book.

of God's wrath. In reality, however, the seals are not part of God's wrath. They are part of man's wrath—specifically, the wrath of one man, the Antichrist.[24]

---

[24] There is something else going on that is encouraging this position. It is a phenomenon described by lawyer Philip Johnson in his book *Darwin on Trial* (Intervarsity Press, 1993), in which he dissects the argument for evolution based on the way the arguments are presented. Johnson writes that, in scientific circles, the theory of evolution is assumed to be true simply because no acceptable alternative exists. Therefore, the evidence—from fossilized remains to the mechanisms of genetics—is investigated, not for the purpose of discovering whether evolution *could have* occurred, but for the purpose of discovering *how* evolution *has occurred*. This, Johnson writes, is where the flaw begins: "There is an important difference between going to the empirical evidence to test a doubtful theory against some plausible alternative and going to the evidence to look for confirmation of the only theory that one is willing to tolerate" (p. 28). In fact, the scientific evidence overwhelmingly supports the idea of "special creation," or the emergence of new species spontaneously, already wholly formed. Genetics, for example, shows that there are biological limits to the amount of change that a species can undergo, and the fossil records reveal that the fundamental characteristic of species is stasis (or lack of significant change), even over millions of years. The fossil record also fails to reveal, as Darwin had hoped, the abundance of transitional life forms that would be required by his theory. The logic used to support the arguments for evolution and the arguments used to support the pretrib rapture are remarkably similar. Let's take Johnson's words and apply them to the pretrib rapture: "There is an important difference between going to the *scriptural* evidence to test a doubtful theory against some plausible alternative, and going to the *scriptural* evidence to look for confirmation of the only theory that one is willing to tolerate." There are no verses that provide direct scriptural evidence for the pretrib rapture. Those that provide indirect evidence are taken out of context or require redefined terms and phrases. For conservative Christians who believe that the Bible is the inerrant Word of God, this should raise serious doubts about the accuracy of the theory. Instead, because the pretrib timing remains the only theory that many are willing to tolerate, they do not allow this lack of evidence to bother them. Johnson writes of a meeting between top mathematicians and leading Darwinists at the Wistar Institute in Philadelphia in 1967. One mathematician argued that it was highly improbable that the eye could have evolved by the accumulation of small mutations, as Darwinism suggested. The Darwinists responded that "[the mathematician] was

The second point, that the Great Tribulation refers to the seals, the trumpets, and the bowls, is also built upon inference. As we have seen, the phrase itself is scriptural, but Jesus uses it to refer to a very specific period of time between the abomination of desolation (the Antichrist's desecration of the temple) and the cosmic disturbances of the sixth seal (see chart on p. 43). Because Dan. 9:27 tells us that the abomination of desolation occurs at the midpoint of "the Tribulation," the Great Tribulation cannot be the full seven years. At most, it can last only three-and-one-half years, and in fact, is much shorter than that. The Great Tribulation corresponds only with the fifth seal, the martyrdom of the saints.

The third point, that Jesus will return to rapture His Church prior to His wrath, *is* supported by scripture. However, God's wrath does not coincide with the start of the Great Tribulation. As we discussed in the last chapter, God's wrath starts *after* the Great Tribulation, as part of the Day of the Lord.[25]

That the pretribulation rapture is built on inference is readily acknowledged by top pretrib scholars. In *The Rapture Question*, one of the founding scholars of pretribulationism, John Walvoord, admits, "One of the problems that face both pretribulationism and posttribulationism is the fact that their point of view is an induction based on scriptural facts rather than an explicit statement of the Bible." Furthermore, in *The Return of the Lord*, Walvoord

---

doing his science backwards; the fact was that the eye had evolved and therefore the mathematical difficulties must only be apparent" (p. 38). Once again, the similarities to the pretrib position are strong. "[The opponents of pretrib theory] must be doing their scripture interpretation backwards; the fact is that the pretrib position is correct and therefore the scriptural difficulties must only be apparent." In both cases—Darwinism and pretrib rapturism—proponents prefer to live with a theory based on faulty data rather than accept a conclusion that is philosophically uncomfortable. I realize that many pretrib scholars have invested tremendous amounts of time and energy into studying the scriptural foundations of the pretrib rapture. However, I humbly submit that if they had not first been taught the pretrib rapture, it is highly unlikely that they would have come up with this timing on their own.

[25] Some pretrib scholars, however, define the Great Tribulation as starting at the midpoint of the 70th Week and extending until Armageddon, a period lasting three-and-one-half years. For a discussion on this subject, see Appendix B.

compounds the problem by stating, "One of the reasons for confusion concerning future events is the failure to analyze correctly the purpose of God in this present age. Some have come to the Bible without the proper method of interpretation" (p. 19). Likewise, Thomas D. Ice, in the theological journal *Bibliotheca Sacra*, notes that, "the timing of the rapture is more the product of one's theology than the prooftexting of specific passages."[26]

This may answer a question readers may be asking themselves as they read this book, which is, "Why do you repeatedly put the phrase 'the Tribulation' or 'the Tribulation period' in quotation marks?" It is because there is no such thing. The seven-year period extending from the opening of the first seal to the Battle of Armageddon, which is commonly called "the Tribulation," is actually the 70th Week of Daniel. "The Tribulation" is a simply a nickname given to this period. However, because the Bible refers to an *actual* time period called "the tribulation" (Matt. 24:29), which is a shortened version of "the great tribulation" (Matt. 24:21, Rev. 7:14), this causes much misunderstanding.

Daniel's 70th Week

In order to fully understand the timing of the rapture, it is necessary to spend a little more time discussing the 70th Week. The phrase comes from Daniel 9:24, in which God determines 70 weeks to deal with the Jewish people:

> Seventy weeks are determined for your people and for your holy city. To finish the transgression, to make an end of sins, to make reconciliation for iniquity, to bring in everlasting righteousness, to seal up vision and prophecy, and to anoint the Most Holy.

Bible scholars agree that the term "weeks," based on the Hebrew word *shbuah*, means "weeks of years," or series of seven-year periods. For this reason, some Bible translations, such as *The New International Version,* translate *shbuah* as "sevens":

---

[26] John Walvoord, *The Rapture Question: Revised and Expanded Edition* (The Zondervan Publishing House, 1979), p. 18; John Walvoord, *The Return of the Lord* (Zondervan Publishing House, 1974); Thomas D. Ice, *Bibliotheca Sacra* (Dallas Theological Seminary, April-June 1990), p. 164.

Seventy "sevens" are determined for your people and for your holy city. To finish the transgression, to make an end of sins, to make reconciliation for iniquity, to bring in everlasting righteousness, to seal up vision and prophecy, and to anoint the Most Holy.

In other words, 70 weeks, or 70 "sevens" (a period of 490 years) is set forth by God to finish what He started. God's purposes for Israel were not abolished when Israel rejected Christ as the Messiah. They were only put on hold.

According to Daniel's prophecy, God's 70-week prophetic time clock started when the walls of Jerusalem were rebuilt by the prophet Ezra in 445 B.C. and continued until the coming of Jesus, the Messiah.[27] Sadly, Daniel foretold that the Messiah would be "cut off," or killed by His people, and God's prophetic time clock would stop. The amount of time elapsing between the start of the 70 weeks and the cutting off of the Messiah would be 69 weeks, or 483 years. Fulfilling Daniel's prophecy to the letter, God's prophetic time clock stopped when Jesus was crucified in A.D. 33.

Out of one of mankind's worst moments, however, rose one of God's greatest acts of mercy. Isaiah prophesied that the cutting off of the Messiah would result in the Lord sending His salvation to the Gentiles.[28] This period, commonly called the Church Age,

---

[27] Ezra 1–6; Daniel 9:25.

[28] Isaiah 42:6, 49:6, 60:3. Some see this parenthesis as the "times of the Gentiles" spoken of by Jesus in Luke 21:24 and Paul in Romans 11:25. While this fits with the theme of the gospel being given as a light to the Gentiles, it does not fit with the concluding characteristics of this time, which are that Jerusalem will no longer be trodden underfoot by Gentiles and that the blindness of the children of Israel will be lifted. Marvin Rosenthal has suggested that the times of the Gentiles began, not with the cutting off of the Messiah, but with the end of the rule of the royal line of David, which occurred when the kingdom of Judah was carried into captivity in 586 B.C. ("12 Messages on Daniel"—1A). In 2 Sam. 7:16, David was promised by God that his house and his kingdom would be established forever. When the Assyrians took Israel captive in 722 B.C., then Judah in 586 B.C., this ended the kingdom of David temporarily. By the time of Jesus, the Israelites had been returned to their homeland but remained under foreign rule as they had for six centuries. They were anxiously looking for their deliverer, a son of the house of David to once again throw off the yoke of foreign oppression and take the throne. When

will last until the gospel has reached every nation (Matt. 24:14). After this prophecy has been fulfilled, God will once again turn His focus back to Israel.

Daniel's 70 Weeks Prophecy

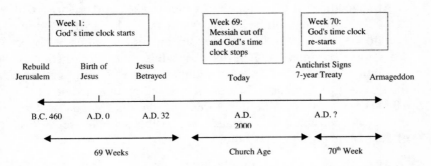

So far, the Church Age has extended nearly 2,000 years, although the rapid fulfillment of end-times prophecy indicates that it may soon be coming to an end. Once God's purposes are fulfilled, the Antichrist will confirm a seven-year covenant with Israel and God's attention will turn back to Israel. At this time, the prophetic time clock will resume (Dan. 9:27) and the countdown to Armageddon will begin.[29] This will be Daniel's 70th Week.

Jesus entered Jerusalem at the end of His ministry and the crowds cried, "Hosanna to the Son of David! Blessed is He who comes in the name of the Lord!" (Matt. 21:9), they were indicating the legitimacy of Jesus' right to rule. Had Israel accepted Jesus as Messiah, the times of the Gentiles would have ended. But the Jews did not accept Jesus, and He was crucified, ending the 69th Week. To this day, there has been no son of David on the throne of Israel, nor will there be until Jesus comes again. When the Son of David touches down, however, He will take back Jerusalem, which is to be the seat of His throne, fulfilling Luke 21:24. Further, the blindness of Israel will be lifted in fulfillment of Romans 11:25. At His Coming, "every eye will see Him, even they who pierced Him" (Rev. 1:7) and "all the tribes of the earth will mourn" (Matt. 24:30). If the time of the Gentiles ends with the beginning of the 70th Week, as some contend, however, this pattern of fulfillment would be lost. Indeed, there would be no event to precipitate these changes.

[29] The fulfillment of the 69 weeks was outlined by Sir Robert Anderson in his 1895 work *The Coming Prince*. Grant Jeffrey gives an excellent

41

There are two prophetic markers relevant to this discussion. The first is the Antichrist's signing of the seven-year covenant with Israel (Dan. 9:27), which signals that the 70th Week has begun. From the time this occurs, there will be one "week" (or period of seven years) until Jesus appears with His heavenly host at Armageddon. At the midpoint of this week, the Antichrist will break the covenant with Israel, take away the daily sacrifices in the (yet to be built) temple, and set up an idol of himself to be worshipped (Dan. 12:11). Jesus called this "the abomination of desolation" (Matt. 24:15). The amount of time elapsing between the setting up of the abomination of desolation and the end of the 70th Week will be another three-and-one-half years.[30] This timetable is accepted by all conservative Bible scholars, regardless of the rapture position they hold.

Daniel's 70th Week

Antichrist Stands in the Temple

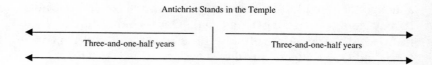

Three-and-one-half years   Three-and-one-half years

Because the time period many people call "the Tribulation" is actually the 70th Week, from this point on, this book will refer to this seven-year period by its proper name, Daniel's 70th Week.

Understanding this background, we can now return to the discussion about the Great Tribulation.[31]

---

synopsis of Anderson's work in his book *Armageddon: Appointment With Destiny*, pp. 27-30. The calculations were worked out using the old Jewish calendar, based on a year of 360 days, which was used at the time that these prophecies were written. Any attempt to work out the dates using the modern 365.25-day calendar will result in error.

[30] As determined by the old Jewish calendar, which used a 360-day year.

[31] An excellent description of the relationship of the Church Age to the 69th and 70th Week, and the resulting impact on interpretation of prophecy, is given by Marvin Rosenthal in his tape series, "12 Messages on Daniel." I will summarize his presentation as follows: There was a 69-week period—made up of a seven-week period, or 49 years, starting with the decree to build Jerusalem in 445 B.C., followed by 62 weeks, or 434 years, for a total of 69 weeks or 483 years—until the Messiah would be

Defining "the Great Tribulation"

The erroneous idea that the Great Tribulation includes all of the events of Revelation is a fundamental tenet of the pretrib doctrine. In most popular treatments of the rapture, the reasoning goes like this: The entire period of God's judgment, which includes the seals, the trumpets, and the bowls, is a time of great destruction. Jesus calls this the "time of great tribulation," but the phrase is sometimes shortened to simply "the Tribulation."[32] Since we are not destined for wrath, believers must be raptured before the Great Tribulation begins.

---

cut off. That began the Church Age, which Paul says was not known in other generations but was made known to him by divine revelation. Paul called this a mystery, something that was always in the plan and program and heart and purpose of God, but in His sovereignty, it was something God chose not to reveal in the Old Testament. As a result, the Old Testament prophets spoke of 69 weeks and one week (for a total of 70 weeks), but they didn't know that there would be an intervening gap (the Church Age) between the 69th and 70th Weeks. They looked down what we now call "the corridor of history" and saw two mountain peaks. The first mountain peak is the First Coming. They wrote about the fact that a child would be born, that a son would be given. They wrote about the fact that His name would be called Emmanuel, "God with us," and the fact that He would be born in Bethlehem in Judea. As they looked down the corridor of time, they also saw the second mountain peak, the Second Coming of Christ, but they did not understand the span between them. Look at how Isaiah writes about it: "For unto us a child is born [that was the first mountain peak], for unto us a son is given [because he was the preincarnate, preexistent son of God]," then there is a comma, "and the government will be upon his shoulder," which refers to His Second Coming. So in one verse, with only a comma in between, Isaiah writes about the First Coming and the Second Coming, with no understanding of the gap in between, because it was a mystery (1 Pet. 1:10-12). Today, we have an advantage over the Old Testament prophets. We are living in the Church Age. What Isaiah was writing about as prophecy is now history to us ("Twelve Messages on Daniel," Tape 5-B, ©Zion's Hope).

[32] Because a straightforward reading of the Olivet Discourse places the rapture after the sixth seal, some pretrib scholars define the Great Tribulation as lasting from the midpoint of the 70th Week to the end, or three-and-a-half years. This puts them in the difficult position of proving that Jesus' coming on the clouds in great glory, which is a defining characteristic of the rapture, actually occurs at Armageddon. The length of the Great Tribulation is discussed in detail in Appendix B.

This is not what scripture teaches. The term "Great Tribulation" is first seen in Matt. 24:21, during the Olivet Discourse. The apostles have just asked Jesus to identify the "end of the age" and the time when Jesus will return. In answer, Jesus gives them a list of very specific signs that will precede this event:

> Now as He sat on the Mount of Olives, the disciples came to Him privately, saying, "Tell us, when will these things be? And what will be the sign of Your coming, and of the end of the age?" And Jesus answered and said to them: "Take heed that no one deceives you. For many will come in my name, saying, 'I am the Christ,' and will deceive many. And you will hear of wars and rumors of wars. See that you are not troubled; for all these things must come to pass, but the end is not yet. For nation will rise against nation, and kingdom against kingdom. And there will be famines, pestilences, and earthquakes in various places. All these are the beginning of sorrows." (Matt. 24:3–8)

Jesus then tells His disciples that the trials will escalate. This will be a terrible time when believers will be killed, false christs will prosper, and lawlessness will abound. However, He also makes it clear that all of these events will occur *prior to His return*:

> Then they will deliver you up to tribulation and kill you, and you will be hated by all nations for My name's sake. And then many will be offended, will betray one another....Then many false prophets will rise up and deceive many. And because lawlessness will abound, the love of many will grow cold. But he who endures to the end shall be saved. And this gospel of the kingdom will be preached in all the world as a witness to all the nations, and then the end will come. (Matt. 24: 9–14)

In the verses that follow, Jesus describes the Antichrist, who has been rising to world domination during this time and is now at the height of his power. He explains how the Antichrist will stand in the temple in Jerusalem and declare himself to be God (or *as* God). When this occurs, the Great Tribulation will begin.

Defining "the Great Tribulation"
(Matt. 24:15-31)

"Therefore, when you see the abomination of desolation, spoken by Daniel the prophet, standing in the holy place….Then let those who are in Judea flee to the mountains. Let him who is on the housetop not go down to take anything out of his house. Let him who is in the field not go back to get his clothes. But woe to those who are pregnant and to those who are nursing babies in those days! And pray that your flight may not be in winter or on the Sabbath.

From Daniel 9:24, we know this is at the midpoint of the 70th Week

For then there will be great tribulation, such as has not been since the beginning of the world until this time, no, nor ever shall be. And unless those days were shortened, no flesh would be saved; but for the elect's sake those days will be shortened.

The Great Tribulation begins. Comparison to the fifth seal of Revelation will show that it is the same event.

Then if anyone says to you, 'Look here is the Christ!' or 'there!' do not believe it. For false christs and false prophets will rise and show great signs and wonders to deceive, if possible, even the elect. See, I have told you beforehand. Therefore if they say to you, 'Look, He is in the desert!' do not go out; or 'Look He is in the inner rooms!' do not believe it. For as the lightning comes from the east and flashes to the west, so also will the coming of the Son of Man be….

Jesus goes to great lengths to tell people not to be deceived—He isn't coming when He is expected. He is talking to believers.

Immediately after the tribulation of those days, the sun will be darkened, and the moon will not give its light; the stars will fall from heaven, and the powers of the heavens will be shaken. Then the sign of the Son of Man will appear in heaven, and then all the tribes of the earth will mourn, and they will see the Son of Man coming on the clouds with great glory. And He will send His angels with a great sound of a trumpet and they will gather together His elect from the four winds, from one end of heaven to the other." (Matt. 24:15-31)

The Great Tribulation ends prior to the cosmic disturbances of the sixth seal. This period is intense, but "cut short" by the rapture for the sake of the elect. Otherwise," no flesh would be saved."

Therefore when you see the "abomination of desolation" spoken of by Daniel the prophet, standing in the holy place..., let those who are in Judea flee to the mountains. Let him who is on the housetop not go down to take anything out of his house. And let him who is in the field not go back to get his clothes. But woe to those who are pregnant and to those who are nursing babies in those days! And pray that your flight may not be in winter or on the Sabbath. For then there will be great tribulation, such as has not been since the beginning of the world until this time, no, nor ever shall be. (Matt. 24:15–21)

It is now understandable why Jesus didn't give the sign of His coming right away. He chose to first warn His children of the perils to come, to prepare and strengthen them for these difficult times. He was particularly concerned about arming His people against deception. Three times after describing the Great Tribulation, He warns them not to be deceived:

Then if anyone says to you, "Look, here is the Christ!" or "There!" do not believe it. For false christs and false prophets will rise and show great signs and wonders to deceive, if possible, even the elect. See, I have told you beforehand. Therefore if they say to you, "Look, He is in the desert!" do not go out; or "Look, He is in the inner rooms!" do not believe it. (Matt. 24:23–26)

After this background, Jesus finally answers the disciples' question:

Immediately after the tribulation of those days, the sun will be darkened, and the moon will not give its light; the stars will fall from heaven, and the powers of the heavens will be shaken. Then the sign of the Son of Man will appear in heaven, and then all the tribes of the earth will mourn, and they will see the Son of Man coming on the clouds of heaven with power and great glory. (Matt. 24:29–31)

The phrase "immediately after" is very clear. The Great Tribulation will begin after the Antichrist stands in the temple and end before the great cosmic disturbances. When will these cosmic disturbances occur? As part of the sixth seal: "I looked when He opened the sixth seal, and behold, there was a great earthquake; and the sun became black as sackcloth of hair, and the moon became like blood. And the stars of heaven fell to the earth, as a fig tree drops its late figs when it is shaken by a mighty wind" (Rev. 6:12–13).

This presents a difficulty for the pretribulation position. Daniel prophesied that the Antichrist will stand in the temple at the midpoint of the 70th Week, or three-and-one-half years from the time that he confirms the covenant with Israel. Jesus' statement in Matt. 24:29, "after the tribulation of those days," puts a limit on the length of this tribulation, only until the sixth seal (remember, 14 judgments—the seven trumpet and seven bowl judgments—are still to come).

Therefore, the Great Tribulation *cannot* refer to the entire 70th Week (or even the last half of it as some pretrib scholars maintain) but only to the portion between the midpoint and the sixth seal.[33]

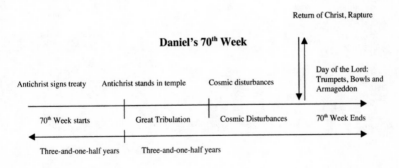

---

[33] In his article, "A Review of the Prewrath Rapture of the Church," Gerald Stanton argues that "the tribulation period," the Day of the Lord, and the Great Tribulation are essentially the same, and criticizes any attempt to limit the Great Tribulation to the time period between the midpoint of the 70th Week and the cosmic disturbances of the sixth seal. He writes, "These descriptions have to do with content, not with duration of that period, and certainly do not designate the timing of the rapture" (*Bibliotheca Sacra*, January-March 1991, Ibid., p. 97). I strongly disagree. Due to the repeated use of words and phrases like "then" and "immediately after" throughout Matthew 24, I believe that the plain meaning of the text is the exact opposite—that they are meant to indicate duration.

Once we look more closely at each of these fundamental premises of the pretrib position, it becomes clear why this position doesn't work. God's wrath is not poured out during the seal judgments (for more on this, see Chapter 2, "What the Bible Says About the Rapture" and Chapter 4, "When Does God's Wrath Begin?"), so there is no reason to require the Church to be raptured prior to the first seal. Even the Great Tribulation, which results in the cry of the martyred saints under the fifth seal, is not God's wrath and concludes before the rapture occurs.

Therefore, the entire premise that, because Jesus will rapture His Church prior to the pouring out of God's wrath, the rapture must be prior to the Great Tribulation is a faulty premise.

4

When Does God's
Wrath Begin?

The fact that the rapture must precede God's wrath is not under debate. On this, both the pretrib and the prewrath positions agree. God has promised that we are not destined for wrath, and the Church will be raptured before this terrible time. But when does God's wrath begin? If it begins with the seals, as the pretribulation position teaches, we are justified in requiring the rapture to occur before the 70th Week. If God's wrath occurs later, after the midpoint of the 70th Week, as the prewrath position contends, a foundational pillar of pretribulationism crumbles.

So when does God's wrath begin? As discussed in Chapter 2, God's wrath is contained in the Day of the Lord, and according to Joel 2:31, the Day of the Lord does not begin until after the opening of the sixth seal. This, in itself, proves that the seal judgments cannot be God's wrath.[34] But because the beginning of God's wrath is so central to the timing of the rapture—indeed, it alone determines the correct reading of rapture doctrine—it would be most helpful if there were multiple confirmations on this point. In fact, there are many.

Use of the Term "Wrath"

The first confirmation comes from the use of the word "wrath." There are 13 uses of the word "wrath" in Revelation, each using the Greek words, *orge* or *thumos*. From the beginning

---

[34] Many pretrib scholars also agree that the Day of the Lord contains God's wrath. The issue, then, is really when the Day of the Lord begins. For a more detailed look at this issue, see Appendixes A and B.

of Revelation until the opening of the sixth seal, both of these words are conspicuously absent. They are not used in the first seal, the rise of the Antichrist; the second seal, the Antichrist's waging of world war; the third seal, the worldwide famine; the fourth seal, widespread death on the earth; or even the fifth seal, the cry of the martyrs. The first time the word "wrath" is used is in Rev. 6:17, after the opening of the sixth seal:

> And the [mighty men of the earth] hid themselves in the caves and in the rocks of the mountains and said to the mountains and rocks, "Fall on us and hide us from the face of Him who sits on the throne and from the wrath of the Lamb! For the great day of His wrath has come and who is able to stand?" (Rev. 6:14–17).

After this, the word "wrath" is used 12 times.

There are some who would argue that the phrase, "His wrath has come" means that God's wrath has already arrived and that the people who are hiding in the caves and the rocks are experiencing His wrath, which started some time earlier. By implication, at the opening of the first seal.

As in English, the Greek verb tense "has come" can have two meanings. The first is an event that has already occurred and the second is an event that is soon to come. The correct reading depends on the context. Since we have already established that God's wrath is associated with the Day of the Lord, and that the Day of the Lord begins after the opening of the sixth seal, this tells us that God's wrath must be imminent, but still in the future.[35]

In order to illustrate this "imminent but still future" use of the phrase *has come,* let's look at an example in the English language. Let's take the example of a young violinist who has been preparing for her first solo concert. On the eve of the event,

---

[35] The debate among theologians as to whether the verb tense "has come," an aorist tense, means "has already come" or "is on the verge of breaking forth" is a lively one. The more discussions one reads on the subject, the more it becomes clear that the correct interpretation will not be determined by Greek grammar alone. The correct reading can be definitively determined only by the context. I believe that, when all relevant verses are taken into account, the case for "is on the verge of breaking forth" is strongest.

she is sitting backstage, warming up, trying to calm the butterflies in her stomach as she listens to the rumble of the crowd. Suddenly, the crowd hushes, her stomach tightens, and her parents give her a warm hug. With a smile, her father says, "Finally, the hour has come." *Has come* — her first concert performance, just moments away, but still a future event.

This verb construction is used several times in the New Testament. The first is in Mark 14:41, when Jesus calls to His followers after they have spent the night in the Garden of Gethsemane, saying, "The hour *has come*; behold, the Son of Man is being betrayed into the hands of sinners." Jesus is referring to His crucifixion, which is still a future event. Another use is in Rev. 19:7, when John describes the destruction of the future Great Harlot of Babylon, writing, "Let us be glad and rejoice and give Him glory, for the marriage of the Lamb *has come* and His wife has made herself ready." Again, this refers to an imminent, but still future, event. As the mighty men hide themselves in the caves and the rocks, John also uses the construction "His wrath *has come*" to refer to an imminent, but still future, event. [36]

Pretrib proponents will argue that the most natural reading of the text gives the opposite impression, that God's wrath has already arrived. However, even pretrib scholar Dr. Renald Showers makes the point that the phrase, "the great day of His wrath is come" cannot be used this way since this is an observation made by the unsaved:

> It is important to note that it is the unregenerate, who will be living on the earth when the sixth seal is broken, who will say, "The great day of his wrath is come" (v.17). The Apostle John did not say this; he simply recorded what they will say. Their statement reveals their conclusion in light of the awesome expression of God's wrath, which they will experience in conjunction with the sixth seal. It is also important to note that this is the statement and conclusion of the unregenerate because they often draw wrong conclusions concerning the works of God. [37]

---

[36] For a more thorough discussion of this verb tense, see Marvin Rosenthal's *Pre-Wrath Rapture of the Church*, Chapter 12.
[37] *Maranatha! Oh Lord, Come!*, p. 120.

51

Although Dr. Showers believes that the sixth seal *is* God's wrath, his conclusion is not drawn from this verse. Therefore, his point about the ability of the unregenerate to consistently draw the wrong conclusions about the activities of God is relevant here. [38]

Furthermore, it is important to notice that the mighty men do not cry, "God's wrath has come." They cry, "the great *day* of God's wrath has come." This distinction is important. Earlier in this book, I defined the Day of the Lord as the terrifying time when God's righteous anger will be poured out upon the wicked and unbelieving. Zephaniah identifies this as "a day of wrath" (Zeph. 1:15) and Isaiah calls it "the day of His fierce anger" (Isaiah 6:13). Joel gives us the signs that will immediately precede this Day: "the sun will turn dark, the moon into blood, and the stars will fall from the sky before the great and terrible day of the Lord" (Joel 2:31)—the sixth seal.

Now, in Rev. 6:17, we have the mighty men crying, "the great day of His wrath has come!" Considering that the world is now on the cusp of the Day of the Lord, could it be that their cry, "the great day of His wrath" is a synonym for the Day of the Lord? That what they are really saying is, "The Day of the Lord has come?" It seems very likely. If so, then the cry, "the great day of God's wrath has come," does not mean the men of the earth are experiencing God's wrath. Rather, it means that they recognize that they are about to enter the Day of the Lord, in which God's wrath is contained.

Differing Use of Angels

There are many other confirmations that the seals are not God's wrath. One of these is the different ways in which the seal judgments and the trumpet and bowl judgments are administered. Throughout the Bible, angels serve as God's messengers, His agents, on earth to accomplish His will. In the six seal judgments, the use of angels as administering agents is absent:

---

[38] Notice (1) that God's wrath occurs as part of the Day of the Lord; (2) and according to Joel 2:31, the Day of the Lord does not start until after the opening of the sixth seal; and (3) the Great Tribulation, which coincides with the fifth seal, occurs *before this time*. Therefore, once again, the Great Tribulation is *not part of God's wrath*.

Now I saw when the Lamb opened one of the seals; and I heard one of the four living creatures saying with a voice like thunder, "Come and see." And I looked, and behold, a white horse. He who sat on it had a bow; and a crown was given to him, and he went out conquering and to conquer.

When I opened the second seal, I heard the second living creature saying, "Come and see." Another horse, fiery red, went out. And it was granted to the one who sat on it to take peace from the earth, and that people should kill one another; and there was given to him a great sword.

When He opened the third seal, I heard the third living creature say, "Come and see." So I looked, and behold, a black horse, and he who sat on it had a pair of scales in his hand. And I heard a voice in the midst of the four living creatures saying, "A quart of wheat for a denarius, and three quarts of barley for a denarius; and do not harm the oil and the wine." (Rev. 6:1–6)

Three other seal judgments follow: the death of up to one-quarter of the earth's inhabitants; the persecution and martyrdom of Jews and Christians by the Antichrist; and the cosmic disturbances that immediately precede the return of Christ. The action in these verses is *passive*: "a crown was given to him"; "it was granted to the one who sat on it"; and "he who sat on it had a pair of scales." In all of these cases, the events are *not* the direct result of action taken by God's angels. Therefore, they are not the direct result of God's active intervention, even though they have been allowed and designed by Him as part of His perfect plan.[39]

Shift to the Day of the Lord

Starting with the trumpet judgments, however, the text changes. At this time, the Lord begins actively interfering with the world's events through His messenger angels. This is what we

---

[39] One of the criticisms of the prewrath position is that it denies God's hand in the seal judgments in order to justify them as not being His wrath. I am *not* making that suggestion. The text makes it clear that Jesus is the one personally breaking the seals and is therefore directly responsible for the consequences. However, the fact that Jesus is responsible for breaking the seals does not make them His *wrath*.

would expect since the trumpets are part of the "great and terrible Day of the Lord."

This shift is described in detail in Revelation 8:

> When He opened the seventh seal, there was silence in heaven for about half an hour. And I saw the seven angels who stand before God, and to them were given seven trumpets.... Then the angel took the censer, filled it with fire from the altar, and threw it to the earth. And there were noises, thunderings, lightnings, and an earthquake. So the seven angels who had the seven trumpets prepared themselves to sound. (Rev. 8:1–6)

The Day of the Lord has begun.

At this point, in contrast to the seals, which were *observed* by angels, the trumpet judgments result from the *direct, active intervention* by angels:

> When He opened the seventh seal, there was silence in heaven for about half an hour. And I saw the seven angels who stand before God, and to them were given seven trumpets....
>
> The first angel sounded: And hail and fire followed, mingled with blood, and they were thrown to the earth. And a third of the trees were burned up and all green grass was burned up.
>
> Then the second angel sounded: And something like a great mountain burning with fire was thrown into the sea, and a third of the sea became blood. And a third of the living creatures in the sea died, and a third of the ships were destroyed.
>
> Then the third angel sounded: And a great star fell from heaven, burning like a torch, and it fell on a third of the rivers and on the springs of water.... (Rev. 8:1–10)

These are followed by three other trumpet judgments: the striking of the sun, the moon, and the stars; locusts swarming from the bottomless pit; and angels being released to kill one-third of mankind. The chronology in each judgment is the same: the angel blows a trumpet and a judgment follows.

Parallel Chronology

We see the same chronology during the bowl judgments:

> Then I heard a loud voice from the temple saying to the seven angels, "Go and pour out the bowls of the wrath of God on the earth."

> So the first [angel] went and poured out his bowl upon the earth, and a foul and loathsome sore came upon the men who had the mark of the beast and those who worshipped his image.

> Then the second angel poured out his bowl on the sea, and it became blood as of a dead man; and every living creature in the sea died.

> Then the third angel poured out his bowl on the rivers and springs of water, and they became blood. (Rev. 16:1–4)

Four other bowl judgments follow: the scorching of men, darkness and pain, the Euphrates drying up, and the great earthquake. These are also administered by angels.

In contrast to the seals, the judgments that make up the Day of the Lord are different in kind. While the seals are passively observed by the living creatures, the trumpets and the bowls result from the *direct, active intervention* of God's angels. Once again, this leads us to the same conclusion: that the trumpets and bowls are part of the God's vengeance and wrath upon the earth during the Day of the Lord, while the seal judgments are not.[40]

---

[40] The difference between God's active and passive will has been contested on the point that the four living creatures, which are often translated "cherubim," are involved in the administration of the seals. However, these creatures do not actively *cause* the seal judgments to happen. Once the seals are broken, the events are *allowed* to happen. The living creatures simply call John to observe events that take place. I do not agree that this places the seals in the same category as the trumpets and the bowls.

God's Passive and Active Will

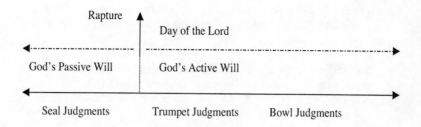

Rapture

Day of the Lord

God's Passive Will | God's Active Will

Seal Judgments | Trumpet Judgments | Bowl Judgments

Adding the Supernatural Element

There is yet another confirmation that the seal judgments are not God's wrath. This is found, not just in how the judgments are administered, but in what they contain. Although the seals will be a time of great turmoil and pain, these trials will be within the realm of natural phenomena, such as war, persecution, and famine. It is only during the cosmic disturbances of the sixth seal that people will realize that something out of the ordinary is happening.

The trumpets and the bowls, on the other hand, contain supernatural elements not found in the seals: water turning to blood, burning mountains falling from the sky, the unnatural occurrences of fire and brimstone. Not only are these judgments greater in severity than the seals, but they can only result from the supernatural intervention of the Creator:

> ... And hail and fire followed mingled with blood... and a third of the sea became blood...a third of the waters became bitter...a third of the sun was struck, a third of the moon, and a third of the stars...smoke arose out of the [bottomless] pit...and a foul and loathsome sore came upon the men who had the mark of the beast and those who worshipped his image...[and the sea] became blood as of a dead man and every living creature in the sea died...the rivers and springs of water [became] blood...and men were scorched with great heat...and there were noises and thunderings and lightnings; and there was a great earthquake, such a mighty and great earthquake as had not occurred since men were on earth. (Rev. 8, 9, 16)

It will be difficult, if not impossible, to rationalize these as natural phenomena.

Martyrs of the Fifth Seal

There is yet another reason that the seals cannot be the wrath of God. Consider this passage from the fifth seal:

> When He opened the fifth seal, I saw under the altar the souls of those who had been slain for the word of God and for the testimony which they held. And they cried with a loud voice, saying, "How long, O Lord, holy and true, until You judge and avenge our blood on those who dwell on the earth?" Then a white robe was given to each of them; and it was said to them that they should rest a little while longer until both the number of their fellow servants and their brethren, who would be killed as they were, was completed. (Rev. 6:9–11)

This passage tells us that an appointed number of believers will be martyred during the fifth seal and no vengeance from God will come until then. If God will not, as He has promised, pour out His wrath upon His children, the fifth seal (and therefore all of the seals before it) cannot be part of God's wrath.[41]

Whose Wrath?

And yet, Luke 21:23 makes it clear that the Great Tribulation is a time of "wrath upon this people." If the Great Tribulation is not God's wrath, whose wrath is it? It is the wrath of

---

[41] Dr. Paul Karleen, in his book, *The PreWrath Rapture of the Church: Is It Biblical?* (BF Press, Langhorne, PA, 1991) contends that the seals are God's wrath based on Luke 21:23, a parallel telling of Jesus' discourse in Matthew 24. See discussion of this verse later in this chapter. John A. McLean tries to place the seals within God's wrath by citing the similarity of the four seals to the four judgments God promises to bring upon His people in "the latter days"—war, famine, pestilence, and beasts. In his article "Another Look at the Prewrath Rapture of the Church," he argues that these are indications of God's wrath, citing Eze. 14:21, Lev. 26:22-26, Deut. 28:21-26, Jer. 15:2-4, and Eze. 5:12-17 (*Bibliotheca Sacra*, Oct-Dec 1991, p. 393). However, the "latter days" also includes the trumpets and the bowls, which unbelieving Israel will have to endure after the believing Jews (as part of the Church) have been raptured. Since the mystery of the Church had not yet been revealed when these prophets were writing, this distinction would not have been clear.

the Antichrist, who is empowered by Satan (Rev.13:2). In Rev. 12:7–12, we are told that there will be a war in heaven in the middle of the 70th Week, and Satan ("the dragon") will be cast to earth. "So the great dragon was cast out, that serpent of old, called the Devil and Satan, who deceives the whole world; he was cast to the earth, and his angels were cast out with him" (v. 9). At this time, the angels cry, "Woe to the inhabitants of the earth and the sea! For the devil has come down to you, *having great wrath*, because he knows that he has a short time."

His fury lit, Satan will begin to persecute the children of Israel, referred to as "the woman" (Rev. 12:13). But the scriptures tell us that the Jews will seek to escape this persecution by fleeing to the wilderness to a place prepared for them by God (v. 14). At this point, Satan (through his puppet, the Antichrist) will turn his fury on the remainder of the woman's offspring, "who have the testimony of Jesus Christ" (v. 17).

This sequence is restated earlier in this chapter: "Then the woman fled into the wilderness, where she has a place prepared by God, that they should feed her there 1,260 days" (v. 6). This period, also referred to as a time, times, and half a time" (v. 14), is a reference to the last three-and-one-half years of the 70th Week. This places this persecution immediately after the abomination of desolation, during the Great Tribulation:

> Therefore when you see the abomination of desolation spoken of by Daniel the prophet, standing in the holy place (whoever reads, let him understand), then let those who are in Judea flee to the mountains. Let him who is on the housetop not go down to take anything out of his house, and let him who is in the field not go back to get his clothes...for then there will be great tribulation, such as has not been since the beginning of the world until this time, no, nor ever shall be. (Matt. 24:15–18, 21)

Remember, Satan has just been thrown out of heaven and is furious. The Antichrist, already an unregenerate soul, becomes his agent to try to eradicate the people of God: "And he [the Antichrist] was given a mouth speaking great things and blasphemies... and it was granted to him to make war with the saints and overcome them. And authority was given him over every tribe, tongue, and nation. All who dwell on the earth will

58

worship him, whose names have not been written in the Book of Life" (Rev. 13:5–8).

So while this will be a time of "great distress in the land and wrath upon this people" (Luke 21:23), this is not the wrath of God. It is the wrath of man, empowered by Satan. In Revelation 6, the martyred saints also attest to this fact, saying that it is the Antichrist who is the author of their deaths, not God: "How long O Lord, holy and true, before You judge and avenge our blood on those who dwell on the earth?" (v. 10). How can they appeal to God for vengeance if He has authored their deaths through His wrath? The fact that they are crying out for vengeance tells us that God's judgment upon the wicked has not yet begun.

This important point is summed up by Marvin Rosenthal:

> In each instance where the great tribulation is used in a prophetic setting, it always refers to the persecution of God's elect by wicked men, never to the wrath of God being directed toward mankind. Prophetically, therefore, the Great Tribulation speaks of man's wrath against man, not God's wrath against man."[42]

The Time of Final Harvest

If God's wrath is contained within the Day of the Lord, does it begin immediately, with the trumpets? Not likely. Although God's wrath will exist during the trumpets as it has existed since the fall of man, the text describes God's final, *end-times* wrath as being contained in the bowl judgments.[43] What is the purpose, then, of the trumpets? Why is there yet another period of waiting?

The trumpets will be the final time of harvest. It may be difficult for the natural mind to imagine that, after all these signs,

---

[42] *The Pre-Wrath Rapture of the Church*, p. 105.

[43] While I take the position that God's final, end-times wrath does not begin until the bowls, many classic prewrath proponents hold to the view that God's wrath begins immediately, with the start of the Day of the Lord, based on Jesus' comparison of the arrival of the Day of the Lord to the arrival of the flood during the days of Noah. Once Noah entered the ark, God's judgment began immediately. Likewise, once the Church is raptured, God's wrath will begin immediately. Neither view affects the timing of the rapture, however, since either case, the rapture is tied to the start of the Day of the Lord and, therefore, before God's wrath.

God will still be waiting for people to come to repentance. However, "the Lord is not slack concerning His promise, as some count slackness, but long-suffering, not willing that any should perish but that all should come to repentance" (2 Peter 3:9). Truly, He is a merciful God, even if it means that He is long-suffering beyond what human beings can understand.

Although God's judgment of the unrepentant world will have begun, the trumpet judgments will also be a time of unparalleled evangelism. In addition to the ministry of those who come to know the Lord after the rapture, there will be three supernatural forces working to spread the Word of God.

First, there will be the 144,000 Jews whom God will preserve according to His promise after the rapture of the Church:

> Then I saw another angel ascending from the east, having the seal of the living God. And he cried with a loud voice to the four angels to whom it was granted to harm the earth and the sea, saying, "Do not harm the earth, the sea, or the trees till we have sealed the servants of our God on their foreheads." And I heard the number of those who were sealed. One hundred and forty-four thousand of all the tribes of the children of Israel were sealed. (Rev. 7:2–4)

Second, God will appoint two supernatural witnesses, likely Enoch and Elijah (or Moses), to preach at the Wailing Wall:

> And I will give power to my two witnesses, and they will prophesy one thousand two hundred and sixty days, clothed in sackcloth….And if anyone wants to harm them, fire proceeds from their mouths and devours their enemies. And if anyone wants to harm them, he must be killed in this manner. These have the power to shut heaven, so that no rain falls in the days of their prophecy; and they have power over waters to turn them to blood, and to strike the earth with all plagues….(Rev. 11:3–6)

Third, once the trumpets begin, God will send an angel to preach the gospel to every creature on earth:

> Then I saw another angel flying in the midst of heaven, having the everlasting gospel to preach to those who dwell

on the earth—to every nation, tribe, tongue, and people—saying with a loud voice, "Fear God and give glory to Him, for the hour of His judgment has come; and worship Him who made heaven and earth, the sea and springs of water." And another followed, saying, "Babylon is fallen, is fallen, that great city, because she has made all nations drink of the wine of the wrath of her fornication." Then a third angel followed them, saying with a loud voice, "If anyone worships the beast and his image, and receives his mark on his forehead or on his hand, he himself shall also drink of the wine of the wrath of God, which is poured out full strength into the cup of His indignation. He shall be tormented with fire and brimstone in the presence of the holy angels and in the presence of the Lamb." (Rev. 14:6–10)

During the trumpet judgments, all excuses will be removed. There will be two supernatural powers present on the earth at that time: the One true God, Creator of heaven and earth; and Satan, embodied in the form of the Antichrist. The world's inhabitants will be forced to choose sides. Either they will serve the Antichrist and lose their souls, or serve the true Lord of heaven and earth and risk losing their lives.[44]

But there is hope in this, too. Those who give up their lives for their faith will gain heaven for eternity. This glorious picture is given to us in Revelation 15. Just as we see the raptured Church in

---

[44] There are people who would reject the assertion that Jesus will be here during the Day of the Lord based on the idea that the Antichrist could not be allowed to reign while Jesus is on earth. Why not? Consider the length of Christ's first ministry. He walked this earth for more than 33 years while His people suffered under the tyranny of Roman rule. This was one of the reasons the Jews were so quick to reject Him as the Messiah. They were tired of their earthly oppression and wanted Him to bring the physical kingdom of God. They did not understand that Jesus wanted to set them free *spiritually*, for His kingdom to reign in their hearts. The parallel between Jesus' First and His Second Comings is strong. As at His First Coming, the world will be suffering under the oppression and reign of the Antichrist, although the suffering will be far more severe. As at His First Coming, He may be fully able and yet not willing to throw off believers' physical yokes, preferring to make them free, not from their earthly circumstances, but in spite of them, by setting them free from sin through His blood on the cross.

61

heaven immediately after the six seals, worshipping Jesus, in this chapter we see these newly martyred saints in heaven immediately after the trumpets, worshipping their King:

> Then I saw another sign in heaven, great and marvelous: seven angels having the seven last plagues, for in them the wrath of God is complete. And I saw something like a sea of glass mingled with fire, and those who have the victory over the beast [through death in Jesus Christ], over his image, and over his mark, and over the number of his name, standing on the sea of glass, having harps of God. They sing the song of Moses, the servant of God, and the song of the Lamb, saying: "Great and marvelous are Your works, Lord God Almighty!" (Rev. 15:1–4)

Once again, what a beautiful picture of the redeemed, glorifying their King! What a comfort this should be to those who face martyrdom in the final days!

Another Look at the Trumpets

It is important to keep in mind that, although the trumpets are part of God's judgment during the Day of the Lord, they are not His final, end-times wrath. The trumpets, like the seal judgments, precede the actual outpouring of God's fury.

At the start of the trumpet judgments, God's wrath is imminent but not immediate. There will be many who come to the saving knowledge of Jesus Christ after the rapture, and God will no more pour out His wrath on these post-rapture believers than He will on pre-rapture believers. It is appropriate, then, that the word "wrath" is not associated with the trumpet judgments any more than it is associated with the seals. It is not used when the vegetation is burned by hail and fire, mingled with blood. It is not used when one-third of the seas and rivers are turned to blood. It is not used when one-third of the heavens are darkened. Nor is it used when locusts swarm from the bottomless pit or when the angels kill one-third of mankind.

The only time the word "wrath" is used is after the sixth trumpet and before the seventh trumpet, just before the bowls. Here, John once again uses the phrase, "Your wrath has come." "The nations were angry, and Your wrath *has come*, and the time of the dead, that they should be judged, and that You should

62

reward Your servants the prophets and the saints" (Rev. 11:18).

Once again, as in Rev. 6:17, God's wrath is an imminent, but *still future,* event.[45]

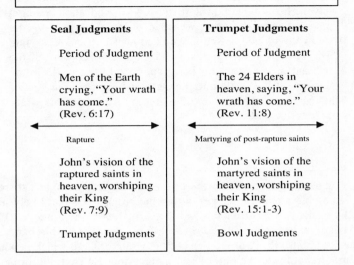

Comparison of "Your Wrath Has Come"	
Seal Judgments	**Trumpet Judgments**
Period of Judgment	Period of Judgment
Men of the Earth crying, "Your wrath has come." (Rev. 6:17)	The 24 Elders in heaven, saying, "Your wrath has come." (Rev. 11:8)
◄——————►	◄——————►
Rapture	Martyring of post-rapture saints
John's vision of the raptured saints in heaven, worshiping their King (Rev. 7:9)	John's vision of the martyred saints in heaven, worshiping their King (Rev. 15:1-3)
Trumpet Judgments	Bowl Judgments

And Now, God's Wrath

That God's wrath is not poured out until the bowls is appropriate because, by this time, all believers will have been raptured, martyred, or protected. Thus, the only people exposed on the face of the earth will be those who cannot or will not repent,

---

[45] This is further confirmed by the fact that, while the phrase, "Your wrath has come" is similar to Rev. 6:17, it is not identical. During the sixth seal, when the mighty men cry, "the great day of His wrath has come," they are announcing the arrival of the Day of the Lord, which contains the trumpets and the bowls. In this passage, the 24 elders, first introduced in Revelation 5, say, "The nations were angry and Your wrath has come." There is an important distinction. While the day of God's wrath *contains* God's wrath, it, in itself, is not entirely God's wrath. It is only now, with the bowl judgments, that God's wrath has arrived. For those wishing more information on the distinction between the trumpets and the bowls, see the Talkin' Rapture column, "Are the Trumpets God's Wrath?" and "Do the Three Woes Tie God's Wrath to the Trumpets?" on the Strong Tower Publishing Web site.

and there will be nothing holding back the wrath of our long-suffering God.[46]

John describes the preparation that goes on in heaven as God readies for this final, terrible time:

> Then another angel came out of the temple which is in heaven, he also having a sharp sickle. And another angel came out from the altar, who had power over fire, and he cried with a loud cry to him who had the sharp sickle, saying, "Thrust in your sharp sickle and gather the clusters of the vine and of the earth, for her grapes are fully ripe.'" So the angel thrust his sickle into the earth and gathered the vine of the earth, and threw it into the great winepress of the wrath of God. (Rev. 14:17–19)

---

[46] Why must this time during the trumpets be allowed? Won't there be people coming to faith in Christ during the bowls, too? Not likely. Rev. 11:10-11 tells us that if anyone worships the beast (the Antichrist) and his image, and receives his mark on his forehead or on his hand, "he himself shall also drink of the wine of the wrath of God, which is poured out full strength into the cup of His indignation. He shall be tormented with fire and brimstone in the presence of the holy angels and in the presence of the Lamb." For believers, there is a strong incentive to faithfulness. But for nonbelievers, there is no such incentive. If they take the mark, they will know that they are choosing the Antichrist over Jesus Christ, but the lie that blankets the earth (2 Thess. 2:11) will cause them to believe that the Antichrist has the power to protect them. At some point, likely very early in the trumpet judgments, they must choose between Jesus as Messiah and Lord or the false god. If they choose the Antichrist, this decision cannot be reversed. Indeed, by the fourth bowl, we see that these decisions have been made: ...*and they blasphemed the name of God who has power over these plagues; and they did not repent and give Him glory* (Rev. 16:9). Indeed, as the waters are being turned to blood, the angel of the waters cries out, *You are righteous, O Lord, the One who is and who was and who is to be, because You have judged these things. For they have shed the blood of saints and prophets, and You have given them blood to drink. For it is their just due* (Rev. 16:5-6). And another angel from the altar cries, *Even so, Lord God Almighty, true and righteous are Your judgments* (Rev. 16:7). These verses give us a strong indication that, by the time the bowls judgments arrive, all of the decisions for Christ or for the Antichrist will be made.

God's wrath has finally arrived. Scripture clearly spells out the arrival of this event four times in the eight verses of Chapter 15 and in the first verse of Chapter 16:

> Then I saw another sign in heaven, great and marvelous: seven angels having the seven last plagues, for in them the wrath of God was complete. (Rev. 15:1)[47]

> Then one of the four living creatures gave to the seven angels seven golden bowls full of the wrath of God who lives forever and ever. (Rev. 15:7)

> Then I heard a loud voice from the temple saying to the seven angels, "Go and pour out the bowls of the wrath of God on the earth." (Rev. 16:1)

At this point, there is no question that the following events are occurring as the wrath of God:

> So the first went and poured out his bowl upon the earth, and a foul and loathsome sore came upon the men who had the mark of the beast and those who worshiped his image.

> Then the second angel poured out his bowl on the sea, and it became blood as of a dead man, and every living creature in the sea died.

> Then the third angel poured out his bowl on the rivers and springs of water, and they became blood. (Rev. 16:2–4)

---

[47] If God's wrath begins with the bowl judgments, why do the angels use the phrase "God's wrath *is complete*"? Does this not mean that God's wrath has already begun? In its most technical sense, the answer is yes. Scripture makes it clear that God's wrath has not waited for the 70th Week. Throughout the Old Testament, God poured out His wrath on unbelieving and rebellious Israel (Ex. 15:7, Ex. 22:24, Nu. 11:33, Nu. 16:46), and today, God's wrath continues to abide on all unbelievers (John 3:36, Eph. 5:6, Co. 3:6). Thus, the Day of the Lord wrath of God will not be the first outpouring of His wrath, although it will be the last. The Day of His Wrath will bring to completion the wrath that has abided on the ungodly for all time, but has been mercifully withheld from full strength until now.

Five other judgments follow: darkness and pain, the gathering of the armies at Armageddon by a league of demons, and the final, devastating earthquake in which the earth is utterly shaken. Revelation 19 then records the arrival of Jesus in the clouds at Armageddon, riding a white horse with the name King of kings and Lord of lords written on His thigh.

This is why, when the seventh trumpet sounds, John records voices in heaven, saying, "The kingdoms of this world have become the kingdoms of our Lord and of His Christ, and He shall reign forever and ever!" (Rev. 11:15). Although Jesus returned to earth before the opening of the seventh seal, it is not until He pours out His wrath that all earthly authority and power is crushed.

Defining God's Wrath

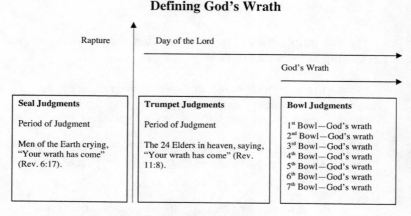

Seal Judgments	Trumpet Judgments	Bowl Judgments
Period of Judgment	Period of Judgment	1st Bowl—God's wrath
		2nd Bowl—God's wrath
Men of the Earth crying,	The 24 Elders in heaven, saying,	3rd Bowl—God's wrath
"Your wrath has come"	"Your wrath has come" (Rev.	4th Bowl—God's wrath
(Rev. 6:17).	11:8).	5th Bowl—God's wrath
		6th Bowl—God's wrath
		7th Bowl—God's wrath

More Confirmations of God's Wrath

There are yet additional proofs that God's wrath does not occur until the bowls. Among these is the phrase, "and that you should reward Your servants the prophets and the saints." This leads to the question: Reward the prophets and the saints for what? This takes us back to the fifth seal:

> When He opened the fifth seal, I saw under the altar the souls of those who had been slain for the word of God and for the testimony which they held. And they cried with a loud voice, saying, "How long, O Lord, holy and true, until You judge and avenge our blood on those who dwell on the earth?" Then a white robe was given to each of them; and it was said to them that they should rest a little while longer until both

the number of their fellow servants and their brethren, who would be killed as they were, was completed. (Rev. 6:9–11)

Earlier, it was pointed out that if these saints were crying out to God to avenge their deaths, He cannot be the author of their deaths through His wrath. Thus, if at the end of the trumpets God's vengeance is still to come, the trumpets cannot be His wrath. Rather, the trumpet judgments will be a time of salvation for the 144,000 and many others who come to a saving knowledge of Jesus Christ during this time. Although some of these believers will be protected during the remainder of the 70th Week (Rev. 12:6), scripture strongly implies that many will be killed in the fury of the Antichrist.

Once this persecution is complete, the martyrs' prayers will be answered. God will avenge their deaths, and our long-suffering Savior will finally pour out His wrath.

The nations were angry, and Your wrath *has come,* And the time of the dead, that they should be judged, *And that You should reward Your servants the prophets and the saints.* (Rev. 11:18)

Protection in the Midst of Wrath

Does this mean that all those who come to faith in Christ will be killed? No. The Bible tells us that some of those who come to faith during the 70th Week remain alive to populate the Millennial earth. The only believers that the New Testament describes as surviving this terrible time are the faithful remnant of Israel ("And so all Israel shall be saved"— Romans 11:26), who will be protected by God in the wilderness until the end of the 70th Week. However, many Old Testament passages tell us that at least some Gentiles will survive, as well. In particular, these prophecies describe how, during the Millennial kingdom, the people of "the nations" will come up to the temple in Jerusalem to worship. In order for this to happen, at least some Gentiles must survive the 70th Week.

Even though believers will be alive on earth during the bowl judgments, God will still be faithful to His promise: "For God did not appoint us to wrath but to obtain salvation through our Lord

Jesus Christ" 1 Thess. 5:9).[48] Consider how He protected the Hebrews during the plagues of Egypt. When the Egyptians were plagued with boils, flies, and frogs, the Hebrews and their livestock were untouched. When the Angel of the Lord (a preincarnate form of the Lord Jesus Christ) passed by in the night to take the life of the firstborn, the children of the unbelieving Egyptians were taken, but the children of those Hebrews who had covered their lintels with the blood of the Passover Lamb remained alive.

This principle of protection in the midst of wrath can also be found in the writings of the prophets. For example, Isaiah writes: "Come, my people, enter into your rooms, and close your doors behind you; hide for a little while, until the indignation runs its course. For behold, the Lord is about to come out from His place to punish the inhabitants of the earth for their iniquity" (Isa. 26:20–21).[49] And in Eze. 14:12–20, Ezekiel describes the land of

------

[48]Writes Douglas Moo: "The judgments and wrath of God are clearly selective. The demonic locusts of the fifth trumpet are ordered to harm 'only those people who did not have the seal of God on their foreheads' (Rev. 9:4), while the first bowl is poured out only on 'the people who had the mark of the beast and worshiped his image' (Rev. 1:2). And the recipients of a number of the plagues are said to refuse to repent (Rev. 9:20-21; 16:9, 11)—an indication that only unbelievers are affected by them" *Three Views on the Rapture*, p. 175.

[49]Douglas Moo points out that the context of this passage sounds very much like the Day of the Lord, but even if it is not, the principle of protection through wrath has been established. In this case, scripture tells us that a multitude of Jews—and likely Christians, as well—will hide in the desert, where they will be sheltered for three-and-one-half years (Rev. 12:6). There will likely be other forms of protection, as well: "It is frequently stated that believers are divinely protected from these judgments. Two characteristic texts can be cited. In Rev. 14:9-10, the angel proclaims, 'If anyone worships the beast and his image and receives his mark on the forehead or on the hand, he, too, will drink of the wine of God's fury, which has been poured full strength into the cup of his wrath.' The conditional nature of this warning ('if') demonstrates that the wrath here is inflicted only on unbelievers. The fact that tribulation believers, whoever they are, will be kept from God's wrath, is indicated also in Rev. 18:4, where God's people are warned to 'come out' of the harlot Babylon 'so that you will not share in her sins, so that

Israel during God's judgment of famine, pestilence, the sword, and wild beasts: "Son of man, when a land sins against Me by persistent unfaithfulness, I will stretch out My hand against it; I will cut off its supply of bread, send famine on it, and cut off man and beast from it. Even if these three men, Noah, Daniel, and Job, were in it, *they would deliver only themselves* by their righteousness" (v. 13).

God has many ways of protecting His people during times of judgment and wrath. During the end times, this can happen in one of three ways: by rapture, by martyrdom, or by divine protection. Apparently, God uses all three. This is not to say that all believers will escape harm during the 70th Week. Clearly, these will be perilous times. All we can say for certain is that they will escape God's *wrath*.

---

you will not receive any of her plagues.'" *Three Views on the Rapture*, p. 89.

5

Will the Church
Endure the Great Tribulation?

One of the arguments used to support the pretribulation rapture is that the Church will not go through the Great Tribulation. Therefore, the rapture will occur before this terrible time. There are many rationales for this position, but first, let's look at what the plain meaning of the scriptures has to say.

The first time the phrase the "great tribulation" is used is in Matthew 24. This chapter is opened by Jesus' disciples asking, "Tell us, when will these things be? And what will be the sign of Your coming and of the end of the age?" (v. 3). In answer, Jesus tells them there will be wars and rumors of wars, nation rising against nation, kingdom against kingdom, and famines, pestilences, and earthquakes in various places. He then describes the abomination of desolation in the temple in Jerusalem, which will occur at the midpoint of the 70th Week. He follows this description by saying,

> For then there will be great tribulation, such as has not been since the beginning of the world until this time, no, nor ever shall be. (v. 21)

This is followed by the command to flee Jerusalem, which is where the persecution will start. Then Jesus goes on to say,

> Immediately after the tribulation of those days, the sun will be darkened, and the moon will not give its light; the stars will fall from heaven, and the powers of the heavens will be shaken. Then the sign of the Son of Man will appear in heaven, and

70

then all the tribes of the earth will mourn, and they will see the Son of Man coming on the clouds of heaven with power and great glory. (v. 30)

In His answer to the disciples—the future New Testament Church—we see the following order: the beginning of the 70th Week, the Great Tribulation, the arrival of Jesus in power and glory, and the rapture of the Church. The plain meaning of this passage, then, is that the Church will endure the Great Tribulation.

During the ministry of the Apostle Peter, the return of the Lord was also a common subject of his writings. In 1 Peter 4, we see the same succession of events. Peter writes,

> But the end of all things is at hand; therefore be serious and watchful in your prayers…. Beloved, do not think it strange concerning the fiery trial which is to try you, as though some strange thing happened to you; but rejoice to the extent that you partake of Christ's sufferings, that when His glory is revealed, you may also be glad with exceeding joy. Yet if anyone suffers as a Christian, let him not be ashamed, but let him glorify God in this matter. For the time has come for judgment to begin at the house of God; and if it begins with us first, what will be the end of those who do not obey the gospel of Christ? (1 Peter 4: 7, 12–13, 16–17)

Here, we see Peter believed that the Church was living during the end times ("the end of all things is at hand"), and as the end-times Church, Christians would go through the fiery trial. And not just any fiery trial, Peter wrote, but *the* fiery trial—the specific trial preordained by God. Once having passed through this trial, he assured Christians that they would see the returning Messiah, "that when His glory is revealed, you may also be glad with exceeding joy." This pattern matches that given by Jesus in Matthew 24—the beginning of the end times, the Great Tribulation, then Christ's appearance in the clouds with power and great glory.

This concept is reiterated earlier in the chapter, when Peter wrote,

> In this [the living hope believers have through the resurrection of Jesus Christ] you greatly rejoice, though now for a little while, if need be, you have been grieved by

various trials, that the genuineness of your faith, being much more precious than gold that perishes, though it is tested by fire, may be found to praise, honor, and glory at the revelation of Jesus Christ. (1 Peter: 6–7)

Contrary to the common assertion that the Great Tribulation is only for unbelieving Israel, Peter consistently refers to this trial as also being part of the plan of a holy, sovereign God for the Church. Notice that Peter says, "For the time has come for judgment to begin at the house of God; *and if it begins with us first...*" While God will use this time to deal with the unbelieving nation of Israel, His testing and refinement will start at home, with His own children.

Was the Discourse Given Only to Israel?

In spite of the clear teaching of the scriptures, there are many who maintain the belief that the Church will not go through the Great Tribulation because it is a time of trial specifically and exclusively for the nation of Israel. This argument follows two lines of reasoning:

1. Daniel's 70 Weeks prophecy was given to the nation of Israel. Because the Church was not part of the first 69 Weeks, it will not be part of the 70th Week either.[50]
2. When Jesus gave the Olivet Discourse, the New Testament Church had not yet been formed. Therefore, the contents of Jesus' sermon (and therefore the corresponding passages in Revelation) apply only to Israel, not to the Church.

Both of these are arguments by implication, not direct from the scriptures. The plain meaning of the scriptures is that the

---

[50] The view that parts of scripture relating to the 70th Week apply only to Israel and not to the Church comes from the dispensational theology. Dispensationalism is a framework for interpreting scripture that breaks human history down into "dispensations," or distinct, non-overlapping (and mutually exclusive) time periods in which God uses different methods to govern mankind. Nowhere in scripture, however, does it tell us that God created such dispensations. This was simply an induction based on observations made by scholars about the activities of God. These observations were then turned into a rigid theological system that, as would be expected from a human product, creates errors and inconsistencies when applied categorically to the Word of God.

Church *will* go through the Great Tribulation. The "70th Week is only for Israel" argument relies entirely on inductive lines of reasoning that do not hold up under biblical scrutiny.

Let's start with the argument that the Church cannot be part of the 70th Week because it was not part of the original 69 weeks of the 70 Weeks prophecy. This approach forces a break between God's dealings with the Church and His dealings with Israel that I do not see in scripture. God has always had separate plans for the Jews and the Gentiles, for believers and unbelievers, but they have never operated independently. When Moses led the people out of Egypt, God had a plan for the Jews: to lead them into the land of promise and to make them into a distinct group of people for His glory. But He also had a plan for the Egyptians: to judge them for their rebellion and idolatry. But even these purposes were not mutually exclusive. Not only did God use the Jews to judge the Egyptians, but He also used the Jews to bless the Egyptians by taking with them a multitude who desired to serve Him. He also used the Egyptians to bless the Jews by giving them gold, silver, and other treasures they would later need to build the tabernacle in the wilderness.

God's purposes throughout the period of the Judges were similarly indistinct. God's purpose for the Jews was to discipline them, break them of their idolatry, and deliver to them the land of promise. God's purpose for the Gentiles was to judge them for their idolatry and ultimately lead them to faith and obedience in Him. God used the pagan nations to discipline Israel and Israel to discipline the pagan nations. At the same time, He also used Israel to bless the pagan nations by spreading the knowledge and love of Himself by which many Gentiles partook of the blessings of salvation. Ruth and the prostitute Rahab even became part of the bloodline of Christ.

This pattern continues throughout the 69 weeks. Even as Israel was rejecting her Messiah, she was fulfilling God's prophecy to bless all of the Gentile nations by giving them the gospel (Gen. 12:3). In turn, God's program for the Church was used to bless the Jews by provoking them to jealousy (Romans 10:19) and thereby turning them to the gospel. Indeed, through the evangelism of the Church, including Jewish Christians, many Jews have come to a saving knowledge of their Messiah.

There is simply no explicit biblical reason to require the

Church to be removed from the earth prior to the 70th Week. God's use of the 70th Week to complete His plan for the Gentiles does not, in any way, keep Him from bringing about His perfect plan for Israel. Rather, this overlapping of purposes is what we might expect. Not to mention that there are compelling reasons for the Church to be here during the first part of the 70th Week.

Who Was Jesus Talking To?

The other argument used to remove the Church before the start of the 70th Week comes from the Olivet Discourse, which gives us some of the greatest detail about the events that will transpire during this time. Because the Church was unknown to the audience to whom Jesus spoke, the reasoning goes, the entire context of His discussion should be applied only to Israel.

Grant Jeffrey is among the prophecy teachers promoting this view. He writes,

> It is easy to forget that, at this point, before the crucifixion of our Lord and the coming of the Holy Spirit at Pentecost, there was no such thing as a Christian Church....One of the classic mistakes in interpretation is to take this conversation between Christ and His Jewish disciples concerning the Messianic kingdom and read back into it the reality of the Christian Church, which did not come into existence until the Jews rejected Christ and God breathed life into His body of believers on the day of Pentecost. Since Christ does not mention the Church to His disciples in this conversation, the plain interpretation is that Israel is the primary focus of the prophecy of Matthew 24.[51]

While I agree that the most intense effects of the Antichrist's reign will be felt by the Jews living in and around Jerusalem during the 70th Week, I also believe that it is a mistake to assume that Christians were excluded from this discussion. While the audience was unaware of the future formation of the Body of Christ, Jesus certainly wasn't. He repeatedly referred to mysteries

---

[51] *Armageddon: Appointment With Destiny*, p. 171. It is also worth noting that the necessity of removing the Olivet Discourse from the prophetic future of the Church indicates just how compelling the parallel between Matt. 24:31 and the other rapture passages (1 Thess. 4:16–17 and 1 Cor. 15:51–52) is.

such as the sending of the Holy Spirit, His crucifixion, and the spiritual kingdom of God that were not to be understood by Jewish and Gentile believers until some time later.

It is also important to remember that the disciples to whom Jesus spoke were *the same disciples who became the foundation of the Church at Pentecost*. If I tell a child—say she is age six—about the many mysteries of becoming a woman, she would look up at me with wide eyes, sweet and loving, but without comprehension. But as she blossomed into a woman, she would come to understand those things in the fullness of time. Liken this to Jesus' discussion on the Mount of Olives. He told these mysteries to His disciples, who had not yet, but would one day soon, become the New Testament Church. He told them great mysteries, things they would only understand in the fullness of time. To suggest that His discussion related, not to the Church, but exclusively to Israel is without basis.

Writes Dr. Gleason Archer, professor of Old Testament at the Trinity Evangelical Divinity School:

> If the apostles and disciples [present at the Olivet Discourse who later] constituted the Christian church at the descent of the Holy Spirit on the Day of Pentecost were not true members or representatives of the Christian church, then who ever could be? Apart from the two books composed by Luke, the entire New Testament was composed by Jewish believers. For the first five years of the existence of the Christian church, during which several thousands of believers were added to its ranks, there was scarcely a non-Jew to be found in the entire company. All of the other admonitions and warnings addressed to the Twelve were unquestionably intended for them personally and found fulfillment or application in their later careers. How could it be that the Olivet Discourse, and that alone, was an exception to this principle? .... Such an interpretation as this appears to violate completely the principle of literal or normal interpretation that underlies the grammatical-historical [reading] of Scripture...If, then, we are to follow the normal use of language and take the wording of the Olivet Discourse in its ordinary and obvious meaning, we have no choice but

to understand it as addressed to representatives of the Christian church, namely the apostles themselves.[52]

The fact that the Olivet Discourse is relevant to the Church is also clear from the fact that Jesus kept saying, "you." When *you* see the abomination of desolation, when *you* see these things beginning to occur. He was clearly referring to the disciples in their future identities as members of the Church, not as their identities as Old Testament Jews that they would leave behind.

Dr. Douglas Moo, assistant professor of the New Testament at the Trinity Divinity School, explains as follows:[53]

> Matthew 24:15–28 clearly describes the second half of Daniel's week: the Antichrist has set himself up in the temple (v. 15), the greatest distress in world history is being experienced (v. 21), and Christ's coming is to take place suddenly (vv. 26–28). But the second person plural ("you") continues to be used throughout these verses. In other words, if the church must be included in the first part of the discourse because of the second person plural pronoun, it can hardly be excluded from the second part.[54]

Not only this, but prewrath advocate Robert Van Kampen points out that this same discourse is surrounded front and back with clear references to the Church:

---

[52] *Three Views on the Rapture*, p. 123.

[53] I cite Douglas Moo several times in this book, and students of the posttrib rapture position will recognize him as a strong posttrib proponent. His arguments are useful because both the prewrath and posttrib positions take the rapture verses cited in 1 Corinthians 15 and 1, 2 Thessalonians as the same event described in Matt. 24:31; and they both believe that the Church will go through the Great Tribulation. Where they differ is in the endpoint of the Great Tribulation. Prewrath sees it as ending prior to the opening of the sixth seal, sometime after the midpoint of the 70th Week; posttrib sees it as ending at Armageddon. This leads to very different conclusions about the length of time the Church will be present during the 70th Week—prewrath just after the midpoint and posttrib until the end. Thus, while I cite Moo's scholarship, his points must be understood in the context as it appears here.

[54] *Three Views on the Rapture*, p. 165.

"You are Peter, and upon this rock I will build My *church*" (Matt. 16:18); "And if he [an unrepentant believer] refuses to listen to them, tell it to the *church*; and if he refuses to listen even to the *church*, let him be to you as a Gentile and tax collector" (Matt. 18:17); and His instructions for the Lord's Supper, which were undeniably intended for the *church*. (Matt. 26:26–30)

Writes Van Kampen, "How is it then that one decides to throw out the Olivet Discourse, making it applicable only to Israel, when everything taught in the larger context of this discourse pertains directly to the church?" [55]

Van Kampen reinforces this point by citing Matt. 28:19–20, in which Jesus gives to His disciples the Great Commission, "Go therefore and make disciples of all the nations, baptizing them in the name of the Father and of the Son and of the Holy Spirit, teaching them to observe *all the things that I have commanded you*." He then asks, "What does 'all that I commanded you' mean if it does not include everything Christ taught His disciples in that particular gospel, the gospel of Matthew?" He also points to the words of Paul in 1 Tim. 6:3: "If anyone teaches otherwise and does not consent to wholesome words, *even the words of our Lord Jesus Christ....*" Neither Jesus nor Paul gave a qualification. All of the words of the Lord Jesus apply to the Church. [56]

It is also worth noting that, when Jesus made a direct reference to Dan. 11:31, saying, "Therefore, when you see the abomination of desolation standing in the holy place," He did not apply Daniel's distinctively Jewish phrase "the time of Jacob's

---

[55] *The Rapture Question Answered: Plain and Simple*, pp. 101-2.

[56] *In The Rapture Question Answered: Plain and Simple*, Van Kampen also gives an interesting test regarding Jesus' coming in glory in the Olivet Discourse. He challenges readers to present to pretrib proponents the following test: Read Matt. 24:27-40, which pretrib proponents claim refers to Armageddon, not the rapture. Then ask whether the pretrib rapture position allows date-setting as to when the rapture will occur. They will typically reply that we cannot know "the day or the hour." Then, Van Kampen continues, ask how this person came to this conclusion. Most will respond, "But of that day and hour no one knows, not even the angels of heaven, nor the Son, but the Father alone" (Matt. 24:36), which comes out of the passage that pretrib proponents claim refers to Armageddon. "You can't have it both ways!" he writes (p. 107).

Trouble" to the Great Tribulation, which He describes a few verses later. If the Great Tribulation were only for Israel, why did Jesus not use this well-known Jewish phrase?

Letters to the Churches

In determining whether the Olivet Discourse is meant only for Israel, it is also important to remember the letters to the six churches in Revelation 2 and 3. Jesus warns the corrupt, compromising, loveless, lukewarm, and dead churches to repent of their sins and to overcome; He warns the persecuted church to endure and overcome; and He promises to protect the loving church from the coming hour of trial. The natural question leading from these passages is, "Overcome what?" and "What trial?" After a brief interlude, Jesus answers these questions by describing the six seals. Because the letters to churches immediately precede the description of the seals, the plain reading of the text is that these churches will endure the seal judgments.

There is yet more evidence that the Church will enter the 70th Week. The compromising church is warned that, if it does not repent, Jesus will "come quickly," a reference to His Second Coming. The corrupt church is warned that, if it does not repent, it will be thrown into "great tribulation," a reference to the Great Tribulation. And to the dead church of Sardis, Jesus says: "Therefore if you will not watch, I will come upon you as a thief, and you will not know what hour I will come upon you" (Rev. 3:3), a clear reference to 1 Thess. 5:2: "For you yourselves know perfectly that the Day of the Lord comes as a thief in the night."

These end-times references, along with Jesus' admonition to repent and overcome, strongly suggest that these letters apply, not just to the first century churches to which they were addressed, but also to believers during the 70th Week.

Comparison to Other Rapture Verses

For those still not convinced that the Great Tribulation is meant for the Church, consider that scripture places it prior to a clear reference to the rapture. Jesus describes the Great Tribulation in Matt. 24:21, then says:

> Immediately after the tribulation of those days, the sun will be darkened, and the moon will not give its light; the stars will fall from heaven, and they will see the Son of Man coming on the clouds of heaven with power and great glory.

And He will send His angels with a great sound of a trumpet and they will gather together His elect from the four winds, from one end of heaven to the other. (Matt. 24:30–31)

We know this is the rapture by comparing it to 1 Cor. 15:52: "In a moment, in the twinkling of an eye, at the last trumpet. For the trumpet will sound, and the dead will be raised incorruptible, and we shall be changed"; and 1 Thess. 4:16–17: "For Lord Himself will descend from heaven with a shout, with the voice of an archangel, and with the trumpet of God. And the dead in Christ will rise first. Then we who are alive and remain shall be caught up together with them in the clouds to meet the Lord in the air."

Some pretrib proponents use the term "God's elect" in Matt. 24:31 as evidence that the Great Tribulation is only for Israel since Israel is called God's "elect." However, Paul repeatedly uses the term "elect" to refer to both Jewish and Gentile believers (Romans 8:33, Col 3:12).[57] The Gentiles became part of the Jewish "branch" at the moment of salvation ("being a wild olive tree, [you] were grafted in among them," Romans 11:17). As grafts into the branch of the olive tree, Christians will not be exempt from the Great Tribulation that will come upon God's people.[58]

In John's description of the martyrdom of believers, the wording also tells us that these are believers in Christ, not unbelieving Jews: "When He opened the fifth seal, I saw under the altar the souls of those who had been slain for the Word of God and for the testimony which they held" (Rev. 6:9). We are no longer under the Old Covenant, so the Word of God and the

---

[57] While pretrib scholars would like to present a united front, suggesting that all pretrib scholars are in agreement that the term "elect" in this context cannot include the Church, they are not. Even John Walvoord admits that "pretribulationists are somewhat confused on this issue" (*The Rapture Question, Revised and Updated*, p. 59).

[58] Douglas Moo also makes this point: "A second reason for thinking that the Olivet Discourse is directed to the church is the use of the term 'elect.' The word is used to describe those who are on earth during the events portrayed in the Discourse and therefore presumably denotes those addressed (Matt. 24:22, 24, 31). Yet this word, denoting one graciously chosen by God, is consistently used in the New Testament to refer to members of the *church*; there is no verse in which there is indication that any restriction is in mind" (*Three Views on the Rapture*, p. 194).

testimony that they held must refer to the New Covenant. These are Christians who have been slain for remaining steadfast amidst the persecution.[59]

Other Evidence From Revelation

There is other evidence that the Church will undergo the Great Tribulation. Rev. 13:7–10 describes the reign of the Antichrist and his power to make war and overcome the saints: "It was granted to him to make war with the saints and to overcome them. And authority was given him over every tribe, tongue, and nation.... *Here is the patience and the faith of the saints.*"[60]

Where have we seen the patience and faith of the saints before? When Paul boasts of the Thessalonians for their great faithfulness:

> ...so that we ourselves boast of you among the churches of God for *your patience and faith in all your persecutions*

---

[59] For those holding the position that Matthew 24 applies only to Israel, I would pose the following question: Should we throw out all of the Old Testament, too, since it was written to a Jewish audience? This would mean throwing out books like Joel, Zechariah, and Isaiah, which contain some of the most important end-times passages. Further, if we throw out Matthew 24, should we also throw out passages like 1 Cor. 15:52 and 1 Thess. 4:16-5:8 — which are at the core of the church's rapture theology — since they refer to the same events and even contain identical wording? In a larger context, you would have to throw out *all* of the books of Matthew, Mark, Luke, and John — and all of the Lord's teachings with them — since these, too, were written before the formation of the Church. So, how do those using dispensationalism to support a pretrib rapture decide which scriptures to accept and which to reject? This leads me to wonder if they are using something I call "selective dispensationalism," or dispensationalism only in the rapture context. If this is the case, it alone makes this view suspect.

[60] At this point, those holding to dispensational theology would protest, saying, "But the saints during the 70th Week aren't Church saints. They are 70th Week saints." There is not one word of scripture to support the suggestion that these are not members of the Church. Dispensationalism is used largely as the supporting structure for pretrib theology and for this reading of this passage. And yet, take away this artificial human framework and anyone reading the New Testament from front to back would read "saints" as having the same meaning from one book to another.

80

and tribulations that you endure, which is manifest evidence of the righteous judgment of God, that you may be counted worthy of the kingdom of God, for which you also suffer; since it is a righteous thing with God to repay with tribulation those who trouble you, and give you who are troubled rest with us when the Lord Jesus is revealed from heaven with His mighty angels. (2 Thess. 1:4–7)

The simple combination of "patience" and "faith" of the saints might not seem like a powerful correlation until we realize that, in this same passage, Paul promises that this patience and faith will be rewarded with something very special: "rest with us when the Lord Jesus is revealed from heaven with His mighty angels" (v. 7). For the generation living during the end times, this "rest," or cease from labor, will come at the rapture.

The relationship between the Great Tribulation and the rapture can also be seen in Revelation 13, where we are told that the Antichrist will be given power over *"all tribes, tongues, and nations,"* and will overcome the saints. This power is granted to him for 42 months, starting at the midpoint of the 70th Week, which is also the starting point of the Great Tribulation. In Matthew 24, the Great Tribulation is followed by the cosmic disturbances and the gathering of the elect. In Revelation, the martyrdom of the saints is followed by the cosmic disturbances and a vision of the raptured Church in heaven. Who are these people? "[The] great multitude which no one could number, of *all nations, tribes, peoples, and tongues*...that come out of the great tribulation."[61]

---

[61] In order to avoid the conclusion that this is the raptured Church, many pretrib scholars suggest that a better reading of this passage would be those "coming out of the great tribulation" rather than "have come out of the great tribulation." By making this "coming out" occur over time rather than all at once, this eliminates the need to identify the precipitating event as the rapture. Instead, "those who come out" are identified as martyred "70th Week saints," a new dispensation of believers after the Church has been removed. Robert Van Kampen, however, has pointed out that this phrase is a participle, not a verb, and the time denoted by a Greek sentence is fixed by the verb in context. In this case, the verbs "have washed" and "made" are both in the past tense, referring to an event that has already been completed before the eyes of the onlookers. "The point is that it is these verbs that tell us the timing of

The Church will undergo the Great Tribulation, but this persecution will be cut short by the rapture (Matt. 24:22).

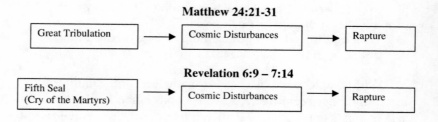

Matthew 24:21-31

| Great Tribulation | → | Cosmic Disturbances | → | Rapture |

Revelation 6:9 – 7:14

| Fifth Seal (Cry of the Martyrs) | → | Cosmic Disturbances | → | Rapture |

We also see this persecution in Rev. 12:13–17:

> Now when the dragon [Satan, who controls the Antichrist] saw that he had been cast to the earth, he persecuted the woman who gave birth to the male Child [Israel, who brought forth Jesus Christ, the Savior]. But the woman was given two wings of a great eagle, that she might fly into the wilderness to her place, where she is nourished for a time and times and half a time [three-and-one-half years, placing this event at the midpoint of the 70th Week], from the presence of the serpent.... And the dragon was enraged with the woman, and he went to make war with the rest of her offspring, who keep the commandments of God and have the testimony of Jesus Christ.

---

the event being described, not the participle. In this case, the present participle is being used to vividly describe a past event, something that has just happened. This is also why one of the elders refers to this great multitude as having already arrived. 'These who are clothed in the white robes, who are they, and from where have they come [*elthon*]?'—the verb *elthon* being the past tense of the Greek verb 'to come.' Certainly, if the elder had been witnessing an ever increasing multitude, getting larger as he watched, the past tense of the verb 'to come' would not have been the appropriate tense to use. Rather, he would have asked, 'Who are they and from where are they coming?' But that is not how the question is posed...[thus] we see that this great multitude must describe the raptured saints and the resurrected 'dead in Christ,' now standing before the throne of God" (*The Rapture Question Answered: Plain and Simple*, p. 160).

The Antichrist begins his persecution in and around Jerusalem (Matt. 24:16), but when the Jews flee to the wilderness, he turns his attention to the remaining thorns in his side, the true believers who make up the Church of Jesus Christ.

Taking the Sorrows Out of the 70th Week

Two other points need to be made here. Some proponents of the pretribulation rapture try to get around many of these arguments by saying that the rise of false christs, wars and rumors of wars, and the great famine described as part of "the beginning of sorrows" do not occur during the 70th Week of Daniel. Nor do they correlate with the seal judgments. Rather, they define this as a general time period of moral and spiritual decline that precedes Daniel's 70th Week. In most cases, they believe this is the period we live in today. They place the beginning of the 70th Week with the abomination of desolation (Matt. 24:15). Therefore, if Jesus' coming in glory in Matt. 24:30 is Armageddon, the Great Tribulation must last seven years.

This creates several difficulties. First, these events so perfectly correlate with the six seals that it would be difficult to argue that these are not the same events (see Chapter 10). Second, this places the start of the 70th Week *after* the Antichrist stands in the temple in Jerusalem, a clear contradiction with Daniel 9:27, which tells us that this event occurs at the midpoint. Third, this places the rapture at the end of the 70th Week, not at the beginning, which is the opposite of what they are trying to prove. Fourth, when the disciples ask Jesus when He is coming back, this interpretation requires Him to skip over the rapture—the blessed hope of all believers—altogether. And fifth, it places the Great Tribulation and the abomination of desolation before the Day of the Lord, which is a contradiction with Joel 2:31.[62]

---

[62] Some pretrib scholars get around this by creating two days of the Lord: a broad Day of the Lord, which they see as referring to the entire 70th Week; and a narrow Day of the Lord, which they see as referring specifically to the day that Jesus comes with the heavenly host at Armageddon. This approach reflects the consistent pattern of redefining words to make them fit a predetermined point of view. For a more detailed look at the broad and narrow Days of the Lord, see Appendix A.

The End of the Age

There is a final difficulty relevant to this discussion, which is that it misplaces the end of the age. In order for the pretrib doctrine to work, proponents must contend that "the end of the age" coincides with Jesus' return at Armageddon, not the rapture. This argument comes from Matt. 24:6–14, in which Jesus continually reminds His listeners that "the end has not yet come":

> And you will hear of wars and rumors of wars. See that you are not troubled; for all these things must come to pass, but the end is not yet. For nation will rise against nation, and kingdom against kingdom. And there will be famines, pestilences, and earthquakes in various places. All these are the beginning of sorrows. Then they will deliver you up to tribulation and kill you, and you will be hated by all nations for My name's sake.... And because lawlessness will abound, the love of many will grow cold. But he who endures to the end shall be saved. And this gospel of the kingdom will be preached in all the world as a witness to all the nations, and then the end will come.

According to this reasoning, if the rapture is pretribulational, and if, at the time of the rapture, the end has not come, "the end of the age" must be Jesus' bodily return at Armageddon. However, Jesus taught that the end of the age occurs with His physical return to earth as conquering King; and according to Joel 2:31, Matt. 24:29-30, and Rev. 6:12–13, this return (and therefore the end of the age) occurs after the opening of the sixth seal and before the Day of the Lord:

> The sun shall be turned into darkness, and the moon into blood, before the coming of the great and awesome Day of the Lord. (Joel 2:31)

> Immediately after the tribulation of those days, the sun will be darkened, the moon will not give its light; the stars will fall from heaven, and the powers of the heavens will be shaken. Then the sign of the Son of Man will appear in heaven, and then all the tribes of the earth will mourn. (Matt. 24:29)

I looked when He opened the sixth seal, and behold, there was a great earthquake, and the sun became black as sackcloth of hair, and the moon became like blood. And the stars of heaven fell into the earth, as a fig tree drops its late figs when it is shaken by a mighty wind. (Rev. 6:12–13)

Daniel's 70th Week

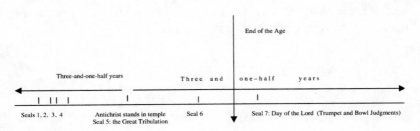

This is exactly what Jesus told the disciples in Matthew 24. In verse 3, Jesus' disciples asked Him, "Tell us, when will these things be? And what will be *the sign of Your coming and of the end of the age?*" After describing the beginning of sorrows, the abomination of desolation, and the Great Tribulation, Jesus answered the disciples' question in verse 30:

> Then the sign of the Son of Man will appear in heaven, and then all the tribes of the earth will mourn, and they will see the Son of Man coming on the clouds of heaven with power and great glory. And He will send His angels with a great sound of a trumpet, and they will gather together His elect from the four winds, from one end of heaven to the other.

They asked a direct question and Jesus gave a direct answer. His return, and therefore the end of the age, will occur after the Great Tribulation and the cosmic disturbances of the sixth seal.

Further Confirmation

Further confirmation that the end of the age cannot occur at Armageddon, as pretribulationists claim, is given in Matthew 28. In this chapter, Jesus tells His disciples that their ministry will extend to the "end of the age" (Matt. 28:18–20). If "the end of the age" is at Armageddon, then by pretribulationists' own argument, this would require the Church to be in residence upon the earth until Armageddon. In fact, both of these passages place the end of the age at the return of Christ at the rapture.

6

What About Imminence?

In almost any discussion of the rapture, the issue of imminence arises. The term "imminence" describes the expectant attitude taken by the early church toward the soon return of Christ. Nowhere in the scriptures, however, do we find the actual word "imminence." This is a term adopted by scholars to describe the joyful anticipation that the apostles exhibited for the return of the Savior.[63] Within the last century, pretrib scholars have begun defining the imminent return of Christ as an event that could happen at any moment, without warning. This definition is frequently used to support the teaching that there is no event or series of events that must occur beforehand.

The distinction between imminence as an attitude of expectation and imminence as an "any moment" return is important. If it is true that no event (or events) must precede Jesus' return, then a pretribulational rapture is the only possible option. If, on the other hand, the Bible does not require an "any moment"

---

[63] In a personal correspondence with Gary Vaterlaus, instructor of biblical research and education for Sola Scriptura Ministries, he writes, "Interestingly enough, in the Latin Vulgate by Jerome, we *do* find the word 'imminent.' Here is the verse: 'Now we request you, brethren, with regard to the coming of our Lord Jesus Christ, and our gathering together to Him, that you may not be quickly shaken from your composure or be disturbed either by a spirit or a message or a letter as if from us, to the effect that the day of the Lord has come' (2 Thess. 2:1–2). The Latin says, 'to the effect that the day of the Lord is imminent.' In other words, the only time the word 'imminent' is used in relation to the return of Christ, it is telling us that His return is *not* imminent."

coming, then one of the most important arguments for the pretrib rapture disappears. Thus, it is not surprising that the "any moment" interpretation has become crucial to—and, in fact, is often held to be synonymous with—the pretrib doctrine.

Is Jesus' Return Imminent?

There is no question that imminence, in the sense of expectation, is found throughout the New Testament. It can be seen in passages such as "looking for that blessed hope and glorious appearing of our great God and Savior, Jesus Christ" (Titus 2:13), "eagerly waiting for the revelation of our Lord Jesus Christ" (1 Cor. 1:7), and "Therefore let us not sleep, as others do, but watch and be sober" (1 Thess. 5:6). All of these passages suggest a lifestyle of heightened watchfulness and preparation for the coming of the Lord.

But does this mean that the Lord could appear at any moment? There is not one verse of scripture that says so. In fact, this would be in direct contradiction to the many signs that Jesus gave to believers to help them discern when His Second Coming is approaching. In Matthew 24, for example, Jesus tells us that His arrival will be preceded by the gospel being preached to all nations, the abomination of desolation spoken of by Daniel the prophet [the desecration of the temple by the Antichrist], the Great Tribulation, and the cosmic disturbances of the sixth seal.

Immediately after describing His arrival in glory, Jesus repeats the importance of these signs by giving the parable of the fig tree. "Now learn this parable from the fig tree: When its branch has already become tender and puts forth leaves, you know that summer is near. So you also, when you see all these things, know that it is near—at the doors!" (vv. 32–33). What things? All the things Jesus has just described: the beginning of sorrows, the preaching of the gospel to all nations, the abomination of desolation, the Great Tribulation, and the cosmic disturbances of the sixth seal.

Paul repeats one of these preconditions in 2 Thess. 2:3–4: "Let no one deceive you by any means; for that Day will not come unless the falling away comes first, and the man of sin is revealed, the son of perdition, who opposes and exalts himself above all that is called God or that is worshiped, so that he sits as God in the temple of God, showing himself that he is God."

Pretrib proponents would like us to believe that to "eagerly wait" for something requires an any-moment event. This is not the case. Children eagerly await summer vacations starting right after Christmas. They eagerly await events like birthdays months in advance. Adults eagerly await events that are even further ahead, like meeting their future mates, entering retirement, or receiving answers to prayer—all of which may be seen as imminent, as well. Does the fact that many things must intervene between the hope and the fulfillment take away from the sense of expectancy? Absolutely not. Nowhere in scripture does it say that earnest expectation requires an "any moment" fulfillment. In fact, in describing His plan for the end times, God tells the prophet Habakkuk, "For the vision is yet for an appointed time; but at the end it will speak, and it will not lie. *Though it tarries, wait for it;* because it will surely come" (Hab. 2:3). In this context, the fulfillment of this promise is clearly in the future, yet Habakkuk is still told to wait.

Douglas Moo agrees, noting that none of the many words used to describe the nearness of the *parousia*, or the believer's expectation of it, require an "any moment" sense of imminence:

"Wait for" (applied to the *parousia* in Luke 12:36; Titus 2:13; Jude 21), is used of Paul's expectation of the resurrection of the just and the unjust (Acts 24:15)—yet the latter does not occur until after the Millennium. "Await eagerly" (used of the *parousia* in 1 Cor. 1:7) can refer to creation's longing for deliverance (Rom. 8:19), which deliverance comes only after the tribulation. "Expect," is used by James of the *parousia* in 5:7, but the analogy in the context is with a farmer who waits for his crops—certainly not "any moment!" "Look for" (cf. Matt. 24:50; Luke 12:46 with reference to the Second Coming) is the word used by Peter to exhort believers to "look for" the new heavens and the earth (2 Peter 3:12–14). "Be near" and the adjectival form applied to the *parousia* in numerous texts are used of Jewish feasts and the seasons of the year (e.g., John 2:13, Matt. 21:34)—and these, obviously, are not "any moment" events. A number of other terms, "watch"; "be awake"; "be sober"; "look at" are used to exhort believers to an attitude of

spiritual alertness and moral uprightness in the light of the
second return, but imply nothing as to its time.[64]

What About Jesus' Unexpected Return?

But what about the warnings that people will be unprepared
for Jesus' coming? Doesn't this mean that the rapture could
happen at any moment? Pretrib support for this interpretation
comes from passages like Matt. 24:36 and 1 Thess. 5:1–2:

> But of that day and hour no one knows, not even the angels
> of heaven, but My Father only.... For as in the days before
> the flood, they were eating and drinking, marrying and
> giving in marriage, until the day that Noah entered the ark,
> and did not know until the flood came and took them all
> away, so also will the coming of the Son of Man be. (Matt.
> 24:36–39)

> But concerning the times and the seasons, brethren, you have
> no need that I should write to you. For you yourselves know
> perfectly that the Day of the Lord so comes as a thief in the
> night. (1 Thess. 5: 1–2)

On the surface, these passages do seem to teach that
believers and unbelievers alike will be taken by surprise by His
coming, but a closer reading shows that this is not the case. In 1
Thess. 5:2, Paul writes, "For you yourselves know perfectly that
the Day of the Lord so comes as a thief in the night," but two
verses later, he clarifies for believers, *"But you, brethren, are not
in darkness, so that this Day should overtake you as a thief"* (v. 4).
In context, this passage tells us that Jesus' coming should be a
surprise *only to the unbelieving world.* Many proponents of the
"any moment" return of Christ cite the first verse of this passage
but ignore the second.

Pretrib proponents would argue, however, that it is
impossible for the scriptures to teach believers to be looking for
Jesus and to be watchful of His coming without also teaching that
He could come at any moment. But this is exactly what the
scriptures teach. In Luke 21:28, after Jesus describes the
abomination of desolation, the Great Tribulation, and the cosmic

---

[64] *Three Views on the Rapture*, p. 208.

90

disturbances, He says, "Now, when these things begin to happen, *look up and lift up your heads*, because your redemption draws near."[65] Although believers should always be living lifestyles of constant readiness and vigilance, Jesus is clearly referring to a unique series of supernatural events (Luke 21:25–26, Matt. 24:29, Mark 13:24–25) that will cause believers to look with literal expectation of His appearing. This is the same level of expectation we would have if we heard footsteps around a corner or someone's key in the lock of the door.

The Sign of the Son of Man

In addition to these clearly prophesied events, the Bible tells us that there will be one final, unmistakable event that will signal Christ's return. In Matthew, Jesus Himself calls this "the sign of the Son of Man" (v. 30). Although we do not know what this will be, we do get a hint of what it will be like, for Jesus says, "so as

---

[65]One of the ways that pretrib scholars get around the cosmic disturbances as a prophetic marker is by proposing that they occur more than once in history. In his critique of Rosenthal's book, *The Pre-Wrath Rapture of the Church*, Gerald Stanton writes of the author's claim that there is only one unique set of cosmic disturbances: "But that can hardly be dogmatized, for the predicted Tribulation will not be limited to one display of cosmic power, making Rosenthal's argument uncertain at best" (*Bibliotheca Sacra*, p. 100). However, the series of cosmic disturbances mentioned in Matthew 24 and Revelation 6 are not just *any* cosmic disturbances. They are very *specific* disturbances used in a unique combination only to describe the start of the Day of the Lord. Furthermore, each time they are mentioned, they are mentioned all together and in the same order—the sun going dark, the moon going dark or turning to blood, and the stars falling from the sky. The other cosmic disturbances, such as the stars falling (Rev. 8:10), one-third of the sun, moon, and stars being darkened (Rev. 8:12), and the scorching heat from the sun (Rev. 16:8) do not follow this pattern. They are either mentioned as individual disturbances or, as in the case of Rev. 8:12, contain details that are significantly different from this precise triple-disturbance event. It is interesting that, earlier in the article, Stanton criticizes Rosenthal for what he sees as the author's ignoring of the close wording of Isaiah 2:19 and Rev. 6:15, which state that the wicked shall hide in the holes of the rocks and caves of the earth as "a fact far too specific to be lightly ignored" (p. 98), yet he does not seem to consider the unique combination of darkened sun, moon, and falling stars to be specific enough to be taken seriously.

lightning flashes from the east to the west, so shall the coming of the Son of Man be" (v. 29). No matter what this event, believers will know. God's signs are not meant to be ambiguous—we will look up.

By the time of His appearing, the Lord will have given us many indicators of His coming. He will have given us the Antichrist's confirming of the seven-year covenant with Israel, the abomination of desolation, the five seal judgments, including the Great Tribulation, the dramatic cosmic disturbances of the sixth seal, and this final, unmistakable sign. When the sun turns dark and the moon turns to blood, millions of believers all over the world will look into the sky with one accord. And when the sign of the Son of Man flashes from east to west, our hearts will quicken—"Here He comes!" The Day of the Lord should come as a thief *only for an unbelieving world.*

That believers will know when the time approaches does not conflict with Jesus' teaching that "no man will know the day or the hour." Jesus said that our redemption "draws near." There will be a period following these events when believers will anticipate, but not be able to calculate, the return of the Savior.

As in the Days of Noah

Another verse often cited by pretrib proponents in support of the "any moment" return of Christ is Jesus' comparison of His Second Coming to the days of Noah. Immediately following the description of the rapture in Matt. 24:29–31, Jesus warns:

> For as in the days before the flood, they were eating and drinking, marrying and giving in marriage, until the day that Noah entered the ark and did not know until the flood came and took them all away, so also will the coming of the Son of Man be. Then two men will be in the field: one will be taken and the other left. Two women will be grinding at the mill: one will be taken and the other left. Watch therefore, for you do not know what hour your Lord is coming. (Matt. 24:38–42)

Pretrib poponents use this passage as evidence that Jesus cannot come during the seals or at any other time during the 70th Week because, at the time of His appearing, people will be living normal everyday lives, not perishing under the kind of intense war, famine, and persecution that will come from the judgment of God. This is why His coming will be such a surprise.

Not so. First, there is no mention of carefree living; only that people's lives will be going on as usual. Second, in Noah's time, who was eating and drinking in a carefree manner as if the world would go on forever? Who was marrying and giving in marriage as if no judgment was coming? Not Noah and his family. They were building the ark, knowing that one day soon, within their lifetimes, God would destroy the earth. Noah, in particular, was preaching, calling his neighbors to repent and turn to the one true God (2 Peter 2:5).

In the days of Noah, God's judgment wasn't some day in the distant, uncertain future. God did not tell him to build the ark *in case* it came before he died. God told him when the flood was coming—soon:

> And God said to Noah, "The end of all flesh has come before Me, for the earth is filled with violence through them; and behold, I will destroy them with the earth. Make yourself an ark of gopherwood; make rooms in the ark, and cover it inside and outside with pitch.... And behold, I Myself am bringing floodwaters on the earth, to destroy from under heaven all flesh in which is the breath of life; everything that is on the earth shall die. But I will establish My covenant with you; and you shall go into the ark—you, your sons, your wife, and your sons' wives with you...." (Gen. 6:13–14, 17–18)

Jesus made a similar promise to the believers who will witness the beginning of end-times events:

> Now learn this parable from the fig tree: When its branch has already become tender and puts forth leaves, you know that summer is near. So you also, when you see all these things, know that it is near—at the doors! Assuredly, I say to you, this generation will by no means pass away till all these things take place. (Matt. 24:32–33)

Just as Noah labored many years to build the ark, this ought to be a picture of the Church laboring for the gospel before and during the seal judgments. Jesus said, "and this gospel of the kingdom will be preached in all the world as a witness to all the nations, and then the end shall come." From the time the Antichrist signs the covenant with Israel, signifying the beginning of Daniel's 70ᵗʰ Week, we will know that Christ's return is "at the doors." As we watch the seals unfold, we should be laboring even more earnestly, as Noah labored, for the gospel in a world blinded to its impending doom.

In the day of the flood, God Himself shut the door of the ark before judgment arrived (Gen. 7:16). So, too, will Jesus Himself rapture His Church before the Day of the Lord. Can you imagine the emotions of the people in Noah's time, stuck outside the ark, watching the water fall and realizing that Noah had been right? How much more will the hearts of unbelievers fail when they see Jesus coming in the clouds, watching the rapture of His glorious Bride, knowing that they have been left behind? Jesus said, "And all the tribes of the earth shall mourn" (Matt. 24:30).

Blinded to the Truth

What about the everyday nature of "eating and drinking, marrying and giving in marriage?" Once again, pretrib proponents use these scriptures to show that the rapture must occur prior to the opening of the seals because people are conducting normal, everyday activities. They contend that none of these events is likely to be occurring at the time of Christ's return. I disagree. Remember, we are dealing with an unbelieving world, which the Bible says has been blinded by the hardness of their hearts:

> Hearing you will hear and shall not understand, and seeing you will see and not perceive; for the hearts of this people have grown dull. Their ears are hard of hearing, and their eyes they have closed, lest they should see with their eyes and hear with their ears, lest they should understand with their hearts and turn, so that I should heal them. (Matt. 13:13)

> But even if our gospel is veiled, it is veiled to those who are perishing, whose minds the god of this age has blinded, who do not believe, lest the light of the gospel of the glory of Christ, who is the image of God, should shine on them. (2 Cor. 4:3–4)

This is especially true when we consider that the rapture will follow the first six seals which, except for their intensity, could be explained as natural phenomena. Already, we are undergoing a period of unprecedented carnage from civil wars and holy wars to ethnic cleansing. In Third World countries, bodies are piling up from the worst famine in modern history. The last decade has brought so many fires, floods, hurricanes, and earthquakes that news headlines such as "record-setting" and "unprecedented" barely bring a second glance. When we hear about new deadly, incurable diseases and destructive abnormalities of nature that mystify scientists, it has become, well, *normal*. The world will easily rationalize the seal disasters as natural phenomena, as well.

Didn't the Disciples Believe in Imminence?

One of pretrib proponents' favorite arguments for the "any moment" return of Christ is that the disciples and the early church fathers believed that Jesus could come at any time. They point out that when Paul used phrases like "waiting for the revelation of our Lord" (1 Co. 1:7) and "looking for that blessed hope and glorious appearing of our great God and Savior, Jesus Christ" (Titus 2:13), he did not add any qualifiers. Thus, he must be teaching that Jesus could come at any time and that all believers, including the apostles, should be looking for Him always.

There are several problems with this approach. First, it is dangerous to build doctrine upon inference. Nowhere in scripture does it say that Jesus could come without warning. Keep in mind that the term "imminent" is a descriptive term applied by modern theologians and does not actually appear in the Bible. The doctrine of imminence was not coined until the Niagara Bible Conference in the late 1800s. Even then, there was great division as to what the term "imminent" actually meant. Pretrib proponents held that it meant "at any time," while others held that it meant "within any generation," but not necessarily at any time, since many prophetic markers must be fulfilled first.

Pretrib scholars gain support for their interpretation by claiming that an "any moment" rapture appears in early church writings. An objective look at those writings, however, shows this assessment to be incorrect. Writers such as Justin Martyr, Tertullian, Ireneaus, and other church fathers from the first, second, and third centuries were very clear in their expectations that the Church would endure the persecution of the Antichrist. Consider the following statements: "the man of apostasy, who...shall venture to do unlawful deeds on the earth against us the Christians" (Martyr); "Heresies, at the present time, will no less rend the church by their perversion of doctrine than will Antichrist persecute her at that day by the cruelty of his attacks" (Tertullian); and "Now, concerning the tribulation of the persecution which is to fall upon the Church from the adversary..." (Hyppolytus).

The fact that the early church fathers expected the Church to enter the 70th Week couldn't be more obvious. For a detailed look at this subject, see Appendix F.

Simply Impossible

Not only do the scriptures *not* teach an "any moment" coming of Christ, but it would have been impossible for many of the end-times prophesies to be fulfilled until the modern day. For example, Jesus told us that the gospel must be preached in all nations before the end would come (Matt. 24:14). At the time this prophecy was given, it would have been physically impossible for the infant Church to carry the gospel to every nation on earth.

There are other prophecies that could not have been fulfilled in the time of the early church, as well. John tells us about the Antichrist, who will have power over "all kindreds, tongues, and nations" and who will prevent all men "rich or poor, bond or free" from buying or selling without his mark on their hands or on their foreheads. How could any government, even one as powerful as first-century Rome, have prevented every person across the globe from buying and selling without the mark? Rome did not have the manpower nor the technology to fulfill this prophecy. Nor did Rome likely know that the ancient civilizations in the Americas even existed. No generation has witnessed the political and military climate to fulfill this prophecy until now.

So, was scripture wrong when it told believers throughout the ages to be looking for Jesus? No. Paul never said that Jesus could come at any time. He said only that we should always maintain a *lifestyle* of expectancy. This lifestyle is one of hope, focused on heavenly things, not earthly things, and it serves as a catalyst for evangelism and holy living. It is a lifestyle that reminds us that we are wanderers and strangers here, and that we should always be looking heavenward and longing to be with Christ in our eternal home. This truly is the heartbeat of God for believers of all ages.

96

Does Prewrath Destroy Imminence?

Throughout this book, I suggest that the prewrath rapture should, by its very nature, be a catalyst for holy living. Some would ask: "How can post sixth-seal rapture do such a thing? Wouldn't it be a catalyst for complacency? After all, if there are events that must unfold before Jesus can return, what's the hurry?" In any other generation but ours, I might agree. But we are living in a time in which we can almost hear the hoofbeats of the four horsemen, creating a new sense of urgency. Like the watchman on the tower, we cry, "Wake up! Wake up!" Far from causing complacency, for the first time, it causes us to know what real imminence is like. We should be anxiously waiting for Him every moment of our lives, preparing for His return by walking in holiness, sowing into the fruits of the Spirit, and growing in spiritual maturity.

According to *Webster's Dictionary*, the word *imminence* means "ready to take place, especially hanging threateningly over one's head." Because of the days in which we live, the physical return of Jesus Christ is doing just that. In fact, we can say His return is hanging more threateningly now than 1,000 years ago or even 100 years ago. We can almost palpably feel it.[66] Even 100 years ago, we had no way of knowing what was going on in countries on the other side of the globe. The Antichrist could have stood in Jerusalem, confirmed the seven-year covenant, initiating the 70th Week of Daniel, and no one outside the Middle East would have known about it. Only when Christ appeared in the sky and the Church was transformed into millions of heavenly bodies would those on the other side of the world have realized that something was happening.

We are in a unique time in history. Via satellite television and streaming Internet video, we can watch moment by moment as international history unfolds. Night after night on the evening news, we watch the countries of the Middle East align exactly as the prophets foretold 4,000 years ago. With modern advances in transportation, telecommunications, and printing and translation, we can literally count the number of nations left before the Great Commission is fulfilled. As we watch hundreds of Old and New Testament prophecies coming to pass before our eyes, we have a sense of imminence greater than any generation in history has ever experienced.

Every day that I awake, I am looking for Jesus. Not the opening in the clouds—not yet—but I am listening for His footsteps. After decades of watching Israel scratch and scrape to maintain her foothold against a powerful array of Arab neighbors, any day I could see the confirming of the seven-year covenant that will signal the 70th Week has begun. Any day, I could be informed that the world's major banks have joined together to share information and laid the foundation for the cashless system that will one day enable the mark of the beast. Every day I watch the political jostling that will one day trigger the rage of Russia against Israel and ignite the biblical war of Gog and Magog (Russia and her Arab alliance) against the Holy City of Jerusalem.

So does the prewrath position compromise imminence? Far from it! For the first time in history, we are experiencing what *real* imminence is like.[67]

---

[67] Robert Van Kampen has cited a very early noncannonical work as supporting the prewrath position. He cites *Didache* or *The Teaching of the Lord through the Twelve Apostles*, written sometime between A.D. 70 and A.D. 140. "The *Didache* sees the Olivet Discourse not as a reference to the battle of Armageddon, but as a reference to the second coming of Christ; '...ye know not the hour in which our Lord cometh,' when 'they that endure in their faith shall be saved [delivered]' from 'the world deceiver,' from 'the fire of testing...but they that endure in their faith shall be saved [delivered]...then shall the signs of truth appear...a sign of a rift in the heaven...a voice of a trumpet...a resurrection of the dead...the Lord coming upon the clouds of heaven.' The early Christians believed this document to be Christ's very teaching passed on to the church through His disciples. Whether this is true is immaterial, but in order for the document to be accepted as it was by the earliest followers of Jesus and His disciples, the teaching in the book must have been consistent with the earliest Christians' memories and understanding of what Christ taught. Clearly, the early church believed that the Olivet Discourse of Christ referred to the rapture of the church. And, just as clearly, the early church also thought this specific instruction to be important enough to be passed along to all the new converts after His resurrection. And the *Didache* is living proof of that" (*The Rapture Question Answered: Plain and Simple*, pp. 191-2).

7

'He Who Restrains'
(Or Will the Church See the Antichrist?)

A common argument in favor of the pretrib rapture is that the Antichrist cannot rise to power until the Holy Spirit has been removed from the earth, which takes place at the rapture of the Church. Once the Holy Spirit's restraining influence is removed, the Antichrist is free to confirm the seven-year covenant with Israel, which kicks off the 70th Week of Daniel. By this reasoning, the Church must be raptured prior to the 70th Week.

This argument comes from Paul's admonition in 2 Thess. 2:3–8: "Let no one deceive you by any means; for that Day will not come unless the falling away comes first, and the man of sin is revealed, the son of perdition, who opposes and exalts himself above all that is called God or that is worshipped, so that he sits as God in the temple of God, showing himself that he is God.... And now *you know what is restraining*, that he may be revealed in his own time. For the mystery of lawlessness is already at work; only *he who now restrains will do so until he is taken out of the way.* And then the lawless one will be revealed...."

The pretrib position essentially reads the last two sentences this way: "For the mystery of lawlessness is already at work; only the [Holy Spirit] who now restrains will do so until [H]e is taken out of the way [at the rapture]. And then the lawless one will be revealed..." In some Bibles, "He" is capitalized, implying that the Holy Spirit is the restrainer specified in the Greek text.

If the Holy Spirit is the restrainer, this would fit the pretrib argument nicely, but it doesn't work.[68] First, because the Holy

---

[68] John Walvoord is among the prominent pretrib scholars who identify the restrainer as the Holy Spirit. In *The Rapture Question*, he states, "The chief proof text concerning the return of the Holy Spirit to heaven is

Spirit's job is not to restrain people from sin. His job is to convict them of it. The Bible tells us that the Holy Spirit teaches, convicts, comforts, intercedes, guides, strengthens, sanctifies, and regenerates (John 16:8,13; John 14:26; John 16:13; Romans 8:26; Romans 15:16; John 3:5), but nowhere does it say that He restrains the act of sin.[69] As God's children, born of His Spirit, it is our responsibility to *resist* sin by relying on Him. If His job were to restrain sin, this would violate our free will.

Furthermore, it is not the believer's ability to resist sin that is in view here. This passage is describing an external force of lawlessness and the restrainer as one who holds back this external force—a function never attributed to the Holy Spirit. *The Amplified Version* translates this passage this way: "For the mystery of lawlessness— that hidden principle of rebellion against constituted authority—is already at work in the world, [but it is] restrained only until he who restrains is taken out of the way." Similarly, *The New International Version* reads, "For the secret power of lawlessness is already at work; but the one who now holds it back will continue to do so till he is taken out of the way."

Third, the Holy Spirit cannot be the restrainer because He cannot be removed from the earth without creating a contradiction of scripture. Jesus said that He would send us a Helper, the Holy Spirit, who would be a comfort and teacher to all believers. "He redeemed us in order that the blessing given to Abraham might

---

found in 2 Thess. 2:6-8, in connection with the lawless one..." (p. 78). However, several sentences later, he admits, "Expositors of all classes have had a field day in attempting to identify this restrainer." One page later, he further admits that the exegesis of key words of the passage are "themselves indecisive." While pretrib scholars would like to present themselves as having a rock solid case, even they, themselves, admit they do not.

[69] According to dispensational theology, the Holy Spirit restrains from sin because the indwelling of the Holy Spirit operates as a "ruling factor" in God's administration over human beings, even though the scriptures never say so. One of the proof texts frequently cited is Gen. 6:3, "Nevertheless I will not strive with man forever," which is a reach at best. Because this sentence is immediately concluded by "yet his days shall be 120 years," a more reasonable conclusion is God is choosing to delay His judgment on the wickedness of mankind. Indeed, the Noahic flood followed soon after.

come to the Gentile through Christ Jesus, so that by faith we might receive the promise of the Spirit" (Gal. 3:14). This promise is not only for believers before the rapture. It is a promise for *all* believers: "But the manifestation of the Spirit is given to *each one* for the profit of all..." (1 Cor.12:7). If scripture is to continue to be without contradiction after the rapture, the Spirit must remain.[70]

Salvation Without the Spirit?

Scripture is also very clear that people will be saved after the rapture. This includes the nation of Israel, who finally accepts Jesus as her Messiah. In fact, the scriptures suggest that there will be an evangelical explosion throughout the 70th Week (Mal. 4:5–6, Eze. 37:1–14, Romans 11:26, Rev. 14:6, Rev. Rev. 15:2–4). The removal of the Holy Spirit would make this impossible because, as Gleason Archer has pointed out, apart from the influence of the Holy Spirit, there can be no such phenomenon as conversion:

> Since no sinner can ever be brought to repentance, faith, and surrender to the lordship of Christ except by the power of the Holy Spirit, it is utterly inconceivable that during an era of total removal of the Spirit Himself from the world scene there could be so much as a single conversion, to say nothing of such a numerous company such as this!"[71]

Many pretrib proponents have tried to reconcile the removal of the Holy Spirit at the rapture with the subsequent evangelistic explosion by suggesting that the Holy Spirit is not removed entirely, but only in part. This is a strange argument, considering that the Holy Spirit is a person, not a quantitative entity that can be divided up. To suggest that He is removed enough to allow the

---

[70] The reference to all believers is significant because it refutes the pretrib contention that this promise is only for the dispensation of the Church, a distinction never made in scripture. John Walvoord, who repeatedly criticizes posttribulationists by "arguing from silence" uses this very argument to support this view, writing that "neither Gundry nor anyone else can prove that the baptizing work of the Spirit that forms the Church is ever seen in the Tribulation" (*The Rapture Question*, p. 243).

[71] *Three Views on the Rapture*, p. 128.

Antichrist to arise but not enough to prevent salvation is such a stretch that I am surprised that reputable scholars suggest it.[72]

Another way pretribulationists try to get around these problems is to suggest that the restrainer is not the Holy Spirit but the Church. When the Church is removed, this allows the man of sin to be revealed. This is another strange argument, considering that, throughout the scriptures, the Church—the Bride of Christ—is identified as feminine. In 2 Thess. 2:8, the restrainer is masculine.

Who Is the Restrainer?

So if the restrainer is not the Holy Spirit, who is he? Most likely, he is Michael the Archangel, who is identified as the historical protector [restrainer] of Israel. This identification is made in Daniel 10:13–21, when Daniel is given a vision of what will occur in the latter days. In verse 13, the delivering angel explains why he has been delayed in bringing the vision: he was fighting with the "prince of Persia" (likely demonic forces) "and behold, Michael, one of the chief princes, came to help me." Later, in verse 21, the angel says, "No one upholds me against these except Michael, your prince."

The verb "upholds" is translated "holdeth" in the King James. According to *Strong's Exhaustive Concordance*, this verb, *chazaq*, means "to bind, restrain, or conquer." Thus, Michael is referred to both as the prince of the Hebrew people and *one who binds, restrains, or conquers*. In his audio tape series on Revelation, Marvin Rosenthal notes,

> When Paul discusses the restrainer in this passage in 2 Thessalonians, he is almost quoting from the book of Daniel, which he would have known extremely well.[73]

Further identification of Michael as the restrainer comes from Daniel 11, in which the prophet describes the Antichrist's

---

[72] John Walvoord is among those pretribulationists who makes this suggestion. He writes, "Pretribulationists agree that the removal of the Spirit is not complete, for the Holy Spirit is still omnipresent and still exercises some restraint, as the Book of Revelation makes plain in the protection of the 144,000" (*The Rapture Question*, p. 243).
[73] "12 Messages on Daniel," audiocassette (© Zion's Hope).

102

rise to power, his defilement of the Jewish temple, and his taking away of the Jewish sacrifices. Daniel then describes the Antichrist's dreadful persecution of God's people and admonishes them to remain steadfast, all of which are consistent with the sequence of events in Matthew 24 and Revelation 6.

At this time, Michael stands up:

> At that time Michael shall stand up, the great prince who stands watch over the sons of your people, and there shall be a time of trouble, such as never was since there was a nation, even to that time. And at that time your people shall be delivered, every one who is found written in the book. (Dan. 12:1)

The phrase "Michael stands up" jumps out. He *stands up*. What does this mean? In our English reading of this phrase, it means literally to stand up, such as after sitting. But the Hebrew word *amad* has little to do with the physical act of being vertical or horizontal. Rather, it can have several meanings, including "appoint, arise, cease, confirm, continue, dwell, endure, establish, and leave."

Marvin Rosenthal writes:

> Speaking of the one who will hinder the Antichrist, Paul said, "only he who now hindereth will continue to hinder until he be taken out of the way" (2 Thess. 2:7). The word hindereth means to hold down, and the phrase taken out of the way means to step aside. Therefore, the one who had the job of hindering the Antichrist will step aside; that is, he will no longer be a restraint between the Antichrist and those the Antichrist is persecuting.

> ...Further, Daniel has already said that Michael will stand up during "a time of trouble, such as never was since there was a nation even to that same time." The unprecedented time of trouble can only refer to the Great Tribulation. Since Daniel is told that this great trouble relates to his people — and his people are the Jews — this can only be "the time of Jacob's Trouble" (Jer. 30:7), which is a synonym for the Great Tribulation. It is at that time that the archangel Michael will stand up.

But what does the Hebrew word for stand up (*amad*) mean? Rashi, one of Israel's greatest scholars ...understood stand up to literally mean [to] stand still. The meaning, according to one of Israel's greatest scholars, would be to stand aside or be inactive. Michael, the guardian of Israel, had earlier fought for her (Dan. 10:13, 21), but now this one "who standeth for the children of thy people" would stand still or stand aside. He would not help; he would not restrain; he would not hold down.

The Midrash, commenting on this verse, says, 'The Holy One, Blessed be He, said to Michael, "You are silent? You do not defend my children."[74]

Although the most intense effects of the Great Tribulation will likely be experienced by the Jews living in and around Jerusalem, it is important to remember that Gentile believers, "being a wild olive tree, were grafted in among them" (Romans 11:17). As grafts into the olive tree, Christians will not be exempt from the perilous times that will come upon God's people.

For greater detail on Rosenthal's argument, see Appendix C.

Should We Look for the Antichrist?

Having a solid understanding of the identity of the restrainer in 2 Thessalonians helps to answer another common challenge to the prewrath position: If we are supposed to look for the Antichrist as a sign, why didn't any of the writers of the New Testament tell us to do so? In fact, three of them did:

Matthew, recording the words of Jesus in Matthew 24:

When you see the abomination of desolation spoken of by Daniel the prophet standing in the holy place...then let those who are in Judea flee to the mountains...For then there will be great tribulation, such as has not been since the beginning of the world until this time, no, nor ever shall be...Then the sign of the Son of Man will appear in heaven, and then all the tribes of the earth will mourn, and they will see the Son of Man coming on the clouds of heaven with power and great glory.... (vv. 15–30)

---

[74] *Pre-Wrath Rapture of the Church*, pp. 257-8.

Mark, recording the words of Jesus in Mark 13:

So when you see the abomination of desolation spoken of by Daniel the prophet, standing where it ought not...then let those who are in Judea flee to the mountains....For in those days there will be tribulation, such as has not been since the beginning of the creation which God created until this time, nor ever shall be....Then they will see the Son of Man coming in the clouds with great power and glory. (vv. 14–26)

And Paul in 2 Thessalonians:

Let no one deceive you by any means; for that Day [the Day of the Lord] will not come *unless the falling away comes first, and the man of sin is revealed,* the son of perdition, who opposes and exalts himself above all that is called God or that is worshipped, so that he sits as God in the temple of God, showing himself that he is God [the abomination of desolation].... (2 Thess. 2:3–4)

8

'Kept From the Hour'

It is by affliction chiefly that the heart of man is purified, and that the thoughts are fixed on a better state. Prosperity has power to intoxicate the imagination, to fix the mind upon the present scene, to produce confidence and elation, and to make him who enjoys affluence and honors forget the hand by which they were bestowed. It is seldom that we are otherwise than by affliction awakened to a sense of our imbecility, or taught to know how little all our acquisitions can conduce to safety or quiet, and how justly we may inscribe to the superintendence of a higher power those blessings which in the wantonness of success we considered as the attainments of our policy and courage.

—Samuel Johnson (1709–1784)

There are many who embrace the pretrib position, despite its lack of scriptural foundation, based on one verse: "Because you have kept My command to persevere, I also will keep you from the hour of trial which shall come upon the whole world, to test those who dwell on the earth" (Rev. 3:10). How can we go through the seal judgments, they protest, when God has promised to keep us from them? Clearly, God will rapture us before the beginning of the 70th Week.

There are five reasons this argument doesn't hold up:

1. The Lord has promised to keep all believers only from His *wrath*—the bowl judgments that are part of the Day of the Lord—not from periods of trial or tribulation.
2. The Lord made the promise, "I will keep you from the hour of trial" only to *one* church, the faithful church, the Church of

Philadelphia, not to all six churches addressed in Revelation.

3. The "hour of trial" does not cover the entire 70th Week, but only the period of the six seals.

4. The Greek verb "to keep" does not necessarily mean "to remove," as the pretrib position suggests.

5. There are compelling reasons for the Church to be present during the seal judgments, including the need to experience God's loving but refining hand and as a witness to the unsaved world during the end-times harvest.

So what about "kept from the hour of trial"? Flaws in the pretrib position repeatedly arise from inaccurate definitions of terms. We have already seen how misleading the wrong definition of God's wrath and the Great Tribulation can be. "Kept from the hour of trial" falls prey to the same error in thinking.

A Closer Look at "to Keep"

Let's look at the phrase more closely. Pretrib proponents take "kept from the hour of trial" to mean that God will keep—by physically removing—His children from this time of great destruction. But the Greek word used for "to keep," *tereo*, does not mean "to remove." It means "to guard from loss or injury, by keeping the eye upon," and comes from the root *teros*, which means "a watch."[75] There is nothing in this definition that implies "to remove," and yet this is exactly what pretrib proponents claim.

In fact, many Bible versions do not translate this phrase "keep you from." The *New American Bible* translates this "save you from"; *The Living Bible* translates it "protect you from"; and *The Amplified Bible* translates it "keep you (safe) from." In its footnotes, *The New International Version* explains, "The Greek for this phrase can mean either 'keep you from undergoing' or 'keep you through.'"

In either case, it does not mean "to remove."[76]

---

[75] *Strong's Exhaustive Concordance of the Bible.*

[76] Among the theologians who read "kept" as meaning "removed," the evidence usually comes from their reading of the word *ek*, or "from." Their position is that to be "kept from" means to be prevented from ever entering. The only way to prevent the Church from ever entering the period of trial, they reason, is to rapture her beforehand. Other scholars, however, disagree that *ek* can be read this way. They see it as meaning "protected in the midst of." Although there are many exhaustive and

It is interesting to note that, according to the *Oxford English Dictionary*, the verb "to keep" dates back to 1,000 A.D. The original sense may have been "to lay hold on with the hands, and hence with the attention; to keep an eye on, watch." Some other early meanings have a very personal, intimate sense: "to ward off, intercept, watch, care for, dutifully abide by, preserve, and protect." What a beautiful picture of God watching over His Church! In a Medieval castle, a "keep" was an innermost stronghold, a central tower serving as a last defense: another wonderful illustration of the true Body of Christ.

John Wycliffe, the Medieval (14th century) English church reformer who paved the way for Martin Luther and the Reformation, likely understood this relationship quite well. While identifying the hour of trial as a specific time period associated with the 70th Week, he did not see the Church being physically removed from the period of testing. Nor did he see the rapture as a form of divine deliverance from this hour. *The Wycliffe Bible Commentary* has this to say on the subject of Rev. 3:10:

> Though so worthy, this church was nevertheless to know a time of severe trial. Note carefully that the word is "trial" here, not *tribulation*. But in the trial the believers were to be divinely kept. (See John 17:15 ["I pray not that thou shouldest take them out of the world, but that thou shouldest keep them from evil"]).

"The Hour of Trial"

The second part of the phrase is "the hour of trial." The Greek word translated "trial" here is *periasmos*, which is sometimes translated "temptation" or "testing." In the *King James Version*, this verse is translated "hour of temptation." In the *New American Standard*, *New Living*, and *Contemporary English* versions, it is translated as "the hour of testing." The same word, *periasmos*, is used in the familiar verses: "Lead us not into temptation *(periasmos)*, but deliver us from the evil one" (Matt. 6:13); "Watch and pray, lest you enter into temptation *(periasmos)*" (Mark 14:38); and "Now, when the devil had ended

---

technical discussions on this subject, it is most likely that it will be contextual clues, not grammar itself, that will ultimately decide the issue.

every temptation *(periasmos)*, he departed from Him until an opportune time" (Luke 4:13).

This word, *periasmos*, is in no way associated with God's wrath. Rather, it implies a time when believers will be tried and tested for their faithfulness, as Jesus was tested in the wilderness.[77]

From where will the temptation *(periasmos)* come? During the Beginning of Sorrows, and intensified during the Great Tribulation, the Antichrist will create a tempting alternative to the suffering and persecution that will occur under his reign. Will God's people buy into the Antichrist's satanically empowered system? Or will they stand firm, even at the expense of their lives? This will be a time characterized by famine, war, and natural disasters. Will believers act unselfishly, sharing their food, medical provisions, and shelter? Or will they hoard for themselves and their families, allowing others to go without? How will believers respond to God during this time? Will they lift up the name of Jesus and give Him glory? Or will they grumble and complain against Him, allowing bitterness and resentment to grow in their hearts?[78] The persecution and testing during the six seals will be intense, and so will be the temptation *(periasmos)*. What will God's people do?

---

[77] Robert Van Kampen makes this point, noting that *peirasmos* means "a putting to the proof," either for good or evil. He then argues that the temptation, or testing, that will come during the seal judgments is from Satan, not God. "Let no one say when he is tempted, 'I am being tempted by God'; for God cannot be tempted by evil, and He Himself does not tempt anyone" (James 1:13); "For this reason, when I could endure it no longer, I also sent to find out about your faith, for fear that the tempter might have tempted you, and our labor should be in vain" (1 Thess. 3:5); and "Stop depriving one another, except by agreement for a time that you may devote yourselves to prayer, and come together again lest Satan tempt you because of your lack of self-control" (1 Cor. 7:5). Every form of the word 'tempt' in these three verses comes from the root *peirazo*, which is derived from the same root word as *peirasmos*. They all say the same thing: Satan is the source of all peirazo, not God" (*The Rapture Question Answered: Plain and Simple*, pp. 173-4).

[78] This was the mistake that the Israelites made in the wilderness of Sin, turning an 11-day journey from Egypt to Canaan into a 40-year sojourn.

Marvin Rosenthal makes an interesting observation about this time period based on the Bible's many parallels of the believer's life to that of a spiritual battle:

> Soldiers are not tested during rest and relaxation in the comfort and safety of the rear echelon. They are tested in the thick of the conflict. The soldiers of Alexander the Great were anxious to experience battle and prove their loyalty and courage to their great leader in combat. Only then could the solider cut an "A" for Alexander into his body. It was a mark (*stigmata*) he was proud to bear. The Apostle Paul had this concept in mind when he wrote, "for I bear in my body the marks (*stigmata*) of the Lord Jesus" (Gal. 6:17). When the Antichrist is personally present—empowered by Satan (Rev. 13:4) and demanding that the world bow down and worship—the true church will be given its greatest opportunity to demonstrate unfailing love and devotion to her sovereign Lord by refraining from bestowing upon a false lover the glory due only to her true Bridegroom.[79]

Many would argue that God would not bring such trials on the Church because He is a loving God and this would make Him responsible for their sin. Neither of these arguments holds true.

There is nothing in the nature of a loving God that prevents Him from testing His people. In the words of Solomon, "Do not despise the chastening of the Lord, nor detest His correction: for whom the Lord loves He corrects, just as a father the son in whom he delights" (Proverbs 3:11–12). Paul picks up on this theme in Hebrews 12:7–11: "If you endure chastening, God deals with you as with sons; for what son is there whom a father does not chasten? But if you are without chastening, of which all have become partakers, then you are illegitimate and not sons...." David also talks extensively about God's testing. In the Psalms, he writes, "For You, O God, have tested us; You have refined us as silver is refined. You brought us into the net. You laid affliction on our backs....We went through fire and through water, but You brought us out to rich fulfillment" (Psalm 66:10–12—also see Psalms 7:9; 17:3).

---

[79] *Pre-Wrath Rapture of the Church*, pp. 137-8.

Nor does this testing, if it causes believers to stumble, make God responsible for their sin. In the words of Paul, "No temptation has overtaken you except such as is common to man; but God is faithful, who will not allow you to be tempted beyond what you are able, but with the temptation will also make the way of escape, that you may be able to bear it" (1 Cor. 10:13). In other words, God *does* allow (or even place) tests, or temptations, in the paths of His people as a way to test the faithfulness of their hearts. But He never tempts them to sin (James 1:12–13); nor, if they stumble, is He responsible for their sin, since in His goodness and mercy, He also provides—and expects us to take—the path of escape.

The conclusion? In no sense can the phrase "I will keep you from the hour of trial" be used to support the interpretation that the Church will be raptured to protect believers from the testing associated with the six seals. Rather, it strongly supports the idea that the Church will be present during this period of intense trial and testing; but in the midst of it, God will supernaturally protect one group of believers, the Church of Philadelphia, which He has described as His true and faithful Bride.

Evidence From Daniel

Additional evidence comes from Daniel 11, a parallel telling of the Beginning of Sorrows and the Great Tribulation. Immediately after Daniel's description of the "abomination of desolation," in which the Antichrist stands in the Jewish temple and declares himself to be God, Daniel records the hour of severe persecution that Jesus calls the Great Tribulation. Paralleling Rev. 3:10, he writes, "And those of the people who understand shall instruct many; yet for many days they shall fall by sword and flame, by captivity and plundering. *Now when they fall, they shall be aided with a little help.*"

What form will this help take? The Bible does not say. There is, however, a strong parallel between some of the bowl judgments and the plagues sent upon the ancient Egyptians, giving rise to the possibility that God's people will be protected during parts of the 70th Week in much the same way that ancient Israel was protected during the time of Moses. Douglas Moo writes: "It is argued that, since the time of testing comes upon the 'whole inhabited earth,' only physical removal can effectively protect the church. This is so, however, only if the tribulation is of such a nature that its ravages fall indiscriminately upon all men. But we

111

have already argued that this is not the case; many biblical parallels, as well as texts within Revelation itself, demonstrate... His ability to keep His people from its effects."[80] Although Moo believes that the Church will undergo God's wrath, a point with which I disagree, his point about protection is well taken.

What method God uses to protect His children will be left for us to discover. But we can be sure of one thing: God is faithful to His word, and the Church of Philadelphia will receive some form of supernatural aid.

Does God Play Favorites?

"I will keep you from the hour of trial." Why is this promise made to one church and not to the others? Jesus Himself answers this question: "I know your works. See, I have set before you an open door, and no one can shut it; for you have a little strength, have kept My word, and have not denied My name.... Because you have kept My command to persevere, I also will keep you from the hour of trial which shall come upon the whole world, to test those who dwell on the earth" (Rev. 6:8,10).

This is God's gift to those who have been faithful, who have kept His commandments, and who have been steadfast through His trial by fire in their lives. They have not despised His chastening, but have loved Him with all their hearts, souls, and minds (Mark 12:30). Jesus confirms this in Luke 21:34, saying, "Watch therefore, and pray always that you may be counted worthy to escape all these things that will come to pass, and to stand before the Son of Man."[81]

The other churches, Jesus tells us, with the exception of the Persecuted Church, have tried to straddle the fence of worldliness and godliness. Because they have not kept His commandment to

---

[80] *Three Views on the Rapture*, p. 97.

[81] In interpreting this passage—as in many similar passages, such as Matt. 24:21-26—John Walvoord interprets this command, "Watch, therefore," not in relation to the rapture, but in relation to the separating of believers from nonbelievers at Armageddon. "They indeed will watch, for His coming is their only hope." If this were the correct interpretation, why would believers need to watch? To wait expectantly? To avoid being deceived? Believers will know the exact day that Jesus will come at Armageddon— seven years plus 30 days after the Antichrist's confirming of the covenant with Israel. Under Walvoord's interpretation, these exhortations to watch and guard from deception make little sense.

112

persevere, they have strayed from the path of true obedience, faith, and love. Instead of promising them protection, He commands them to repent and overcome.

This exhortation is given to:

• The Loveless Church:

I know your works, your labor, your patience, and that you cannot bear those who are evil.... Nevertheless I have this against you, that you have left your first love...**repent**.... **To him who overcomes** I will give to eat from the tree of life, which is in the midst of the Paradise of God. (Rev. 2:2–7)

• The Compromising Church:

I have a few things against you, because you have there those who hold the doctrine of Balaam, who taught Balak to put a stumbling block before the children of Israel, to eat things sacrificed to idols, and to commit sexual immorality.... **Repent**.... **To him who overcomes** I will give some of the hidden manna to eat. And I will give him a white stone, and on the stone a new name written which no one knows except him who receives it. (Rev. 2:14–17)

• The Corrupt Church:

I have a few things against you, because you allow that woman Jezebel, who calls herself a prophetess, to teach and seduce My servants to commit sexual immorality and eat things sacrificed to idols.... Indeed I will cast her into a sickbed, and those who commit adultery with her into great tribulation, unless they **repent** of their deeds.... **And he who overcomes**, and keeps My works until the end, to him I will give power over the nations.... (Rev. 2:18–28)

• The Dead Church:

I know your works, that you have a name that you are alive, but you are dead.... **Repent**.... **He who overcomes** shall be clothed in white garments, and I will not blot out his name from the Book of Life. (Rev. 3:1–5)

• The Lukewarm Church:

> I know your works, that you are neither cold nor hot. I
> could wish you were cold or hot. So then, because you are
> lukewarm, and neither cold nor hot, I will vomit you out of
> my mouth...**repent**.... **To him who overcomes** I will grant
> to sit with Me on My throne, as I also overcame and sat
> down with My Father on His throne. (Rev. 3:14–21)

Nowhere is the Church of Philadelphia (the Loving Church)
given either the command to repent or to overcome. The other five
churches that have wandered away from their Shepherd will
undergo God's loving hand of discipline. The Loving Church,
which has stayed close to Her Lord, is exempt.

This protection in the midst of trial is part of a biblical
pattern. God's favor often rests on the faithful, while the
compromising or unfaithful are tested. For example, Ezekiel 14
describes the land of Israel during God's judgment of famine,
pestilence, the sword, and wild beasts. God prefaces each by
saying that even if Noah, Daniel, and Job were in it, they would
deliver only themselves by their righteousness. He then repeats
this caveat with each judgment.

First the famine:

> Even if these three men, Noah, Daniel, and Job, were in it,
> they would deliver only themselves by their righteousness.
> (v. 14)

Then the wild beasts:

> Even though these three men were in it, as I live, says the
> Lord God, they would deliver neither sons nor daughters;
> only they would be delivered and the land would be desolate.
> (v. 16)

Then the sword:

> Even though these three men were in it, as I live, says the
> Lord God, they would deliver neither sons nor daughters, but
> only they themselves would be delivered. (v. 18)

114

Then the pestilence:

> Even though Noah, Daniel, and Job were in it, as I live, says the Lord God, they would deliver neither son nor daughter; they would deliver only themselves by their righteousness. (v. 20)

The context of delivery from these judgments is not that Noah, Daniel, or Job would be physically removed from these trials or prevented from ever entering them. It is that they would be protected and delivered out from the midst of them. The similarity to the protection of the Church of Philadelphia in the midst of the seal judgments—"and I will keep you from the hour of trial that shall come upon the whole earth"—is striking. This lends further support that "kept from the hour" means "kept through" or "protected in the midst of" rather than "removed," as in the rapture.

What about the Persecuted Church? This church is given the command to overcome, but this is not accompanied by the need to repent. Therefore, the great persecution that is about to come upon them is not associated with any chastening. Jesus said, "Do not fear any of those things which you are about to suffer. Indeed, the devil is about to throw some of you into prison that you may be tested....Be faithful unto death, and I will give you the crown of life.... He who overcomes shall not be hurt by the second death" (Rev. 2:10–11).

Considering the newly opened doors for evangelism throughout Eastern Europe and in many Middle Eastern countries, I believe that these believers may represent the Persecuted Church. During the 70th Week of Daniel, these newly evangelized countries will be the heart of the Revived Roman Empire, where the Antichrist's power and dominion will be at its height. These new believers, many just babes in Christ, will by God's grace be given a crash course in faith, perseverance, and obedience.

Undergoing the Fire

In all cases, this refining and testing should not be seen as an act of punishment, but as an act of mercy. This is God's loving preparation for believers' entrance into eternity. Remember, God's thought is not for our short-term comfort, but for our long-term gain. Writes Paul in Phil. 1:6: "Being confident in this very thing, that He who has begun a good work in you will complete it until the day of Jesus Christ." And Solomon writes in Prov. 3:11: "Do not despise the chastening of the Lord, nor detest His correction: for whom the Lord loves He corrects, just as a father the son in whom he delights."

No one likes correction. But our response to it reveals much about the condition of our hearts. Do we repent, as Jesus has commanded us to do? Do we surrender our wills and allow Him to restore us to a right relationship with Him? Or do we stiffen our necks and rebel against His Holy Spirit?

Notice the wording in Paul's letter to the Philippians: "He who has begun a good work in you will complete it until *the day of Jesus Christ.*" The Day of the Lord has many names, all of which use the same formation: "the day of" plus a reference either to the Lord in one of His many names or to His anger, wrath, or vengeance. Among these incarnations are: "the Day of His Wrath," "the Day of His Fierce Anger," "the Day of the Lord's Vengeance," "the Day of the Lord's Anger," and "the Day of Jesus Christ." Thus, Paul's letter could easily have read, "He who has begun a good work in you will complete it *until the Day of the Lord.*" We have already identified the start of the Day of the Lord: after the opening of the sixth seal and prior to the seventh. This means that God has until after the opening of the sixth seal to test, chasten, and perfect us.

The purpose of the Great Tribulation is to test and purify believers. This is also made clear in the book of Daniel. After describing the Antichrist's defilement of the temple (the abomination of desolation), which occurs just before the Great Tribulation, Daniel writes, "And some of those of understanding [believers] shall fall, to refine them, purify them, and make them white, until the time of the end; because it is still for the appointed time" (Dan. 11:35).

This provides some of the clearest evidence, not just for the fact that the Church must go through the Great Tribulation, but why. We will be tried and tested as David called it, as "through fire." This is a time of final cleansing and purification for the Church. (While the Old Testament exclusively addresses the nation of Israel, "those of understanding," especially in the context of end-times subjects, are likely Jewish Christians—something that was still a mystery to the ancient prophets but which, from our perspective today, seems clear. By implication, then, this would include Gentile Christians, as well.)

Despite the clarity of the scriptures on this point, this cleansing will take believers by surprise. Daniel anticipates their confusion and panic by telling them that, despite these circumstances, the end is not yet, for "it is still for the appointed time."[82] Jesus uses almost identical language in Matthew 24. Immediately after describing the abomination of desolation and the Great Tribulation, He warns believers three times *not to look for Him*, for the end is not yet:

> Then if anyone says to you, "Look, here is the Christ!" or "There!" do not believe it. For false christs and false prophets will rise and show great signs and wonders to deceive, *if possible even the elect*. See, I have told you beforehand. Therefore, if they say to you "Look, He is in the desert!" do not go out; or "Look, He is in the inner rooms!" do not believe it. For as lightning comes from the east and flashes to the west, so also will the coming of the Son of Man be. (Matt. 24:22–27)

During the six seals, believers will be looking for Jesus to remove them from their persecution, famine, and other terrible circumstances. But God has a better plan, and Jesus is telling them not to be deceived: "See, I have told you beforehand."

A Biblical Pattern

This refining and testing is part of a consistent biblical pattern. Throughout their writings, Paul and Peter both consistently herald the biblical virtue of perseverance in tribulation while claiming exemption from wrath.

---

[82] In this passage, many people interpret "the end" as referring to Armageddon. Jesus, however, defined "the end of the age" in Matthew 24 as His physical arrival on earth, which occurs immediately following the sixth seal (Matt. 24:29-30).

Comparison of Daniel 11:31-35 and Matthew 24

Daniel 11:31–35	Matt. 24: 15-26
"And forces shall be mustered by him, and they shall defile the sanctuary fortress; then they shall take away the daily sacrifices, and place there **the abomination of desolation**.	"Therefore when you see **the abomination of desolation** spoken of by Daniel the prophet, standing in the holy place (whoever reads, let him understand), then let those who are in Judea flee to the mountains...
Those who do wickedly against the covenant he shall corrupt with flattery; but the people who know their God shall be strong, and carry out great exploits. And those of the people who understand shall instruct many; yet for many days they shall fall by sword and flame, by captivity and plundering. Now when they fall, they shall be aided with a little help; but many shall join with them by intrigue.	For then there will be great tribulation, such as has not been since the beginning of the world until this time, no, nor ever shall be. And unless those days were shortened, no flesh would be saved, but for the elect's sake those days will be shortened.
And some of those of understanding shall fall, to refine them, purify them, and make them white, until the time of the end; *because it is still for the appointed time.*	*Then if anyone says to you, 'Look, here is the Christ!' or 'There!' do not believe it.* For false christs and false prophets will rise and show great signs and wonders to deceive, if possible, even the elect. *See I have told you beforehand. Therefore if they say to you, 'Look, He is in the desert!' do not go out; or 'Look, He is in the inner rooms!' do not believe it."*

For example, Romans 5:3,9: "...but we glory in tribulations, knowing that tribulation produces perseverance; and perseverance, character; and character, hope [but] we shall be saved from wrath through him." And 1 Peter 4:12: "Beloved, do not think it strange concerning the fiery trial which is to try you, as though some strange thing happened to you: but rejoice to the extent that you partake of Christ's sufferings, that when His glory is revealed, you may also be glad with exceeding joy."

Notice that Peter did not say "*if* fiery trials are to try you," or "the fiery trial which *may* try you." He was quite certain that believers must endure certain physical, emotional, and spiritual hardships that are necessary for growth. In 1 Peter 4:13, as part of the same context in which he writes about the "fiery trial," he also uses the phrase, "...when His glory is revealed." The Greek word for "revealed" is *apokalupto*, the same word that is often used to describe the appearing of Christ at His return. Similar wording is used in Matt. 29:31: "...and they will see the Son of Man coming on the clouds of heaven with power and great glory...." When Peter wrote about the fiery trial, he was likely speaking of the Great Tribulation, which will occur immediately before Christ's appearance at the rapture.

Also remember that Jesus desires His Bride to be "without spot or wrinkle" (Eph. 5:27). If Jesus were to come for the Church today, could we truly say that she could be described this way? We may be spotless *positionally*—in our legal standing before God—but purification and sanctification only come by trial and testing. For Jesus to come for a spotless Bride, she must be refined, purified, and tested. Peter could not have made it any more clear when he wrote, "For the time has come for judgment to begin at the house of God" (1 Peter 4:17). Is this testing the hand of a wrathful God? Not at all. It is the hand of a God of infinite love.

Wrote an unnamed poet:

He sat by a fire of sevenfold heat,
As he watched by the precious ore,
And closer he bent with a searching gaze
As he heated it more and more.

He knew he had ore that could stand the test,
And he wanted the finest gold
To mold as a crown for the King to wear,
Set with gems with a price untold.

So he laid our gold in the burning fire,
Though we fain would have said him "nay,"
And he watched the dross that we had not seen,
And it melted and passed away.

And the gold grew brighter and yet more bright;
But our eyes were so dim with tears,
We saw but the fire—not the Master's hand—
And questioned with anxious fears.

Yet our gold shone out with a richer glow,
  As it mirrored a form above
That bent o'er the fire, though unseen by us,
  With a look of ineffable love.

Can we think that it pleased his loving heart
  To cause us a moment's pain?
Ah, no! but he saw through the present cross
  The bliss of eternal gain.

So he waited there with a watchful eye,
  With a love that is strong and sure,
And his gold did not suffer a bit more heat
  Than was needed to make it pure.
              —Anonymous

9

Where Does Pretrib Come From?

Because there is no direct scriptural basis for the pretrib doctrine, it is amazing to me that so many of today's prophecy teachers adhere to it. I repeatedly watch highly respected prophecy teachers and television personalities give two verses to substantiate their positions: "we are not destined for wrath" and "the Lord comes as a thief in the night," even though the first is taken out of context and the other refers, not to believers, but to the unbelieving world.

I have read the writings of one television personality and prophecy teacher who, in order to make his pretrib position fall together, requires that all of the events of Revelation happen simultaneously, even though they are clearly delineated by words such as "then" and "after" that indicate consecutive events.

I have watched video productions of the rapture and the end times in which the rapture happens silently, mysteriously, leaving the world to wonder how millions could disappear instantly—"could it be aliens? new biological weapons? spontaneous combustion?"—even as the actors read 1 Thess. 4:16–17, "For the Lord Himself will descend from heaven with a shout, with the trumpet of God...." (For a discussion of the fact that the rapture will not be a silent mystery but a worldwide event, see Chapter 13, "Every Eye Will See.")

So where do people get the idea that there will be a pretribulation rapture? Despite the widespread misconception that the pretribulation view was held by the early church, pretribulationism is a modern interpretation. Although there has been much speculation about the influence of the visions of a

121

young Scottish girl named Margaret Macdonald, the development of the pretribulation rapture is generally attributed to John Darby of the Plymouth Brethren, who formalized the theory around 1830. Prior to this time, the return of Christ was seen as a singular event. Jesus would return to earth once, to rapture His Church, to redeem lost Israel, and to judge the wicked and rebellious world, and this was seen either as a midtribulational or posttribulational event. Darby was the first to formally theorize that Jesus would return in two stages: first in spiritual form to rapture the Church, then in bodily form seven years later to judge the world. This allowed Jesus to return triumphantly at Armageddon while keeping the Church out of the 70th Week.

Classic Bible scholars, including John Wesley, Charles Spurgeon, Matthew Henry, John Knox, John Hus, John Calvin, Isaac Newton, John Wycliffe, and John Bunyan, among others, did *not* hold to a pretribulation rapture view.[83]

A Little History

How did Darby's unusual interpretation of the scriptures win such widespread acceptance? In order to understand this, it is necessary to look at some of the issues surrounding the biblical scholarship of the time.

The Book of Revelation was not written until about 90 A.D. Thus, in the early church, any budding end-times theology would have arisen from the gospels and epistles. It is only John's detailed description of the seal, trumpet, and bowl judgments—written more than three decades later—that allows readers to place Jesus' coming in the timeline of 70th Week events. When one considers only the gospels and epistles, a posttribulational rapture is the most reasonable interpretation, and indeed, the writings of the earliest church fathers indicate that the infant church was posttribulational. By the time Revelation began to circulate, clarifying the fine points of prophetic timing, the first century church was in the midst of dire persecution, and as John Walvoord has pointed out, such studies took a back seat to the very real tribulations of the day.

Even though the early church was posttribulational, there is little question that most believers expected Jesus to return in their

---

[83] This list is taken from Marvin Rosenthal's *Pre-Wrath Rapture of the Church*, p. 54.

122

lifetimes. When their brethren began to die, and in fact, many died horrific martyrs' deaths, it is not surprising they began to wonder if Jesus had already come and they had missed it, or perhaps, if He was coming at all. Even as early as the book of 1 Thessalonians, which was written around 51 A.D., Paul appears to be comforting those who thought that perhaps the Day of the Lord had come and gone (1 Thess. 4:13–1 Thess. 5:2).

By the fourth century, as the persecutions continued, Catholic theologian Augustine proposed something that many believers were starting to be ready to hear: Perhaps the Second Coming, the rapture, and the Day of the Lord were not to be taken literally after all. Perhaps the kingdom of God was not a literal kingdom, and there would be no physical, earthly millennial kingdom over which Christ would rule. Instead, Augustine proposed that the kingdom of God is spiritual, fulfilled "in the hearts of faithful men." The Millennium, he suggested, will not be a literal, future time period in which Christ will reign. Rather, the Millennium is here, now, manifest in the Body of Christ in the Church Age in which we live.

Origins of Amillennialism

Augustine was not, of course, the first to put forth this theory. Credit is given to fourth century theologian Origen, the chief proponent of the allegorical method of interpretation of his time. Despite the fact that his interpretation contradicted the clear, established teachings of the church fathers, Origen's view (which was highly influenced by Greek philosophy) flourished. Until this time, the church had been exclusively premillennial, or *chialistic*, believing in a literal, thousand-year reign of Christ.

Gary Vaterlaus, instructor of biblical education and research for Sola Scriptura, attributes the widespread acceptance of amillennialism to four main factors:

> 1. A strong anti-Jewish bias that grew from a belief that God had cast away the nation of Israel and, consequently, a belief in the supremacy of the Church;
>
> 2. An overreaction to many heretical movements that, in addition to their heresies, taught a literal thousand-year reign of Christ. In reacting to these heresies, the Church threw the baby out with the bath water.

3. Influence from Greek culture and thought that placed superiority of the spiritual world over the material;

4. Conversion of Emperor Constantine to Christianity in 307 A.D., raising the status of the organized church from an entity of persecution to one of respect and great power.[84]

Although Origen's allegorical method of interpretation ultimately led him to develop and teach such deviant doctrines as the belief that the souls of men existed in a previous state, a denial of the bodily resurrection, and a belief in universal salvation for all men (even demons, for which he was ultimately declared a heretic), his teachings had a profound influence on those who would come after him, including Augustine. And because this view—called amillennialism, or "no millennium"—answered the nagging question in believers' hearts: "Why has Christ not come for us?" fourth-century Christians were ready to believe it.

Amillennial theology carried through what has commonly come to be known as the "Dark Ages," or the decline in Europe between 500 A.D. and 1000 A.D. after the fall of the Roman Empire. During this time, the scriptures were largely spiritualized, if they were read at all. Few common people could read and write, leaving issues of faith in the hands of the religious system.

The amillennial period was followed by a postmillennial period, which also spiritualized the Millennium, but taught that Christ would come to set up His kingdom after man had prepared the world through faithful preaching of the gospel.

Between these two lengthy periods of scholarship, a literal reading and interpretation of end-times prophecy was all but impossible. It was only with the Protestant Reformation in the 1500s that the church returned to extensive Bible study and literal reading of the scriptures. Initially, this return extended only to theological issues on doctrines such as faith, grace, and atonement, so eschatology remained where it left off—postmillennial.[85]

Haste Makes Waste

By the time Darby developed the novel interpretation of the two-stage return of Christ in the early 1800s, the scholarly

---

[84] "Amillennialism: Examining Its 'Origens,'" *Parousia*, Summer 2001.
[85] Both of these positions remain popular today. The point is that they were unchallenged, since a return of any kind to a literal reading of the scriptures did not occur until the Reformation.

community was hungry to take the scriptures fully literally again. Since posttribulationism requires some degree of allegorization, this desire now extended to the end-times scriptures for the first time in 1500 years. Thus, despite pretribulationism's poor exegetical foundation, Darby's efforts, which returned to a premillennial framework for the scriptures, appealed to a large segment of the scholarly population. Overlooking the theory's scriptural problems, scholars seized upon it, gradually refining it to where it is today.

Its popularity among the nonscholarly community, however, arose only after the view was adopted by Charles Scofield, who promoted it in his *Scofield Reference Bible* in 1909.

> The pretribulational view made its way into the United States in the 1880s, and with it, unfortunately, came friction and division.... The *Scofield Reference Bible* of 1909 and the revised edition of 1917, which included pretribulation rapturism as a major part of its prophetic teaching, more than any other force popularized the pretribulation view of the rapture. Untold multitudes became pretribulationists as a result of Scofield's notes which, because attached to his reference Bible, became highly authoritative in the minds of many. Most of the early Bible conferences, Bible colleges, and seminaries, under the influence of those early pretribulationist leaders, adopted the pretribulational position.[86]

The initial appeal of the pretrib doctrine is not surprising. On a popular level, pretrib theology was then, as it is now, a pleasing doctrine. Its logic is simple and easy to follow. And because this interpretation results in the Church not having to go through any of the 70th Week, it stuck.[87] In fact, despite its lack of

---

[86] *Pre-Wrath Rapture of the Church*, pp. 55–56. This is not to say that Darby was the only person to suggest a two-stage return of Christ. He is simply credited with being the first to formalize it into a cohesive theology.

[87] There are those who would point out that many of the early church fathers believed in an imminent rapture, thus requiring us to hold to an imminent, "any moment" return of Christ. However, as discussed in Appendix F, while the church fathers did hold to a biblical sense of expectation, they believed that the Church would see the Antichrist and

direct scriptural support, it has grown to become a foundational doctrine for most Bible-believing churches, missions, and evangelical organizations today. Under the circumstances of its advent, this is understandable.

The tragedy arises when you consider that this teaching *continues* to perpetuate despite its clear scriptural error, especially considering the high literacy rate in today's society, which ought not to have let such inaccuracy go unchecked. We are not living in the Middle Ages, when the scriptures were inaccessible to the average believer. Especially in Westernized countries, most Christians have their own Bibles, if not several, in their native tongues. And yet, even when they discover discrepancies between the scriptures and the teachings of their churches, they are too often willing to accept the conclusions of others than to study the scriptures for themselves.

Equally disturbing is the level of importance to which the pretrib rapture theory has risen in Christian theological circles. In some cases, it is placed in the company of such fundamental tenets of the Christian faith as the virgin birth, the blood atonement, and the deity of Christ. It has even become part of churches' doctrinal statements. Those who admit to *not* holding the pretribulation position may even risk having their salvation questioned.

Tragic Consequences

In the conclusion of his book *The Rapture Question Answered: Plain and Simple*, Robert Van Kampen has written about some of the consequences of taking prewrath as a doctrinal position:

> In spite of the strong biblical argument for the prewrath position, and in spite of the consequences of what will happen to the church if the pretribulation view is wrong, scores of men in Christian leadership have told me that if they were to publicly teach the prewrath rapture position, they would lose their jobs.

---

undergo severe persecution before the return of Christ. Thus, their attitude of expectancy cannot be equated with pretribulationism. The idea of a two-stage, pretribulational return of Christ was unknown until at least the fifth century and was not formally espoused until the early 1800s.

Marvin Rosenthal (whose relationship with me was discussed in some detail in Chapter 2) is a perfect example of what can happen if you change your view. He was thrown out of the Jewish ministry to which he had devoted his life, even though he was personally responsible for building the Friends of Israel ministry from a handful of employees to one of the largest, conservative missions to Jews in the world today....

...Charles Cooper, a Dallas Seminary grad, held a teaching position at Moody Bible Institute. He was extremely popular with the students, was a speaker at Moody Founders Week, at Moody's Pastors Conference, at Bible conferences that sponsored Moody weeks [and many other events].... Like Marv Rosenthal, he became convinced of the biblical basis for the prewrath view of Christ's return...[and] was given a choice: support the pretrib position and your job is secure; [or] support the prewrath position and you must leave.... He resigned.

These are only two examples of the stories that I hear from pastors, missionaries, teachers, even board members that have been forced to leave ministries they had given their time and resources to, faithfully, over many years!.....

...Today, many pastors...kiddingly refer to themselves as "closet prewrathers," knowing that if they went public with their convictions on this particular issue, they would pay the price and be expelled from the association, labeled, like Marv Rosenthal, as proponents of "false teachings."[88]

Such a thing should not occur within the Body of Christ. How could this have happened?

Satanic Deception?

There is a possible answer, although a decidedly uncomfortable one. I believe that the pretrib doctrine could be a form of satanic deception. After all, if Satan cannot prevent the 70th Week, what's his next best option? To face a strong Church? A spiritually prepared Church? Or a weak and defenseless one? Satan is a defeated foe—defeated two thousand years ago by

---

[88] *The Rapture Question Answered: Plain & Simple*, pp. 198–202.

Christ's blood on the cross—but he is also a roaring lion, seeking whom he may devour (1 Peter 5:8). If he is going to be destroyed, he wants to take as many people with him as possible. What better way to do this than to keep the Church blinded to the timing of Christ's return? After all, why would the Bride prepare herself for something she thinks she will never have to endure?

To do this, Satan uses the perfect tool: the Word of God. From the moment that he tempted Eve in the garden, Satan has used God's own words, twisting and misinterpreting them. To Eve, he said, "Has God indeed said, 'You shall not eat of every tree of the garden?'...You will not surely die. For God knows that in the day you eat of it your eyes will be opened and you will be like God, knowing good and evil" (Gen. 3:1–5). When Jesus was tempted in the desert, what did Satan use? Scripture! He taunted the Lord with the words of David: "If you are the Son of God, throw Yourself down. For it is written: 'He shall give His angels charge over you,' and 'In their hands they shall bear you up, lest you dash your foot against a stone'" (Matt. 4:6–7).

In his magazine, *Zion's Fire*, Marvin Rosenthal has written many articles showing the errors in the pretrib position and has set forth the prewrath argument as the better scriptural alternative. Even in the early days, it was apparent that the resistance to this position was spiritual, not scriptural. In the July/August 1997 issue of *Zion's Fire*, he addressed this issue forthrightly:

> In the March/April issue of *Zion's Fire*, I wrote an article entitled "The Church's Trojan Horse." In the article, I shared my understanding of the biblical chronology of Christ's second coming. I reminded my readers that Satan is the father of lies (John 8:44). And in that connection I wrote:
>
> "At the end of the last century, he inserted a falsehood into the Bible-believing Church of America. It entered deceptively, much like a 'Trojan Horse.' It remains inside the camp and is now so ingrained in the mind-set of many believers that to even question its biblical basis is to subject oneself to scorn and intimidation. I refer, of course, to the Trojan Horse of pretribulation rapturism."
>
> No one takes issue with the statement that Satan is the father of lies. But suggest that many Christians, however

unintentionally, have been deceived into believing one of his lies — well, that's another story — that pushes a "hot" button.... I knew [that these words] would not endear me to some of my brethren, but I also believed that they are true and need desperately to be said.

...I fear that those who do not believe the Church will be here when the Antichrist arises will, by that very fact, be the most confused and vulnerable when he does appear. If left unchallenged, for Satan, it will be a coup. If, believing as I do, I do not blow a trumpet — if I do not sound an alarm — then I am an unfaithful watchman.

I agree completely. Furthermore, I would add that, if this is a form of Satanic deception, it is no coincidence that the pretrib doctrine has arisen to such popularity and influence in the first generation in history that could, potentially, be the generation to witness the return of Christ.

I am not suggesting that pretrib proponents are not godly, Spirit-filled people. I believe that many of them are. But even godly people have their blind spots, and these blind spots can serve Satan well. For Satan knows that it is better to use sweets and honey than horns and hooves. 2 Corinthians 11:14 tells us that Satan transforms himself "into an angel of light," and what a tempting light the pretrib position is to a Christian community that, in all its humanness, does not want to believe that they will have to endure the kind of hardships for which the Word of God tells us to prepare.

10

Matthew, Revelation, and Daniel:
Three Descriptions of the Same Events

Throughout this book, I refer to the passages in Matthew 24, Revelation 6, and Daniel 11–12 as describing the same events—the seals, the trumpets, and the bowls—in the same order. This provides an important framework for understanding end-times prophecy, especially the timing of the rapture. Not everyone sees it this way, however, so this chapter will give the evidence for this conclusion.

I will start with Matthew 24 and Revelation 6. In both passages, Jesus describes world war, followed by world famine, intense persecution and martyrdom of believers, and a unique set of cosmic disturbances in the sun, moon, and stars. All of these events occur in an end-times context, in the same order, immediately before the visible manifestation of Christ. We know that both passages are consecutive because words such as "then" and "after," as well as other textual clues, tell us that they are.[89]

From a straightforward reading, it would be difficult to argue that the beginning of sorrows, the Great Tribulation, and the cosmic disturbances described in Matthew 24 are not the same as those described in Revelation 6.[90]

The comparison is as follows:

---

[89] Jesus also indicates to John that He is giving a consecutive telling of end-times events. In Rev. 4:1, He says, "Come up here, and I will show you things which must take place *after this*."

[90] Although he adheres to a pretrib interpretation, this same conclusion is reached by Dr. Renald Showers in *Maranatha! Our Lord Come!*, p. 25.

The First Seal

Matt. 24:6: And you will hear of wars and rumors of wars. See that you are not troubled; for all these things must come to pass, but the end is not yet.

Rev. 6:1– 2: Now I saw when the Lamb opened one of the seals; and I heard one of the four living creatures saying with a voice like thunder, "Come and see." And I looked and behold, a white horse. He who sat on it had a bow; and a crown was given to him, and he went out conquering and to conquer.

The Second Seal

Matt. 24:7: For nation shall rise against nation and kingdom against kingdom.

Rev. 6:3–4: When he opened the second seal, I heard the second living creature saying, "Come and see." Another horse, fiery red, went out. And it was granted to the one who sat on it to take peace from the earth, and that people should kill one another; and there was given to him a great sword.

The Third and Fourth Seals

Matt. 24:7–8: And there will be famines, pestilences, and earthquakes in various places....

Rev. 6:5–8: When He opened the third seal, I heard the third living creature say, "Come and see." So I looked, and behold, a black horse, and he who sat on it had a pair of scales in his hand. And I heard a voice in the midst of the four living creatures saying, "A quart of wheat for a denarius, and three quarts of barley for a denarius; and do not harm the oil and the wine."

When He opened the fourth seal, I heard the voice of the fourth living creature saying, "Come and see." So I looked, and behold, a pale horse. And the name of him who sat on it was Death, and Hades followed with him. And power was given to them over a fourth of the earth, to kill with sword, with hunger, with death, and by the beasts of the earth.

The Fifth Seal

Matt. 24:15–21: Therefore when you see the abomination of desolation spoken of by Daniel the prophet, standing in the holy place (whoever reads, let him understand), then let those who are in Judea flee to the mountains....For then there will be great tribulation, such as has not been since the beginning of the world until this time, no, nor ever shall be.

Rev. 6:9–11: When He opened the fifth seal, I saw under the altar the souls of those who had been slain for the word of God .... And they cried with a loud voice, saying, "How long, O Lord, holy and true, until You judge and avenge our blood on those who dwell on the earth?" Then a white robe was given to each of them; and it was said to them that they should rest a little while longer until both the number of their fellow servants and their brethren, who would be killed as they were, was completed.

The Sixth Seal

Matt. 24:29: Immediately after the tribulation of those days, the sun will be darkened, and the moon will not give its light; the stars will fall from heaven, and the powers of the heavens will be shaken.

Rev. 6:12–13: I looked when he opened the sixth seal, and behold, there was a great earthquake; and the sun became black as sackcloth of hair, and the moon became like blood. And the stars of heaven fell to the earth, as a fig tree drops its late figs when it is shaken by a mighty wind.

Between the Sixth and Seventh Seals

Matt. 24:30: Then the sign of the Son of Man will appear in heaven, and then all the tribes of the earth will mourn, and they will see the Son of Man coming on the clouds of heaven with power and great glory.

Rev. 6:15–16: And the kings of the earth, the great men, the rich men, the commanders, the mighty men, every slave and every free man, hid themselves in the caves and in the rocks of the mountains, and said to the mountains and rocks, "Fall on us and hide us from the face of Him who sits on the throne…."

Still, there are critics who would argue that this comparison cannot be made, that these are not the same events in the same order. I would urge them to sit down and read these passages side by side. Imagine sitting on the Mount of Olives, listening to Jesus speak about the events to come at the end of the age. Then imagine sitting at the feet of John the apostle, listening as he recounted the tale of the amazing things he saw. There can be no mistaking the correlation. Marvin Rosenthal has pointed out that the similarity, even in the wording, should be expected since John was one of the disciples present when Jesus gave the Olivet Discourse.

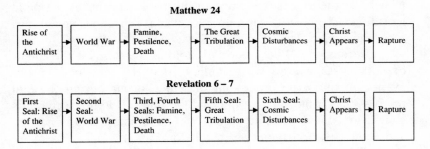

Matthew 24

| Rise of the Antichrist | → | World War | → | Famine, Pestilence, Death | → | The Great Tribulation | → | Cosmic Disturbances | → | Christ Appears | → | Rapture |

Revelation 6 – 7

| First Seal: Rise of the Antichrist | → | Second Seal: World War | → | Third, Fourth Seals: Famine, Pestilence, Death | → | Fifth Seal: Great Tribulation | → | Sixth Seal: Cosmic Disturbances | → | Christ Appears | → | Rapture |

Similarity of Intent

Not only is there a direct correlation between Matthew 24 and Revelation 6, but to suggest that these are not the same events in the same order also ignores the *instructive* nature of the text. Remember, Jesus is answering His disciples' direct question: "Tell us, when will these things be? And what will be the sign of Your coming and of the end of the age?" (Matt. 24:3). Jesus is not speaking in parables or in riddles to confuse. As the author of truth, He has been asked a direct question and is giving a direct answer:

> For everyone who asks receives, and he who seeks finds, and to him who knocks it will be opened. For what man is there among you who, if his son asks for bread, will give him a stone? Or if he asks for a fish, will he give him a serpent? If you then, being evil, know how to give good

133

gifts to your children, how much more will your Father who is in heaven give good things to those who ask Him! (Matt. 7:8–11)

For those who don't accept that the events of Matthew 24 are the same as the seals of Revelation 6, I must ask the following question: Was Jesus being deceptive? Both of these passages are Jesus' own accounts: His recounting of end-times prophecy on the Mount of Olives and His direct revelation of end-times events to the Apostle John. Remember that the book of Revelation takes its title from its opening verse: "The Revelation of Jesus Christ, which God gave Him to show His servants—things which must shortly take place. And He sent and signified it by His angel to His servant John" (Rev. 1:1). In fact, when Jesus calls John to heaven to witness the events described in the book, He makes a simple and direct promise, "Come up here and I will show you things which must take place after this" (Rev. 4:1).

Because the Bible has clearly told us that Jesus is the author of both passages, are we to believe that He described similar events, in the same order—all of which occur during the end times—and yet they are not one and the same? I do not accept this conclusion, for this would create confusion, and "God is not the author of confusion, but of peace" (1 Cor. 14:33).

Tying the Great Tribulation to the Fifth Seal

There is more evidence that the events in the Olivet Discourse are the same as the seal judgments. This comes from the fact that the Great Tribulation and the fifth seal (the cry of the martyrs) are the same event. The use of the word "tribulation" in this context is *thlipsis*, which is often translated "tribulation" or "affliction." While it occurs 20 times in the New Testament, it only occurs five times in an end-times context. All five refer to the Great Tribulation.

The first two uses of *thlipsis* are in Matthew's telling of end-times events:

For then there shall be great tribulation [*thlipsis*] such as has not been since the beginning of the world until this time, no, nor ever shall be....Immediately after the tribulation [*thlipsis*] of those days, the sun will be darkened, and the moon will not give its light .... (Matt. 24:21, 29)

134

The second two are in Mark's telling of these same events:

> For in those days there will be tribulation [*thlipsis*], such as has not been since the beginning of the creation which God created until this time, nor ever shall be....[A]fter that tribulation [*thlipsis*], the sun will be darkened, and the moon will not give its light; the stars of heaven will fall.... (Mark 13:19, 24, 25)

Notice that, in both accounts, Jesus says that the tribulation He has just described is unique. It will be a tribulation "such as has not been since the beginning of the creation which God created until this time, nor ever shall be." There was none like it in the past and there will be none like it in the future. This is why it is called *the* Great Tribulation—there is only one.

The last use of *thlipsis* in this context is in Rev. 7:13–14:

> After these things I looked, and behold, a great multitude which no one could number, of all nations, tribes, peoples, and tongues, standing before the throne and before the Lamb.... These are the ones who come out of the great tribulation [*thlipsis*].... (Rev. 7:9,14)

The "great tribulation" that causes the death of the martyrs in the fifth seal is clearly the same Great Tribulation described in Matthew 24 and Mark 13. Therefore, if the Great Tribulation is the same as the fifth seal, it is reasonable (and even imperative) to conclude that the triple sign in the heavens (the sun, moon, and the stars) that follows the Great Tribulation is the same triple sign in the heavens (the sun, moon, and the stars) of the sixth seal. From here, we must also conclude that the beginning of sorrows corresponds with the first, second, third, and fourth seals.

Confirming the Rapture

This confirms another fact, as well, that not only is the fifth seal the same as the Great Tribulation, but that Christ's return and the rapture occur after the opening of the sixth seal. In Matthew 24, the order is as follows:

First, the Great Tribulation:

For then there will be great tribulation, such as has not been since the beginning of the world until this time, no, nor ever shall be.... (Matt. 24:21–22)

Then the cosmic disturbances:

Immediately after the tribulation of those days, the sun will be darkened, and the moon will not give its light; the stars will fall from heaven; and the powers of the heavens will be shaken. (Matt. 24:29)

Then the appearance of Christ:

Then the sign of the Son of Man will appear in heaven, and then all the tribes of the earth will mourn, and they will see the Son of Man coming on the clouds of heaven with power and great glory. (Matt. 24:30)

Then the rapture:

And He will send His angels with a great sound of a trumpet, and they will gather together His elect from the four winds, from one end of heaven to the other. (Matt. 24:31)

Now look at the events in Revelation 6. First, there is the great martyrdom of God's people:

When He opened the fifth seal, I saw under the altar the souls of those who had been slain for the word of God and for the testimony which they held. (Rev. 6:9)

Then the cosmic disturbances:

I looked when He opened the sixth seal, and behold, there was a great earthquake; and the sun became black as sackcloth of hair, and the moon became like blood. And the stars of heaven fell to the earth, as a fig tree drops its late figs when it is shaken by a mighty wind. (Rev. 6:12–13)

136

Then the appearance of Christ:

> And the kings of the earth, the great men, the rich men, the commanders, the mighty men, every slave and every free man, hid themselves in the caves and in the rocks of the mountains, and said to the mountains and rocks, "Fall on us and hide us from the face of Him who sits on the throne...." (Rev. 6:17)

Then the raptured Church in heaven:

> After these things I looked, and behold, a great multitude, which no one could number, of all nations, tribes, peoples, and tongues, standing before the throne and before the Lamb, clothed with white robes, with palm branches in their hands and crying out with a loud voice, saying, "Salvation belongs to our God who sits on the throne and to the Lamb!" ...Then one of the elders answered, saying unto me, "Who are these who are arrayed in white robes? And where did they come from?" And I said unto him, "Sir, you know." And he said to me, "These are the ones who come out of the great tribulation." (Rev. 7:9–10, 13)

From a straightforward reading of the text, we must conclude that Revelation 6 and Matthew 24 refer to the same events in the same order and that the Second Coming of Christ and the rapture occur after the opening of the sixth seal.

Daniel 12 and the 70th Week

If there is any doubt remaining that Matthew 24 and Revelation 6 refer to the same events in the same order, and that the return of Christ follows the sixth seal, perhaps it will be dispelled by a look at Daniel 11 and 12. These prophetic books, written approximately 600 years before Jesus' Olivet Discourse, provide yet a third telling of the same events in the same order.

Daniel 10 and 11 describe the rise of Antiochus IV, or Antiochus Epiphanes, a ruler from Syria several centuries before the birth of Christ. Antiochus IV is infamous for seeking to outlaw practice of the Mosaic Law and for putting a statue of Zeus in the Temple of God. He followed these atrocities by butchering a large number of Jews. Most conservative biblical scholars agree that he is given to us as a type of Antichrist to provide insight into the

Antichrist's character and reign. Many also agree that the reference to "the time of the end" in Daniel 11:40 shifts the narrative exclusively from the historical activities of Antiochus Eiphanes to the activities of the Antichrist during the 70th Week. This being the case, the description of battles and military intrigue described in Daniel 11 correlate with Jesus' description of the beginning of sorrows (wars and rumors of wars and nation rising against nation) and the first and second seals (the rise of the Antichrist).

Then, in Dan. 11:31, we see the word-for-word correlation with Jesus' reference to the abomination of desolation (Matt. 24:15), which occurs at the midpoint of the 70th Week:

> *Dan. 11:31:* And forces shall be mustered by him, and they shall defile the sanctuary fortress; then they shall take away the daily sacrifices and place there the abomination of desolation.

> *Matt. 24:15:* Therefore when you see the abomination of desolation spoken of by Daniel the prophet, standing in the holy place (whoever reads, let him understand), then let those who are in Judea flee to the mountains.

Jesus' reference to the abomination of desolation "spoken by Daniel the prophet" establishes that these two passages are describing the same event. Although Daniel does not make specific reference to the famine mentioned as part of the third seal, he does outline the fourth and fifth seals:

> Those who do wickedly against the covenant, he shall corrupt with flattery, but the people who know their God shall be strong, and carry out great exploits. And those of the people who understand shall instruct many; yet for many days they shall fall by the sword and flame, by captivity and plundering. (Dan. 11:32,33)

138

Matthew 24	Revelation 6
Matt. 24:6 "And you will hear of wars and rumors of wars. See that you are not troubled; for all these things must come to pass, but the end is not yet."	**Rev. 6:1-2** "Now I saw when the Lamb opened one of the seals…And I looked and behold, a white horse. He who sat on it had a bow; and a crown was given to him, and he went out conquering and to conquer."
Matt. 24:7 "For nation will rise against nation, and kingdom against kingdom."	**Rev. 6:3-4** "When I opened the second seal… Another horse, fiery red, went out. And it was granted to the one who sat on it to take peace from the earth, and that people should kill one another; and there was given to him a great sword."
Matt. 24:7 "And there will be famines, pestilences, and earthquakes in various places. All these are the beginning of sorrows."	**Rev. 6:7-8** "When He opened the third seal… I looked and behold, a black horse, and he who sat on it had a pair of scales in his hand. And I heard a voice …saying, 'A quart of wheat for a denarius, and three quarts of barley for a denarius; and do not harm the oil and the wine.' When He opened the fourth seal…I looked, and behold, a pale horse. And the name of him who sat on it was Death, and Hades followed with him. And power was given to them over a fourth of the earth, to kill with sword, with hunger, with death, and by the beasts of the earth."
Matt. 24:21 "For then there will be great tribulation, such as has not been since the beginning of the world until this time, no, nor ever shall be."	**Rev. 6:9-11** "When He opened the fifth seal, I saw under the altar the souls of those who had been slain for the word of God and for the testimony which they held. And they cried with a loud voice, saying, 'How long, O Lord, holy and true, until You judge and avenge our blood on those who dwell on the earth?'"
Matt. 24:29 "Immediately after the tribulation of those days, the sun will be darkened, and the moon will not give its light; the stars will fall from the heaven, and the powers of the heavens will be shaken."	**Rev. 6:12-13** "I looked when He opened the sixth seal, and behold, there was a great earthquake; and the sun became black as sackcloth of hair, and the moon became like blood. And the stars of heaven fell to the earth…."
Matt. 24:30 "Then the sign of the Son of Man will appear in heaven, and then all the tribes of the earth will mourn, and they will see the Son of Man coming on the clouds of heaven with power and great glory.	**Rev. 6:15–16** And the kings of the earth, the great men, the rich men … every slave and every free man, hid themselves in the caves and in the rocks of the mountains, and said to the mountains and rocks, "Fall on us and hide us from the face of Him who sits on the throne…"

At the beginning of Chapter 12, as in Matthew 24 and Revelation 6, there is another near word-for-word correlation with the persecution and martyrdom of the Great Tribulation:

> At that time, Michael shall stand up, the great prince who stands watch over the sons of your people; and there shall be a time of trouble, such as never was since there was a nation, even to that time. (Dan. 12:1)

Compare this to the Olivet Discourse:

> Therefore when you see the abomination of desolation spoken of by Daniel the prophet, standing in the holy place...then let those who are in Judea flee to the mountains.... For then there will be great tribulation, such as has not been since the beginning of the world until this time, no, nor ever shall be. (Matt. 24:15, 21)

Even the wording, "and there shall be a time of trouble, such as never was since there was a nation, even to that time," is nearly identical to Matt. 24:21. As would be expected in corresponding passages, the word for "trouble" used in Daniel, *tsarah*, has the nearly identical translation as the Greek word for "tribulation," *thlipsis*, used in Matthew, Mark, and Revelation.[91]

Just as God's plan of glorious deliverance (in the form of the rapture) follows the Great Tribulation in Matthew 24, so, too, does it follow in this passage of Daniel:

> At that time your people shall be delivered, every one who is found written in the book. And many of those who sleep in the dust of the earth shall awake, some to everlasting life, some to shame and everlasting contempt. (Dan. 12:1–2)

---

[91] *Strong's Exhaustive Concordance of the Bible.*

Comparison of Matthew 24, Revelation 6, and Daniel 11, 12

Matthew 24	Revelation 6	Daniel 11, 12
Matt. 24:6 "And you will hear of wars and rumors of wars. See that you are not troubled; for all these things must come to pass, but the end is not yet."	*Rev. 6:1, 2* "Now I saw when the Lamb opened one of the seals; and I heard one of the four living creatures saying with a voice like thunder, 'Come and see.' And I looked and behold, a white horse. He who sat on it had a bow; and a crown was given to him, and he went out conquering and to conquer."	*Daniel 11:21-22* And in his place shall arise a vile person, to whom they will not give the honor of royalty; but he shall come in peaceably, and seize the kingdom by intrigue. With the force of a flood they shall be swept away from before him and be broken, and also the prince of the covenant."
Matt. 24:7 "For nation will rise against nation, and kingdom against kingdom."	*Rev. 6:3, 4* "When He opened the second seal, I heard the second living creature saying, 'Come and see.' Another horse, fiery red, went out. And it was granted to the one who sat on it to take peace from the earth, and that people should kill one another; and there was given to him a great sword."	*Daniel 11:5* He shall stir up his power and his courage against the king of the South with a great army. And the king of the South shall be stirred up to battle with a very great and mighty army; but he shall not stand, for they shall devise plans against him. Yes, those who eat of the portion of his delicacies shall destroy him; his army shall be swept away, and many shall fall down slain. …At the appointed time he shall return and go toward the south; but it shall not be like the former or the latter. For ships from Cyprus shall come against him; therefore he shall be grieved, and return in rage against the holy covenant, and do damage…
Matt. 24:7,8 "And there will be famines, pestilences, and earthquakes in various places. All these are the beginning of sorrows."	*Rev. 6:7,8* "When He opened the third seal, I heard the third living creature say, 'Come and see.' So I looked, and behold, a black horse, and he who sat on it had a pair of scales in his hand. And I heard a voice in the midst of the four living creatures saying, 'A quart of wheat for a denarius, and three quarts of barley for a denarius; and do not harm the oil and the wine.' When He opened the fourth seal, I heard the voice of the fourth living creature saying, 'Come and see.' So I looked, and behold, a pale horse. And the name of him who sat on it was Death, and Hades followed with him. And power was given to them over a fourth of the earth, to kill with sword, with hunger, with death, and by the beasts of the earth."	

Matthew 24	Revelation 6	Daniel 11, 12
Matthew 24:15, 21 "Therefore when you see the abomination of desolation spoken of by Daniel the prophet, standing in the holy place...then let those who are in Judea flee to the mountains...For then there will be great tribulation, such as has not been since the beginning of the world until this time, no, nor ever shall be."	*Rev. 6:9,11* "When He opened the fifth seal, I saw under the altar the souls of those who had been slain for the word of God and for the testimony which they held. And they cried with a loud voice, saying, 'How long, O Lord, holy and true, until You judge and avenge our blood on those who dwell on the earth?' Then a white robe was given to each of them; and it was said to them that they should rest a little while longer until both the number of their fellow servants and their brethren, who would be killed as they were, was completed."	*Daniel 11:31* "And forces shall be mustered by him, and they shall defile the sanctuary fortress; then they shall take away the daily sacrifices and place there *the abomination of desolation.*" *Daniel 12:1* "At that time, Michael shall stand up, the great prince who stands watch over the sons of your people; *and there shall be a time of trouble, such as never was since there was a nation, even to that time.*"
Matt. 24:29 "Immediately after the tribulation of those days, the sun will be darkened, and the moon will not give its light; the stars will fall from heaven, and the powers of the heavens will be shaken."	*Rev. 6:12, 13* "I looked when He opened the sixth seal, and behold, there was a great earthquake; and the sun became black as sackcloth of hair, and the moon became like blood. And the stars of heaven fell to the earth, as a fig tree drops its late figs when it is shaken by a mighty wind."	
Matt. 24: 30-31 "Then the Sign of the Son of Man will appear in the heaven, and then all the tribes f the earth will mourn, and they will see the Son of Man coming on the clouds of heaven with power and great glory. And He will send His angels with a great sound of a trumpet, and they will gather together His elect from the four winds, from one end of heaven to the other."		*Daniel 12:1,2* "At that time your people shall be delivered, every one who is found written in the book. And many of those who sleep in the dust of the earth shall awake, some to everlasting life, some to shame and everlasting contempt."

How do we know this is the rapture and not some other form of deliverance? The rising of the dead is one of the fundamental characteristics of this historic moment. "For the dead in Christ shall rise first. Then we who are alive and remain shall be caught up together with them in the clouds to meet the Lord in the air" (1 Thess. 4:16–17). So, too, in Dan. 12:2, do we see the rising of the dead as a prelude to the delivery of God's people: "and many of those who sleep in the dust of the earth shall awake."

In fact, the Hebrew word Daniel uses for delivered is *malat*, which means "to escape (as in slipperiness); to release or rescue; ...preserve, save speedily and surely."[92] This isn't merely a removal, but a massive evacuation—the rapture.[93]

---

[92] Ibid.

[93] Of course, the rapture was a mystery at the time this passage was written (1 Cor. 15:51), but there can be little question that the rapture is part of this event. Not only is the rising of the dead one of the fundamental characteristics of this historic moment, but this will happen only once (1 Cor. 15:21–25)— at the end of the age, at the bodily return of Christ.

11

The Last Trump(et)

Another way to determine the timing of the rapture is to determine when the last trumpet will be blown. For Paul writes, "Behold, I tell you a mystery: We shall not all sleep, but we shall all be changed in a moment, in the twinkling of an eye, *at the last trumpet*. For the trumpet will sound and the dead will be raised incorruptible, and we shall be changed" (1 Cor. 15:51–52). I love the use of the trumpet in this context because the sounding of the trumpet has profound meaning for the nation of Israel: as the call to worship, the call to ceremony, and the call to war. In this case, it is all three.

Along with the trumpet, this verse contains several defining characteristics of the rapture:

- The trumpet will be blown.
- We will be given new, glorified bodies.
- The dead will be raised.

Compare this to the description in 1 Thess. 4:15–17:

For this we say to you by the word of the Lord, that we who are alive and remain until the coming of the Lord will by no means precede those who are asleep. For the Lord Himself will descend from heaven with a shout, with the voice of an archangel, and with the trumpet of God. And the dead in Christ will rise first. Then we who are alive and remain shall be caught up together with them in the clouds to meet the Lord in the air. And thus, we shall always be with the Lord.

Once again, we see the same set of defining characteristics:

• Jesus will come in the clouds.
• The trumpet will be blown.
• The dead will rise.
• Believers will meet Jesus in the air.

In Matt. 24:30–31, Jesus describes this scene once more:

Then the sign of the Son of Man will appear in heaven, and then all the tribes of the earth will mourn, and they will see the Son of Man coming on the clouds of heaven with power and great glory. And He will send His angels with a great sound of a trumpet, and they will gather together His elect from the four winds, from one end of heaven to the other.

Again, we see the following characteristics:

• Jesus coming on the clouds.
• The blast of the trumpet.
• The gathering of the elect.

Even the passage in Daniel describes two of the key elements of the rapture:

And at that time your people shall be delivered, every one who is found written in the book. And many of those who sleep in the dust of the earth shall awake, some to everlasting life, some to shame and everlasting contempt. (Dan. 12: 1–2)

In this passage, we see:

• The rising of the dead.
• The miraculous delivery of God's people.

All of these passages clearly describe the same event, particularly when you take into consideration the larger context in which these events take place (see Chapter 10). Therefore, if the rapture occurs at the last trumpet, and the rapture is described in Matt. 24:31—after the Great Tribulation, after the unique series of cosmic disturbances, and after "the sign of the Son of Man"—then the last trumpet will be blown at this time, too.

Furthermore, since we know that the cosmic disturbances described in Matthew 24 are the same as those in the sixth seal, we must come to the same conclusion that we have drawn many times before: that the last trumpet, and therefore the rapture, will follow the sixth seal.

Multiple Raptures?

There are those who would argue that all of these verses do not refer to the same rapture, but to several *different* raptures. They believe that Jesus will rapture His Church in stages, each at a different time during the 70th Week. The multiple rapture theory allows readers to see Jesus' coming in glory in Matt. 24:31 as *a* rapture without doing damage to hope in the pretribulation rapture. This commonly involves the teaching that there are three separate raptures: one occurring prior to the 70th Week, one in the middle of the 70th Week, and one at the end.

The idea that Jesus raptures His Church in stages presents several scriptural problems. First, the New Testament writers made it very clear that Jesus returns only once, using language such as "waiting for the [singular] revelation of our Lord...." (1 Cor. 1:7); "our Lord Jesus Christ at His [singular] coming" (1 Thess. 2:19); and "Therefore be patient, brethren, until the [singular] coming of the Lord" (James 5:7). To suggest that Jesus makes one or more trips to the sky, appearing visibly, but not fulfilling His prophetic Second Coming, implies deception, either on the part of Jesus or on the part of the New Testament writers. Even if there were evidence that Jesus could come visibly but not physically prior to His return (although all direct scriptural evidence is to the contrary), Paul makes it clear in 1 Cor. 15:52 that there is only one rapture, and this will be "at the last trumpet."

Those holding to the multiple rapture view have a third difficulty, as well. This is the same difficulty as those who would dispute that Matthew 24, Revelation 6, and Daniel 11 and 12 do not describe the same events in the same order. The descriptions are strikingly similar, and in several cases are almost identical,

Characteristics of the Rapture

There are four characteristics of the rapture that appear, in part or whole, in all of the rapture verses. This clearly indicates that they represent the same event. They are:
1. Jesus appearing in the clouds.
2. The sound of the trumpet.
3. The rising of the dead.
4. The delivery of God's people.

Matt. 24:30-31
"Then the sign of the Son of Man will appear in heaven, and then all the tribes of the earth will mourn, and they will see the Son of Man coming on the clouds of heaven with power and great glory. And He will send His angels with a great sound of a trumpet, and they will gather together His elect from the four winds, from one end of heaven to the other."

1. Jesus appearing in the clouds.
2. The sound of the trumpet.
3. The delivery of God's people.

1 Cor. 15:51-52
"Behold, I tell you a mystery: We shall not all sleep, but we shall all be changed, in a moment, in the twinkling of an eye, at the last trumpet. For the trumpet will sound, and the dead will be raised incorruptible, and we shall be changed."

1. The sound of the trumpet.
2. The rising of the dead.
3. The delivery of God's people.

1 Thess. 4:15-17
"For this we say to you by the word of the Lord, that we who are alive and remain until the coming of the Lord will by no means precede those who are asleep. For the Lord Himself will descend from heaven with a shout, with the voice of an archangel, and with the trumpet of God. And the dead in Christ will rise first. Then we who are alive and remain shall be caught up together with them in the clouds to meet the Lord in the air."

1. Jesus appearing in the clouds.
2. The sound of the trumpet.
3. The rising of the dead.
4. The delivery of God's people.

Daniel 12:1-2
"At that time Michael shall stand up, the great prince who stands watch over the sons of your people; And there shall be a time of trouble, such as never was since there was a nation, Even to that time. And at that time your people shall be delivered, every one who is found written in the book."

1. The rising of the dead
2. The delivery of God's people.

even using identical wording. This puts those who suggest these are not the same events in a difficult position.[94]

What About Armageddon?

What about Jesus' return at Armageddon? This passage also describes Jesus coming on the clouds. Couldn't this be a description of the rapture? No. Revelation 19 gives us a very clear description of Jesus coming on the clouds and it is not the same as the rapture:

> Now I saw heaven opened, and behold, a white horse. And He who sat on him was called Faithful and True, and in righteousness He judges and makes war. His eyes were like a flame of fire, and on His head were many crowns. He had a name written that no one knew except Himself. He was clothed with a robe dipped in blood, and His name is called the Word of God. And the armies in heaven, clothed in fine linen, white and clean, followed Him on white horses. (Rev. 19:11–14)

The fact that Jesus is coming on the clouds is the only similarity to the verses describing the rapture. This is a very different event, with a very different set of identifying characteristics.

Let's look more closely at those characteristics:

• He appears in the heavens on a white horse.
• His eyes are like flame.
• He is clothed in a robe dipped in blood.
• The armies of heaven follow on white horses.

There is no blast of the trumpet, no rising of the dead, and no deliverance of God's people. Plus, horses play a very prominent role in this passage, something that not one of the other rapture verses mentions. Matthew 24:29 also tells us that, just

---

[94] Not only is the similarity of the wording and in content of these verses strong evidence that they are the same events, but the entire context of Matthew 24 and 1 and 2 Thessalonians is the same, as well. In *Three Views on the Rapture*, Douglas Moo provides a chart showing the dramatic similarities between the Olivet Discourse and the two epistles (p. 194).

prior to Jesus' return, the sun will turn dark, the moon will not give its light, stars will fall from the sky, and the powers of the heavens will be shaken. There is no such description before His triumphal entry in Revelation 19. This combination of cosmic disturbances is mentioned much earlier, as part of the sixth seal.

Jesus' arrival at Armageddon is a *different* event for a different purpose: to defeat the beast and his false prophet. His physical return occurred much earlier, after the opening of the sixth seal when He raptured His Church.[95]

This, along with other evidence, explains why the trumpet—Israel's historic call to war—is not blown at this time. There are a great many details in Rev. 19:11–21, but a trumpet blast is not one of them. Was this an oversight of some kind? Not at all. The reason is that *war has already been declared.* It was

---

[95] To support the contention that the Son of Man in Matt. 24:31 does not refer to the rapture but to Jesus' Coming at Armageddon, many scholars refer to Daniel 7, which describes the Messiah coming on the clouds, then immediately setting up His Millennial kingdom. Because Jesus borrows from the language of this passage in His Olivet Discourse, this leads to their conclusion that Matt. 24:30–31 is also Armageddon, no matter how many similarities there may be to the sixth seal. There are several considerations to be taken here. First, in a technique called "telescoping," prophetic literature often uses the foreshortening of two events so that they appear to be temporally successive, even if they are separated by long spans of time (Isa. 61:1-2, Dan. 12:1-2, John 5:29). This is the case here. There are also several non-consecutive events described in this passage that tell us that, not only are the events foreshortened, but they are nonconsecutive as well. This includes the books being opened prior to the slaying of the beast and Jesus' coming on the clouds after the beast has been cast into the fire. For these reasons, this passage should not be used to override the clear order of events given by Jesus in the New Testament. Douglas Moo makes this point as well, saying, "Inasmuch as the rapture is clearly revealed only in the New Testament, the decisive evidence for its timing with respect to the [great] tribulation must come from the New Testament also. Furthermore, it is sound hermeneutic procedure to establish a doctrine on the basis of the texts that speak most directly to the issue" (*Three Views on the Rapture*, p. 172). It must also be remembered that even Daniel did not understand many of his own visions (Dan. 12:8). Therefore, Jesus' description in the Olivet Discourse should be used to interpret Daniel's vision rather than the other way around.

declared approximately three years earlier, when the trumpet was blown as the Lord Jesus came on the clouds to declare the Day of the Lord. This is simply the final battle of an ongoing war.[96]

Matt. 24:31 Is Not Armageddon

One of the most common arguments against the prewrath position is that Matt. 24:30, Jesus' coming in glory after the Great Tribulation, is a reference to Armageddon, not the rapture:

> Then the sign of the Son of Man will appear in heaven, and then all the tribes of the earth will mourn, and they will see the Son of Man coming on the clouds of heaven with power and great glory. (Matt. 24:30)

In the previous chapter of this book, this argument was invalidated by the scriptural evidence that the cosmic disturbances described in this passage are the same as those in the sixth seal. This places Jesus' return in glory after the midpoint of the 70th Week, but before the trumpets and the bowls.

In addition, there are six more reasons that Matt. 24:30–31 cannot refer to Armageddon:

1. It would contradict Jesus' statement that no one knows the hour or the day of His return. When Jesus made this statement (Matt. 24:36), it was in the context of His coming in glory described five verses earlier. If this coming in glory refers to Armageddon, as pretribulationists would have us believe, this would create a serious scriptural problem. We know that there will

---

[96] Although Paul Feinberg argues in favor of the pretrib position, he also makes a strong argument that Christ's return at the rapture and His return at Armageddon in Revelation 19 are not the same event. That argument can be used here: "In the central rapture passage dealing with this issue, 1 Thess. 4:13-18, the time of the resurrection of the dead saints is clearly stated to be *during* the descent of Christ to the earth. Those raptured, living and dead saints, will be caught up to meet the Lord in the air. Contrast that information with what is found in Revelation 19-20. There, the order seems to be: the descent of Christ, the slaying of His enemies, the casting of the beast and the false prophet into the lake of fire, the binding of Satan, and *then* the resurrection of the saints. It seems as though the resurrection of the dead will be *during* the descent at the rapture, but *after* the descent at [Armageddon]" (*Three Views on the Rapture*, p. 84).

150

be exactly seven years and 30 days (1260 days plus 30 days—Dan. 9:24, Dan. 12:11) between the time the Antichrist confirmed the covenant with Israel and the time that Jesus fights the battle of Armageddon at the end of the 70th Week.[97] Therefore, if this

---

[97] Although, for the sake of simplicity, this book makes few distinctions between the seal, trumpet, and bowl judgments in their relationship to the 70th Week, the 70th Week likely ends with the sixth trumpet. Explains Gary Vaterlaus, instructor of biblical education and research for Sola Scriptura: "When comparing Dan. 9:24–27, Rev. 11:14, and Rev. 10:7, the 70th Week appears to end just before the blowing of the seventh trumpet. As described in Revelation 11, the witnesses are granted 1260 days to prophesy and conclude their prophecy on the last day. They are killed the day after, then are raised and ascend to heaven three and one-half days later. After this, the sixth trumpet judgment (second woe) is announced as being past (Rev. 11:14). The blowing of the seventh trumpet (Rev. 11:15) seems to be the fulfillment of the 70 Weeks prophecy of Daniel 9:24 ('everlasting righteousness' coming to Israel). Furthermore, Rev. 10:7 states, 'but in the days of the voice of the seventh angel, when he is about to sound, then the mystery of God is finished, as He preached to His servants the prophets.' This 'mystery' takes us back to the completion of the Church—the salvation of Israel—as Paul taught in Romans 11:25-26: 'For I do not want you, brethren, to be uninformed of this mystery, lest you be wise in your own estimation, that a partial hardening has happened to Israel until the fullness of the Gentiles has come in; and thus all Israel will be saved' At the blowing of the 7th trumpet, the kingdom of the world also reverts back to God Almighty: 'And the seventh angel sounded; and there arose loud voices in heaven, saying, "The kingdom of the world has become the kingdom of our Lord, and of His Christ; and He will reign forever and ever"' (Rev. 11:15), which appears to be the fulfillment of Dan. 9:24 and the anointing of the 'Most Holy,' that is, Christ as King. Furthermore, in Dan. 12:7 we are told that the reign of the Antichrist will be for a 'time, times and half a time,' or 1,260 days. Afterwards, Daniel asks, 'what will be the outcome of these events?', and the angel tells him that from the midpoint, it would be 1,290 days, or 30 more days beyond the end of the 70th Week (Dan. 12:11), that the outcome is the destruction of the desolator, the Antichrist: 'And he will make a firm covenant with the many for one week, but in the middle of the week he will put a stop to sacrifice and grain offering; and on the wing of abominations will come one who makes desolate, even until a complete destruction, one that is decreed, is poured out on the one who makes desolate.' So, the 'outcome of these events,' which occurs 30 days after the end of the 70th Week, is the

151

passage refers to the battle of Armageddon, and if that battle occurs exactly seven years and 30 days after the confirming of the covenant, we *will* know the day, since it was set by the prophet Daniel. The only satisfactory resolution to this problem is that Jesus' coming in glory in this passage does *not* refer to Armageddon, but to His return for the Church at the rapture.

2. *It would contradict Jesus' answer to His disciples.*

In the early part of the chapter, Jesus' disciples asked Him, "What will be the sign of Your coming and the end of the age?" Essentially, they were asking, "When is the end of the age *for us?*" These disciples were soon to become the foundation of the New Testament Church at Pentecost. If Matt. 24:30–31 does not refer to the rapture, then Jesus did not answer their question. When He told the disciples that He will appear in the clouds with the blast of the trumpet and the archangel of God, He will not really be "back," so to speak. This would make the pretrib's belief in a "partial" or "spiritual" return (as opposed to a bodily return) of Christ a form of divine tease.[98]

---

seventh bowl, or the battle of Armageddon, when the Antichrist is destroyed. The nature of the bowls is so severe that they could not go on for long or else all life would be destroyed. Thus, the bowls are concentrated in about a 25-day period."

[98] If the Church is raptured when Jesus comes after the opening of the sixth seal, and the resurrection of the dead occurs at that time, how are we to reconcile John's description of those sitting on the thrones in Rev. 20:4, which occurs immediately after Armageddon? This is one of the arguments used by posttribulationists to justify the rapture of the Church at the end of the 70th Week. However, since this vision occurs *after* Armageddon, it does not support one of these views over the other. The phrase, "This is the first resurrection," simply identifies those who are seated on the thrones, whenever they came out in relation to the 70th Week. Nor does the description of the seated give us a definitive answer. Some texts, such as King James, read, "And I saw thrones, and they sat upon them, and judgment was given unto them...," which implies an act in progress. Other versions, such as the New International, read, "I saw thrones on which *were seated* those who *had been* given authority to judge...," which implies an act taken in the past, but how far in the past is not specified. I believe that, in this context, the prewrath reading is most consistent with the character of God since the ones who have proven themselves through the fire have earned, through their faithfulness, the right to judge. Those who become believers after the

3. Who is Jesus talking to when He tells us not to be deceived?

In Matt. 24:23–26, Jesus tells believers three times not to be deceived by false prophets during the Great Tribulation, that "the time is not yet." And yet we know from Dan. 12:11 that the exact duration between Antichrist's confirming of the covenant with Israel and the day that Jesus destroys him at Armageddon will be 1290 days. If Matt. 24:29–31 refers to Armageddon, as pretribulationists claim, why would Jesus' warning be necessary? Once the 70th Week begins, believers will know the exact number of days until this terrible battle, so there is no reason for them to be looking for Him before then.

4. Who are the multitudes in Dan. 11:32–35, Matt. 24:23–26, Rev. 6:9–11, and Rev. 7:9–10?

If the Church is raptured prior to the 70th Week and Israel does not recognize Jesus as the Messiah until He comes at Armageddon, who are the multitudes of believers in these verses? They cannot refer to unbelieving Jews because Daniel calls them "those of understanding," and Jesus refers to them as looking for Him, the Messiah Jesus. If they are not believers undergoing the persecution of the Great Tribulation, these descriptions do not make sense.

5. What causes 144,000 Jews to suddenly become believers after the cosmic disturbances of the sixth seal?

As discussed in the next chapter, something causes a massive, worldwide salvation experience — 144,000 unbelieving Jews suddenly becoming sealed with the Holy Spirit after the opening of the sixth seal. If this is not caused by Jesus coming on the clouds to rapture the Church, what causes it?

6. If Jesus is coming to rescue the Jews at Armageddon, and Matt. 24:30–31 refers to Armageddon, why would they mourn?

Jesus tells us that when He comes on the clouds of heaven, in glory and with the blast of the trumpet, "all of the tribes of the earth will mourn" (Matt. 24:30, Rev. 1:7). Considering that Jesus'

---

rapture — who have seen the risen Christ in bodily form, leaving no doubt as to the truth of scripture — while remaining faithful, were not operating under the same level of faith. Thus, those seated in Rev. 20:4 are believers raptured earlier, after the opening of the sixth seal. This passage does not signify that the rapture has occurred at this time.

153

arrival at Armageddon will bring the destruction of the Antichrist, the judgment of the rebellious nations, the restoration of the Jews to their homeland in everlasting peace, and usher in the physical kingdom of God, this will be a time of joy for God's people. Scripture also tells us that, by the end of the 70th Week, all Israel, the believing remnant preserved for the sake of God's Holy name, will be saved. Thus, the Jews should be welcoming Jesus as their Savior and King at Armageddon, receiving Him with ecstatic joy. When would there be time or reason to mourn?

Once again, a satisfactory resolution to these questions can only be found if Jesus' coming on the clouds in Matt. 24:30–31 is the rapture of the Church after the sixth seal. It eliminates contradiction with the statement that "no one knows the hour or the day." It eliminates the possibility that Jesus is being deceptive in answering the disciples' question, "When are you coming back?" It explains why Jesus was so concerned that believers not be deceived by false prophets. It explains the identity of the multitudes in Daniel, Matthew, and Revelation. It explains the instant salvation and sealing of 144,000 Jews. Finally, it gives the Jews a time period for mourning after the appearance of the Messiah that does not conflict with the joyousness of His return.[99]

When Is the Last Trumpet?

This leaves one final question to be answered: If the rapture occurs after the opening of the sixth seal, how can it occur, as Paul describes it, at "the last trumpet" (1 Cor. 15:52)? After all, following the rapture of the saints, there are still seven trumpet judgments to come. There is no definitive answer to this problem. However, there are three things that we do know:

1. There is overwhelming scriptural evidence for the timing of the rapture—after the sixth seal. Placing the rapture after the seventh trumpet would contradict all of the clear, direct scriptural evidence given elsewhere in scripture. If we use the principle of

---

[99] While arguing for the pretrib position, Paul Feinberg acknowledges these similarities but believes that the contrasts between these passages outweigh them (*Three Views on the Rapture*, p. 231). These contrasts, however, create no contradictions in the biblical text and are easily explained by the fact that they are describing different aspects of the same event, much as the gospels provide complementary accounts of Jesus' life and ministry.

interpreting the unclear by the clear, we cannot throw out all of this evidence based on one verse.

2. When Paul penned 1 Corinthians, Revelation had not yet been written. In fact, it would not be written until approximately four decades later, so Paul may have had no knowledge of the trumpet judgments when he wrote this passage. It is possible that he was simply making an analogy that would have been easily understood by his audience: the call to assembly, which was used in the Roman games or a military context. In these cases, there was a preliminary trumpet, sometimes two, with the last being the call to assembly. Such an analogy would make sense in this context, since the New Testament writers frequently made cultural analogies to clarify points.

3. The last trumpet, or the trumpet call of God, could not be the seventh trumpet of Revelation—or any of the trumpets of Revelation, for that matter—because, in Revelation, those who are blowing the trumpets are angels. At the rapture, it is Jesus Himself who initiates the blast (Matt. 24:31, 1 Thess. 4:16). This is why the trumpet is called "the trumpet of God" (1 Thess. 4:16).

This distinction, in itself, separates "the last trumpet" from the trumpets of Revelation.

Identifying the First Trumpet

Robert Van Kampen has suggested that, in order to define the second trumpet, we ought to look for the first trumpet. In order to do this, we must look for a time in which God has blown a trumpet before. Indeed, we find one:

> Then the Lord will be seen over them, and His arrow will go forth like lightning. *The Lord God will blow the trumpet*, and go with whirlwinds from the south. The Lord of hosts will defend them; they shall devour and subdue with slingstones. They shall drink and roar as if with wine; they shall be filled with blood like basins, like the corners of the altar. The Lord their God will save them in that day, as the flock of His people. They shall be like the jewels of a crown, lifted like a banner over His land. (Zech. 9:14–15)

155

Van Kampen has suggested that this trumpet blast, which was prophesied during the Jews' return from captivity in Babylon, is the first trumpet.[100]

Indeed, earlier in this passage, God says that His hand will specifically be against Greece, likely a reference to the Maccabbean revolt that began in about 160 B.C. when the Jews revolted against the Greek ruler Antiochus Epiphanes, the precursor to the Antichrist (this uprising is detailed in the apocryphal books of 1 and 2 Maccabbees).

Writes Gary Vaterlaus,

> At this time, God blew His trumpet and delivered His people from oppression. In the same way, God will once again, and for the last time, blow His trumpet and deliver His people from oppression [prior to the outpouring of the Day of the Lord]. This will be the last blast of the trumpet of God.[101]

The Rapture in Revelation

But even if we do not hear the actual trumpet blast in Revelation (could this be because the book was written from John's perspective, which was in heaven, not on earth?), the Lord does not leave us entirely without evidence of the rapture. Although John does not describe the trumpet itself being blown at the end of Chapter 6, John does give us a description of the *results* of this trumpet blast—the raptured Church.

In Revelation 7:9, we read:

> After these things I looked, and behold, a great multitude, which no one could number, of all nations, tribes, peoples, and tongues, standing before the throne and before the Lamb, clothed with white robes, with palm branches in their hands and crying out with a loud voice, saying, "Salvation belongs to our God who sits on the throne and to the Lamb!" (Rev. 7:9–10)

---

[100] *The Sign*, 3rd Revised Edition (Crossway Books, 2000), p. 151.
[101] Personal correspondence with the author.

12

Dry Bones Live

In an earlier chapter, we discussed how the phrase "the four winds" ties the rapture to Rev. 7:1. But the four winds have yet another purpose in identifying the timing of the rapture. This is by tying the return of Christ to the redemption of Israel through the sealing of the 144,000 of the tribes.

Who are these 144,000?

For centuries, God disciplined His people for their persistent idolatry by allowing them to be conquered by pagan nations—first the Babylonians, then the Medo-Persians, then the Greeks, and finally the Romans. But when even these efforts did not cause His people to be faithful, God broke fellowship with them and scattered them across the earth, as the prophets foretold:

> Then I saw that for all the causes for which backsliding Israel had committed adultery, I had put her away and given her a certificate of divorce; yet her treacherous sister Judah did not fear, but went and played the harlot also. (Jer. 3:8)

> Bring charges against your mother, bring charges; for she is not My wife nor am I her Husband! Let her put away her harlotries from her sight and her adulteries from between her breasts.... I will not have mercy on her children, for they are the children of harlotry, for their mother has played the harlot. (Hosea 2:2–5)

For the Israelites, this separation from God resulted in a period commonly called "the dispersion." During this time, God scattered the people of Israel just as He scattered the rebellious and arrogant people of Babel:

> Son of man, when the house of Israel dwelt in their own land, they defiled it by their own ways and deeds.... Therefore I poured out My fury on them for the blood they had shed on the land, and for their idols with which they had defiled it. So I scattered them among the nations, and they were dispersed throughout the countries. I judged them for their ways and their deeds. (Eze. 36:17–19)

This dispersion lasted from Rome's destruction of the temple in A.D. 70 until the re-establishment of the nation of Israel in 1948. At that time, God began to gather His people back into their own land in fulfillment of end-times prophecy.

Faithful to His promise, God preserved a remnant for His name's sake:

> But I had concern for My holy name, which the house of Israel had profaned among the nations wherever they went. Therefore say to the house of Israel, Thus says the Lord God: "I do not do this for your sake, O house of Israel, but for My holy name's sake.... For I will take you from among the nations, gather you out of all countries and bring you into your own land. Then I will sprinkle clean water on you, and you shall be clean; I will cleanse you from all your filthiness and from all your idols. I will give you a new heart and put a new spirit within you; I will take the heart of stone out of your flesh and give you a heart of flesh. I will put My Spirit within you and cause you to walk in My statutes, and you will keep My judgments and do them. Then you shall dwell in the land that I gave to your fathers; you shall be My people and I will be your God." (Eze. 36:21–28)

Notice that there are two parts to this prophecy: (1) that God would fully restore His people to the land that He promised to Abraham; and (2) that He would fully restore His people to their position of fellowship with Him.

We see this same two-part prophecy in Hosea:

> Therefore, behold, I will allure her, will bring her into the wilderness, and speak comfort to her. I will give her

158

vineyards from there, and the Valley of Achor as a door of hope. She shall sing there, as in the days of her youth, as in the day when she came up from the land of Egypt. And it shall be, in that day, says the Lord, that you will call Me My Husband, and no longer call Me My Master. For I will take from her mouth the names of the Baals [false gods], and they shall be remembered by their name no more. (Hosea 2:14–17)

For decades, many have taught that the Old Testament prophecies about the restoration of Israel were fulfilled when Israel became a nation. But this fulfillment was incomplete. While Israel has been re-gathered in the land of Abraham, God's people are still in denial about the identity of their Savior. Thus, the second part of this prophecy has yet to be fulfilled. This fulfillment has everything to do with the rapture.

The Sealed of God

In Revelation 7, we read about 144,000 Jews who are sealed immediately before the trumpet judgments are blown:

And he cried with a loud voice to the four angels to whom it was granted to harm the earth and the sea, saying, "Do not harm the earth, the sea, or the trees till we have sealed the servants of our God on their foreheads." And I heard the number of those who were sealed. One hundred and forty-four thousand of all the tribes of the children of Israel were sealed:

of the tribe of Judah twelve thousand were sealed;
of the tribe of Reuben twelve thousand were sealed;
of the tribe of Gad twelve thousand were sealed;
of the tribe of Asher twelve thousand were sealed;
of the tribe of Naphtali twelve thousand were sealed;
of the tribe of Manasseh twelve thousand were sealed;
of the tribe of Simeon twelve thousand were sealed;
of the tribe of Levi twelve thousand were sealed;
of the tribe of Issachar twelve thousand were sealed;
of the tribe of Zebulun twelve thousand were sealed;
of the tribe of Joseph twelve thousand were sealed;
of the tribe of Benjamin twelve thousand were sealed.
(Rev. 7:2–8)

159

The use of the term "seal" in this context is interesting because throughout the New Testament, the term "seal" is applied only to believers. The Greek word for "sealed" is *sphragizo*, which means "to stamp (with a signet or private mark) for security or preservation."[102] According to scripture, sealing comes with the filling of God's Holy Spirit through a saving relationship with Jesus Christ: "In Him you also trusted, after you heard the word of truth, the gospel of your salvation; in whom also, having believed, you were sealed with the Holy Spirit of promise" (Eph. 1:13). And, "Now He who establishes us with you in Christ and has anointed us is God, who also has sealed us and given us the Spirit in our hearts as a guarantee" (2 Cor. 1:21–22).

Nowhere in Revelation does it tell us that these Jews become believers after they are sealed. They simply are sealed. For this to be true, they must *already be believers*.[103] Today, the nation of Israel is largely a secular people. Israel rejected her Messiah two thousand years ago, and despite many evangelistic efforts, this view has remained largely unchanged. For the 144,000 to be sealed all at once, something dramatic must have happened. What would cause a spontaneous repentance of so many heart-hardened Jews?

The appearance of Christ Himself:

Behold, He is coming with clouds, and every eye will see Him, even they who pierced Him. And all the tribes of the earth will mourn because of Him. (Rev. 1:7)

The use of the terms "all the tribes of the earth" is a uniquely Jewish phrase, used to describe the 12 tribes of Israel. A similar phrase, "all the tribes of the earth," is used in Matthew 24:

Then the sign of the Son of Man will appear in heaven, and then all the tribes of the earth will mourn, and they will see the Son of Man coming on the clouds of heaven with power and great glory." (Matt. 24:30)

---

[102] *Strong's Exhaustive Concordance of the Bible.*
[103] It is commonly argued that these are seals of protection during the last half of the 70th Week, not seals of the Holy Spirit. There is no question that they serve a protective role, but based on the number of other scriptural indicators, I am suggesting that they are both.

This tells us that the 144,000 are likely observant Jews who know the teachings of the prophets, who have heard the saving gospel of Jesus Christ, but like their forefathers, have rejected Jesus as "the Gentile's Messiah." When Jesus appears in the heavens to rapture the Church, they will realize their mistake, and although it will be too late for them to be taken in the rapture, they will serve Him in the exalted position of the 144,000 preserved as God's servants in the post-rapture world.

John describes these Jews' relationship with Jesus in Rev. 14:2–5:

> I heard the sound of harpists playing their harps. They sang as it were a new song before the throne, before the four living creatures, and the elders; and no one could learn that song except the 144,000 who were redeemed from the earth. These are the ones who were not defiled with women, for they are virgins. These are the ones who follow the Lamb wherever He goes. These were redeemed from among men, being firstfruits to God and to the Lamb. And in their mouth was found no deceit, for they are without fault before the throne of God.

Now compare this with the promise in Eze. 36:28:

> I will take the heart of stone out of your flesh and give you a heart of flesh. I will put My Spirit within you and cause you to walk in My statutes, and you will keep My judgments and do them. Then you shall dwell in the land that I gave to your fathers; you shall be My people and I will be your God.

The sealing of the 144,000 begins the fulfillment of the second half of the Old Testament prophecies about the restoration of Israel. As the gospel is spread during the 70th Week, Ezekiel's words will be completely fulfilled once the last of the faithful remnant of Israel accepts Jesus as Messiah at the end of the 70th Week. But this fulfillment will start with these "firstfruits to God" (Rev. 14:4) who immediately recognize and accept Jesus as their long-awaited Messiah at His bodily return. From this point, God will lift the blindness from the eyes of His people, and as the prophets predicted, "so all of Israel shall be saved" (Romans 11:26). By the end of the 70th Week, the last of the remnant of

Israel, preserved for the sake of God's Holy name, will come to know Him as Lord and Savior (Dan. 9:24).[104]

Times of the Gentiles

There is additional evidence that the sealing of the 144,000 is directly related to their salvation at the rapture. This comes from the Apostle Paul, who writes: "For I do not desire, brethren, that you should be ignorant of this mystery, lest you should be wise in your own opinion; that blindness in part has happened to Israel until the fullness of the Gentiles has come in" (Romans 11:25).

In other words, God has ordained a spiritual blindness upon Israel as punishment for their rebellion and sin:

> Hearing you will hear and shall not understand, and seeing you will see and not perceive; for the hearts of this people have grown dull. Their ears are hard of hearing, and their eyes they have closed, lest they should see with their eyes and hear with their ears, lest they should understand with their hearts and turn, so that I should heal them. (Matt. 13:13)

In God's mercy, however, this blindness will be lifted after the completion of a time called "the times of the Gentiles."

When are the times of the Gentiles? It is the time when Israel has no legitimate ruling king. For the northern kingdom of Israel, this began in 722 B.C., when the nation was carried away captive to Babylon. For the southern kingdom of Judah, this

---

[104] The suggestion that Israel is saved over the period of the last half of the 70th Week differs from the common teaching that Israel is saved all at once, at the end. According to Dan. 9:24, God has determined 70 weeks for the nation of Israel, to finish the transgression, to make an end of sins, and to make reconciliation for iniquity. To finish something implies the completion of an ongoing process. Although, in the dry bones prophecy, the army "lived, and stood on their feet," this does not require the salvation of Israel all at once. It simply says, "they lived, and stood." The Old Testament practice of telescoping allows for a gradual fulfillment over a period of years (especially considering the 6,000-year history of the Israelites; the three-and-one-half years of the latter half of the 70th Week is rapid, to say the least). I see the fulfillment of Romans 11:26 beginning with the 144,000, continuing over the last half of the 70th Week, and being brought to a conclusion at the end of the Week, with the salvation of the last member of the remnant.

162

happened some years later, in 586 B.C. Since that time, there has been no legitimate heir on the throne. In fact, there has not even been a legitimate *claim* to the throne except one, Jesus Christ. Although Jesus was rejected at His First Coming, at His Second Coming, He will return as the Lion of the Tribe of Judah. No longer the Suffering Servant, He will be the long-awaited King. The times of the Gentiles will be at an end. When He appears in the clouds in glory to take His Bride, the veil will be lifted from the eyes of Israel and many will accept Him as Savior.

This relationship is recognized by John Walvoord, who writes, "Apparently, the very act of the rapture of the church serves to confirm to those who are honestly seeking their Messiah, and the only Savior. Overnight, after the church is caught up, many of Israel have their eyes opened to the truth and immediately become the evangels of the period. The special blindness which was Israel's judgment during the time of Gentile blessing is removed, and the Jew resumes his place."[105]

Walvoord, however, sees this event occurring at the beginning of the 70th Week with the spiritual, not physical return of Christ, which is the standard pretrib position. Furthermore, he contends that Jesus does not claim His throne until Armageddon. To this I must ask: How can the times of the Gentiles be at an end, as the pretrib position maintains, if Jesus does not physically return to claim His throne until seven years later? It makes much more sense that the times of the Gentiles come to an end with the physical return of the Savior after the opening of the sixth seal.[106]

---

[105] *The Return of the Lord*, p. 99.

[106] Walvoord gets very close to the prewrath position when he says, "It seems clear that before Christ returns, Israel will turn to Him and will formally acknowledge her sin. Zechariah 12:10 speaks of this: 'And I will pour upon the house of David, and upon the inhabitants of Jerusalem, the spirit of grace and of supplication; and they shall look unto me whom they have pierced, and they shall mourn for him, as one mourneth for his only son...' The passage goes on to describe the mourning and the cleansing from sin that follows. It is apparently the divine preparation for the return of their Messiah" (p. 100). Walvoord sees this pouring out of the spirit of grace and the turning of Israel from her sin as occurring prior to Christ's physical return, but he does not make the connection with Rev. 1:7: "Behold, He is coming with clouds, and every eye will see Him, even they who pierced Him. And all the

Dry Bones Live

That the rapture is the trigger event that enables the sealing of the 144,000 is confirmed by yet another Old Testament prophecy, the "dry bones" prophecy (Eze. 37:1–14). During a vision, God places Ezekiel in the midst of a valley full of dry bones and asks. "Son of man, can these bones live?" Ezekiel answers, "O Lord, you know!" The vision then describes how God gathers together the dry bones and covers them with sinews and flesh, "but there was no breath in them."

> Also He said to me, "Prophesy to the breath, prophesy, son of man, and say to the breath, 'Thus says the Lord God: "Come from the four winds, O breath, and breathe on these slain, that they may live."'" So I prophesied as He commanded me, and breath came into them, and they lived, and stood upon their feet, an exceedingly great army. (vv. 9–10)

Prophecy teachers have long agreed that the dry bones represent Israel, a prophecy that was fulfilled in 1948 when the bones were given flesh as the reborn and acknowledged nation. However, the prophecy is clear: Even once Israel is reborn, she will remain dry, spiritually dead, until God puts His Spirit in her. The fact that *breath is given to these dry bones* is important, because the only way to be raised from spiritual death to life is through salvation in Jesus Christ:

> Therefore, just as through one man sin entered the world, and death through sin, and thus death spread to all men, because all sinned...even so through one Man's righteous act the free gift came to all men, resulting in justification for life. (Romans 5:12–18)

> For the wages of sin is death, but the gift of God is eternal life in Christ Jesus our Lord. (Romans 6:23)

---

tribes of the earth will mourn because of Him," which clearly *does* refer to His physical return. In spite of this, Walvoord's own interpretation fits better with the prewrath reading of scripture than it does with pretrib.

164

According to God's own Word, the raising from death to life of these dry bones refers to salvation. This can be seen in Eze. 17:13–14: "Then you shall know that I am the Lord, when I have opened your graves, O My people, and brought you up from your graves. *I will put My Spirit in you, and you shall live.*" Just as in the prophecies of Jeremiah and Hosea, something gives life (salvation) to these bones, for the Spirit cannot live in an unsaved soul but is evidence of being born again. Once again, this is confirmed by Paul. Speaking of the unbelief of the nation of Israel, he writes, "For if their being cast away is the reconciling of the world [by bringing salvation to the Gentiles], what will their acceptance be but life from the dead?" (Romans 11:15).

In the dry bones prophecy, we are told that this salvation happens suddenly and dramatically. Indeed, Romans 11:26 tells us that, by the end of the 70th Week, less than three-and-one-half years later, "all Israel shall be saved." What would cause "an exceedingly great army" to be saved so rapidly? As in Revelation 7, the reference to the four winds ties this to the bodily return of Christ following the opening of the sixth seal.

Let's compare the dry bones passage to the sealing of the 144,000:

Rev. 7:1–8: After these things, I saw four angels standing at the four corners of the earth, holding the four winds of the earth, that the wind should not blow on the earth, on the sea, or on any tree. Then I saw another angel ascending from the east, having the seal of the living God. And he cried with a loud voice to the four angels to whom it was granted to harm the earth and the sea, saying, "Do not harm the earth, the sea, or the trees till we have sealed the servants of our God on their foreheads." And I heard the number of those who were sealed. One hundred and forty-four thousand of all the tribes of the children of Israel were sealed.

Here we have:

• The bodily return of Christ.
• The reference to the four winds.
• The sealing (through the salvation and the spiritual coming to life) of the 144,000.

Comparison of the Four Winds in Matthew 24, Revelation 6, and Ezekiel 37

Matthew 24	Revelation 6	Ezekiel 37
		Ezekiel 37:1-6 "The hand of the Lord came upon me and brought me out in the Spirit of the Lord, and set me down in the midst of the valley; and it was full of bones. Then He caused me to pass by them all around, and behold, there were very many in the open valley; and indeed they were very dry. And He said to me, 'son of man, can these bones live?' So I answered, 'O Lord God, You know.' Again, He said to me, 'Prophesy to these bones, and say to them, 'O dry bones, hear the word of the Lord! Thus says the Lord God to these bones: 'Surely I will cause breath to enter into you, and you shall live. I will put sinews on you and bring flesh upon you, cover you with skin and put breath in you; and you shall live. Then you shall know that I am the Lord.
	Rapture	
Matt. 24:31 "And He will send His angels with a great sound of the trumpet, and they will gather together His elect **from the four winds**, from one end of heaven to the other."	*Rev. 7:1-2* "After these things I saw four angels standing at the four corners of the earth, **holding the four winds of the earth...** Then I saw another angel ascending from the east, having the seal of the living God. And he cried with a loud voice to the four angels to whom it was granted to harm the earth and the sea, saying, 'Do not harm the earth, the sea, or the trees till we have sealed the servants of our God on their foreheads.'"	*Ezekiel 37:9-10* "Thus says the Lord God: 'come from the four winds, O breath, and breathe on these slain, that they may live.'" So I prophesied as He commanded me, and breath came into them, and they lived, and stood upon their feet, an exceedingly great army.'"

166

Eze. 37:13–14: Thus says the Lord God: "Come from the four winds, O breath, and breathe on these slain, that they may live."

In this passage, we also see:

• The reference to the four winds.
• The giving of the Holy Spirit that raises the dry bones from death to life.

These 144,000 of the tribes of Israel are the firstfruits of Ezekiel's prophecy. After the revelation of the Messiah Jesus, whom they have rejected for two thousand years, they suddenly receive — and accept — God's revelation of His truth. For the first time in centuries, the dry bones of the nation of Israel *live*.

13

Every Eye Will See

Blessing and honor, glory and power, be unto the Ancient of Days. From every nation, all of creation, bow before the Ancient of Days. Every tongue in heaven and earth shall declare Your glory. Every knee shall bow at Your throne in worship. You shall be exalted, O God, and Your kingdom shall not pass away, O Ancient of Days. [107]

In all of the popular treatments of the rapture in books, lectures, and movies, the rapture is a big mystery to the unbelieving world. Suddenly, millions across the globe are missing. Cars crash, planes fall from the sky, husbands and wives find themselves sitting alone at the dinner table without their spouses and children. Amidst the devastation, these poor souls are left rubbing their eyes in wonder, searching for answers that are provided by the deceiving Antichrist.

This makes for an exciting book or motion picture, but it isn't what scripture teaches. Scripture teaches that Jesus will return to the earth in the same way that He ascended—in bodily form—with the blast of a heavenly trumpet that draws our attention to the sky, where He will be visible to all.

This fact is told to us many places in scripture, but nowhere more clearly than in the Book of Acts. After Jesus' ascension into heaven, the angel gave this message to the dazed disciples, who continued to gaze skyward: "Men of Galilee, why do you stand gazing up into heaven? This same Jesus, who was taken up from

---

[107] "Ancient of Days," words by Gary Sadler, music by Jamie Harvill, ©1992 Integrity's Hosanna! Music.

you into heaven, will so come in like manner as you saw Him go into heaven" (Acts 1:9).

In like manner. The disciples watched Jesus ascend to heaven in bodily form. When believers see Him again, it will also be in bodily form.

Revelation 1:7 adds one very important detail of this event: *He will be seen by every living person.* "Behold, He is coming with clouds, and every eye will see Him, even they who pierced Him. And all the tribes of the earth will mourn because of Him." Jesus confirmed this detail in Matt. 24:30: "Then the sign of the Son of Man will appear in heaven, and then *all the tribes of the earth* will mourn, and they will see the Son of Man coming on the clouds of heaven with power and great glory."

This is hardly a silent descent, leaving the removal of the Church a great mystery. The Church will be whisked away all right, but the entire world will watch.

There is yet another supernatural occurrence that will add to the drama of this event, and that is the raising of the dead. Consider what happened in the moments that followed Jesus' death on the cross: "In that moment the curtain of the temple was torn in two....The earth shook and the rocks split. The tombs broke open and the bodies of many holy people who had died were raised to life. They came out of the tombs, and after Jesus' resurrection they went into the holy city and appeared to many people" (Matt. 27:51–53). Both Paul and the prophet Daniel tell us that something similar will happen at the time of the rapture. We see this described in three separate passages:

> And at that time your people shall be delivered, every one who is found written in the book. And many of those who sleep in the dust of the earth shall awake. (Dan. 12:1–2)

> For the trumpet will sound, and the dead will be raised incorruptible, and we shall be changed. (1 Cor. 15:52)

> For this we say to you by the word of the Lord, that we who are alive and remain until the coming of the Lord will by no means precede those who are asleep. For the Lord Himself will descend from heaven with a shout, with the voice of an archangel, and with the trumpet of God. And the dead in Christ will rise first. (1 Thess. 4: 15–16)

What a surprise for the unbelieving world! The earth will split, coffins will open, and the dead will once again see the sun. How much time will elapse between this event and the rapture of all believers is uncertain. However, it is almost certain that, if the world has time to see Jesus coming in the clouds, it will also have time to see the dead standing in worship of their King.

If there is still any question about what is going on when Jesus returns, it will be dispelled when the world sees believers' transformation into new, heavenly bodies. We know from the bodily manifestations of Jesus and the angels that heavenly bodies can be seen by the natural world (Gen. 19:1, Heb. 13:2, John 20:27). Likewise, the transformation of the dead and the living will be witnessed by those who are left behind. As believers are transformed and taken up into heaven, the unbelieving world will watch in wonder and in horror.

This makes Jesus' comparison of the rapture to the days of Noah even more compelling: "But as the days of Noah were, so also will the coming of the Son of Man be" (Matt. 24:37). Many people tend to focus on the activities during this time, the eating and drinking, the marrying and giving in marriage. But as he awaited the flood, Noah was "a preacher of righteousness" (2 Peter 2:5). The Greek word for preacher is *kerux*, meaning one who proclaims or publishes, especially news of the gospel. Noah wasn't quietly building the ark, keeping its purpose to himself. He was building with one hand and preaching with the other, warning the inhabitants of the earth of their impending doom.

People back then weren't different from those today. Noah was likely mocked. His neighbors probably stood around and made fun of the ridiculous floating vessel in the middle of the desert. People might have even traveled from one side of the Mediterranean Basin to the other, just to gawk. But one thing is for certain, when the flood waters came and the mockers were stranded outside, not one of them was in doubt as to why. They may not have believed God's words before the waters fell, but you can bet that they believed as the waters were coming down. But by the time it became clear that God's judgment had arrived, it was too late. So it will be at Christ's coming at the rapture.

The coming of Jesus in bodily form, visible to the entire world, plays the same role as the flood waters during Daniel's 70th Week. There will be no more excuses for those who are left behind. The gospel will have been proclaimed to the ends of the earth. Unbelievers will have seen the bodily form of Jesus and will know that He is Lord. They will have seen the raising of the dead and the transformation at the rapture, and they will know that they have missed it. When Jesus arrives in the clouds, with the blast of the trumpet and the voice of the archangel, they will not be in doubt as to why. And, as in the days of Noah, it will be too late.

This lesson is so important that the Bible makes the comparison between Christ's Second Coming and the days of Noah three times (Matt. 24:37; 1 Peter 3:20–22; and 2 Peter 2:5). Fortunately, because the gospel will have reached every tribe, tongue, and nation, there will be plenty of Bibles in every language readily available after the rapture, no longer needed by their owners, who have been caught up into heaven.

The Sign in Heaven

There are those who would have us believe that at His coming, Jesus will be seen only by believers, that somehow our spiritual condition entitles us to see His glory while others will not—hence the "silent disappearance" theory. The mourning of the Jewish tribes, however, clearly invalidates this position.

> Then the sign of the Son of Man will appear in heaven, and then all the tribes of the earth will mourn, and they will see the Son of Man coming on the clouds of heaven with power and great glory. (Matt. 24:30)

> Behold, He is coming with clouds, and every eye will see Him, even they who pierced Him. And all the tribes of the earth will mourn. (Rev. 1:7)

All around the globe, the 12 tribes of Israel will join the millions of unbelievers whose jaws drop in one accord at the sight of the Lord God Himself, and they will mourn for the Messiah they should have recognized long ago (Zech. 12:10). What a sad day for God's chosen people!

But, in God's unique and wonderful way, there is hope in this, too. Remember, since the beginning of the 70th Week, there will have been an evangelistic explosion. Christians, knowing that time is short, will be forsaking all to spread the gospel. After all, what will their homes, their finances, and their lives profit them when their Lord is coming *for certain* in a matter of months or years? Jesus' coming will validate all that the proclaimers of the gospel have said. For those looking for a sign, the "coming of the Son of Man" will be infallible proof. And unlike those who missed out on boarding Noah's Ark, those who miss the rapture will be given a second chance to know God's grace, even if it means giving up their lives under the Antichrist.

That God would give such a sign to unbelievers has a lot of company throughout the Bible. Since the beginning of mankind, God has given the world signs as clear indicators of His power, His majesty, and the immutability of His Word. These signs have been clear, often supernatural, and visible to believers and unbelievers alike. In Exodus, for example, Moses was told to cast his rod to the ground as a sign to the Israelites that the Lord had appointed him to lead them out of Egypt. If they did not believe him, he was to put his hand to his bosom, first to make it leprous, then to restore it to health. If they still did not believe, he was to pour water from the river onto dry land and it would become blood (Ex. 4:1–9). Israel would require all three. Later, Moses would perform even greater signs before the Pharaoh.

Thousands of years later, God would give the greatest sign: His Son, Jesus Christ, who would be born of a virgin (Isaiah 7:14). Jesus would use signs as well, validating His earthly ministry by raising the dead, giving sight to the blind, healing the lame, and fulfilling all of the Messianic prophecies of the Old Testament. After all of these, when the Israelites demanded yet another sign, He gave them the sign of the prophet Jonah, referring to His death and resurrection three days later (Matt. 12:39).

Thus, when Jesus says that there will be a sign of His coming, should we expect it to be a secret known only to believers? Or like His other signs, will it be a declaration before the entire world?

Eternal Damnation and the Mark

The global viewing of Jesus in bodily form will play an important part in the events of Revelation. One of these is God's warning that anyone who takes the mark of the beast will be damned forever. On one hand, this seems like a severe punishment for one mistake. On the other hand, in light of Jesus' coming in bodily form, it makes a lot of sense. There will be no question

172

about who is Lord of heaven and earth. Those who take the mark will be openly rejecting the Lordship of Christ.

What is the mark of the beast? Along with the identification of the Antichrist with the number 666, this mark is one of the most identifying characteristics of the 70th Week. Even people who have never read the Bible or been to church know that, along with Armageddon, these two things have something to do with "the end of the world," even if they don't know why.

The mark of the beast and the number "666" come from Rev. 13:1–18:

> Then I stood on the sand of the sea. And I saw a beast [the Antichrist] rising up out of the sea, having seven heads and ten horns, and on his horns ten crowns, and on his heads a blasphemous name....And I saw one of his heads as if it had been mortally wounded, and his deadly wound was healed. And all the world marveled and followed the beast. So they worshipped the dragon [Satan] who gave authority to the beast; and they worshipped the beast, saying, "Who is like the beast? Who is able to make war with him?"

> And he was given a mouth speaking great things and blasphemies, and he was given authority to continue for forty-two months [three-and-one-half years, from the midpoint of the 70th Week to the end]. Then he opened his mouth in blasphemy against God, to blaspheme His name, His tabernacle, and those who dwell in heaven. It was granted him to make war with the saints and to overcome them [the Great Tribulation]. And authority was given him over every tribe, tongue, and nation. All who dwell on the earth will worship him, whose names have not been written in the Book of Life of the Lamb slain from the foundation of the world.

> ...Then I saw another beast [the false prophet] coming up out of the earth, and he had two horns like a lamb and spoke like a dragon. And he exercises all the authority of the first beast in his presence, and causes the earth and those who dwell in it to worship the first beast, whose deadly wound was healed. He performs great signs, so that he even makes fire come down from heaven on the earth in the sight of men.

And he deceives those who dwell on the earth by those signs which he was granted to do in the sight of the beast, telling those who dwell on the earth to make an image to the beast who was wounded by the sword and lived. He was granted power to give breath to the image of the beast, that the image of the beast should both speak and cause as many as would not worship the image of the beast to be killed.

He causes all, both small and great, rich and poor, free and slave, to receive a mark on their right hand or on their foreheads, and that no one may buy or sell except one who has the mark or the name of the beast, or the number of his name. Here is wisdom. Let him who has understanding calculate the number of the beast, for it is the number of a man: His number is 666.

What a terrifying picture of the world before the return of Jesus Christ! During this time, God's people will be tested for their faithfulness, and God's Word will provide them with the strength, warning, and encouragement they will need to keep them from being deceived by the lying wonders present during the last half of the 70th Week (Matt. 24:24, Rev. 13:4).

Revelation 13 tells us, for example, that once the Antichrist is in the public eye (following the confirming of the seven-year covenant with Israel, when he is propelled to worldwide fame), he will be wounded in the head so severely that he will be taken to be dead. Through the power of Satan, he will miraculously be given life and the world will be amazed and praise him: "Who is like the beast? Who can make war with him?" (Rev. 13:4).

With this supernatural event as his witness, the Antichrist will seize this opportunity to stand in the temple in Jerusalem and declare himself to be God or in place of God (hence *Anti*christ — or against Christ), and place there an idol that Jesus referred to as "the abomination of desolation spoken of by Daniel the prophet." At this point, the Antichrist, whose conquest of nations will have brought him to world power, will require all people over whom he rules to worship him. The punishment for disobedience will be death. The false prophet, who will also be empowered by Satan, will be able to do all types of supernatural wonders in the name of the Antichrist, further strengthening his claim to deity.

Now "under the power of God," the Antichrist will require all people, from infants to senior citizens, to take a mark on their hands or foreheads without which they cannot buy or sell. This mark, like the *stigmata* of Jesus on believers, will permanently identify those who take it with the Antichrist. God has warned that the taking of the mark will cause the person to be lost forever:

> Then a third angel followed them, saying with a loud voice, "If anyone worships the beast and his image, and receives his mark on his forehead or on his hand, he himself shall also drink of the wine of the wrath of God, which is poured out full strength into the cup of His indignation. He shall be tormented with fire and brimstone in the presence of the holy angels and in the presence of the Lamb. And the smoke of their torment ascends forever and ever; and they have no rest day or night, who worship the beast and his image, and whoever receives the mark of his name." (Rev. 14:9–11)

Many people question the fairness of this warning because it seems so harsh. How could one decision cause you to be forever separated from God? In light of the manifestation of Jesus in bodily form, this becomes more understandable. There will be no saying "I didn't know." All will know the identity of the Creator of heaven and earth. All will know that He will not tolerate their sin. They will see the deceiver, the Antichrist, who does wonders by the power of Satan and exalts himself in the place of God. Face to face with the two opposing powers—the true God and the false god—they will be forced to choose sides.

Even after the rapture has occurred, by God's grace, the gospel will still be heard. God will preserve 144,000 of the tribes of Israel, who will likely evangelize the shocked and bewildered world (Rev. 7:3, 14:1). He will send two witnesses to preach righteousness at the Wailing Wall (Rev. 11:6–7). And He will send an angel to preach the gospel to every creature on earth, saying, "If anyone worships the beast and his image, and receives his mark on his forehead or on his hand, he himself shall [be] tormented with fire and brimstone in the presence of the holy angels and in the presence of the Lamb" (Rev. 14:9–10).

God is truly merciful, but He draws boundaries, too. The mark of the beast is one of them. If anyone takes the mark, they cannot say they weren't warned.

14

Don't Be Fooled

The idea that trial and testing is a part of the life of a believer is not popular among churches today. As a result, many Christians will be shocked and completely unprepared for the severe tribulation and testing of the six seals. They will be wondering where Jesus is, why He is tarrying, and, for some, perhaps whether He is coming at all. In His discourse on the Mount of Olives, Jesus anticipated these concerns and repeatedly warned His followers not to be deceived. He described the abomination of desolation, the Great Tribulation, and the many false christs that will appear to take advantage of believers' fears. His language was strong:

> Then if anyone says to you, "Look, here is the Christ!" or "There!" do not believe it. For false christs and false prophets will rise and show great signs and wonders to deceive, if possible even the elect. See, I have told you beforehand. Therefore, if they say to you "Look, He is in the desert!" do not go out; or "Look, He is in the inner rooms!" do not believe it. For as lightning comes from the east and flashes to the west, so also will the coming of the Son of Man be. (Matt. 24:23–27)

How will we know when the real Christ has come? Jesus told His followers that there will be no mistaking it: "For as lightning comes from the east and flashes to the west, so shall the coming of the Son of Man be."

Many proponents of the pretrib position have used the phrase "as lightning flashes from the east to the west" to

177

emphasize both the suddenness of Christ's appearing and its imminence. In light of the unmistakable signs of His coming, however, I believe it refers not to its imminence but to its unmistakable identity. When Jesus arrives, there will be no question. He will arrive in glory to take home His Bride and, as in the parable of the rich man's feast (Luke 14:16–24), all of those who spurned the invitation will be left out of the party.

Parable of the Foolish Virgins

Because the pretribulation rapture position teaches that believers do not need to spiritually prepare for the seal judgments, many Christians will be spiritually weak during this time of battle. Sadly, this, in itself, is also a fulfillment of prophecy. Jesus was painfully aware of believers' lack of spiritual readiness during the end times and continually emphasized the theme of preparedness. Three times in His description of the Great Tribulation, He warned believers to endure their suffering patiently and not to look for Him until the appointed time:

> 1. Then if anyone says to you, "Look, here is the Christ!" or "There!" do not believe it.
> 2. For false christs and false prophets will rise and show great signs and wonders to deceive, *if possible even the elect*. See, I have told you beforehand.
> 3. Therefore, if they say to you, "Look, He is in the desert!" do not go out; or "Look, He is in the inner rooms!" do not believe it. (vv. 23–25)

As if this weren't warning enough, immediately after Jesus' description of the rapture and His glorious return, He returned to the theme of preparedness once again. This time, He likened His return to the times of Noah: "For as in the days before the flood, they were eating and drinking, marrying and giving in marriage, until the day that Noah entered the ark, and did not know until the flood came and took them all away, so also will the coming of the Son of Man be" (vv. 38–39).

Just when His followers might have thought that they'd gotten the message, Jesus illustrated this point yet again in the parable of the foolish virgins (Matt. 25:1–13):

> Then the kingdom of heaven shall be likened to ten virgins who took their lamps and went out to meet the bridegroom.

Now five of them were wise, and five were foolish. Those who were foolish took their lamps and took no oil with them, but the wise took oil in their vessels with their lamps. But while the bridegroom was delayed, they all slumbered and slept. And at midnight a cry was heard: "Behold, the bridegroom is coming; go out to meet him!" Then all those virgins arose and trimmed their lamps. And the foolish said to the wise, "Give us some of your oil, for our lamps are going out." But the wise answered, saying, "No, lest there should not be enough for us and you; but go rather to those who sell, and buy for yourselves." And while they went to buy, the bridegroom came, and those who were ready went in with him to the wedding; and the door was shut.

At this point, Jesus' followers might have said, "Okay, okay, Jesus, we get the point!" But Jesus was anticipating a time—today's spiritually unprepared world—when these warnings would be sorely needed.

For this reason, I think it is important to understand that all of the women in this parable were virgins. In other words, they were either believers or professed believers.[108] It is also important to understand that the groom comes at midnight, *at the darkest hour*, when he is least expected. Although many prophecy teachers use this passage to illustrate the importance of being prepared for Christ's return, they miss the fact that it may also be a reference to its *timing*. If so, then the bridegroom comes at the darkest hour, after a time of prolonged distress and despair (not in a time of prosperity and plenty, as is commonly taught). His arrival is so late that the virgins are actually sleeping.

In the context of the return of the bridegroom, this parable tells us that Jesus' return will also be much later than expected, not in time to save believers from the severe persecution of the Great Tribulation. This is the reason for Jesus' warning: "See, I have told you beforehand."

---

[108] Is there a reason that Jesus chose virgins or was He just making an illustration? Some believe that Jesus used the illustration of virgins to mean all believers. Others take the reference simply to mean young, unmarried women. Either reading does not affect the use of this story for this illustration—preparedness.

Proof of Imminence?

Many pretrib proponents like to use the last verse of this passage: "Watch therefore, for you know neither the day nor the hour in which the Son of Man is coming," as proof of an any-moment rapture. Indeed, this element of surprise is reiterated many times throughout the New Testament. But does it really mean that the rapture could occur at any moment? This warning also occurs one chapter earlier, in Matt. 24:42–44: "Watch therefore, for you do not know what hour your Lord is coming. But know this, that if the master of the house had known what hour the thief would come, he would have watched and not allowed his house to be broken into. Therefore you also be ready, for the Son of Man is coming at an hour you do not expect."

In both passages, Jesus is addressing the apostles, who are believers or (in the case of Judas) a professed believer. This is somewhat a mystery. For the unbelieving world, it makes sense that His coming, no matter when it occurs, would take them unawares. This was Paul's message in 1 Thess. 5:2: for "the Day of the Lord will come as a thief in the night." But for believers, how could this be? Pretrib proponents insist that this is because He could come at any minute. And yet, we have already established that this day will be preceded by many clear warning signs and should not be a surprise to God's children. For as Paul says, "But you, brethren, are not in darkness, so that this day should overtake you as a thief" (1 Thess. 5:4).

So how can believers be warned of the signs and seasons and still have the day take them unawares? Could it be that, because they expect Jesus to return prior to the 70th Week—pretribulationally—the time they least expect is *after the 70th Week of Daniel has begun?* If the lesson of the parable of the foolish virgins is that Jesus will arrive when He is least expected, is not a non-pretribulational rapture the time they least expect?

In the parable of the wise and foolish virgins, Jesus used the illustration of a Jewish wedding. Jewish weddings were generally celebrated at the rising of the evening star. According to the parable, the bridegroom was delayed until midnight, perhaps up to seven hours, well beyond what tradition would have expected. So, too, will the coming of the Bridegroom be delayed, well beyond what much church tradition is expecting.

15

God Wouldn't Do That

Many people balk at the claim that God's wrath does not start with the seal judgments on the assumption that God would not put His children through such perils. "The seals are too harsh to be anything but His wrath," they say. This assumption raises its head in almost every discussion I have had with believers in a pretribulation rapture. However, God has used such judgments in the past, and He will again.

Consider the lessons recounted in Judges 20. This chapter tells the story of the nation of Israel's rise against the Benjamite tribe of Gibeah, whose men have brutally raped and slain a Levite's concubine. In response to this crime, the children of Israel gather before the Lord at Mizpah to determine the course of battle. Four hundred thousand foot soldiers, "men who drew the sword," were represented. In addition, there were 27,000 men "who drew the sword" of the Benjamites.

The Israelites, whom God had already been disciplining for their rebellion and idolatry, went up to the house of God and asked, "Which of us shall go up first to battle against the children of Benjamin?"

The Lord replied, "Judah first!"

And the men of Israel went out to battle against Benjamin, and the men of Israel put themselves in battle array to fight against them at Gibeah. Then the children of Benjamin came out of Gibeah, and on that day, cut down to the ground, 22,000 men of the Israelites. (vv. 20–21)

Understandably, the Israelites were confused. They were on the side of justice. They had asked God what they should do. And yet, they had just suffered a terrible, bloody defeat.

The next day, the dazed congregation gathered again before the Lord and asked, "Shall I again draw near for battle against the children of my brother Benjamin?"

And the Lord said, "Go up against him."

> And Benjamin went out against them from Gibeah on the second day, and cut down to the ground 18,000 more of the children of Israel; all these drew the sword. (v. 25)

The now beleaguered Israelites were likely terrified to inquire of the Lord again. Yet, in spite of their bewilderment, they went up once more. "Shall I yet again go out to battle against the children of my brother Benjamin, or shall I cease?" they asked. And the Lord said, "Go up, for tomorrow I will deliver them into your hand." On that day, it was the Benjamites' turn to be judged, for 25,100 Benjamites were killed. Only 600 survived.

In these three days, there were more than 65,000 men slain. God did not just *allow* this terrible slaughter. He *sent these men into battle*, knowing what the outcome would be. These numbers might seem small in comparison to up to one-quarter of the earth's population during the six seals, but considering that Israel's fighting force was only 400,000 men, their losses amounted to 10% of their fighting population. For a nation that had been told to go into the land of Canaan and possess it, this was a terrible loss. For the Benjamites, who lost 96 percent of their able-bodied men, it was devastating.

God's Judgment in Habakkuk

Another example can be found in the book of Habakkuk. The book opens with Habakkuk's cry to the Lord, asking for justice against the apostate nation of Israel. They had continued in their pattern of rebellion and idolatry and Habakkuk was crying out, wondering why judgment had not been forthcoming.

> O Lord, how long shall I cry, and you will not hear? Even cry out to You, "Violence!" And you will not save. Why do you show me iniquity, and cause me to see trouble? For plundering and violence are before me. There is strife, and contention

arises. Therefore the law is powerless, and justice never goes forth. For the wicked surround the righteous. Therefore perverse judgment proceeds. (Hab. 1:2–4)

Habakkuk got his answer, but it was not what he expected. For God replied, "Look among the nations and watch—be utterly astounded!...For indeed, I am raising up the Chaldeans, a bitter and hasty nation...terrible and dreadful...more fierce than evening wolves" (vv. 5–8). Habakkuk was shocked. The Chaldeans were a warlike, aggressive people who served dreadful pagan gods. The Lord's description of them as "bitter," "terrible," and "fierce" likely struck terror into his heart.

Indeed, this was judgment far more severe than Habakkuk was looking for, which we see in his reply:

Are You not from everlasting, O Lord my God, my Holy One? We shall not die. O Lord, you have appointed them for judgment; O Rock, You have marked them for correction. You are of purer eyes than to behold evil and cannot look on wickedness. Why do You look on those who deal treacherously and hold Your tongue when the wicked devours a person more righteous than he? (vv. 12–13)

Considering the nature of the Chaldeans, it is understandable why Habakkuk was horrified. "God, why would you do that?" he cries. "They are so much worse than we are!"

The *Nelson Study Bible* gives this analysis:

Habakkuk's point seems to be that God's holiness should have prohibited Him from using a "dirty" instrument like Babylon to accomplish His purposes in judging and reproving His own people. Habakkuk wondered how God would look on as the wicked Babylonians perverted justice. "A person more righteous than he." This was the ethical dilemma that faced Habakkuk: The Judeans were less corrupt and idolatrous than the Babylonians, who were being used to judge them for their sins.

The parallels to the six seal judgments are strong. "God wouldn't do that," some would argue. "He wouldn't bring such destruction upon His people, let alone use such a personification of evil as the Antichrist." This was exactly the argument Habakkuk was making—and lost.

Others would use the argument, "But this was under the Old Covenant. God doesn't use those methods today. We are under grace." This is also a losing argument. The Bible tells us that not only were God's righteous judgments just punishment for the people's sins, but they serve as warnings for us today. Paul explains, "Now these things became our examples, to the intent that we should not lust after evil things as they also lusted...and they were written for our admonition, upon whom the ends of the ages have come. Therefore, let him who thinks he stands take heed lest he fall" (1 Cor. 10: 6, 11–12).

Although it may be difficult to comprehend, the judgment recounted in Judges was both just and part of the plan of a loving, holy God. In our natural minds, it may be difficult to fully comprehend, but the pattern that God has established is that He *does* do that. In the context of books like Judges and Habakkuk (not to mention 1 and 2 Kings and 1 and 2 Chronicles), which recount the habitual pattern of rebellion and apostasy of God's people, these judgments are the culmination of God's repeated efforts to turn His people from their sin. They are at the same time both harsh and loving, as part of His perfect plan to purify His people and make them a holy congregation.

God's Judgment in Revelation

The seals of Revelation will accomplish the same purpose. The purpose of the seal judgments is to refine and test God's people. This can be seen in Jesus' parables about the end of the age in Matthew 13. In this chapter, Jesus gave two parables about the kingdom of God with reference to the end times. In the parable of the wheat and the tares, the harvest is designed to separate the "sons of the kingdom" from the "sons of the wicked one":

> The kingdom of heaven is like a man who sowed good seed in his field; but while men slept, his enemy came and sowed tares among the wheat and went his way. But when the grain had sprouted and produced a crop, then the tares also appeared. So the servants of the owner came and said to him, "Sir did you not sow good seed in your field? How then does it have tares?" He said to them, "An enemy has done this." The servants said to him, "Do you want us then to go and

gather them up?" But he said, "No, lest while you gather up the tares you also uproot the wheat with them. Let both grow together until the harvest, and at the time of the harvest I will say to the reapers, 'First gather together the tares and bind them in bundles to burn them, but gather the wheat into my barn.'" (Matt. 13:24–30)

As Jesus pointed out, tares were weeds sown into a farmer's crop by his enemies. In the early stages of the plants' growth, it was impossible to tell the two apart. If the farmer attempted to pull out the tares, he risked pulling up the wheat, as well. It was only when the plants were mature, at the time of harvest, that it was clear which was which. Jesus went on to say that, for humanity, this harvest will come at the end of the age, when "the Son of Man will send out His angels and they will gather out of His kingdom all things that offend, and those who practice lawlessness, and will cast them into the furnace of fire. There will be wailing and gnashing of teeth. Then the righteous will shine forth as the sun in the kingdom of their Father" (Matt. 13:41–43).

When is the end of the age? This is exactly the question asked by Jesus' disciples earlier in this same chapter. "Tell us, when will these things be? And what is the sign of Your coming and the end of the age?" (v. 3). To this question, Jesus answered by describing the beginning of sorrows—the first, second, third, and fourth seals (vv. 5–8); the abomination of desolation and the Great Tribulation (vv. 15, 21); the cosmic disturbances (v. 29); and then, finally, His triumphal return (vv. 30–31). At this time, the physical Kingdom Age, with Jesus coming to claim His rightful throne, has begun. Judgment, which begins during the Day of the Lord, has begun, as well.

The parable of the wheat and the tares is a perfect illustration for *why* the events must occur in this order. Before the Church can be presented to Christ as the spotless Bride, she must go through the "hour of testing" (Rev. 3:10), during which professing believers will be "refined, purified, and made white" (Dan. 11:35). Those who are true believers in Jesus will stand firm for their faith, while those who are merely professing will stumble under the threat of famine, persecution, or death. The wheat (true believers) and the tares (professing Christendom), once indistinguishable, will be ready for harvest.

185

Parable of the Dragnet

The second parable is the parable of the dragnet:

> Again, the kingdom of heaven is like a dragnet that was cast into the sea and gathered some of every kind, which when it was full, they drew to shore; and they sat down and gathered the good into vessels, but threw the bad away. So it will be at the end of the age. The angels will come forth, separate the wicked from among the just, and cast them into the furnace of fire. There will be wailing and gnashing of teeth. (Matt. 13:47–50)

Like the wheat and the tares, this parable illustrates the fate of professing Christendom. Jesus said to His disciples, "Follow me, and I will make you fishers of men" (Matt. 4:19). In one of His last instructions, He commanded, "Go therefore and make disciples of all the nations, baptizing them in the name of the Father and of the Son and of the Holy Spirit" (Matt. 28:19). In other words—go fishing. Yet many sit in churches today, having been caught by the dragnet and accepted the teachings of Christ, perhaps even having gone through the physical act of being baptized into His death and resurrection, without truly being regenerated. Like the fish of every kind, they remain mixed with the good fish until the end of the age. Once again, this is in perfect agreement with the seals as a time of testing prior to the return of Christ at the harvest.[109]

These parables give further confirmation that the seals are a time of purification for the Church prior to the end of the age. The judgment of the wicked begins during the trumpets and bowls, which are administered by angels during the Day of the Lord. This judgment begins with the bodily return of Christ at the rapture, after the opening of the sixth seal.

---

[109] Earlier, I argued that the seals were not God's wrath based in part on the lack of angels as administrating agents. This argument is consistent with both of these parables. In both parables, the harvest at the end of the age comes at the hand of angels, which do not begin their active participation in the 70th Week until the trumpet judgments, which begin with the return of Christ at the end of the age.

Chapter 19, "Does God Create Evil?" takes a look at this subject in more detail and discusses God's use of judgments and adversity to accomplish His perfect purposes in our lives.

16

Are the Letters to the Churches for Us Today?

In Chapter 8, we took a look at the letters to the seven churches in Revelation 2 and 3. In these letters, which were written to the loveless, compromising, corrupt, lukewarm, persecuted, dead, and loving churches, Jesus gives very sobering exhortations. To five of the churches, He tells them to repent and to overcome or they will be thrown into fiery judgment. One is told to hold fast despite the terrible persecution it is about to experience. And one, the loving Church of Philadelphia, is promised that it will be "kept" from the hour of trial.

The context of these letters is the 70th Week of Daniel, and the fiery trial is the Great Tribulation. The idea that the Church will be present during the Great Tribulation and that God will allow only one group of believers to be "kept" is very uncomfortable for most Christians. For this reason, many pretrib proponents redefine the letters to the seven churches in a way that makes the Church of Philadelphia, which Jesus promises to "keep from the hour of trial," apply to all believers in the modern day.

Proponents of this position generally use one of three arguments:

1. The seven churches are literal churches that were in existence at the time Revelation was written. This makes this passage irrelevant for us today.
2. The seven churches are not literal churches. They represent seven church "ages," from the first century to the end of the 70th Week. Today's church age is Philadelphia, making the other letters irrelevant for the Church today.

3. The seven churches are not literal churches. They represent six types of unbelieving (or false) churches and one true church, the Church of Philadelphia, making the other six letters irrelevant for us today.

The last two of these arguments fall back on dispensational theology, the bedrock on which the pretrib doctrine is laid. Dispensationalism is a man-made framework for interpreting the scriptures that, in practice, makes certain scriptures relevant only to specific time periods and not to believers as a whole. Dispensationalism, like its progenitor pretribulationism, relies on inference, not on direct scriptural support, and can introduce error into the otherwise plain meaning of the text. Needless to say, I do not hold a dispensational view.

Are They Literal Churches?

On the first point, it is true that these churches were seven actual churches at the time Revelation was written. This is not, however, a good argument for dismissing these letters for today. If we are going to make this assertion, we should throw out all of the New Testament books, since these were also letters written to specific individuals, groups, or churches at the time. Paul wrote "to the Corinthians," for example, or "to the Galatians." The books of 1 and 2 Timothy were written to this young man of God, preparing him for a leadership position. The gospel of Luke was written to encourage a believer named Theophilus.[110]

---

[110] In his tape series, "13 Messages on Revelation," Marvin Rosenthal points out that the writer of Revelation is repeatedly called a prophet, and prophets typically wrote about conditions and events that were contemporary at the time but that also had a broader fulfillment at the end of the age. This is the case for the desecration of the temple in Jerusalem by Antiochus Epiphanes, for example, and is the case here. While these churches were contemporary to John's writing, they reflected or paralleled a larger fulfillment during the 70th Week. For this reason, Rosenthal also takes issue with many scholars' interpretation of Rev. 1:19—"Write these things which you have seen [commonly interpreted as referring to Rev. 1], and the things which are [commonly interpreted as Revelation 2 and 3], and the things which will take place after this [Revelation 4 on]"—as support for the preterist-only (or end-times events fulfilled in past history) view of the seven churches.

Another reason we cannot excuse these passages is that this would require us to take them out of context. By definition, Revelation describes the events of the 70th Week. In the opening verses, Jesus makes this clear by telling John, to whom this vision is given, to record "things that must shortly take place." This is biblical language for the Second Coming of Christ. Jesus is giving this revelation to John as a message to His children about the end times. This is followed by warnings and specific instructions to the seven churches, with very strong commandments to six of these churches to overcome and a promise to one that it will be kept from the hour of trial.

The natural questions that arise from these letters are, "Overcome what?" and "What trial?" Jesus immediately answers these questions by describing the seal judgments. If the Body of Christ will not undergo these trials, which is the straightforward reading of the text, what would be the point of Jesus' message? Clearly, these letters were intended as an encouragement and warning to believers during this time of severe testing. Lifting these letters out of context and applying them only to first century churches is not merited.

On this point, Marvin Rosenthal makes the following observation:

> John knew these churches. They were his contemporaries. In fact, he had been the pastor at Ephesus [the loveless church]. So in these letters, John was writing to his contemporaries, addressing specific problems that they were experiencing. However, these seven churches were also singled out because they accurately reflect the problems within Christendom at the end of the age. Therefore, this is a warning to professed Christendom inside the 70th Week. If we are actually approaching the end of the age, I can think of no body of truth that is more relevant to believers than the content of those letters to the seven churches in Revelation 2 and 3.[111]

What About Church Ages?

The second argument in favor of removing the modern Church from the rebuke of these letters is made by making these

---

[111] "13 Messages on Revelation," audiocassette © Zion's Hope, Orlando, FL). Paraphrased for clarity.

letters refer, not to specific bodies of believers, but to seven "church ages," during which the corporate church is said to embody each of these characteristics. In this teaching, all modern-day believers comprise the Church of Philadelphia.

The seven "ages" are as follows:[112]

1. Ephesus (Rev. 2:1–7): the loveless church at the end of the apostolic age, through the first century.
2. Smyrna (Rev. 2:8–11): the persecuted church beginning in the second century.
3. Pergamos (Rev. 2:12–17): the compromising church of imperial favor that reigned when the Emperor Constantine made Christianity the national religion in the third century.
4. Thyatira (Rev. 2:18–29): the corrupt church of the Roman Catholic papacy starting in the fourth century.
5. Sardis (Rev. 3:1–6): the dead church that spawned the Reformation beginning in 1500s.
6. Philadelphia (Rev. 3:7–13): the loving church of the "latter day outpouring" present today through the end of the age.
7. Laodicea (Rev. 3:14–22) the lukewarm church, which will be present through the end of the age.

While there are certainly interesting parallels between church history and these letters, these time periods were created to fit these passages, not the other way around. Revelation contains very concrete descriptions of people, places, and events, and Jesus tells us that its purpose is to prepare believers for the time of great trial and difficulty before His return. To suggest that these are church "ages" and not end-times churches requires the reader to abandon the normative reading of the text and switch to an allegorical one. Allegory can be a dangerous thing because it allows readers to interpret the passage in just about any way they please, which is exactly what pretrib scholars do.

This reading also creates the same problem described earlier: The context of Revelation is the 70th Week, so to suggest that only two of the seven churches described in these letters will actually enter the 70th Week takes the letters out of context.

---

[112] Renald Showers, *There Really Is A Difference: A Comparison of Covenant and Dispensational Theology* (Friends of Israel Gospel Ministry, 1990).

Furthermore, the "church age" teaching creates a false picture of the Church today. If this interpretation is correct, and we are living in the age of the Church of Philadelphia, then the modern Church must be fundamentally characterized as loving, purified, and ready to be taken up into heaven. This is exactly the position taken by John Walvoord: "Eventually, as the scriptures anticipate, He will present them [the Church] to Himself as a Bride which is spotless, a glorious church, not having spot or wrinkle or any such thing, but holy and without blemish. This purpose of God is in the process of being fulfilled."[113]

A realistic look, however, shows us that this is simply not the case. The Church is no more spotless or without blemish now than at any other time in church history.[114] The fundamental characteristics of the churches described by Jesus—loveless, persecuted, compromising, corrupt, dead, lukewarm, and loving—have been manifest in *every* stage of church history and in *every* church body since the ascension of Christ. As a whole, the Body of Christ is filled with love, faithfulness, and grace, but it is also filled with hypocrisy, compromise, and sin. As in every other time in church history, believers are at all levels of spiritual development. Some are walking in blessed fellowship with the Savior; others are babes in Christ, just taking their first steps. Some are lukewarm, not having truly submitted their hearts and wills to Jesus Christ; others are backslidden, struggling with their flesh. Corruption and false doctrine can be found even within the leadership of the Church.[115]

---

[113] *The Return of the Lord*, p. 21.

[114] It is interesting that scholars who take the "church age" position—that the entire body of believers making up the Body of Christ today also comprise the purified, sanctified Church of Philadelphia—will, in the same argument, point out that postmillennialism lost its momentum when the Church realized that human beings were not capable of ushering in the Millennium through their own efforts. It is ironic that these scholars are able to recognize the failings of humanity as a whole, but the frailty of the Body of Christ escapes notice. Either this, or we are forced to conclude that those who are not spotless or wrinkle-free at the beginning of the 70th Week are not truly saved, a conclusion that the Bible does not justify.

[115] It is this falsehood that will allow the false church, the harlot of Babylon, to arise. In his book, *A Different Gospel*, D. R. McConnell

192

The "church age" teaching also fails in its assessment of the Church of Laodicea, the lukewarm church, which dispensationalists teach will exist after the rapture. I highly doubt this will be a lukewarm body of believers. Rather, scripture teaches that those who are living during the last half of the 70th Week, under the persecution of the Antichrist, will be anything but lukewarm. Rather, they will be clinging fervently to their faith and to the promise of eternal salvation in Christ. The books of Revelation and Daniel refer to the 70th Week as a time of unparalleled evangelism. This is not a likely description for a lukewarm church.[116]

Six False Churches and One True Church?

The third attempt at dismissing these letters as not applying to the entire Body of Christ today is that they refer to six "false" churches and one true Church, the Church of Philadelphia. This approach doesn't hold up any better than the others.

First, Jesus never said that these were false churches. In fact, the persecuted church is never told to repent, only to overcome,

---

discusses the danger of false teaching creeping into the Church today: "It is a strange curiosity that those Christians who are most adamant that ours is the generation that will see the Lord's return—and the end-time deception and apostasy associated with His return—look for signs of this deception *outside* the church, in such conspiracies as the New Age movement, and in such cults as Mormonism, Jehovah's Witnesses, and Christian Science. Admittedly, these movements pose potential threats to the church, but perhaps we would do better to look for the deception of the End Times where Jesus and the New Testament predicted it would occur: *within* the church, within groups that call themselves Christian but which actually preach a different gospel" (*A Different Gospel* [Hendrickson Publishers, 1988], p. xv).

[116] Many pretrib scholars identify the church of Laodicea as the apostate church of the 70th Week, the harlot of Babylon. This is made difficult, considering that the dispensational approach used to justify much of the pretrib position requires the Church to no longer be in existence during this period. Dispensationalism identifies those who come to Christ during this time as "tribulation saints" or "70th Week saints," terms that are not used in the Bible. If the Church is no longer in existence, then the church of Laodicea is not really a church in the New Testament sense of the word. However, Jesus makes no distinction between the first six churches and this supposedly last, apostate end-times church. This is a reading that is entirely unsupported by the text.

disqualifying it as a false church. And even among those told to repent, there are signs of spiritual life. The church at Ephesus (the loveless church), for example, is praised for its works of faith, patience, and sensitivity to false doctrine:

> I know your works, your labor, your patience, and that you cannot bear those who are evil. And you have tested those who say they are apostles and are not, and have found them liars; and you have persevered and have patience, and have labored for My name's sake and have not become weary. (Rev. 2:2–3)

The church at Pergamos (the compromising church) is given similar praise:

> I know your works, and where you dwell, where Satan's throne is. And you hold fast to My name, and did not deny My faith even in the days in which Antipas was My faithful martyr, who was killed among you, where Satan dwells. (Rev. 2:13–14)

It is difficult to argue that these are false churches. Works, patience, and holding fast to Jesus' name are characteristics of believers, even if they resist God's teaching in other areas of their lives. Moreover, in Rev. 1:12–13, John sees the seven golden lampstands, which are symbolic of the testimony of believers, and Jesus, "one like the Son of Man," standing in the midst of them. Jesus does not stand in the midst of false churches.[117]

Second, the "six false churches and one true church" interpretation would once again place the entire Body of Christ in the Church of Philadelphia, which creates the false impression of the Church today: that all believers have kept His commandment to persevere and are walking in wisdom, truth, and love. As nice as this picture is, it is not true. A more accurate picture is the one portrayed in these letters: a Church body that is comprised of believers at all different levels in their spiritual walks. And like a classroom, in which only students who have maintained an "A" average all semester are exempt from the final exam, only the

---

[117] For more on this subject, see Marvin Rosenthal's "13 Messages on Revelation," Tape 2 (© Zion's Hope).

Church of Philadelphia, those believers who have achieved a level of spiritual maturity in Christ, will be protected ("kept") during this final hour.

It has always been my hope and desire that, when Jesus comes, I will be found in the Church of Philadelphia. However, as I was writing this book, the letters to the churches caused me to take a look at my own life. In particular, I contemplated the loveless church, for some of those characteristics started sounding uncomfortably familiar. I contemplated how this church labored for the gospel, tested false apostles, and exhibited sensitivity to doctrine to the letter of the law without the accompanying compassion and love. I thought of the many criticisms I had levied at churches or individuals for straying from the core of the gospel. I thought of the many organizations I had condemned for allowing false doctrine or compromise to seep in. I thought of the many individuals I had chastised for allowing persistent sin to remain in their lives. I suddenly wondered if my desire to encourage obedience in the Lord had turned into intolerance—not of sin—but of people. I wondered if I had become so enthusiastic for testing false teachers and false doctrine that I, too, *had lost my first love.* The thought chilled me. Since that time, this concern has been a subject of prayer and meditation for me.

And this is the heart, I believe, of Jesus' message to the churches: that we would use them for reflection on our own relationships to Him. These warnings were given *to believers*—not to false churches—as red flags, highway billboard signs, red rocket flares to bring us back on track in case we have lost our way. To deny the relevance of these messages is to undermine one of the fundamental purposes for which they were given.

Why Isn't the Word "Church" Used?

One of the common arguments for the pretribulation rapture is that the word "church" is not used after the fourth chapter of Revelation. This, pretrib supporters would have us believe, lends support to the argument that the rapture occurs prior to the opening of the seals. This form of debate is commonly called "arguing from absence," which means arguing from the lack of information rather than arguing against errors or flaws.

I like Robert Van Kampen's explanation of this issue, since it speaks directly to one of the main subjects repeatedly addressed by end-times texts: the separation of the wheat and the chaff.

The fact that the word "church" is not used in the heart of the book only validates once again the fact that it will not be the church in general that undergoes Antichrist's persecution. On the contrary, it will be the faithful remnant within the church [since the false professors will capitulate to his request to worship him and take the mark rather than face persecution and martyrdom] that will stand true to Christ during these difficult times.

It is also interesting and significant to note that John, the recorder of the book of Revelation, also penned the gospel of John and the epistle of 1 John. He doesn't use the word "church" in either of those books. In addition, the word "church" is never used in the three classic rapture passages referred to by pretribulationists — 1 Thess. 4:13–17; 1 Cor. 15:51–53; or John 14:1–3. Also, except for general references in the first verses of 1 and 2 Thessalonians, neither of those two great prophetic books uses the word "church" either.

...When the real trouble begins, the "hard labor," so to speak, the church in general will fall away from the faith — the apostasy — when most people's love for Christ will grow cold. Therefore, it will not be the church in general that stands firm for Christ, but only the true believers (i.e. the saints, overcomers, bond-servants, elect of God — that will "endure to the end" through the difficult events detailed in the heart of the book of Revelation, before the great persecution by Antichrist is cut short by the events associated with the sign given in the sun, moon, and stars. For that reason, John uses the word "saint" to depict the genuine bond-servant of Christ, not the word "church."

That is why the word "saint" is used 13 times in the heart of the book (see 5:8, 8:3–4, 11:18, 13:7, 10, 14:12, 16:6, 17:6, 18:20, 24, 19:8, 20:9), and the word "church" is avoided altogether.

In fact, the book of Revelation isn't even addressed to the church in general, but to the true bond-servants of Christ. It is "the revelation of Jesus Christ, which God gave Him [Christ] to show His bond-servants" (1:1). Revelation does, however, contain severe warnings to seven specific churches about what will happen to them when the adversity hits. But even then, in each instance, Christ separates those "who have ears to hear"—genuine bond-servants of Christ who listen carefully to what the Spirit is telling these churches— from the specific church that He is reprimanding.[118]

---

[118] *The Rapture Question Answered: Plain and Simple*, p. 134.

17

Does Jesus Come Twice?

Many people reject the idea that Jesus comes to earth in bodily form prior to the Battle of Armageddon, thinking that this requires Jesus to come twice—once at the rapture and once to defeat the Antichrist. How can He return in bodily form to rapture the Church after the sixth seal and then appear in the sky over Armageddon without coming twice?

This is a valid question. However, the Bible tells us that Jesus returns only once—at the rapture—and *remains on earth during the administration of the judgments of the Day of the Lord.* When the armies see Him at the battle of Armageddon, He is simply manifesting Himself in the rightful role that He assumed on arrival, as King of kings and Lord of lords.

That Christ's appearance at the rapture and His physical return to earth occur at the same time is made clear in 2 Thess. 2:1. In this passage, Paul refers to them in the same breath, as part of the same event: "Now, brethren, concerning the coming of our Lord Jesus Christ and our gathering together to Him...." In other words, when Jesus comes at His one and only bodily return, this will also be the time that the Church is delivered.

This concept of "our gathering together to Him" (the rapture) as occurring at His bodily return is repeated throughout scripture. Here are just three examples:

> ...and they will see the Son of Man coming on the clouds of heaven with power and great glory... [and they—the angels] will gather together His elect from the four winds, from one end of heaven to the other. (Matt. 24:29–31)

For the Lord Himself will descend from heaven with a shout.... Then we who are alive and remain shall be caught up together with them in the clouds to meet the Lord in the air. (1 Thess. 4:16–17)

I go to prepare a place for you. And if I go and prepare a place for you, I will come again and receive you unto myself. (John 14:2–3)

Christ: The Executor of Judgment

If Jesus comes to earth after the opening of the sixth seal, what will He be doing during the time period of the trumpets and the bowls? Executing the Day of the Lord judgments. Many of us have the idea that it is God the Father who is the executor in these final days. It is not—it is Christ Himself. In 1 Cor. 15: 21–25, Paul writes, "For since by man came death, by Man also came the resurrection of the dead. For as in Adam all die, even so in Christ all shall be made alive. But each one in his own order: Christ the firstfruits, afterward those who are Christ's at His coming. Then comes the end, when He delivers the kingdom to God the Father, when He puts an end to all rule and all authority and power. For He must reign till He has put all enemies under His feet."

There are three important points made in this passage: (1) "the end" is associated with Christ's coming; (2) "the end" will see the raising of the dead, which according to 1 Thess. 4:16–17 occurs at the rapture; and (3) Jesus must stay and continue in this role until all of His enemies have been vanquished. He cannot come to rapture the Church, then go away again to return another time.[119] Later in Revelation, we also see that it is Jesus Himself who executes wrath during the bowl judgments: "Now out of [Jesus'] mouth goes a sharp sword, that with it He should strike the nations. And He Himself will rule them with a rod of iron. He

---

[119] Another important point is that Christ's reign clearly precedes the vanquishing of His enemies. The text does not say, "For He must reign *once* He has put all enemies under His feet." It says, "*until* He has put all enemies under His feet." This does not require Christ's reign to start before Armageddon, of course, since Jesus will allow Satan to stir up one final rebellion at the end of the Millennium, but the text certainly allows, and strongly implies, it.

Himself treads the winepress of the fierceness and wrath of Almighty God" (Rev. 19:15).

Think back to the Olivet Discourse, recorded in Matthew 24. At the beginning of this chapter, the disciples asked Jesus when He will come back and when will be "the end of the age." They were not asking a philosophical question. The Jewish people had been battling pagan rule for centuries. They wanted to know when their Messiah would establish His physical kingdom and liberate them from oppression. They did not understand Jesus' puzzling words, "the kingdom of God is at hand," in light of His unwillingness to overthrow the authority of Rome. If the Messiah had come, why were they still under Roman oppression?

The apostles did not understand that, at His First Coming, Jesus had come to set up His spiritual kingdom and to free them from their bondage of sin, not their physical circumstances. It would not be until His Second Coming that He would sit on the throne of David and that His physical kingdom, and with it the peace and prosperity of Israel, would be established.

But Jesus did answer the disciples' question, even if they didn't know it at the time. When they asked about the end of the age, Jesus outlined a series of events that would not take place for at least another 20 centuries. He described the beginning of sorrows, the Great Tribulation, and the cosmic disturbances that will usher in the Day of the Lord. He then described "the sign of the Son of Man," His coming on the clouds with power and great glory, and the gathering together of the elect in the rapture. Thus, Jesus tells us that His physical return and His overthrow of earthly power will begin at that time—after the opening of the sixth seal. No longer the suffering Servant, He will come as the conquering King who personally "delivers the kingdom to God the Father ... [and] ... must reign till He has put all enemies under His feet."

The Bible tells us that, in an earthly sense, Jesus is the reigning King from the moment He appears in the clouds, through the trumpet and the bowl judgments, through the Battle of Armageddon, and through the Millennium and beyond. To suggest that Jesus comes in the clouds to take His Church but that the "end of the age" does not begin until several years later when He comes back "fully" a second time is not warranted by scripture.

Jesus on the Holy Hill

The idea that Jesus is here on earth during the Day of the Lord judgments is foreign to most Christians. Not because it is unscriptural, but simply because they have never considered it. And yet, why should it seem so strange? Jesus' First Coming spanned a period of 33 years. Why should His Second Coming not extend through the 70th Week?

For those who actually want to see Him in residence on the earth during this time, Jesus gives us this picture in Rev. 14:1:

> Then I looked, and behold, a Lamb standing on Mount Zion [the holy hill in Jerusalem], and with Him one hundred and forty-four thousand, having His Father's name written on their foreheads.

This physical appearance is also seen in Zech. 14:3–4:

> Then the Lord will go forth and fight against those nations, as He fights in the day of battle. And in that day, His feet will stand on the Mount of Olives.[120]

This appearance on Mt. Zion may also have been prophesied by King David. In Psalm 102:13–16, David writes,

> So the nations shall fear the name of the Lord, and all the kings of the earth Your glory. For the Lord shall build up Zion; He shall appear in His glory. (vv. 15–16)

---

[120] Despite his pretrib position, prophecy expert Dr. Renald Showers also places the moment of Jesus' touchdown on Mt. Zion as the defining moment of His kingship. He writes, "Zech. 14:4, 9 disclosed the fact that Messiah will be King after His feet have touched down on the Mount of Olives at His Second Coming" (*There Really Is a Difference*). Showers places this event at the end of the 70th Week, however, at His coming at Armageddon. But if Armageddon is Jesus' first physical appearance, as Showers suggests, why do we see Him standing on the Mount of Olives in Rev. 14:1? And if this occurs at Armageddon rather than after the sixth seal, why are the Jews commanded to flee until the coming of the Lord Jesus sometime later, accompanied by the saints, in verse 5 (compare to 1 Thess. 3:13)?

Furthermore, in Psalm 2:2, David speaks about "the kings of the earth," who "take counsel together against the Lord and against His anointed." Several verses later, he goes on to say, "I have set My King on My holy hill of Zion" (Psalm 2:6). While this Psalm is a wedding song written for the king of Israel, it has traditionally been interpreted as having a dual fulfillment in the First Coming of Christ. In light of Rev. 14:1, however, it may also have a fulfillment in the end times. It is likely that the leaders of the earth, under strong delusion from the Antichrist, will "take counsel together against the Lord and against His anointed" at this time, just as they did 2,000 years ago.[121]

An even more direct reference to the physical presence of Christ on earth during the reign of the Antichrist is made by the prophet Daniel. In describing the Antichrist's supreme arrogance, Daniel writes,

> And in the latter time of their kingdom, when the transgressors have reached their fullness, a king shall arise, having fierce features, who understands sinister schemes. His power shall be mighty, but not by his own power. He shall destroy fearfully. And shall prosper and thrive.... He shall

---

[121] A look at Zechariah 14 may shed some interesting light on other events in Revelation. Zechariah writes, "Then the Lord will go forth and fight against those nations as He fights on the day of battle. And in that day his feet will stand on the Mount of Olives, which faces Jerusalem on the east, and the Mount of Olives shall be split in two, from east to west, making a very large valley; half of the mountain shall move toward the north and half of it toward the south. Then you shall flee through My mountain valley, for the mountain valley shall reach to Azal" (Zech. 14: 3–5). In this passage, Jesus creates an earthquake that rends the earth in two, providing assistance to fleeing Israel. This is exactly what we see in the second half of the 70th Week: "Now when the dragon saw that he had been cast to the earth, he persecuted the woman who gave birth to the male child. But the woman was given two wings of a great eagle, that she might fly into the wilderness to her place, where she is nourished for a time and times and half a time [three-and-one-half years] from the presence of the serpent. So the serpent spewed water out of his mouth like a flood after the woman, that he might cause her to be carried away by the flood. But the earth helped the woman, and the earth opened its mouth and swallowed up the flood which the dragon had spewed out of his mouth" (Rev. 12:13-16).

destroy many in their prosperity. *He shall even rise against the Prince of princes.* But he shall be broken without human means. (Dan. 8:25)

Throughout Daniel's prophecies, one theme runs consistently among them: the Antichrist's kingdom will be broken by supernatural means at the end of the age, cut short by the arrival of the Messiah. Therefore, this reference to the "Prince of princes" refers to the Second Coming of Jesus Christ, once again providing strong evidence that Jesus will be in residence upon the earth during the Antichrist's reign.

His Coming (*Parousia*)

That Jesus' Second Coming spans a period of months or years is also confirmed by the use of the noun "to come" (*parousia*), which the New Testament writers often used to refer to the return of the Christ. For example, "But each one in his order: Christ the firstfruits, afterward those who are Christ's at His coming [*parousia*]" (1 Cor 15:23); "For what is our hope, or joy, or crown of rejoicing? Is it not even you in the presence of our Lord Jesus Christ at His coming [*parousia*]?" (1 Thess. 2:19); and "Therefore be patient, brethren, until the coming [*parousia*] of the Lord" (James 5:7).

According to *Strong's Exhaustive Concordance*, the noun *parousia* means a "being near, i.e. advent (often, return; especially of Christ to punish Jerusalem, originally the wicked), or by implication, physical aspect—coming, presence." The idea of Jesus' coming as "being near, a presence," is very different from the picture that is painted of Jesus swooping down out of the clouds, snapping up His Bride, and racing away again. *Parousia* implies that when Jesus comes, He comes to stay. W. E. Vine confirms this in his reference work, *Vine's Expository Dictionary of New and Old Testament Words*, saying, "*Parousia* does not signify merely a coming, it includes or suggests the presence which follows the arrival."[122]

Indeed, this is how the word *parousia* was commonly used at the time the New Testament documents were written. The term was frequently used in ancient manuscripts, called *papyri*, to

---

[122] *Vine's Expository Dictionary of New and Old Testament Words* (Thomas Nelson, 1997).

designate the special visits of kings—again, the concept of "coming to stay."[123]

Marvin Rosenthal condenses the argument nicely:

> *Parousia* is derived from two Greek words, *para* meaning "with" and *ousia* meaning "being." *Parousia*, then, denotes two things: an arrival and a consequent presence with. The Greek scholar W.E. Vine illustrates this by referring to a papyrus letter in which a lady speaks of the necessity of her *parousia* in a place in order to attend to matters relating to her property (a coming and a continued presence in order to accomplish certain matters).
>
> On at least two occasions, the Apostle Paul uses the word *parousia* in the sense of his [own] presence. Quoting what others had said about him, he wrote, "For his letters, say they, are weighty and powerful, but his bodily presence (*parousia*) is weak, and his speech contemptible" (2 Cor. 10:10). And again, "Wherefore, my beloved, as ye have always obeyed, not as in my presence (*parousia*) only but now much more in my absence, work out your own salvation with fear and trembling" (Phil 2:12)....
>
> And of the Antichrist, Paul wrote, "whose coming [*parousia*] is after the working of Satan with all power and signs and lying wonders" (2 Thess 2:9). The coming [*parousia*] of the Antichrist includes his continuing presence to perform his satanic work of false signs and lying wonders. The coming [*parousia*] of Christ will include His continuing presence to rapture the church and His Day of the Lord judgment of the wicked.[124]

Compare this word *parousia* with another word translated "coming" in the New Testament—*exerchomai*. "When He had come to the other side, to the country of the Gergesenes, there met Him two demon-possessed men, coming [*exerchomai*] out of the tombs" (Matt. 8:28). Here, the word "coming" has a very different meaning: "to come forth, depart out of, proceed forth." This is more of the meaning that the pretrib position wants to apply to

---

[123] *Three Views on the Rapture*, p. 176.
[124] *Pre-Wrath Rapture of the Church*, p. 217.

204

Christ's coming at the rapture, and yet this is a different word that is never used in the context of the Second Coming.

In addition to *parousia*, there are two other words used in scripture to refer to the Second Coming. One of these is *erchomai*, which has a great variety of applications, including "accompany, appear, bring, come, and enter." In one instance, the term "coming" is translated from *apokalypsis*, which means "to disclose or bring to light," as in, "so that you come behind in no gift, waiting for the coming [*apokalypsis* or self-disclosure], of our Lord Jesus Christ" (1 Cor. 1:7).

Some scholars have tried to use the New Testament writers' use of these differing Greek words to suggest that there is more than one coming of Christ: one at the rapture and another at Armageddon. In light of all of the scriptural evidence that there is only one coming, however, it makes much more sense to view the variety of words for "coming" as being for the purpose of describing the different aspects, or characteristics, of Jesus' one and *only* return. Think of a family that has been suffering from the loss of a child who had been kidnapped several months before. Suddenly, the doorbell rings and the father opens the door to see his daughter, radiant with joy, on the doorstep. Her coming could be described several ways: *erchomai* (physical arrival), *apokalypsis* (revelation or bringing to light that she is alive and safe), and *parousia* (she is home, and home to stay).

There is another word used to describe the return of the Lord, *epiphaneia,* which carries with it the visible manifestation of a hidden deity.[125] This term is usually translated "appearing." As with *parousia, erchomai*, and *apokalypsis*, there is no reason to believe that this refers to another coming, but rather illuminates another aspect of the same coming. After all, can the coming of Christ be *epiphaneia* (a revelation of hidden deity) without being other things, too, such as *erchomai* (physical arrival) and *apokalypsis* (revelation or bringing to light)?

Oswald T. Allis' defense of the use of these words to describe the different aspects of Christ's one and only return can be found in Appendix E.

---

[125] *Expository Dictionary of Bible Words*, ed. Lawrence Richards.

Arguments Against *Parousia*

One pretrib argument against the prewrath rapture is that Jesus can't possibly remain on earth after He claims His Bride because scripture promises that, after death, "we will forever be with the Lord" (1 Thess. 4:17). How can we be up there and He be down here? Doesn't this contradict scripture?

First, let me appeal to common sense. When I married my husband, I promised him that I would be with him until my dying day. One day, I was called away to Belgium. Did the fact that I was half a continent and the full width of the Atlantic Ocean away from him mean that I had broken my promise? Of course not! So, as the Bride of Christ, why would the comings and goings of the Lord mean that we were no longer with Him? This also relates to the commonly asked question about Jesus' return with the angels at Armageddon. Just because His physical return was sometime earlier does not prevent Him, at the appointed time, from going back to heaven to get His troops.

Second, in a scriptural context, to be "separated from the Lord" means to be spiritually separated from, cast away from, or out of fellowship with Him. Just as in marriage or other covenant agreement, to be "forever with" doesn't necessarily mean to be with physically, every moment of the day. It means we will be forever in fellowship with that person and of one mind and spirit. There is no reason that we cannot be "forever with the Lord" and be in two separate places.[126] This puzzle is reminiscent of the

---

[126] The terms "up here" and "down there," also reflect our limited human understanding of where God is and how He interacts with us. Dr. Hugh Ross, an astrophysicist, evangelical Christian, and founder of the organization Reasons to Believe, puts these logistical issues in terms of a multidimensional universe. Because our universe exists in a four-dimensional envelope (length, width, height, and time), God must live outside these four dimensions — in a fifth dimension — or more. As evidence of the extra-dimensional nature of Christ, Ross points to Jesus' activity following His resurrection when He walked through a wall, then ate fish with His disciples. "The disciples understood the impossibility of a physical body passing through physical barriers. That is why they concluded that the form of Jesus in front of them had to be ghostly or spiritual and not physical. But Jesus proved His physical reality by allowing the disciples to touch Him and by eating food in front of them. Though it is impossible for three-dimensional physical objects to pass

promise that Jesus gave the night before He was to be crucified when He told His disciples that He would be leaving them shortly, and yet earlier, He had promised to be with them always.[127]

For these reasons, the phrase "we shall ever be with the Lord" *cannot* be used to undermine the clear scriptural teaching that Jesus will remain here after the Church has been transported to heaven. We should also consider the fact that Jesus and the Father are One (John 10:30). Therefore, even if Jesus is on earth and we are in heaven with the Father, we are still with Jesus.[128]

---

through three-dimensional physical barriers without one or the other being damaged, Jesus would have no problem doing this in His extra dimensions" (*The Creator and the Cosmos: How the Greatest Scientific Discoveries of the Century Reveal God* [NavPress, 1995]).

[127] Many pretrib scholars use Jesus' promise in John 14:2–3 to support the contention that the Church cannot be in heaven while Jesus is on earth administering His Day of the Lord judgments, as the prewrath position suggests. This is because Jesus promises us that when He comes again and receives the Church unto Himself, "where I am you may be also." However, such a promise does not require an unbroken period of time. Consider one of the most important covenants in the Bible, the Davidic covenant. In 2 Sam. 7:16, God promises that David's kingdom will endure forever and that David's seed will forever be on the throne. And yet, in 589 B.C., the last of the kings, Zedekiah, watched his two sons be executed before his eyes, after which the kingdom of Judah followed her sister Israel into captivity. To this day, there has been no son of David on the throne of Israel. God's promise will only be fulfilled when Jesus returns in glory to rule forever. Therefore, to require the phrase, "that where I am you may be also" to refer to an unbroken period of time, especially when eternity is in view, is not warranted by scripture. For more on this, see Appendix B.

[128] One pretrib proponent suggested to me that this view compromises the beautiful picture we are given of the Marriage Supper of the Lamb. The Bible paints a glorious picture of the Bride of Christ, sitting with Her Husband to dine on Her wedding night in celebration of their beautiful union, forever unbroken. This Marriage Supper differs from the White Throne Judgment and occurs immediately after the judgment of believers, including the trial of works by fire and the giving of crowns. "How can all of these glorious promises be fulfilled if Jesus is physically on the earth, sitting in judgment During the Day of the Lord?" he asked. The obvious answer, which is that Jesus is omnipotent and omnipresent, is somehow unsatisfying. There is, however, a satisfying resolution to this paradox found by considering the multiple time dimensions in which

Coming With All His Saints

There is another seeming paradox that pretrib proponents raise when it is suggested that Jesus' one and only bodily return occurs after the opening of the sixth seal. In 1 Thess. 3:16–17, one of the clearest and most detailed passages on the rapture in the New Testament, Paul writes that Jesus will come "with all His saints." If He is coming to take us in the rapture, they ask, how can He be coming with believers?

In *Zion's Fire*, Rosenthal gives a concise answer to this question:

> Much of the criticism came over my comment concerning the Pauline expression "with all his saints." I stated that the word "saints" in 1 Thess. 3:13 was not referring to believers, but rather to angelic beings; that at Christ's second coming, He would not be accompanied by the raptured and glorified Church, as many teach, but by a great angelic army. I expressed my view of the text this way: "Paul wrote these words to the Thessalonians: 'To the end he may establish your hearts unblameable in holiness before God, even our Father, at the coming [*parousia*] of our Lord Jesus Christ with all his

---

God operates. Dr. Hugh Ross gives an excellent treatment on a related subject in his book, *Beyond the Cosmos*. The fact that God can listen to the prayers of billions of people at one time, giving each His undivided attention, can be satisfactorily resolved when one considers that God could easily be operating in an equal number of time dimensions as there are people. Similarly, the ability of Jesus to spend time in revelry with the Church after the rapture is not compromised by His responsibility for being on earth to administer His judgments if it is considered in the context of multiple time dimensions. This is not a replacement for the scriptural support given in this book, but an augment to it. It is interesting that John Walvoord inadvertently provides support for this position in *The Rapture Question* when he disputes George E. Ladd's contention that the rapture and judgment of Christians must be posttribulational because the seven-year period taught by pretrib is too short for the judgment of two hundred million Christians. Walvoord writes, "This argument would seem to border on the ridiculous—God is not subject to the same limitations as men.... While the judgment of the church is properly distinguished from millennial judgments, we can infer from such judgments as that of the sheep and the goats (Matt. 25:31-46) that there is no divine problem in judging millions at once" (p. 85).

208

saints'" (1 Th. 3:13). Then I went on to say: "Saints in this verse is an unfortunate and inappropriate translation. 'Saints' in this verse does not refer to believers. The Greek word *hagios* should be translated 'holy ones' and is a reference to angelic beings. These angelic beings will accompany Christ at His coming [*parousia*]" (cf. Matt. 25:31, 2 Th. 1:7–8; Rev. 19:14).[129]

Further evidence is found when you consider that Rev. 19:14 elaborates on this return by saying that Jesus will come with His armies on white horses with "fine linen, white and clean." Among the pretrib camp, the assumption is made that these armies are the Church because Rev. 19:8 describes the saints as being given linen that is "clean and white." However, the saints are not the only ones wearing clean, white linen. God's holy angels wear clean, white linen, too:

> ...and the seven angels who had the seven plagues came out of the temple, clothed in linen, clean and bright, and girded around their breasts with golden girdles." (Rev. 15:6)

Considering this evidence, along with the fact that the Church is never identified as the army of God—indeed, this is a term reserved exclusively for angels (the word "hosts," the term that is often used, implies military ranks)—the *"armies"* seen in Rev. 19:14 must be angels, not the Church.

This is, in fact, exactly what Paul tells us in 2 Thess. 1:7–8. In this passage, he explains that this host at Armageddon is comprised of angels, coming with Christ to deal out retribution:

> Since it is a righteous thing with God to repay with tribulation those who trouble you, and to give you who are troubled rest with us when the Lord Jesus is revealed from heaven with His mighty angels, in flaming fire taking vengeance on those who do not know God, and on those who do not obey the gospel of our Lord Jesus Christ. (1 Thess. 1:6–8)

---

[129] For a very thorough treatment of this subject, see Rosenthal's argument in his article, "Coming With All His Saints," in the July–August 1997 issue of *Zion's Fire*.

18

Is Revelation Consecutive?

A straightforward reading of Matthew 24 and Revelation 6–16, taking the events literally and consecutively unless there is a compelling reason to do otherwise, teaches that God's wrath does not start until after the opening of the sixth seal. Because of the clarity of the scriptures on this point, many proponents of the pretribulation rapture argue that the judgments described in Revelation cannot be read consecutively. In general, this argument comes in one of three forms:

1. Revelation is not consecutive in any part;
2. The seal judgments are consecutive, but they serve as an overview of (and therefore run concurrent with) the trumpets and the bowls;
3. All three periods of judgment—the seals, the trumpets, and the bowls—are consecutive within themselves, but the periods of judgment overlap.

Personally, I believe that a straightforward reading of Revelation, combined with a dose of common sense, should be enough to convince the reader of the error of this thinking. However, enough prophecy experts teach one of these three theories that touching on this subject would be helpful.

Why Was Revelation Written?

In order to determine whether the judgments described in Revelation are consecutive, we first need to determine the frame of reference of the book. Revelation 1 introduces us to the writer of this book, John the Apostle, and the authority on which he writes, the Lord Jesus Christ. As early as the first verse, the text tells us that Jesus has chosen to reveal the details of the 70th Week to John during the apostle's exile on the island of Patmos:

> The Revelation of Jesus Christ, which God gave Him to show His servants things which must shortly take place. And He sent and signified it by His angel to His servant John, who bore witness to the word of God, and to the testimony of Jesus Christ, to all things that he saw. (Rev. 1:1–2)

Overview Interpretation 1

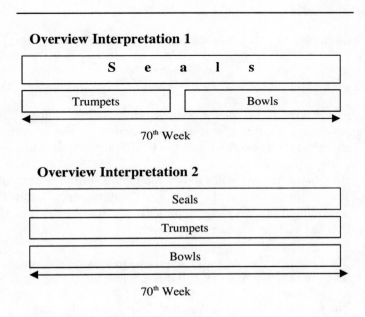

Overview Interpretation 2

Overview Interpretation 3

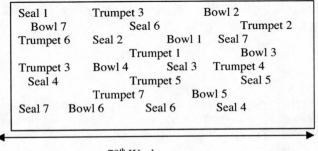

In Revelation 2 and 3, Jesus gives John a message for the seven churches, including the famous promise, "I will keep you from the hour of trial," given to the Church of Philadelphia. To the other six churches, He gives the command to repent (except to the persecuted church) and to overcome. This leads to two important questions: "What trial will the Church of Philadelphia be kept from?" and, "What will the other six churches have to overcome?"

John wastes no time in answering this question. Chapter 4 begins,

> After these things I looked, and behold, a door standing open in heaven. And the first voice which I heard was like a trumpet speaking with me, saying, "Come up here, and I will show you things which must take place after this."[130]

Then John lays out the events, as if telling a story. This straightforward approach is important because, as John wrote at the beginning of the book, it was his intention "to bear witness to all the things [he] saw."

In Chapter 5, we begin to see the events unfold. First, John describes the opening of the scroll, which represents the 70th Week. As each of the seals holding closed the scroll is broken, this unleashes the corresponding seal judgment:

> Now when He had taken the scroll, the four living creatures and the twenty-four elders fell down before the Lamb, each having a harp, and golden bowls full of incense, which are the prayers of the saints. And they sang a new song, saying: "You are worthy to take the scroll, and to open its seals; for You were slain and have redeemed us to God by Your blood...." Then I looked, and I heard the voice of many angels around the throne.

---

[130] Some pretrib proponents use this verse to prove that the rapture occurs prior to the opening of the six seals. In this argument, the phrase "Come up here" is used, not just to refer to John's taking up into heaven, but to symbolize all believers being taken to heaven in the rapture. Other than the fact that the timing fits with the pretrib position, there is no scriptural reason to equate the two.

212

Already, phrases like "Now when He had taken the scroll," and "Then I looked," indicate consecutive order.

In Chapter 6, each of the seal judgments is described in detail. In these descriptions, John continues to use words that indicate the consecutive nature of these judgments, not the least of which is his ordering of the seals from one to seven.

The use of words such as "when," "until," and "then," also indicate consecutive order:

> Now I saw when the Lamb opened one of the seals; and I heard one of the four living creatures saying with a voice like thunder, "Come and see." And I looked, and behold, a white horse....**When** He opened the second seal, I heard the second living creature saying, "Come and see." Another horse, fiery red, went out....**When** He opened the third seal, I heard the third living creature say, "Come and see." So I looked, and behold, a black horse....**When** He opened the fifth seal, I saw under the altar the souls of those who had been slain for the word of God and for the testimony which they held....**Then** a white robe was given to each of them; and it was said to them that they should rest a little while longer, **until** both the number of their fellow servants and their brethren, who would be killed as they were, was completed....I looked **when** He opened the sixth seal, and behold, there was a great earthquake...and the stars of heaven fell...then the sky receded as a scroll...and the kings of the earth...hid themselves in the caves and in the rocks of the mountains, and said to the mountains and rocks, "Fall on us and hide us from the face of Him who sits on the throne and from the wrath of the Lamb!"

When Chapter 7 opens, this pattern continues. Once again, we see consecutive order:

> **After these things**, I saw four angels standing at the four corners of the earth, holding the four winds of the earth, that the wind should not blow on the earth, on the sea, or on any tree. **Then I saw another angel ascending from the east,** having the seal of the living God. (vv. 1–2)

> **After these things**, I looked, and behold, a great multitude which no one could number, of all nations, tribes, peoples,

and tongues, standing before the throne and before the Lamb, clothed with white robes. (v. 9)

Then one of the elders answered, saying to me, 'Who are these arrayed in white robes, and where did they come from?' (v. 13)

The same language continues through the trumpet and the bowl judgments.

Only the Order Seen?

Some pretrib proponents make the case that the use of the term "then" could indicate that this is the order only in which John saw the events, not the order in which they occurred. In answer to this, and to the whole question of consecutive order in Revelation, I must defer to the first verses of this book: "The Revelation of Jesus Christ, which God gave Him to show His servants things which must shortly take place. And He sent and signified it by His angel to His servant John, who bore witness ... to all things that he saw" (Rev. 1:1–2). With some clearly identified exceptions, Revelation is, by Jesus' own command, a straightforward telling of events. To suggest that these events are actually in a different order than they appear undermines the purpose of the book—"to show His servants things that must shortly take place"—and requires that God deliberately created a false impression. This is not an acceptable conclusion.

Keep in mind that not only does the straightforward nature of the text strongly imply consecutive order, but John was asked to "bear witness" of the things he saw. The Greek verb used here is *martureo*, which comes from the root word *martus*, which means "to be a witness, to testify or bear record." It is the same word that is used by John the Baptist when he bore witness of Jesus in the wilderness: "And John bore witness [*martureo*], saying, 'I saw the Spirit descending from heaven like a dove, and He remained upon Him.... And I have seen and testified [*martureo*] that this is the Son of God" (Luke 1:32–34). John the Apostle also used it to describe the actions of the townspeople who saw Jesus raise Lazarus from the dead: "Therefore the people, who were with Him when He called Lazarus out of his tomb and raised him from the dead, bore witness [*martureo*]" (John 12:17).

214

In addition to the translation, "to bear witness of the truth," this verb also carries the implication, *so that the hearers might believe*. Not only does John's use of the verb *martureo* imply that the events in Revelation are consecutive, but consecutive order is also consistent with God's character. When has God ever made His central truths an unsolvable puzzle? Or made it His intention to deceive? With the extraordinary emphasis in the New Testament placed on the return of Christ and the need for believers to remain steadfast as they await their deliverance, what purpose would be served by telling the events out of order? In overlapping order? Or in any other order that would obscure the truth?

Certainly, there is a purpose for prophetic symbolism and parables in the scriptures. There are even instances when, because of the hardness of the hearers' hearts, God has chosen to obscure His truth rather than make it plain (Mark 4:12, Matt. 18:4). But in these cases, Jesus always revealed the true meaning of these sayings to His disciples at a later time. As Jesus described the judgments that will occur throughout the 70th Week, He was not being obscure. Nor was He being obscure when He called John to view the events from heaven. He said, "Come up here, and I will tell you the things that must take place after this." It was His intention to bring to light—not to hide.

In fact, at His First Coming, it was Jesus Himself who first indicated that these descriptions are in consecutive order. In the Gospel of Luke, after describing the beginning of sorrows, the Great Tribulation, and the cosmic disturbances (a parallel telling of the seal judgments), He said, "Now, when these things begin to happen, *look up and lift up your heads*, because your redemption draws near" (Luke 21:28). What good would it do to tell His audience to lift their heads "when these things begin to happen" if the events were not in consecutive order?

Symbolism Points to Consecutive Order

The symbolism used in Revelation also points to consecutive order. The judgments of Revelation are contained in a scroll, which in Jesus' time was usually a piece of rolled parchment. Documents of a sensitive nature were often rolled up tightly and sealed with a small piece of clay impressed with a signet, called a *bulla*. Only authorized persons could break the seal. In the case of the scroll in Revelation, it is sealed with seven seals, the sign of perfection, and the only one authorized to break the seals is Jesus, the perfect Lamb of God:

> Then I saw a strong angel proclaiming with a loud voice, "Who is worthy to open the scroll and to loose its seals?" And no one in heaven or on the earth or under the earth was able to open the scroll or to look at it. So I wept much because no one was found worthy to open and read the scroll, or to look at it. But one of the elders said to me, "Do not weep, Behold, the Lion of the tribe of Judah, the Root of David, has prevailed to open the scroll and to loose its seven seals." And I looked, and behold, in the midst of the throne and of the four living creatures, and in the midst of the elders, stood a Lamb as though it had been slain, having seven horns and seven eyes, which are the seven Spirits of God sent out into all the earth. Then He came and took the scroll out of the right hand of Him who sat on the throne. (Rev. 5: 2–3, 6–7)

Illustration of the Revelation 5 Scroll

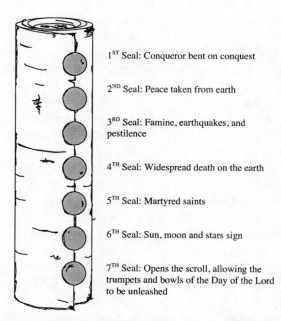

1ST Seal: Conqueror bent on conquest

2ND Seal: Peace taken from earth

3RD Seal: Famine, earthquakes, and pestilence

4TH Seal: Widespread death on the earth

5TH Seal: Martyred saints

6TH Seal: Sun, moon and stars sign

7TH Seal: Opens the scroll, allowing the trumpets and bowls of the Day of the Lord to be unleashed

Graphic courtesy of Dave Bussard, *Who Will Be Left Behind and When?* (Strong Tower Publishing, 2002)

216

It is important to notice that the document cannot be opened until all of the seals have been broken. This means that the scroll cannot be unrolled—and therefore the trumpets and bowls cannot be unleashed, or revealed—if even one seal is still in place. This further undermines the "overview" interpretation since, even in the symbolism, the opening of the seals must precede the blowing of the trumpets and the outpouring of the bowls. Furthermore, because all of the bowl judgments are contained within the seventh trumpet, the bowls cannot be poured out until the last of the trumpets has been blown. There is a clear order of succession.

What About Signs and Metaphors?

Not all of the events described in Revelation occur in consecutive order, however. There are four topics in Revelation for which Jesus uses a consecutive telling of events to get His point across: the seal judgments; the trumpet judgments; the bowl judgments; and the description of His Millennial reign, the final defeat of Satan, and His creation of a new heaven and a new earth. These comprise about half of the book of Revelation.

The other half is made up of signs, heavenly events, and general descriptions of people, places, and things that are of great importance during the 70th Week but that are not necessarily described in a strict chronological order. Typically, these descriptions provide additional background to what has just been discussed. They are not, however, mixed in randomly. Scripture makes it clear when it takes a break from the straightforward narrative and when it returns.

For example, the first three chapters of Revelation provide background to the reader about the purpose and content of the book. It establishes that this is a vision given by Jesus to the Apostle John about the 70th Week. In the first three chapters, John describes his vision of heaven, Jesus standing in the midst of the seven lampstands, and the letters to the seven churches.

In chapters four and five, John describes the throne room of heaven, introduces the scroll containing the judgments of God, describes the search for One worthy to open the scroll, and introduces the seal judgments. In Chapter 6, he describes each of these judgments, which he identifies by name: the first seal, the second seal, and so on. Then, once all seven seals have been described, in Chapter 7, John gives us a glimpse of what is happening in heaven: the joy of the angels, the triumphant arrival of the Church ("those who come out of the great tribulation"), and the preparations for the Day of the Lord. In chapters eight and nine, he describes each of the trumpet judgments in detail, just as he described the seals, ordering them from one to seven.

So far, the story has been chronological, but now, some additional details are necessary to give the reader a full understanding of what has just been described. In Chapters 10 through 15, John takes a break from his story and backs up to provide additional details to fill out the picture. These include descriptions of the ministry of the two witnesses, Satan being thrown out of heaven, the rise of the Antichrist and the false prophet, and the giving of the mark, all of which occur during the seal and trumpet judgments, as well.

A Little Background

How do we know John is backing up in chapters 10–15? John gives us a reference point. We know that the fifth seal, the cry of the martyrs, is the same as the Great Tribulation, and that the Great Tribulation occurs immediately after the midpoint of the 70th Week (Matt. 24:15, Dan. 9:27). If the Great Tribulation (Rev. 6:9–11) occurs at the midpoint, then the final trumpet judgment—the point at which John stops his chronological description—is well past this half-way mark.

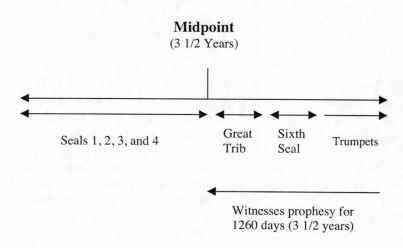

Midpoint
(3 1/2 Years)

Seals 1, 2, 3, and 4

Great Trib

Sixth Seal

Trumpets

Witnesses prophesy for 1260 days (3 1/2 years)

Now, in Rev. 10:11, John is told, "You must prophesy again about many peoples, nations, tongues, and kings." This is the first clue that John is backing up. Next, John hears the voice telling him about the two witnesses who will prophesy outside the temple for 1,260 days (Rev. 11:3). This period, 1,260 days, is the equivalent of three-and-one-half years. This puts the beginning of their ministry at or before the midpoint of the 70th Week. Thus, we know that the description John is giving us covers the earlier period of the seals and the trumpets that he has already described.

Another time John diverges from consecutive order is when he describes the sign of the woman who bore a male Child "who was to rule all nations with a rod of iron," which is described in Chapter 12. This Child is "caught up to God and His throne" (v. 5). The language throughout this passage is highly symbolic. The male Child is clearly Jesus, and the catching up to God and His throne is Christ's ascension in A.D. 33. There is also "Mystery, Babylon," the scarlet woman with the garland of 12 stars who rides the beast, who has been the subject of much speculation over the years. Once this background is given, providing us with many additional clues to the timing, purpose, and nature of the 70th Week, John returns to his story.

In Chapter 15, John lets the reader know he is returning to a chronological description of the judgments by giving us a prelude, or introduction, to the bowls. In Chapter 16, these final, terrible judgments are described. This is followed by a rich, vivid description of the final fall of the great city of Babylon and the exultation in heaven over God's majesty and triumph in Chapters 17 and 18. Then, in Chapter 19, we see the arrival of Jesus on His white horse to bring the last and final temporal judgment of the Day of the Lord, the battle of Armageddon.

When Revelation is seen in this way, as a mixture of signs, visions, and metaphors in conjunction with the straightforward narrative, all of the elements fall together with perfect clarity. Like any other story, some parts are consecutive. Others are not. But these digressions are both clear and important to the central theme. It is a bit like someone stopping a yarn about Aunt Minnie's 90th birthday party to say, "Meanwhile, going on in the kitchen," or "Before I get to that, remember...."

As would be expected in a straightforward narrative, the Bible makes it clear when it is making use of these devices. For example, after describing the seventh trumpet, when John describes the great sign of the woman clothed with the sun, with the moon under her feet, and on her head a garland of twelve stars, the phrase, "Now a great sign appeared in heaven" (Rev. 12:1) makes the shift from the consecutive timeline to symbolism clear. When John gets ready to return to the timeline and describe the bowl judgments, this transition is just as clear: "Then I heard a loud voice from the temple saying to the seven angels, 'Go and pour out the bowls of the wrath of God on the earth'" (Rev. 16:1). Scripture is not obscure about its intent.

Defining Revelation's Structure

Can the use of such divergences be used to support the contention that all of the events in Revelation are non-consecutive? Absolutely not. As I mentioned, these descriptions are *clearly delineated* from the seal, trumpet, and bowl judgments and serve an entirely different purpose. Throughout Revelation, the Apostle John uses many techniques to make his point. If you break the book down into its components, a very well-defined narrative structure becomes visible:

Outline of the Structure of Revelation

I. Description of the general purpose for the 70th Week
General introduction
Warning to the seven churches

II. Description of the 70th Week
Introduction to the seals
Description of the seals
Introduction to the trumpets
Description of the trumpets
Conclusion to the seals and the trumpets

III. Description of God's wrath
Introduction to the bowls
Description of the bowls

IV. Description of Christ's reign
Description of Christ's descent to earth
Description of Christ's Millennial reign
Description of Christ's final defeat of the Antichrist
Description of the creation of a new heavens and earth

It may also help to look at the structure visually:

The Structure of Revelation

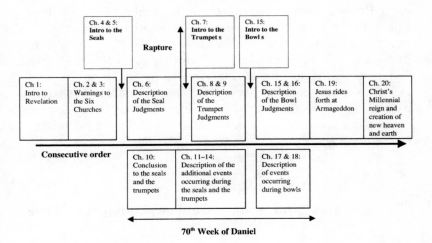

Other Textual Clues

There are many clues in the text that confirm this structure. We have already looked at many of them. One of these is John's repeated use of the phrase "after all these things," a phrase that merits additional discussion.

We first see this phrase used in the introduction to the trumpet judgments. This introduction states, "After these things, I looked and behold, a great multitude which no one could number, of all nations, tribes, peoples, and tongues, standing before the throne and before the Lamb..." (Rev. 7:9). The phrase "after these things" tells us that John sees the multitude standing in heaven after the preceding events—the seal judgments, which John has just described—have concluded.

We see a similar device used after the trumpet judgments. After all seven trumpets have been blown, John records, "And he [the angel with the little book] said to me, 'You must prophesy again about many peoples, nations, tongues, and kings.'" Why "prophesy again"? Hasn't John been prophesying? The answer is that John is instructed to *prophesy again* about the same time period he has just written about in Chapters 6–9: the seals and the trumpets. Thus, in addition to all of the other clues that the

221

judgments of Revelation are consecutive, John has just told us that the prophetic order is the seals, followed by the trumpets, in a clearly delineated order.

Rounding out the textual clues, John tells us that the bowls follow in the prophetic succession. We know this because, after describing the seals and the trumpets and all of the background that goes with them, he says, *"After all of these things* I looked, and behold, the temple of the tabernacle of the testimony in heaven was opened. And out of the temple came the seven angels having the seven plagues....Then one of the four living creatures gave to the seven angels seven golden bowls full of the wrath of God"* (Rev.15:5–7).

The following chart may help to clarify the relationship between these verses.

Use of Textual Indicators to Confirm Consecutive Order

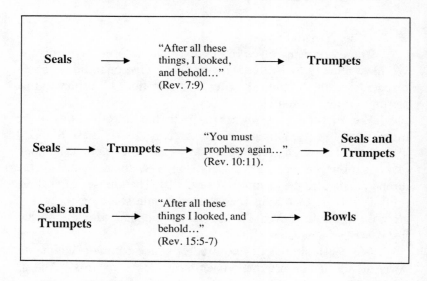

The Bible gives us a very basic rule in understanding its structure—take it literally and consecutively unless there is *compelling textual or contextual evidence* to do otherwise. This is exactly what we see in Revelation—compelling evidence when to read it consecutively and when to read it as background or a metaphor. What the text does not do is give us license for interpretation.

Are the Seals an Overview?

One of the common arguments used to deny the consecutive nature of Revelation is the "seals as an overview" argument. This position argues that the seals serve as an overview or condensed version of the 70th Week, like reading the Cliff Notes before reading the book. According to this line of reasoning, the 70th Week begins with the first seal and ends after the sixth seal, which is opened just prior to Armageddon. The trumpets and the bowls, then, cover the same period, starting at the beginning of the 70th Week and ending with Armageddon.

Overview Interpretation of Revelation

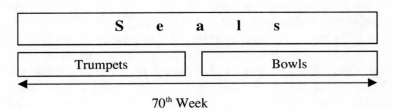

70th Week

This is a clever argument that allows the seals to coincide with Jesus' description of the end times in Matthew 24, while placing Jesus' bodily return at Armageddon, not after the midpoint of the 70th Week. Because the trumpets and the bowls are said to cover the same time period, only in more detail, this makes the great cosmic disturbances of sixth seal coincide with the seventh bowl, the earth utterly shaken.[131]

---

[131] One argument for the overview interpretation is based on the concept of the scroll as it would have been understood in the ancient Jewish culture. The scroll was often used as the last will and testament and could be opened only by the officiating judge. Seals of wax or clay held the scroll closed until the appropriate time. On the scroll opened by Jesus, the number of seals is seven, the number God uses to represent perfection—in this case, representing perfect judgment. According to pretrib theology, the rapture must occur prior to the opening of the scroll because the breaking of the seals indicates Jesus' active involvement in the end times. Like a last will and testament, the purpose and intent of the will is contained within it. Hence, the outer layer of the scroll represents

There are many reasons this doesn't work.

First, there is no compelling textual or contextual reason to read it this way. It is an awkward construction that, in no way, could be devised from a natural reading of the text. It is a necessary construction to support the desired outcome, which, in itself, makes the position suspect.

Second, it requires the seals to be part of God's wrath. And yet, scripture clearly and repeatedly establishes that God's wrath is associated with the Day of the Lord, which begins after the opening of the sixth seal (Joel 2:31). This creates a fatal flaw for the summary interpretation. If the Day of the Lord must *follow* the sixth seal, the sixth seal cannot be *part of it*.[132]

Third, the overview interpretation puts the advocates of this interpretation back into the position of having to explain the rapture verse in Matt. 24:30–31 as Jesus' coming at Armageddon, creating many scriptural inconsistencies (see Chapter 11).

Fourth and finally, the seal judgments simply don't read like a summary. A summary is a condensed version of the original, hitting the highlights in a shortened form. We see no such character for the seal judgments. They contain very detailed descriptions, such as the sun turning dark and the moon turning to blood, that are not mentioned in the trumpets or the bowls.

---

an overview of the details contained inside. I love the imagery that this picture evokes: Jesus, our perfect Judge, opening His last will and testament for the earth. However, as discussed in an earlier chapter, this model actually fits the prewrath timing, not the pretrib timing. The nature of sealed scrolls is that all of the exterior seals must be broken before the scroll can be unrolled. In this case, *all seven seals* must be broken before the trumpets can be blown, strongly implying consecutive order. This is confirmed by the fact that the seven trumpets are contained within the seventh seal, so once again, all seven seals must be broken before the trumpets can be blown. Further, the seven bowls are contained within the seventh trumpet, so all seven trumpets must be blown before the bowls can be poured out. This imagery, that the trumpets and the bowls cannot be unleashed until all seven seals are broken, is also appropriate since the trumpets and the bowls represent the Day of the Lord: the seals must be broken and the scroll opened before that Day can begin.

[132] Some scholars try to solve this problem by creating two days of the Lord: one that covers the entire 70th Week and one that refers only to Jesus' touchdown at Armageddon. See Appendix A.

Likewise, in the trumpets and the bowls, we see very unique judgments, such as the burning of one-third of the earth's vegetation and one-third of the waters turning to blood, that are not mentioned in the seals. It does not make sense that Jesus would tell John to write an overview of the 70th Week that omits key elements of the event being summarized. Nor does it make sense that Jesus would tell John to write an overview that contains unique events not described in the event itself.

The overview interpretation stretches credulity even further when we consider that this view requires Jesus to have given the summary judgments an entirely different name (the seals) than the events they are purported to describe (the trumpets and the bowls).

By all accounts, the seals, the trumpets, and the bowls are different judgments for different purposes.

Six More Reasons

There are six additional reasons that the seals cannot be a summary of the trumpet and the bowl judgments.

First, this would make them God's wrath. However, 1 Cor. 15:22–24 tells us that, during the time of His wrath, Jesus puts an end to all authority and power. Yet according to Rev. 6:2, the Antichrist is given power (a crown) and allowed to rise to great authority, including authority to persecute God's elect (Rev. 13:7). If the Antichrist is allowed to rise to power during this time, it cannot be the time of God's wrath.

Second, if the seals are an overview of the trumpets and the bowls, this would make them part of the Day of the Lord. However, Isaiah tells us of the Day of the Lord, "the eyes of the arrogant man will be humbled and the pride of men brought low; the Lord alone will be exalted on that day (Isaiah 2:11). And yet, Jesus tells us that, at the midpoint of the 70th Week, the Antichrist will exalt himself in the temple, claiming to be God. Therefore, if the Antichrist will exalt himself during the seals, the seals cannot be part of the Day of the Lord.[133]

Third, there are an appointed number of believers set by God who will be martyred during the fifth seal. Since we are not destined for wrath, the fifth seal cannot be part of God's wrath since God will not direct His wrath against His own people.

---

[133] Dave Bussard, *Who Will Be Left Behind and When?* (Strong Tower Publishing, 2002).

225

Significance of the Use of Seals, Trumpets, and Bowls
As Agents for Judgment in Revelation

Judgment	Historical Significance	Meaning in End Times Context
Seal	Important documents were rolled up as a scroll and sealed with clay impressed with a signet, or bullae. These seals could not be opened except by an authorized person at the risk of death.	In Rev. 5:2, the angel cries with a loud voice, "Who is worthy to open the scroll and to loose its seals?" This ushers in the 70th Week and completes God's perfect plan to redeem the earth. Only the Lion of the Tribe of Judah, the Root of David, the Messiah Jesus, is found to be worthy. Only once the seals are broken can the scroll be unrolled, revealing the events of the Day of the Lord, or the trumpet and bowl judgments. It is Jesus Himself who breaks the seals.
Trumpet	In ancient Israel, trumpets were used to call together a congregation to worship or to war.	After the rapture of the church between the sixth and seventh seals, the angel blows the trumpet in Revelation 8 to signify that war has been declared on the enemies of God. The Day of the Lord has begun. From this point on, angels are the agents by which the judgments come.
Bowl	Shallow bowls were typically used for Jewish ceremonial washing. After washing, the contents of bowls could be quickly thrown out, their contents being useless and dirty.	Old Testament prophets typically used the term "to pour out" to refer to God's wrath upon the Earth. Thus, the use of bowls in Revelation 15 to depict the pouring out of God's wrath upon the Earth is appropriate.

My thanks to Marvin Rosenthal for his explanations in his tape series, "Thirteen Messages on Revelation," on which this chart is based.

Fourth, Revelation 7:9 makes it clear that the trumpet judgments occur after the seals, not concurrent with them. *"After all these things*, I looked, and behold, a great multitude which no one could number...."* Likewise, Rev. 15:5–7 makes it clear that the bowls occur after the seals and the trumpets: *"After these things* I looked, and behold, the temple of the tabernacle of the testimony in heaven was opened. And out of the temple came the seven angels having the seven plagues...."

Fifth, the structure of Revelation, as described earlier, makes it clear that the seals and the trumpets comprise the portion of God's judgment that is not His wrath.

Sixth, throughout scripture, seals, trumpets, and bowls have distinct symbolic meanings in the history of Israel (see chart on the preceding page). The seals indicate the authenticity of revelation; the trumpets, the declaration of war; and the bowls, fiery judgment. When the judgments in Revelation are viewed in consecutive order, this symbolism becomes very helpful in illuminating the meaning of the scriptures. If these judgments overlap, this symbolism becomes meaningless, and even serves to confuse the issue.

When all of these factors are taken into consideration, it becomes clear that the seal judgments and the trumpet and the bowl judgments cannot occur simultaneously, as the overview position requires.

Comparison to the Plagues of Egypt

There is also a strong parallel to the plagues of Egypt in Exodus 5–11 that provides further evidence of the consecutive nature of these judgments.

Although God is not constrained to past patterns and often acts in unique and unpredictable ways, He also uses patterns to reflect His consistency of character. He used patterns of sevens to illustrate perfection (the seven days of creation, the seven-year cycle of the year of rest, the seven stars and seven golden lampstands in Revelation 1); He used the Passover Lamb and the sacrificial system to foreshadow the perfect sacrifice of Jesus on the cross; and He used the pattern of the days of Noah to illustrate the deliverance of His people at the time of the rapture.

In this case, there are four characteristics of the plagues of Egypt that are very strong parallels to the trumpets and the bowls. These characteristics are shown in the following chart:

Comparison of the Judgments in Egypt to the Judgments in Revelation

Judgments in Egypt	Judgments in Revelation
1. The judgments are consecutive.	1. The judgments are consecutive.
2. The judgments are administered by an agent: Moses.	2. The judgments are administered by agents: God's angels (trumpets and the bowls).
3. The judgments are supernatural.	3. The judgments are supernatural.
4. The judgments grow in intensity with each new plague.	4. The judgments grow in intensity with each new disaster or plague.

Furthermore, consider the judgments God showed to Egypt:

• Waters turning to blood.
• Frogs blanketing the earth.
• Egyptians plagued with lice.
• Unbearable flies.
• Egyptian's livestock diseased and killed.
• Boils that cover man and beast.
• Destructive hail killing man, beast, and vegetation.
• Locusts covering the earth.
• Darkness covering the earth.
• Death of the firstborn.

Many of these judgments, such as the waters turning to blood, boils, hail, locusts, and darkness, will also be brought upon the earth during the Day of the Lord, although in much greater intensity. Many others, although not specifically mentioned by name, are possible and even likely.

The language used in Revelation, the structure, the textual clues, and the parallels to other areas of scripture strongly point to consecutive order for the seal, trumpet and bowl judgments. Furthermore, to suggest that the seals, the trumpets, and the bowls are not in consecutive order would create more scriptural contradictions and problems than is profitable to cover here.

These arguments do not exhaust the need to read the judgments of Revelation in a consecutive fashion. However, I hope that they are convincing enough that the reader will allow John to do as He was commanded: to bear witness to the things he has seen and let the scriptures speak for themselves.

19

Does God Create Evil?

Sometimes He calms the storm / With a whisper, "Peace, be
still."/ He can settle any sea, but it doesn't mean He will. /
Sometimes He holds us close, while the wind and waves rage
all around. / Sometimes He calms the storm. / Sometimes He
calms the child...

—Scott Krippayne, "Wild Imagination"[134]

There are some readers who would reject the prewrath
argument solely on the belief that God does not bring plagues
upon His people. Therefore, they cannot accept that the Church
will be present on earth during the seals. God's judgment, they
believe, will only be for the unbelieving world. "How could God
create a period of famine, plagues, and bloodshed that will kill
millions of people, including His own children?" they argue. "That
is not a loving God." I agree that this is difficult to understand.
However, the Bible is very clear that God *does* cause such things
to happen and He will do so again during the 70th Week in order to
accomplish His perfect, loving will.

How can this be? First, we must be careful not to put a
human spin on the acts of God. Throughout the Old Testament,
God frequently used famine, captivity, and disease to discipline
His people and break them of idolatry. The Hebrew word used for
these events is *ra*, which means "bad or (as a noun) evil: adversity,
affliction, calamity, displeasure, distress, exceedingly great grief."

---

[134] Scott Krippayne, "Wild Imagination," Word Records; lyrics and
music by Tony Wood and Kevin Stokes.

In English versions of the text, this word is often translated "disaster," "calamity," or "evil."

Repeatedly, God makes it clear that He is the author of disaster and calamity for His purposes. In Isaiah 45:7, He says, "I form the light and create darkness. I make peace and create calamity [*ra*]. I, the Lord, do all these things." In the *King James Version*, the word *ra* is translated "evil." Thus, Isaiah 45:7 reads, "I form the light and create darkness. I make peace and create evil [*ra*]. I, the Lord, do all these things."

The *King James Version* translates *ra* as "evil" 425 times. It is the same word, for example, that is used in Isaiah 5:20: "Woe to those who call evil good, and good evil, who put darkness for light and light for darkness." The word is used again in Isaiah 13:11, in the description of God's purposes for the great Day of the Lord: "I will punish the world for its evil [*ra*], and the wicked for their iniquity; I will halt the arrogance of the proud, and will lay low the haughtiness of the terrible." Whether you translate the word *ra* as disaster, calamity, or evil makes no difference. After 425 verses, God makes it clear that it is part of His divine plan.

This is not to say that *all* disasters and calamities are created by God. Some are the devices of Satan, for the Bible tells us that Satan is like "a roaring lion, seeking whom he may devour" (1 Peter 5:8). But nowhere does the Bible say that all disasters and calamities are created by Satan. In fact, it says the opposite (see Chapter 15). The difference between a calamity created by God and a calamity created by Satan is that Satan uses it to turn people away from God. God uses it to bring His people back.

It is important, however, to distinguish between events that are physically or emotionally painful and events of moral corruption, something that the word *ra* does not distinguish. This is why some of the more recent Bible editions translate *ra* as "disaster" or "calamity" rather than "evil."

As in all areas of difficulty in the Bible, God's use of *ra* must always be seen in its proper context, which is as part of the plan of a perfect, holy, and righteous God in whom "there is no darkness at all" (1 John 1:5). In the lives of His children, all things created by God are good and perfect, even if they are difficult or painful. Paul clarified this point when he wrote, "All things work for good for those who love the Lord and are called according to His purpose" (Romans 8:28).

Good Uses of Evil

One of the best examples of a good use for evil (*ra*) in my own experience comes from a friend whose son was born with an incurable disease of the nervous system. When I met his son, the boy was 16. His speech, his ability to talk, the position of his hands and arms, head, and legs were all severely affected by the disease. But despite these physical challenges, and despite the fact that the doctors had not expected him to live to see puberty, he was a happy, well-adjusted teenager. When my friend first told me about his son's disease, my flesh immediately cried out, "What a terrible thing to happen to a man of God!"

Then he shared something with me. Of my friend's own immediate family (his parents and siblings), he was the only one who had a personal relationship with Jesus. He had tried many times to share the gospel with them, but their hearts were hard. When his family discovered his son's disease, they had been horrified. But their shock quickly turned to amazement when, instead of being devastated or blaming God for their circumstances, my friend and his wife thanked God for their child. They watched as this couple bore with grace and patience the trips to the hospital, the cost of the medical treatments, and the daily rituals of caring for their son. They watched as he and his wife glorified God every day for the blessing their son brought to their lives. They were baffled. How could this couple have peace and joy? How could they be so happy and content? And yet, as the years passed, it became quite clear that this was no act. This was a joyful, loving family, full of the peace of the Lord.

Through this experience, my friend was able to share with his family the power of God in a very practical way that words could never do. As he shared this story with me, he leaned over earnestly and said, "My son is not angry with God for this disease. He loves the Lord. He has many wonderful Christian friends and is a blessing to us all. If this disease was necessary to reach the hearts of my family, then so be it."

That conversation humbled me deeply and taught me an important lesson about the things of God. Had this humble servant and his wife seen their son's disease as a curse instead of a blessing, the outcome might have been very different.

Use of Tragedy for Good

The spirit of what God was doing through this family can be applied to many other events in the Bible and to our own lives. God frequently uses tragedy and calamity to bring about His good and perfect purposes. One of those uses came during the Israelites' rebellion in the wilderness on their way to Canaan.

In Numbers 21, Moses recorded the Israelites' wandering in the wilderness. It had been years since God freed them from their bonds in Egypt, but He continued to perform many miracles as He led them toward the land of promise. The Israelites, however, were frustrated and restless. Every morning, God provided them with manna to feed themselves and their families, yet they did not thank Him for this miraculous provision. Instead, they complained against God and Moses, saying, "Why have you brought us up out of Egypt to die in the wilderness? For there is no food and no water, and our soul loathes this worthless bread" (Num. 21:5).

How patient God is! When the Israelites first began complaining in Egypt, He sent them a deliverer. After Moses led the Israelites out of Egypt, they complained about the pursuing Egyptian army, so He parted the Red Sea. Then, when they complained that they had only bitter water to drink, He turned the waters sweet. When they complained that they had no water, He brought liquid from a rock. And how did Israel thank Him? During the 40 days that God gave Moses the Levitical law, they built and worshiped the golden calf.

Now, God's people were complaining once again. Finally, God had had quite enough. His longsuffering and mercy turned to discipline:

> So the Lord sent fiery serpents among the people, and they bit the people; and many of the people of Israel died. Therefore the people came to Moses, and said, "We have sinned, for we have spoken against the Lord and against you; pray to the Lord that He take away the serpents from us." So Moses prayed for the people. Then the Lord said to Moses, "Make a fiery serpent, and set it on a pole, and it shall be that everyone who is bitten, when he looks at it, shall live." (Num. 21:6–8)

Many people have been taught that anything uncomfortable or painful may be *allowed* by God, but its origin must ultimately be from Satan. This passage makes it clear that this is not always the case. Even the people's statement, "Pray to the Lord that He take away the serpents from us," tells us that the Israelites acknowledged that this plague was from God. God is our Father, but His role is not to make our lives comfortable and easy. It is to teach us, grow us, and prepare us for eternity. Sometimes this includes blessing, but often it requires discipline.

Personal discipline we understand, since an individual's personal sin clearly requires personal punishment. What we find difficult to understand is *corporate* discipline, when God punishes an entire nation at once, judging (or testing) the innocent along with the guilty. This is the case of the examples given here and, in the future, during Daniel's 70th Week.

It is important to remember that God's purposes are good, even if we have trouble understanding them right away. This is usually because our perspective is limited and earthly, while His perspective is eternal. Life is a training ground, a period of preparation for the eternal blessings that He has for us.

We must remember, too, that God's judgment is always fair and it is His will that all men be saved and come to repentance (1 Peter 3:9). If God's disciplinary actions lead to death, those who have eternal salvation will be blessed with the fast-track to heaven—no more suffering and no more toil. If a soul is eternally lost, we can be certain that no number of additional chances would have saved him or her. Therefore, if God can use the timing of the loss of that soul to keep a weak child from going astray, to bring an erring child to repentance, or even simply to magnify His name, He has turned tragedy into good.

God's Warning to Obedience

It is from this perspective that God's discipline becomes easier to understand. Especially when considering that the Israelites had been repeatedly warned that He would visit judgment on them for their rebellion and idolatry. This is why, in Numbers 21, there was no question as to why God had sent the fiery serpents. Earlier, God had given the people this warning:

> If you walk in My statutes and keep My commandments, and perform them, then I will give you rain in its season, the land shall yield its produce, and the trees of the field shall yield their fruit....But if you do not obey Me, and do not observe

234

all these commandments, and if you despise My statutes, or if your soul abhors My judgments, so that you do not perform all My commandments, but break My covenant, I also will do this to you: I will even appoint terror over you, wasting disease and fever which shall consume the eyes and cause sorrow of heart. And you shall sow your seed in vain, for your enemies shall eat it. I will set My face against you and you shall be defeated by your enemies. Those who hate you shall reign over you, and you shall flee when no one pursues you. And after all this, if you do not obey me, then I will punish you seven times more for your sins. I will break the pride of your power; I will make your heavens like iron and your earth like bronze. And your strength shall be spent in vain.... (Lev. 26:3–4,14–20)

It is God, Himself, who will bring these judgments. There can be no blaming Satan for the hand of God. "I, the Lord, do all these things."

God's Discipline in Judges

In Judges, we see God's repeated use of war to discipline and test His people. This period occurred after the Israelites entered Canaan and God gave them specific instructions to destroy the pagan nations inhabiting the land. The Israelites were not to make covenants with them; nor were they to intermarry with them. The Israelites were to utterly destroy these nations both as judgment on the nations for their rebellion and to protect the Israelites from being led back into idolatry, a habit to which they were particularly prone.

The Israelites made some half-hearted attempts at obedience, but their fleshly desires led them to do the very things God wanted them to avoid. Before the conquest of Canaan could be complete,

Then the children of Israel did evil in the sight of the Lord, and served the Baals [foreign gods]; and they forsook the Lord God of their fathers, who had brought them out of the land of Egypt; and they followed other gods from among the gods of the people who were all around them, and they bowed down to them, and they provoked the Lord to anger. They forsook the Lord and served Baal and the Ashtoreths. And the anger of the Lord was hot against Israel. So He delivered them into the hands of plunderers who despoiled them; and He sold them into the hands of their enemies all around, so that they could no longer stand before their enemies. Wherever they went out, the hand of the Lord was against them for calamity, as the Lord had said. (Judges 2:11–15)

The word "calamity" here is the same as the word used in Isaiah 45:7, *ra*. In the *King James Version*, it is translated "evil." Thus, the KJV translates this passage as, "Whithersoever they went out, the hand of the Lord was against them for evil, as the Lord had said." This is not Satan bringing calamity under God's permissive will. It is God Himself bringing these judgments to accomplish His perfect will. Once again, He is using something that is humanly interpreted as bad, or evil, to accomplish His purposes, which are always perfect and good.

The result is played out through the book of Judges. In Judges 3, God began a long period in which He used pagan nations to judge His people: "So the children of Israel did evil in the sight of the Lord. They forgot the Lord their God, and served the Baals and Asherahs. Therefore the anger of the Lord was hot against Israel, and He sold them into the hand of the Cushan-Rishathaim king of Mesopotamia" (Judges 3:7–8). Then, after God rose up Othniel to deliver them, they went back to their old ways. "So the Lord strengthened Eglon king of Moab against Israel, because they had done evil in the sight of the Lord" (Judges 3:12). After God used Ehud to deliver Israel from Eglon, the Israelites were faithful for 80 years. But as soon as Ehud was dead, "the children of Israel again did evil in the sight of the Lord. So the Lord sold them into the hand of Jabin king of Canaan" (Judges 4:1–2). God used the Midianites to discipline the Israelites in Judges 6. And so it went for another several hundred years.

There are those who would protest, saying, "That was the Old Testament. We are under the New Covenant. God doesn't do that anymore." I would remind them that the character of God never changes (Heb. 13:8) and that the New Covenant has nothing to do with God's character. It has to do with the age of grace, the eternal salvation purchased for us by the atoning blood of Jesus Christ, which replaced the sacrificial system and the age of the law. Consider God's judgment on Ananias and his wife for lying to the Holy Spirit in Acts 5. The punishment was death.

Still, there are others who would bristle at the suggestion that God brings judgment on the innocent as well as the guilty, saying, "That's not fair!" I would remind them that we are all living by the grace of God, and by God's grace alone. For the Bible says, "No, there is none righteous. No, not one" (Romans 3:10) and "the wages of sin is death" (Romans 6:23). God is loving, but He is also righteous and holy. No matter how good we think we are, we are still sinful and imperfect. How and when He chooses to judge His people *is* perfect and fits into His perfect plan. Human beings cannot see into the hearts of men. Nor can we see into the future and how all things fit together. God does.

Corporate Discipline in Revelation

This provides a framework for understanding God's judgment in Revelation. In the first half of the 70th Week, God will pour out drought, famine, war, earthquakes, fire and brimstone, and other disasters upon the world. This may seem harsh, but the stakes are high—the world is about to end. People no longer have 20, 30, or 60 years to get their lives right with God. In His perfect wisdom, God will use the most drastic techniques to get the world's attention because He loves them.

God will never pour His wrath upon His children. To His children, it is promised, "For God has not appointed us to wrath, but to obtain salvation through our Lord Jesus Christ" (1 Thess. 5:9). God will, however, discipline and *refine* His people, and He has until the Day of the Lord, which occurs after the opening of the sixth seal, to do it (Phil. 1:6).

For Christians, the period of judgment that takes place during the seals can be compared to cramming before a test. Many put off allowing God to sculpt and mold them, saying, "I've got my whole life to do that. I'll get around to it later." But once the Antichrist confirms the seven-year covenant with Israel, the world as we know it will only be around for another seven years. For "pre-rapture" Christians, their time will be even less. God wants us to have the maximum blessings in heaven, and these blessings can only be obtained through tests of faith and obedience. By putting us through fire, He is not unfairly putting His children through a judgment designed for the world. He is giving laggard students a chance to catch up and good students a chance to excel. He is giving all of His children an opportunity to gain treasures that neither the moth nor rust can destroy. How much He loves us!

Some Christians might protest, saying, "But I live a holy life. I don't need to be put through the fire." Once again, this reveals the limits of our human perspective. No matter how we appear in our own eyes, our righteousness is as filthy rags to God (Isaiah 64:6). Plus, there are many Christians who have spent their whole lives cushioned by material comforts, padded from the world by the church, and so spiritually cautious that they do not step out of their comfort zones to stretch themselves for God. When their works go through the fire at the judgment seat of Christ, will they shine like precious stones? Or will they burn up as hay and stubble (1 Cor. 3:12–15)?

This was what happened to the Israelites in the time of Joshua. In spite of their unfaithfulness, God drove the Canaanites out from before them in the early years. Because the Israelites were obtaining military victories left and right, they mistook God's promises to their forefathers for their own divine right. But God exposed the truth in their hearts. He said, "I also will no longer drive before them any of the nations which Joshua left when he died, so that through them *I may test Israel*, whether they will keep the ways of the Lord, to walk in them as their fathers kept them, or not" (Judges 2:21–22).

So will be the first six seals of Revelation. This will be a time of unparalleled testing for the Body of Christ. It is easy to follow the commandments of God in times of plenty. It is easy to confess faith in Jesus when your life is not at stake. It is during times of stress and persecution that the heart is tested. When all is laid bare, will God's people stand tall for Him? When they themselves have little, will they share with the lost? Under persecution of the Antichrist, will they risk martyrdom to share the gospel? Or will they capitulate to the Antichrist, or run and hide? It is no wonder that Rev. 3:10 calls the six seals the hour of "testing," "trial," or "temptation."[135]

---

[135] Many have tried to re-interpret the words in The Lord's Prayer, "lead us not into temptation," saying that this cannot mean what it seems, since it is not God who leads us into temptation, but Satan. However, God's tempting of the Israelites clearly shows that He *does* lead His people into tempting situations, but the word used for temptation, *peirasmos*, does not necessarily mean being led to sin. It can also be translated "trial" or "proof." This kind of temptation, *peirasmos*, is not for evil but for good.

Many people mistakenly see the first six seals as focused on the world. They are not. God's judgment of the unsaved does not begin with the seal judgments, but later, during the Day of the Lord. The seal judgments are for His children. Read again the letters to the seven churches and the commands of Jesus for the five wayward churches: the loveless church, the corrupt church, the dead church, the compromising church, and the lukewarm church. "Repent," He says, "And overcome, and I will give you the crown of life." He wants to give us one last chance to get it right, to get an "A" on the test.

(Any temptation to sin does not come from God, but from the sin of our own hearts—James 1:14-16). Along these lines, it is interesting that the Church of England has debated changing the Lord's Prayer from "Lead us not into temptation" to, "Save us from the time of trial." *The New American Bible* reads, "Do not subject us to the final test"; and the Anglican Church is debating whether to use the same language. *The New English Bible* has the following note on this verse: "Jewish apocalyptic writings speak of a period of severe trial before the end of the age, sometimes called the "Messianic woes." This petition asks that the disciples be spared that *final test* [sic]."

20

What's the Rush?

It is appointed to men to die once, but after this, the judgment.
—Heb. 9:27

We do not know the day nor the hour of the rapture, but the Bible gives us a general timetable for when this event will be. The return of Jesus, and therefore the rapture, will occur after the midpoint of the 70th Week of Daniel, after the revealing of the Antichrist in the yet-to-be-rebuilt Jewish temple, after the persecution of the saints during the Great Tribulation, and after the cosmic disturbances of the sixth seal.

The implications of this are important. For those who are not believers or who are sitting on the fence at that time, this will be a time of unparalleled proof of the authority of the Word of God. In this unique time in history, we will literally be able to watch the events of prophecy unfold like reading chapters in a book. This is also why the end-times Church should be a preaching Church, seizing opportunities more boldly than at any other time in history because we know the time is short.

Jesus repeatedly referred to the end times as like the days of Noah. Noah knew that time was running out, that his worldly neighbors would soon lose their lives under the judgment of God. Noah knew, too, that there was only one door by which men could be saved. He did not keep this knowledge to himself, but was "a preacher of righteousness," calling a lost and dying world to repentance. The certainty of God's impending judgment gave Noah a boldness he would not have otherwise had, a willingness to risk everything to be obedient to the word of God. If Noah risked all for the gospel because he knew the end was near, how much more burdened for souls should the end-times Church be?

But it isn't just to unbelievers that the truth should be preached. Many believers will need encouragement, too. Too many, even in the Church, are spiritually unprepared for the 70th Week. They are not grounded in the Word of God and are relying on a pretribulation rapture to save them. Thus, when they suddenly find themselves in the midst of world war, natural disasters, famine, and persecution under the Antichrist, there is a danger that they will stumble, questioning the Word of God, even perish. It is the responsibility of those who do know the Word of God, who do know the truth about the sequence of end-times events, to lift them up during these perilous times.

> And some of those of understanding shall fall, to refine them, purify them, and make them white, until the time of the end; because it is still for the appointed time. (Dan. 11:35)

These will be dangerous times, and preaching the Word of God will be dangerous too. It could cost believers their homes, their jobs, their possessions, and even their lives. Even so, as we await the trumpet of God, will we be bold? Will we be witnessing at work? At the grocery store? On street corners, with the Bible in one hand and the newspaper splashed with events of fulfilled prophecy in the other? As we watch the rise of the Antichrist, counting the days until he defiles the Temple Mount, what will our earthly treasures profit when we know *for certain* that the Lord will return in just a few months? or years? The closer the time comes, the bolder we should become.

If we do not lift up the name of the Lord Jesus to a dying world, we must ask ourselves why.

• **Do we value our material possessions?**

If so, Jesus said, "Do not lay up for yourselves treasures on earth, where moth and rust destroy and where thieves break in and steal; but lay up for yourselves treasures in heaven, where neither moth nor rust destroys. For where your treasure is, there your heart will be also" (Matt. 6:19–21).

• **Do we value our lives?**

If so, Jesus said, "Do not fear those who kill the body but cannot kill the soul. But rather fear Him who is able to destroy both soul and body in hell....He who finds his life will lose it, and he who loses his life for My sake will find it" (Matt. 10:28,39).

• **Are we afraid of rejection?**

If so, Jesus said, "The disciple is not above his teacher, nor a servant above his master....Therefore do not fear them. For there is nothing covered that will not be revealed, and hidden that will not be known. Whatever I tell you in the dark, speak in the light; and what you hear in the ear, preach on the housetops" (Matt. 10:24, 26–28).

• **Are we afraid of being shunned by our friends and families?**

If so, Jesus said, "I did not come to bring peace but a sword. For I have come to set a man against his father, a daughter against her mother, and a daughter-in-law against her mother-in-law, and a man's enemies will be those of his own household. He who loves father or mother more than Me is not worthy of Me. And he who loves son or daughter more than Me is not worthy of Me" (Matt. 10:34–37).

• **Do we think that preaching is not our responsibility?**

If so, Jesus said, "Go therefore and make disciples of all the nations, baptizing them in the name of the Father and of the Son and of the Holy Spirit" (Matt. 28:19–20). This was not a suggestion, but an order.

• **Do we not truly believe the gospel that we have professed?**

Is it possible that we have sat in church year after year without ever *really* trusting Jesus as our Savior? If we don't know, trust, and love Him as our own Savior, it isn't likely that we will risk our lives and security to lead others to Him. If so, it's not too late. Paul wrote, "If you confess with your mouth the Lord Jesus, and believe that God has raised Him from the dead, you will be saved. For with the heart one believes unto righteousness, and with the mouth confession is made unto salvation" (Romans 10:9–10).

According to a recent George Barna survey, two-thirds of Americans profess to be religious and 62% claim to have made a personal commitment to Christ, and yet there are many barren lives with no fruit. God is not fooled, nor is He mocked (Gal. 6:7). Jesus made it clear that mere profession is not enough:

Many will say to Me in that day, "Lord, Lord, have we not prophesied in Your name, cast out demons in Your name and done many wonders in Your name?" And then I will declare to them, "I never knew you; depart from Me, you who practice lawlessness!" (Matt. 7:22)

How do we know whether we truly know Jesus as our personal Savior? He has given us a simple test: "Not everyone who says to Me, 'Lord, Lord' shall enter the kingdom of heaven, but he who does the will of My Father in heaven" (v. 21). Throughout the book of 1 John, the Apostle John gave a variety of tests based on the fruit that is born in our lives. The seals will be a time of spiritual inventory. God will give us one last chance to make sure that our hearts are pure before Him. It is to our shame if we miss it!

Prophecy Is Not a Timer

But while the seals will provide proof of the authority and infallibility of the Word of God, the Bible also makes it clear that now, not later, is the time to submit your heart to Jesus. "For now is the day of your salvation" (2 Cor. 6:2). Don't think that you can use prophecy as a timer, telling you how long you can wait.

I remember a friend of mine who had been convicted mightily of the Lord, saying, "I want to give my heart to Jesus, but not right now. There are a few sins that I want to commit first." Her pastor gave her a stern warning: When the Lord calls, obey. Will you say "no" to Almighty God? Now that friend is a blessed saint, forever grateful that her uncommitted sins did not separate her from her Savior. True repentance is required for salvation, and true repentance cannot be put off.

I have another friend who started out much the same, but his end has been very different. Several years ago, he was a professing but backslidden Christian. For a period of time, he was convicted mightily of his sins and felt the strong love of the Lord pulling him back. But unlike my other friend, he found his current and future sins too attractive and decided to wait. "I'll do it later," he said. As he waited, his heart continued to harden. The Lord, in His abundant mercy, continued to reach out, but the harder the conviction came, the harder my friend fought against it. "I'll do it later," he said. Soon, his heart was so hard that he had no interest

243

in God and could no longer hear the Holy Spirit calling him. What a terrible place to be!

The Big Lie

"I'll do it later." That is a lie from Satan. The lie is that we will *want* to do it later. The truth is that the longer we wait, the less likely we are to do it. Sadly, we can even harden our hearts to such a point that, should the Antichrist himself stand in the Temple Mount, we could not repent, even if we wanted to.

One heartbreaking tale came from a young man who had resisted and insulted the Holy Spirit so many times that, on his deathbed, he looked up into the face of the doctor and cried, "I have missed it—at last!"

> "What have you missed?" inquired the physician.
> "I have missed it—at last," again he repeated.
> "Missed what?"
> "Doctor, I have missed the salvation of my soul."
> "Oh, say it is not so. Do you remember the thief on the cross?"
> "Yes, I remember. And I remember that he never said to the Holy Spirit, 'Go your way!' But I did. And now He is saying to me, 'Go your way!'"
> He lay gasping a while. Then, looking up with a vacant, staring eye, he said, "I was awakened and was anxious about my soul a little time ago. *But I did not want to be saved then.* Something seemed to say to me, 'Don't put it off. Make sure of salvation.' I said to myself, 'I will postpone it.' I knew I ought not to do it. I resolved, however, to dismiss the subject for the present. *I resisted and insulted the Holy Spirit.* Now—I have missed it!"
> "You remember," said the doctor, "that there were some who came at the eleventh hour."
> "My eleventh hour," [the lad] rejoined, "was when I had that call of the Spirit. I have had none since—and shall not have. I am given over to be lost." Then he buried his face in the pillow, and again exclaimed in agony and horror, "Oh, I have missed it at last!" and died.
> "Now is the accepted time!" (2 Cor. 6:2). "Today, if you will hear His voice, do not harden your hearts" (Heb. 3:7).[136]

The Bible is clear—we cannot choose the day of our salvation. Too many people think that getting right with God is

---

[136] *Voices from the Edge of Eternity*, compiled by John Meyers (Barbour Press, 1998), p. 52.

something that can be done at their convenience. This is one of the paradoxes in the Bible. On one hand, Jesus promised, "the one who comes to Me I will by no means cast out" (John 6:37). And yet, He also gave the solemn warning, "No one can come to Me unless the Father who sent Me draws him" (John 6:44). God is loving and full of mercy, but He is holy and righteous also. There may be a time when, because of the hardness of our hearts, He ceases to draw us to Himself (Psalm 32:6).

The Unforgivable Sin

When God calls, we must obey. Jesus told His followers that all of the sins of men will be forgiven, except one: "Therefore I say to you, every sin and blasphemy will be forgiven men, but the blasphemy against the Spirit will not be forgiven men" (Matt. 12:31). He repeats this warning in Mark 3:28–29: "Assuredly, I say to you, all sins will be forgiven the sons of men, and whatever blasphemies they may utter; but he who blasphemes against the Holy Spirit never has forgiveness, but is subject to eternal condemnation."

Jesus is not referring to a "once and done" event, but rather to a lifestyle of continual hardening of the heart. It is the Holy Spirit who convicts us of sin and calls us to repentance before God. Blasphemy of the Holy Spirit, or resistance to His call, puts a person in a position forever outside God's grace. Do not try to choose the moment of your own salvation. Do not harden your heart against the calling of God. For once He has laid before us His own life as ransom for our sins, "How shall we escape if we neglect so great a salvation?" (Heb. 2:3).

One of the threads that can be seen in many deathbed testimonies like the one above is that people often see clearly into life after death. Some believers actually see Jesus or the angels, standing in heavenly lights, beckoning to them, or holding their hands. Some unbelievers see the flames, the despair, and know that they have missed their chance at redemption.

This is the pattern set by the days of Noah. For just as in the days of Noah—when God gave the lost *certainty* as to the truth of His Word—it was too late. Similarly, we ought not wait until we see the six seals begin to appear to submit our lives to the Savior. Jesus wants us to act now, on faith. "For blessed are they who have not seen, and yet have believed" (John 20:29). Those who harden their hearts today, saying, "I will give my heart to Jesus

245

when I see the signs appear" cannot be sure that, on the day of their choosing, salvation will be found.

There will be many who would protest this point, saying, "I would never be so blind as all that." But you may not have a choice. For Paul warns that, following the rise of the Antichrist, God will send a strong delusion upon those with rebellious hearts:

> And for this reason God will send them strong delusion, that they should believe the lie, that they all may be condemned who did not believe the truth but had pleasure in unrighteousness. (2 Thess. 2:11–12)

I Want to Be in Philadelphia

What about people who are already believers? These warnings have relevance to us, as well. Jesus was very clear that there will be seven churches during the six seals, only one of which—the Church of Philadelphia, the loving church—will be "kept from the hour of trial" (Rev. 3:10).

Why does Jesus promise to keep the Church of Philadelphia from the hour of trial and not the others? "I know your works. See, I have set before you an open door, and no one can shut it: for you have a little strength, have kept My word, and have not denied My name....Because you have kept My command to persevere, I also will keep you from the hour of trial which shall come upon the whole world, to test those who dwell on the earth" (Rev. 3:8–9).

When the rapture comes, all believers will be taken, no matter their walks with the Lord. According to pretrib theology, there will be no repercussions. When the trumpet blows, all bets will be off, whether believers' hearts are in full submission to the Lord or not. But the Bible teaches that there *will* be repercussions to an unsanctified life and an unsubmitted heart. The Church *will* be here during the first part of Daniel's 70th Week and there will be a time of refinement by fire. Only the Church of Philadelphia will be kept from its most ferocious effects. Believers who think they can make a "deathbed conversion" and enter the Church of Philadelphia at that time are deluding themselves. Jesus' praise that "you have kept my command to persevere" is not something Christians can grab onto at the last minute. It is a reward for faithful service.

Consider the parable of the virgins in Matthew 25. Some were prepared. Others were not. They all had oil, some little, some much. Some had chosen to look ahead and prepare. Others had taken the opportunity for granted. How are we in our own Christian lives? Are we assuming that we can ride on the backs of our friends and families? That we can "borrow" our salvation or faithfulness from others? Are we trusting our membership in a church to save or sanctify us? You can't borrow eternal things when you come up short without them.

Taking Personal Inventory

For unbelievers, this will be the most perilous time of all. At the breaking of the first seal, the trial will begin. For the Church, it will be a time of testing and evangelistic outreach that will last more than three-and-one-half years. But at the sound of the trumpet, all bets will be off. Christ will take those who are prepared. Others will not have an opportunity to see Him coming in the clouds and then suddenly decide they want to be saved. Although their salvation may come afterwards, they may die of disease, of starvation, from natural disasters, or from martyrdom. In Matthew 24, Jesus uses words of immediacy, like "then" and "at that time." He is coming—soon—and for most of the world, it will come as a surprise. Salvation is not something you go out and get at the last minute after you've been caught napping.

Which group are you in?

Adam Clarke, an eminent 19th century scholar, writes: "This parable, or something very like it, is found in the Jewish records ...We read thus: 'Our wise men ... say, "Repent whilst thou hast strength to do it, whilst thy lamp burns, and thy oil is not extinguished; for if thy lamp be gone out, thy oil will profit thee nothing"'... Then he quotes from the Jewish Midrash: "The holy blessed God said to Israel, 'My sons, repent whilst the gates of repentance stand open; for I receive a gift at present, but when I shall sit in judgment, in the age to come, I will receive none.'"[137]

Yes, I would have to agree with Clarke: "What an awful thing to be summoned to appear before the Judge of the quick and the dead!"

---

[137] *Clarke's Commentary* (N.Y.: Abingdon Press), p. 237.

But for those who know Jesus Christ as their Savior, who are His faithful servants, the end for them is glory:

> And I heard a loud voice from heaven saying, "Behold, the tabernacle of God is with men, and He will dwell with them, and they shall be His people. God Himself will be with them and be their God. And God will wipe away every tear from their eyes; there shall be no more death, nor sorrow, nor crying. There shall be no more pain, for the former things have passed away." Then He who sat on the throne said, "Behold, I will make all things new." And he said to me, "Write, for these words are true and faithful." (Rev. 21:3–5)

21

Signs of the Times:
End-Times Prophecy Fulfilled
In This Generation

When Jesus comes, there will be no second chances. Either you will know Him as your Savior and be ready to go with Him, or you will be left behind. Those who are left will either come to belief in Christ and face martyrdom at the hands of the Antichrist, or they will face the wrath and fiery judgment of God.

Many people know that getting right with God is important, but they also think it is something that they have until just before they die to get done. Kind of like cleaning the house before the relatives arrive—important, but not absolutely necessary until the very last minute. This creates a nice mental comfort zone before many people feel that they have to spiff up for the Almighty. Scripture clearly and repeatedly warns against the folly of this kind of thinking, and for the first time in history, we are seeing signs in the world around us that we might not have as much time as we thought we did.

On the Mount of Olives, Jesus' disciples asked Him, "What are the signs of Your coming and the end of the age?" Jesus answered by speaking at length about the series of events that would precede His physical return to earth. He said these events will be so clear, so recognizable, that when they occur, people will look up, expecting to see Him emerge from the clouds at any moment. This is not a lifestyle of waiting and anticipating, although this is something all believers should do, but the kind of literal expectation that comes from hearing footsteps around the corner or someone's key enter the lock (Luke 21:28).

Christians began looking for Jesus the day of His ascension, and with each series of cataclysmic natural disasters, wars, and moral abominations, they searched the prophetic scriptures, wondering if the time had come. Throughout history, the world has experienced "millennial fever," and at times, this has reached a fevered pitch; but the sky has remained empty. The reason is that, despite the terrible nature of the events the world is experiencing—from devastating plagues in Europe˙ in the Middle Ages to catastrophic world wars in the twentieth century—these events do not represent the kind of clear, recognizable prophetic fulfillment that Jesus said they would.

In 1948, everything changed. Almost two thousand years after Jesus spoke on the Mount of Olives, the United Nations formally recognized Israel as a nation. This event, foretold by the prophets as the watershed event for the return of the Messiah, turned the prophetic world electric. In *The Beginning of the End*, John Hagee wrote of the moment, as a young boy, that he and his father listened to the announcement on the radio. "My father put the book he was holding down on the table and said nothing for a long moment. I knew from the look in his eyes that he had been profoundly moved. Then he looked at me and said, 'We have just heard the most important prophetic message that will ever be delivered until Jesus Christ returns to earth.'"[138]

Today, speculation about whether or not we are entering the end times is no longer necessary. Since the rebirth of Israel, the fulfillment of prophecy has been so literal, so rapid, that there can be no question that we are entering into a new phase of human history. Because the groundwork for end-times prophecy is being laid so quickly, many believe that the return of Christ could happen in our lifetimes.

Here are just a few examples:

Rebirth of Israel

There are many end-times prophecies, but there is always one constant among them. The nation of Israel is center stage. Following the destruction of the temple by the Romans in A.D. 70, God disciplined the Jews for their rebellion by scattering them

---

[138] *Beginning of the End*, p. 92.

across the earth. But the scriptures also promised that Israel would be regathered at the time of the end.[139]

> In the latter years, you will come into the land of those brought back from the sword and gathered from many people on the mountains of Israel, which had long been desolate. (Eze. 38:8)

Moreover, the scriptures tell us that the event would occur suddenly, in a single day:

> Shall the earth be made to give birth in one day? Or shall a nation be born at once? For as soon as Zion was in labor, she gave birth to her children. (Isaiah 66:8)

Following the destruction of the temple in A.D. 70, Israel was passed from conquering nation to conquering nation for 2,000 years. After the horrific slaughter of 15 million Jews by Hitler and Stalin, the idea of re-establishing a Jewish state seemed impossible, if not downright ridiculous. Then, against all odds, the Zionist movement took the birth of Israel into labor in the early 1900s. Following the Israelis' successful War of Independence, the nation was formally recognized by the United Nations on May 15, 1948. Overnight—in a single day—Israel again became a nation, just as Isaiah said it would.

Now, for the first time since the first century, there is a literal nation of Israel with which the Antichrist can confirm a seven-year covenant, setting the 70th Week into motion (Dan. 9:27). This critical end-times prophecy has been literally fulfilled.

---

[139] In the chapter, "Israel, O Israel," Hal Lindsey, in his classic, *The Late Great Planet Earth* (Zondervan Publishing House, 1970) lays an excellent foundation for the need for the nation of Israel to be reborn prior to the return of Jesus Christ. Although I disagree with many of Lindsey's theological conclusions, his chapter on the need for the rebirth of Israel is excellent.

Israeli Control of Jerusalem

> Seventy weeks have been decreed for your people and your holy city...." (Dan. 9:24)

The ancient prophets declared that, at the Messiah's return, Israel would not only be its own sovereign state, but that the Jews would be in control of Jerusalem. Although Israel was given nation status in 1948, it was not until the Six-Day War of 1967 that the entire city of Jerusalem was reincorporated into the infant nation. Once again, the return of Jerusalem to Israeli control is an end-times prophecy that has been literally fulfilled.

Return of the Jews to Their Homeland

> Therefore, behold, the days are coming, says the Lord, that they shall no longer say, "As the Lord lives who brought up the children of Israel from the land of Egypt," but, "As the Lord lives who brought up and led the descendants of the house of Israel from the north country and from all the countries where I had driven them." And they shall dwell in their own land. (Jer. 23:7–8)

Not only has today's generation witnessed the revival of the Jewish state, but it has also seen the fulfillment of another end-times prophecy—the mass migration of Jews to Israel from all over the world, especially Russia ("the land of the north"). Jeremiah declared that, not only would the Jews return to Israel, but this return would be so dramatic that it would cause the people to focus more on this event than their exodus from Egypt. Today, in our generation, the Zionist movement has led Jews from all parts of the world to emigrate to Israel by the hundreds of thousands, largely Jews from Russia ("the north country") fleeing persecution under Soviet rule. And with the secularization of the modern Jewish community, few still believe that the Torah reflects their national history. Thus, it is truly the second exodus—not the first—that is remembered, just as the prophets foretold.

The Rebuilding of the Jewish Temple

And forces shall be mustered by him, and they shall defile the sanctuary fortress; then they shall take away the daily sacrifices, and place there the abomination of desolation. (Dan. 11:31)

Because of transgression, an army was given over to the horn [the Antichrist] to oppose the daily sacrifices; and he cast truth down to the ground...and prospered. (Dan. 8:12)

Since the destruction of the Jewish temple in 70 A.D., Jews have had no place for their ceremonial worship. Yet, end-times prophecy tells us that Israel will resume its traditional animal sacrifices prior to (or during) the rise of the Antichrist, since he will bring an end to these sacrifices at the midpoint of the 70th Week. For this prophecy to be fulfilled, Israel must rebuild the temple and reinstate the Levitical system.

Today, under leadership of organizations such as The Jerusalem Temple Foundation and the Temple Institute, plans for rebuilding the temple have begun. A group called the Faithful of the Temple Mount has built a detailed model and is taking donations to fund the rebuilding. Many of the ceremonial articles used in Solomon's temple have been uncovered by archeological digs and the rest are in the process of being reproduced, including the high priest's breastplate, robe, and gold crown, the clothing for the temple priests, the gold lampstand, the bronze laver, and the sterling silver trumpets.[140] By the time the second edition of this book had been released, the Faithful of the Temple Mount had announced the anointing of the two marble cornerstones for the temple and had identified many Levites to serve in the temple. According to its Web site (templemountfaithful.org), the invitation to attend was open to all:

At the dedication ceremony, held October 4, 2001 [the Feast of Tabernacles], the Movement's architect will present the first plans for the Third Temple as well as a large model. The

---

[140] Grant Jeffrey, *Messiah: War in the Middle East and the Road to Armageddon* (Frontier Research Publications, Toronto, Ontario, 1994), pp. 214-233.

golden altar of incense and vessels for the Third Temple will also be brought. Priests dressed in the original Biblical garments will lead the event followed by Levites playing musical instruments in front of many pilgrims and marchers.

Twenty or thirty years ago, the rebuilding of the temple would have been impossible. Today, this end-times prophecy is in the process of being literally fulfilled.

Preaching the Gospel to All Nations

And this gospel of the kingdom will be preached in all the world as a witness to all the nations, and then the end will come. (Matt. 24:14)

For nineteen centuries, this was seen as a metaphor. With human travel limited to foot, horseback, and ship, evangelizing every nation of the world was not possible in a literal sense. Even in 1900, the gospel had to be preached by mouth, letter, or book. Today—in our generation—the gospel has reached into every corner of the globe with satellite television, radio, and the Internet. The Bible has been translated into more than 3,850 languages, representing approximately 98% of the world's population. Christian radio can be heard in 360 languages, reaching 78% of the world's listeners. Evangelists are taking videos of the gospel of Jesus Christ into remote villages in the native language of the peoples. By dividing the globe into what it calls "[one] million population area targets" (MPATs), The Jesus Film Project hoped to show its film to 5 billion people in 271 languages and 1,000 dialects by 2000.[141] As of November, 2001, the organization had more than doubled its language goal, reaching 4.6 billion people in 700 languages. And while it has not yet reached every *language group* in the world, The Jesus Film Project claims that it has reached every *nation*. For the first time in history, this prophecy is in the process of being literally fulfilled.

---

[141] Paul Eschelman, *I Just Saw Jesus* (published by The Jesus Film Project, 1999), p. 9.

The Gospel Reaching All Nations
Through the Jesus Film

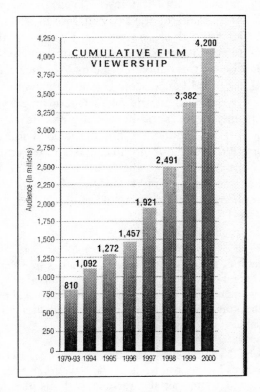

Cumulative Film Viewership of *The Jesus Film* provided courtesy of
The Jesus Film Project and reproduced from its promotional booklet
One Chance to See Jesus, p. 5.

Return to Sanhedrin Laws

Therefore when you see the abomination of desolation
spoken of by Daniel the prophet, standing in the holy place...
let those who are in Judea flee to the mountains. Let him who
is on the housetop not go down to take anything out of his
house. And let him who is in the field not go back to get his
clothes....And pray that your flight may not be on the
Sabbath. (Matt. 24:15–20)

To us, Jesus' command is a riddle. However, to the Jews of the first century, it made perfect sense because biblical Jews were governed by ancient Sanhedrin laws. These laws, which were rabbinical interpretations of the laws of Moses, stated that Jews could not travel more than one thousand paces on the Sabbath since this would constitute work. Jesus' command, "pray that your flight may not be on the Sabbath," seems to indicate that, during the 70th Week, Israel will once again be under the Sanhedrin law.

In our generation, Israel is, in fact, returning to these laws. Israel is passing more and more religious laws, especially regarding the Sabbath regulations, and the Israel Torah Foundation and other orthodox religious groups in Israel are calling for the formation of the Sanhedrin in the Sixth Millennium, which they believe will enable them to build the Third Temple.[142] Yet another end-times prophecy is in the process of being fulfilled.

The Revived Roman Empire

And the fourth kingdom shall be as strong as iron, inasmuch as iron breaks in pieces and shatters everything.... Whereas you saw the feet and toes, partly of potter's clay and partly of iron, the kingdom shall be divided; yet the strength of the iron shall be in it. (Dan. 2:40–41)

And behold a fourth beast, dreadful and terrible, exceedingly strong. It had huge iron teeth; it was devouring, breaking in pieces, and trampling the residue with its feet. It was different from all the beasts that were before it, and it had ten horns. I was considering the horns, and there was another horn, a little one, coming up among them...in this horn were eyes like the eyes of a man, and a mouth speaking pompous words...because of transgression, an army was given over to the horn to oppose the daily sacrifices." (Dan. 7:7–8; 8:12)

During the height of its power, the Roman Empire stretched from Ireland to Egypt and included Turkey, Iran, and Iraq. The Bible tells us that, prior to Jesus' Second Coming, political power will be held by a revived "Roman Empire," which will be made up of a confederation of 10 nations covering much, if not all, of the

---

[142] Ibid., p. 150.

territory of the original empire. The Antichrist will arise from one of these nations and be given power over its massive military, political structure, and economy.[143] Today, many believe that we are witnessing the rapid formation of the Revived Roman Empire in the form of a united Europe, which reconstitutes many of the lands previously held by Rome. In fact, the European Economic Union (EU) is based on the Treaty of Rome (1957).[144]

Covenant With Israel

Then he shall confirm a covenant with many for one week; but in the middle of the week he shall bring an end to sacrifice and offering." (Dan. 9:27)

The 70th Week will not begin mysteriously. When a world leader confirms a seven-year covenant with Israel, we will know that it has begun. If the European Union is the 10-nation confederacy referred to by the prophet Daniel, then it must unite its political and military power to allow the Antichrist to make this covenant. This is happening today. In addition to uniting the countries' currencies, the original plan for the creation of the European Union called for a European Political Union that would involve the creation of a European Defense Army and a European Foreign Policy.[145] Preparation for the fulfillment of this prophecy

---

[143] For a detailed look at this prophecy, see *Messiah: War in the Middle East and the Road to Armageddon*, Chapters 4, 5.

[144] Not all prophecy experts accept this interpretation. By tracing the lineage of Noah's sons Ham, Shem, and Japheth from Genesis 10, Robert Van Kampen developed a theory that the eighth and final beast empire of Satan, the 10-nation confederacy of Revelation, will be entirely of Japhethetic decent (from the line of Japheth). He argued strongly that this beast empire, which will be led by the Antichrist, must be determined by ancestry, not geographic location. According to this line of reasoning, the "people of the prince who is to come" are Germanic/Russian, since this is the ancestry of the peoples who formed the power base of ancient Rome (*The Sign*, pp. 117–141).

[145] In his book *Beginning of the End*, John Hagee suggests that the 1996 assassination of Israeli Prime Minister Yitzhak Rabin set the stage for this covenant by creating "peace at any price" mentality to honor the life and memory of this great leader (pp. 9-10,14). He believes that this move

comes directly from today's news headlines. Take the following report from *The Economist*: "[Since NATO's war with Kosovo, there] has been the emergence of a strong sense among the leading EU countries that they should possess a capacity for collective military actions that is separable or even separate from the ordinary structures of NATO, and thus not always dependant on the military leadership of the United States. This new sense of purpose in defense policy has coincided with formal moves to develop a 'common foreign and security policy' for the EU. The combined effect will be a movement towards a true European diplomacy backed by muscle."[146]

One-World Government

> It was granted to him to make war with the saints and to overcome them. And authority was given him over every tribe, tongue, and nation. (Rev. 13:7)

In the form of a "Revived" Roman Empire, the Antichrist will conquer much of the European and Mediterranean world and have control over nearly all of it. In many places, he will have total, autocratic power. This will require a form of what is commonly called a "one-world government," although the prophet Daniel tells us that the geographic boundaries of the Antichrist's empire will be contained in the greater area of Europe and the Middle East. His political and economic influence, however, will likely be worldwide.

Until our generation, such a massive and powerful federation of nations seemed impossible. Now we are witnessing the rising authority, power, and influence of organizations such as the United Nations, NATO, the International Monetary Fund, the World Trade Organization, the World Health Organization, International Labor Organization, and the World Court, making a

---

will primarily come from secular Zionists who are willing to compromise biblical promises of land granted to Abraham's descendants by God. Because these are secular Jews, even once God miraculously destroys the invading armies of Gog and Magog, they will prefer to make a covenant with a human being (the Antichrist) than to trust the God of their ancestors who has just delivered them.

[146] "My Continent, Right or Wrong," *The Economist*, Oct. 23, 1999.

revived Roman Empire seem puny by comparison. The common terminology used in books and magazine articles is "the New World Order," and one has only to look on the bookshelves of Christian bookstores or go to Web sites like Prophecy Central to pull up a library of information.

The Mark of the Beast

> He causes all, both small and great, rich and poor, free and slave, to receive a mark on their right hand or on their foreheads, that no one may buy or sell except one who has the mark or the name of the beast. (Rev. 13:16–17)

As part of the Antichrist's rise to power, he will cause all people within his dominion to receive a mark on their right hands or on their foreheads without which they will not be able to buy or sell. This is something possible only in our generation. At the time of Christ, a mark such as this might have been accomplished with some form of tattoo, but it would not have been possible to prevent all people from buying or selling, since a certain amount of trading could easily have been done on the underground market.

In today's global electronic society, in which the vast majority of transactions are electronic, this prophecy can finally be fulfilled. Many prophecy experts believe that the mark will be contained in a microchip. Twenty or 30 years ago, society would have been unwilling to accept such methods of electronic identification, but today we have become used to the process of scanning for conducting financial transactions and verifying our identities, whether using cards, retinas, or other body parts. The technology of biometrics, or the mapping and digitizing of our unique biological characteristics, from the patterns on the backs of our eyeballs to the way we smell, is becoming more common. In my own backyard, a fingerprint identification program is being used in three school districts to allow pupils to pay for chicken nuggets, sloppy joes, pizza, and other cafeteria meals by placing their index fingers on small scanner, where a template matches them with their electronic prints. And the technology guru of one of the morning television programs has demonstrated a retinal scanner designed for providing security for the contents of computers and laptops for as little as $200. The leap to a microchip implanted under the skin is not so great.[147]

Once again, this is a critical end-times prophecy that could be fulfilled only in this generation.

One-World Religion

And on her forehead a name was written: Mystery, Babylon the great, the mother of harlots and of the abominations of the earth. (Rev. 17:5)

---

[147] Just how close we are to seeing the fulfillment of this prophecy comes from this condensed version of a report by WorldNetDaily.com. What is particularly frightening is that this report is now four years old: "New implant technology currently used to locate lost pets has been adapted for use in humans, allowing implant wearers to emit a homing beacon, have vital bodily functions monitored, and confirm identity when making e-commerce transactions. Applied Digital Solutions, an e-business-to-business solutions provider, acquired the patent rights to the miniature digital transceiver it has named Digital Angel. The company plans to market the device for a number of uses, including as a tamper-proof means of identification for enhanced e-business security. Digital Angel sends and receives data and can be continuously tracked by global positioning satellite technology. When implanted within a body, the device is powered electromechanically through the movement of muscles and can be activated either by the wearer or by a monitoring facility. 'We believe its potential for improving individual and e-business security and enhancing the quality of life for millions of people is virtually limitless,' said ADS Chairman and Chief Executive Officer Richard Sullivan. 'Although we're in the early developmental phase, we expect to come forward with applications in many different areas, from medical monitoring to law enforcement.' Dr. Peter Zhou, chief scientist for development of the implant and president of DigitalAngel.net, Inc, a subsidiary of ADS, told WorldNetDaily the device will send a signal from the person wearing Digital Angel to either his computer or the e-merchant with whom he is doing business in order to verify his identity. In the future, said Zhou, computers may be programmed not to operate without such user identification. User verification devices requiring a live fingerprint scan are already being sold by computer manufacturers. Digital Angel takes such biometric technology a giant step further by physically joining human and machine (2000 WorldNetDaily.com).

During the Antichrist's rise to power, the world will be dominated by a false religious system the Bible calls "Mystery, Babylon the great, the mother of harlots." Many prophecy teachers refer to this as the coming "one-world religion," although the history of the Babylonian religious practices—which combined astrology and mysticism with their own brand of hedonism—indicates that this religion was very fragmented. "Mystery, Babylon" could thus be a dominant religious philosophy or an established religion.

Whatever form it takes, "Mystery, Babylon" will be pervasive throughout the world. Already we see strong acceptance of the New Age/humanist movement, with its rising interest in "spiritual awareness" and growing acceptance of astrology and mysticism, tying together many of the world's religions. We are also seeing tremendous pressure on the part of major religious groups to de-emphasize their differences (for biblical Christianity, this means disassociating from the divinity of Christ, the blood atonement, and the virgin birth) and focus on the similarities, such as compassion, decency, and respect for diversity as embodied in the philosophy of humanism.

These efforts have been accelerating in a movement called "ecumenicism." We have seen such heresies as the "United Religions 72 Hours Project," which brought together the world's religions for 72 hours of peace under the efforts of religious leaders such as the Dalai Lama alongside the Christian clergy; the Council for the Parliament of the World Religions, which brought representatives from the world's religions to "seek moral and ethical convergence"; the United Religions Initiative, a project designed to set up a united body of the world's religions to "resolve conflicts" between different faiths; and the Interfaith Alliance, a new, non-partisan, faith-based organization with supporters from over 50 faith traditions, including Muslims, Catholics, Protestants, and Jews dedicated to promoting "the positive role of religion as a healing and constructive force in politics and in public life."

One hundred years ago, the idea of one-world religion seemed preposterous. Today, we can almost hear the hoofbeats. And once the true believers are whisked away in the rapture, there will be nothing left to stop the ecumenical tide.

261

False Christs

> For many will come in My name, saying, "I am the Christ," and will deceive many.... For false christs and false prophets will rise and show great signs and wonders to deceive, if possible, even the elect. (Matt. 24:5, 24)

Jesus tells us that the end times will be characterized by false christs. Although there have been false religious systems since the fall of Adam and Eve, never before have there been so many prophesying the coming of Armageddon and claiming to be the Messiah. Just in the last few years, consider Marshall Applewhite, who led followers of the Heaven's Gate cult to commit suicide in April, 1997; the Solar Temple Cult, another UFO cult, blamed for the death of 75 members since 1994; and the Movement for the Restoration of the Ten Commandments, whose 600 members covered themselves in gasoline and went up in a fiery blaze in Uganda in March, 2000.[148]

There have been many others, including Ming Chen, leader of God's Salvation Church, who believed that his followers would dine with God in Garland, TX, in 1998, and who claims that one of his members is a reincarnation of Jesus Christ; Reverend Kim, whose intermittent demonic possessions are the foundation of his claims to be the mouthpiece of God; and the Branch Davidians, whose leader, David Koresh, called himself "the Latter Day Lamb." There have also been a rising number of incidents of visions of the Virgin Mary, creating false spiritual leadership for millions all over the world. There is even growing popularity of the "world teacher" Maitreya and his new-age prophet, Benjamin Crème (who sound eerily like the Antichrist and the false prophet, although this could be by design). Maitreya, who is being presented as a universal savior and healer, is said to have strategic ties to all major religions and the United Nations.[149]

---

[148] http://www.bible-prophecy.com/false.htm.
[149] http://www.shareintl.org/.

The Two Witnesses

> And I will give power to My two witnesses, and they will prophesy 1260 days.....Then those from the peoples, tribes, tongues, and nations will see their dead bodies three-and-one-half days, and not allow their dead bodies to be put into graves. And those who dwell on the earth will rejoice over them, make merry, and send gifts to one another, because these two prophets tormented those who dwell on the earth. (Rev. 11:3, 9–10)

John wrote about two witnesses who would stand in Jerusalem during the reign of the Antichrist and preach the gospel. They will supernaturally resist any attempts at assassination, breathe fire from their mouths, and consume their enemies until their time is fulfilled. At the appointed time, they will be killed and all of the people of the earth will see them and rejoice.

Until this generation, how could all the people of the earth see two dead bodies at the same time? Yet today, with the invention and worldwide adoption of television, we can see them on the CNN Headline News, not to mention the Internet. In fact, the NBC Nightly News recently reported that a new "Web cam" (a small electronic camera that streams video to Web sites 24 hours a day) is pointed—guess where?—at the Wailing Wall (http://aish.com/ wallcam/). There is a 24-hour, worldwide surveillance camera pointed at the exact place that the Bible says these two witnesses will stand. Once again, this lays the foundation for a critical end-times prophecy to be fulfilled.

Russia's War With Israel

> In the latter years, you [Gog—i.e. Russia] will come into the land of those brought back from the sword and gathered from many people on the mountains of Israel, which had long been desolate; they were brought out of the nations, and now all of them dwell safely. You will ascend, coming like a storm, covering the land like a cloud, you and all your troops and many peoples with you.... Persia, Ethiopia, and Libya are with them.... (Eze. 38:8, 9, 5, 6)

When prophesying about the days immediately preceding the return of Christ, Daniel envisioned an alliance of Russia and the Arab nations, particularly Iran, Iraq, and Afghanistan, that will come against Israel. This war, in which the main participants will be Gog and Magog, will be supernaturally cut short as God destroys the aggressors for their long history of persecution of His people. Although the biblical names are not familiar to most readers, historians are able to identify these nations by the regions in which the various biblical tribes settled and the names by which they were originally called. The prophecy gives the added detail that Russia will not only organize the attack, but will supply the weapons for her Arab allies.

Groundwork for the fulfillment of this prophecy has already been laid. Both regions are highly anti-Semitic; and Russia, which was responsible for destroying nine million Jews under Stalin, is the main supplier of weapons to the Middle East. The Arab nations are armed primarily with Soviet weapons (including SAM missiles, AK-47 assault rifles, M-72 tanks, RPG7 anti-tank weapons, and MiG-23 to MiG-39 fighter planes), just as the prophets foretold.[150]

Russia's loyalty lies with her Arab neighbors, as well. During the U.N.-led military action against former Balkan President Slobodan Milosevic, for example, Russia clearly stood behind the Middle Eastern countries rather than taking the side of the U.N. And during the Gulf War, Russia was repeatedly caught supplying military intelligence to Iraq against the U.N.

It is also noteworthy that Gog is identified as the land of Russia, not the larger land mass of the former U.S.S.R. The dissolution of the United Soviet Socialist Republic left Russia—the union's military giant—free to act independently. This is a giant step toward the literal fulfillment of this prophecy in our generation.

---

[150] For a detailed look at this prophecy and the underlying political and military Soviet agenda, see *Messiah: War in the Middle East and the Road to Armageddon*, Chapter 3. For a detailed explanation of how the identities of these nations were determined, see *Armageddon: Appointment With Destiny*, Chapter 7.

Revival of Babylon

> The kings of the earth who committed fornication and lived luxuriously with her will weep and lament for her, when they see the smoke of her burning, standing at a distance for fear of her torment, saying, "Alas, alas, that great city Babylon, that mighty city! For in one hour your judgment has come." (Rev. 18:9–10)

Revelation describes the revival of the ancient city of Babylon and its rise to glory in the last days (Isaiah 13:19, Revelation 18–19). Babylon is located about 20 miles from Baghdad, the capital of Iraq. Although the city sat in ruin for thousands of years, before the U.S.-led war with Iraq, the country's former president, Saddam Hussein, was reported to have spent in the neighborhood of $1 billion to rebuild it, from the famous hanging gardens and the amazing underground water system to the temple of the pagan god Marduk,[151] just as the prophets foretold.

Incidentally, in another prophecy, God promises that He will bring utter destruction on Babylon during the Day of the Lord. His method? The streams will "[turn] to pitch and the dust thereof into brimstone, and the land thereof shall become burning pitch" (Isaiah 34:8–9). Recently, it was discovered that Babylon was built over an underground lake of asphalt and oil, revealing that God has already provided the fuel for its demise.[152]

Rise of Earthquakes and Natural Disasters

> And there will ... [be] earthquakes in various places." (Matt. 24:7)

> ...And there were noises and thunderings and lightnings, and there was a great earthquake, such a mighty and great earthquake as had not occurred since men were on the earth; now the great city was divided into three parts, and the cities of the nations fell.... (Rev. 16:18–19)

---

[151] For a detailed look at this prophecy, see *Messiah: War in the Middle East and the Road to Armageddon*, Chapter 5.

[152] *Armageddon: Appointment With Destiny*, p. 278.

Jesus told us that the 70th Week will be characterized by an unusual frequency and severity of earthquakes all over the globe, with earthquakes strong enough to level entire cities. Although there have always been natural disasters, something strange is happening in our generation. Seismological records indicate that, since 1950—just after the birth of Israel—earthquakes in the range of 6.0 or higher have increased exponentially. John Hagee reports that, in the seventh century, historians recorded 37 earthquakes. In the 15th century, they recorded 115 earthquakes. In the 16th century, they recorded 253 earthquakes. This rose to 640 in the 18th century and 2,119 in the 19th century. Between 1983 and 1992, the number of earthquakes rose from 2,588 to 4,084. [153]

While some may argue that this can be attributed simply to better reporting, prophecy experts argue that, because of their severity, earthquakes in the range of 6.0 or higher have always been accurately and scrupulously tracked. Therefore, this recorded increase is not due to better reporting, but reflects an actual—and exponential—increase in earthquake activity.

Grant Jeffrey also uses earthquakes to show how God is setting the stage for this prophecy to be literally fulfilled. His approach is to watch the number of "killer" earthquakes (defined as 6.5 or higher on the Richter scale):

Rise in the Number Killer Earthquakes

Decade	Number of Major Quakes
1890 to 1899	1
1900 to 1909	1
1910 to 1919	3
1920 to 1929	2
1930 to 1939	5
1940 to 1949	4
1950 to 1959	9
1960 to 1969	13
1970 to 1979	56
1980 to 1989	74
1990 to 1995	125

Source: *Armageddon: Appointment With Destiny*, pp. 233–235.

---

[153] *Beginning of the End*, p. 98.

Other weather patterns are changing, too. Global warming is melting the ice caps, raising the water level, and eroding our shorelines. Topsoil is being destroyed at record levels. We are experiencing record levels of floods, fires, hurricanes, volcanoes, and other natural disasters; and meteorologists warn that changes in global weather patterns mean that we will have hotter, more turbulent weather for the next 100 years or so. One Web site dedicated to end-times prophecy, Prophecy Central, has regular updates on these geological and climatic changes.[154]

War

> For nation will rise against nation, and kingdom against kingdom....All these are the beginning of sorrows. (Matt. 24:7–8)

> When He opened the fourth seal, I heard the voice of the fourth living creature saying, "Come and see." So I looked, and behold, a pale horse. And the name of him who sat on it was Death, and Hades followed with him. And power was given to them over a fourth of the earth, to kill with the sword.... (Rev. 6:7–8)

Along with unparalleled natural disasters, the end times will be characterized by war. War has existed throughout history, but it is entering a new era of destructiveness. Already, we are seeing massive military buildups and weapons capable of destroying, not just entire armies, but entire nations. One single Trident submarine can deliver more devastation than all of the weapons used in World War II combined. And with advanced chemical and biological weapons, we are capable of leveling entire cities with the contents of a single teaspoon. When the world's children start building pipe bombs in their basements, and when children as young as six start committing premeditated murder in their school classrooms with guns, truly this has become a planet characterized by violence and war.

---

[154] www.Bible-prophecy.com.

Widespread Indifference

> And because lawlessness will abound, the love of many will grow cold. (Matt. 24:12)

As the level of evil in the world grows, so does the indifference of its inhabitants. This is not just the sin of unbelievers, but of believers, too (after all, when Jesus gave this prophecy, He was talking to the disciples—believers). We have become so jaded that evil and sin no longer surprise or horrify us. When a child is molested, a woman raped, an elderly person abused, or a baby aborted, we barely notice. Violence and brutality have become commonplace. As Jesus predicted, we have become a society "whose love has grown cold," another sign that we could be what John Hagee calls "the terminal generation."

Widespread Death Through Famine

> And there will be famines...in various places." (Matt. 24:7)

> So I looked, and behold, a black horse, and he who sat on it had a pair of scales in his hand. And I heard a voice in the midst of the four living creatures saying, "A quart of wheat for a denarius [about a day's wages], and three quarts of barley for a denarius, and do not harm the oil and the wine." (Rev. 6:5–6)

The world's population is exploding, and along with it, so are disease and famine. As with war, these things are not new. But Jesus tells us that they will occur with unusual severity prior to His return. During the third and fourth seals, up to one-quarter of the earth's population will die from war, hunger, and disease. Notably, the famine will not affect those of wealth.

Although, like war, famine has been with us throughout history, we are experiencing a new level of severity. In August of 1999, one assistance agency estimated that three-and-one-half million people in North Korea have starved to death since 1995. According to the U.N. Food and Agriculture Organization, nearly 10 million people in sub-Sahara Africa need emergency food; one million in Somalia face food shortages and 400,000 are at risk of starvation; 16 nations, most in East Africa, are said to be facing "exceptional food emergencies." A recent book from the WorldWatch Institute shows that spreading water shortages threaten to reduce the global food supply by more than 10%. Irrigation problems are widespread in the grain-growing regions of central and northern China, northwest and southern India, parts of Pakistan, and much of the western United States, North Africa, the Middle East, and the Arabian Peninsula.

The situation will only get worse. Even as the world's population rises, its agricultural capabilities are diminishing. According to the Annual Study of the U.N. Population Fund, deserts are growing at a rate of 14.8 million acres every year. More than 26 billion tons of topsoil—11% of the world's total—have already been lost. Tropical rain forests, which contribute significantly to our planet's oxygen, are shrinking by more than 27 million acres per year.[155] Nearly half a billion people don't have enough drinking water. This number is expected to increase to 2.8 billion by 2025, or 35% of the world's projected population.[156] As the world's population grows to 8 billion and beyond, this will set the stage for the greatest famine the world will ever know.

Explosion in the World's Population

Timescale	Years	World Population
Until Christ	?	300 million
Christ to Columbus, 1492	1462	500 million
Columbus to WWI, 1918	418	2 billion
WWI to 1962	44	3 billion
1962 to 1980	18	5 billion
1980 to 2000	20	6 billion plus

---

[155] *Armageddon: Appointment With Destiny*, pp. 242-244.
[156] www.Bible-prophecy.com/famplague.htm.

Pestilence

And there will be...pestilences in various places." (Matt. 24:7)

When He opened the fourth seal, I heard the voice of the fourth living creature saying, "Come and see." So I looked, and behold, a pale horse. And the name of him who sat on it was Death, and Hades followed with him. And power was given to them over a fourth of the earth ...[to kill]...with hunger, with death, and with the beasts of the earth. (Rev. 6:7–8)

In today's world of scientific and medical advances, we still cannot stop the ravaging power of disease. It has been reported that 40,000 deaths from malnutrition and disease occur daily. The World Summit for Children has reported that 1,400 children die from whooping cough, 4,000 die from measles, 2,150 die from tetanus, 2,750 die from malaria, 11,000 die from diarrhea, and 6,000 die from pneumonia *every day*. Many diseases are becoming resistant to antibiotics, and new, virulent plagues are arising. A World Health Organization report stated that at least 30 new infectious diseases with no known treatment, cure, or vaccine have emerged in the past 20 years. In addition, many deadly diseases, such as bubonic plague, malaria, smallpox, diphtheria, and yellow fever, are making a comeback. Health officials are calling tuberculosis a disease "out of control."

But perhaps the most frightening plague of all is HIV infection and AIDS. UNAIDS and WHO estimate that more than 30 million people worldwide were living with HIV at the end of 1997, or one in every 100 adults in the sexually active ages of 15 to 49. It is estimated that up to 75% of the population of Africa south of the Saharan Desert will be infected with HIV in the next decade. Up to 50% of Uganda's population is already infected. The situation is so severe in Zimbabwe, where one in four adults is infected, that former President Clinton called it a threat to world security and a national emergency for the United States.

Will We See the Return of Jesus?

For 2,000 years, we had no literal fulfillment of end-times prophecy. Since the rebirth of Israel, the rate of prophetic fulfillment has been exponential. Something is happening, and it is

270

happening now. Contrast the long period of prophetic silence with the current rate of prophetic fulfillment and it is no wonder that many believe that the return of Christ could happen in our lifetimes. These are just a few examples, but there are many more.

There are a number of prophecy teachers who believe that the generation that was privileged to witness the rebirth of Israel is the generation that will also witness the return of Christ. This is based on Jesus' teaching in Matthew 24.

Grant Jeffrey put it well:

> During the closing days of Christ's ministry on earth, He warned us about the terrible events that would constitute the "signs of the times" leading up to the Battle of Armageddon and His Second Coming. He then gave His disciples a clear prediction of when these events would occur—at the rebirth of the nation of Israel. "Now learn a parable of the fig tree; when its branch is yet tender, and puts forth leaves, you know that summer is nigh. So likewise you, when you shall see all these things, know that it is near, even at the doors. Verily I say to you, this generation shall not pass till all these things are fulfilled" (Matt. 24:32–24). The fig tree was used six times throughout the Bible as a prophetic symbol of the nation of Israel.
>
> On May 15, 1948, after almost 1900 years of devastation and persecution, Israel became a nation—in the precise year foretold by the prophet Ezekiel over 2,500 years earlier. Therefore, based on Christ's promise in Matt. 24:32–34, our generation is the first group of Christians in history with a sound foundation for believing that, within our natural life span [40 to 70 years], we will witness the amazing events concerning the Second Coming of Christ.[157]

I must admit, when I first read this statement, it made my blood run cold. It was this statement that, almost single-handedly, pushed me into study of end-times prophecy. Never before had I considered that Jesus might actually return in my lifetime. Suddenly, I took it very seriously.

---

[157] *Armageddon: Appointment With Destiny*, p. 12.

A Different Take on the Fig Tree

Today, I see this prophecy somewhat differently. While Jesus indicates that the rebirth of the nation of Israel signals that "summer is near," the signal He gives for His return is when *all of these things* begin to occur. The formation of the nation of Israel is a singular event. Therefore, we must ask, what are these *things* — plural? Earlier in the chapter, Jesus gave us a description of the opening of the first six seals: the rise of false christs, including the Antichrist, world war and the rise of the Antichrist through bloodshed, worldwide famine and death, the Great Tribulation, and the cosmic disturbances. Because scripture must always be taken in its larger context, I believe these are the events Jesus was referring to. When we see them, we will know without question that His return is "at the doors."

Furthermore, in the parallel parable in Luke 21:30-31, Jesus says, "Look at the fig tree, and all the trees. When they are already budding, you see and know for yourselves that summer is now near." This is another important clue that He is not identifying the fig tree as the nation of Israel. He is simply using an agricultural analogy: Just as you know spring is near when the trees begin to bud, so, too, you will know my coming is near when the signs begin to take place.

Does this mean that the generation that witnessed the birth of Israel is not the terminal generation? No. It certainly could be. This prophecy leaves the question open. Either way, Jeffrey's point is well taken. No matter what your age, whether you are young or whether you are old, we are all witnessing the fulfillment of very precise prophecies that are rapidly paving the way for the return of the Messiah.

Is it fair that we may have less time than our grandparents did? I believe that it is. We are living in an age of almost unparalleled revelation of the power and sovereignty of God. Scientific discoveries on a daily basis are proving beyond the shadow of a doubt that there is intelligent design behind the creation of the universe. People are being healed by the hundreds in Third World countries of paralysis, blindness, and innumerable diseases. Countries that previously wouldn't allow missionaries across their borders are now opening their doors, even if just for a little while. There have been explosions in evangelism throughout Africa, Russia, Eastern Europe, and Latin America. Even Cuba is letting in the gospel—against all reason, against all natural sense. God is pouring out His Spirit now for a reason.

Many people are frightened by what is happening in the world today. But the Word of God provides hope and salvation through God's Son, Jesus Christ, who is the light and hope of the world. Jesus said, "For I did not come to condemn the world, but to save it." John 3:16 tells us that all who believe in Him should have everlasting life.

The exact time of Christ's return may be a mystery, but how to prepare for it is not.

> If you confess with your mouth the Lord Jesus and believe in your heart that God has raised Him from the dead, you will be saved. For with the heart one believes unto righteousness, and with the mouth confession is made unto salvation. (Romans 10:9–10)

If you don't know Jesus as your Savior, don't put off making the decision. If you feel God tugging at your heart, do it today. Scripture makes it clear that we do not come to the Father in our own time. We come in His. None come to the Father unless the Spirit draws them, so when He calls, we must respond. "Behold, now is the accepted time; behold, now is the day of salvation" (2 Cor. 6:2).

If you are waiting for prophecy as a timer, letting you know how long you can wait, don't fall prey to the folly of this kind of thinking. Paul warns that, following the rise of the Antichrist, God will send a strong delusion upon those with rebellious hearts "that they should believe the lie" (2 Thess. 2:11). At the height of prophetic fulfillment, when God's truth is most clear, God will give them over to their rebellion because of the hardness of their hearts, even to the point of blinding them to the truth.

But this doesn't have to happen. Jesus referred to these events as signs by which we could anticipate and be able to prepare for His coming. So the question He asked of His followers in the first century is still a question that He asks of you today:

> Nevertheless, when the Son of Man comes, will He really find faith on the earth? (Luke 18:8)

22

One Final Thought

As the first edition of this book was going to press, I had a conversation with Rev. Charles Cooper of The Sign Ministries (now Sola Scriptura). As part of our discussion, he asked me a question that set me thinking for the next several days. The answer that came to my heart, if born out to be the truth, could change the way I will think about the end times forever.

The question Rev. Cooper asked was this: Do we really have the proper understanding of the promise, "I will keep you from the hour of trial," given to us in Rev. 3:10? Or has the pretrib agenda so set the approach to the study of this verse that we may have missed its true meaning altogether? What would happen if we were to start, not from the premise of challenging the pretrib interpretation, but entirely independent of it? As I got thinking about this question, I had trouble concentrating on anything else.

In Chapter 8 of this book, I pointed out that the word used for temptation, *peirasmos*, can also be translated "trial" or "proof." For this reason, the Church of England has debated changing the Lord's Prayer (Matt. 6:13) from "Lead us not into temptation" to "Save us from the time of trial." Moreover, in *The New American Bible*, the Lord's Prayer reads, "Do not subject us to the final test."

I must admit, I'd always wondered about that line. "Lead us not into temptation...." Why would Jesus tell us to pray such a thing? Temptation is usually associated with sin, and God does not tempt us to sin. Over the last several years, however, it has become clear to me that there is another kind of temptation, that which is referred to as a "trial" or a "proof." There are many places in scripture where God leads His people into tempting situations in order to test their faithfulness. Think of the prideful

Israelites in Judges, who had come to think that their military victories were their birthright. To them God said, "I also will no longer drive before them any of the nations which Joshua left when he died, so that through them *I may test Israel*, whether they will keep the ways of the Lord, to walk in them as their fathers kept them, or not" (Judges 2:21–22). Or the godly King Hezekiah, whose blessed reign was interrupted with a jolting trial: "God withdrew from him, *in order to test him*, that He might know all that was in his heart." (2 Chr. 32:31). David also talked extensively about God's testing. In the Psalms, he writes, "for the righteous God tests the hearts and minds" (Psalm 7:9) and, "His eyelids test the sons of men" (Psalm 11:4).

Testing is a consistent theme throughout the scriptures. But so is God's choice to sometimes be silent during these times. In Psalm 10:1, David writes, "Why do you stand afar off, O Lord? Why do You hide in times of trouble?" In Psalm 13:1, we can almost feel David's pain when he cries, "How long, O Lord? Will you forget me forever?" Then there is the unforgettable, "My God! My God! Why have you forsaken me? Why are You so far from helping me, and from the words of my groaning?" (Psalm 22:1). Of course, God does not remain hidden indefinitely, and in each of these Psalms, David concludes with a powerful response of praise when God ultimately answers his prayer. But between the prayer and the response, the silence is deafening.

Testing All That Is in Our Hearts

It is a sobering scriptural principle that sometimes God withdraws the sense of His presence to test the hearts of those whom He loves. During the 70th Week, the test will be this: Is our love for God conditional or unconditional? Do we love Him because He is the righteous and holy God? Or do we love Him because He is the big Sugar Daddy in the sky? This is exactly the challenge that Satan levied at God in the first chapter of Job: "Have You not made a hedge around him, around his household, and around all that he has on every side? You have blessed the work of his hands, and his possessions have increased in the land. But now, stretch out Your hand and touch all that he has, and he will surely curse You to Your face" (Job 1:10–11).

So the Lord allowed Satan to take Job's children, his property, his health, and all of his possessions. Imagine how Job must have felt. Did God tell Job that He was with him during this time? Did He comfort him? Give him wisdom? Give him direction? No! It was a test of Job's character. Job simply suffered loss after loss, devastation after devastation, without knowing why. And yet, despite the silence, Job remained faithful, and the end for him was restoration and glory. Many of us have wondered how we would react if, like Job, God were to take from us all of our worldly possessions, and even our families. But have we thought about how we might feel if *God were also silent during this time*?

Consider now the promise from Rev. 3:10: "Because you have kept My command to persevere, I also will keep you from the hour of trial which shall come upon the whole world, to test those who dwell on the earth." Could it be that the test to come upon the earth is not primarily a physical one, but a spiritual one? That, as during the period of the Judges and King Hezekiah, God will withdraw the sense of His presence from His people (just as the archangel Michael will withdraw his restraining influence over Israel at the midpoint of the 70th Week) to test them to see all that is in their hearts? Could this be the reason that, in the model prayer, the Lord says, "Do not lead us into temptation," or, alternatively, "Do not subject us to the final test"?

Putting Ourselves to the Test

In Chapter 1, I asked a very personal question. I asked about the believer's attitude when the first half of the 70th Week comes: "But what happens when *you* start losing the security of *your* food, *your* clothing, and *your* shelter? What happens when the earthquakes are tearing *your* neighborhood asunder and just practicing your faith can, and will, get you killed? Spiritual preparation suddenly takes on new meaning." Now add to this the possibility that you will receive no communication from God during this time. You pray and get no answer. You suffer and get no comfort. You are frightened and confused, and get no guidance.

If so, these trials will not be for all believers. They will only be for believers in the loveless, dead, compromising, corrupt, and lukewarm churches described in Revelation 2 and 3. If you have lived your whole life spiritually apathetic, with one foot on either side of the fence, girding yourself up spiritually only when you feel yourself sliding "too far" over the fence, if you are obedient during the first half of the 70th Week, it will be because, for the first time in a long time (or, if you are really honest with yourself,

276

perhaps ever), you have counted the cost and made the choice. If God has chosen to withdraw Himself during this time, being obedient will truly be a choice—an act of the will.

Could this be what this scripture is teaching? Could it be that five of the seven churches will feel no tangible presence of God during the first half of the 70th Week? What a terrifying thought! I think of the times in my own life when the trials have come and God seemed remote and far away. For believers who have come to rely on God's wisdom and strength, there is no thought more fearsome than that they might face a trial alone. Jesus said, "Watch therefore, and pray always that you may be counted worthy to escape all these things that will come to pass, and to stand before the Son of Man" (Luke 21:36).

Of course, Jesus will never leave us physically, for He promised, "Lo, I am with you always, even to the end of the age" (Matt. 28:20). The writer of Hebrews reminds us of this, promising, "He will never leave you or forsake you" (Heb. 13:5). But could it be that many will *feel* like He has forsaken them? In this time of "experiential Christianity," when we are encouraged to test the goodness of God by how it feels, by the manifestation of the Spirit, and by our levels of happiness, health, and prosperity, the need to rely solely on the promise of the Word of God *without experiential confirmation* would be an enormous test.

Jesus in the Garden of Gethsemane

Why shouldn't God put His people to such a proof? He put Hezekiah to one. He put David to one. Most importantly, He put His Son to one. Did Jesus not cry out on the cross, "My God, My God, why have You forsaken Me?" (Mark 15:34). Think about the Garden of Gethsemane. The night before His crucifixion, the Bible tells us that, as He prayed, Jesus was actually sweating blood. *Sweating blood.* Jesus was fully man, but He was also fully God. Did He not know that He would be raised on the third day? Of course He did. So what caused Him so much distress that His blood vessels actually broke from the emotional strain?

The answer lies in His lament: "My soul is exceedingly sorrowful, even to death" (Matt. 26:38); and, "O My Father, if it is possible, let this cup pass from Me" (Matt. 26:39). What cup? The cup of God's wrath (Rev. 14:10), which is poured out in the full strength of His indignation on the perfect, sacrificial Lamb. If the bowl judgments of Revelation are God's wrath at the end of the age, imagine His wrath upon Jesus on the cross. Jesus was about to bear the full wrath of God for the sins of *all* humanity, of *every* age, for *all* time. This is the gift of Jesus Christ, the sacrifice He paid so that we would not have to.

We cannot even begin to imagine what we have been spared. But Jesus could. No wonder He asked, "Let this cup pass from Me!" If you or I thought we were going to endure the full wrath of God, we would sweat blood, too. And no wonder that, feeling the separation from His Father as He hung upon the cross, Jesus cried, "Why have You forsaken Me?"

What a terrible word.

Bound for Glory

But the story doesn't end here. The end for Jesus was glory—just as it will be for the Church. And how did relief come to Jesus as He endured God's wrath on the cross? It was cut short through His death. Scripture records that Pontius Pilate was actually surprised that Jesus had died so soon (Mark 15:44). If what I have just presented regarding Rev. 3:10 is, in fact, the correct reading of scripture, then so, too, will the sense of separation from God experienced by believers be cut short (*koloboo*) through the translation of their bodies at the rapture. ("And unless those days were shortened [*koloboo*], no flesh would be saved," Matt. 24:22). Forsakenness to glory.

This is also the model presented by Psalm 22, from which Jesus is quoting on the cross. Although Jesus felt forsaken by the Father during His final period of testing, Psalm 22 goes on to praise God for His ultimate faithfulness: "Ye that fear the Lord, praise Him; all you the seed of Jacob, glorify Him, and fear Him .... My praise shall be of You in the great congregation: I will pay my vows before them that fear Him...." (vv. 23, 25). Once again, we see God's silence followed by restoration and praise.

If this is the correct reading, God promises that not all will feel forsaken. One church, the loving Church of Philadelphia, who has kept His command to persevere and been counted worthy, will be kept from this hour of trial. These will know that God is with them. They will experience His comfort, wisdom, and grace that will give them joy and patience throughout the 70th Week. I am a tough person. I feel that I can take adversity, war, famine, persecution, and even death. But the thought of feeling separated from God, even in my life now, terrifies me. I cannot begin to imagine what that sense of separation would feel like during the testing of the six seals. Yes, the Lord's Prayer will never seem the same again. Oh, how I want to be in Philadelphia!

This is not to suggest that this is the last word on Rev. 3:10. It is only a suggestion, designed to give believers some food for thought. Perhaps the answer lies elsewhere. Certainly, there is much left yet to discover in the Word of God, and there are lessons yet to be learned. Believers should be open, discerning, and compliant to guidance from the Holy Spirit. As we continue to study and learn from God's infallible Word, may it always be the cry of our hearts:

"Even so come, Lord Jesus."

Epilogue

Several years ago, one well-respected scholar published a study of the rapture that he called, as part of his title, "a definitive study of the rapture." I make no such claim. As of this third edition, I have spent four years studying this subject and have tried to do a prayerful and accurate job. My conclusions differ from those of most mainstream prophecy teachers. In the end, I could be proven right, but in the end, I could also be proven wrong. I do not say this to undermine the credibility of this book. I say it because, ultimately, it is the responsibility of every believer to come to his or her own conclusions about the truth of scripture—all of scripture, not just about the rapture.

Do not take my word on the things written here. Test everything for yourselves. For Paul has commanded us, "Test all things; hold fast what is good" (1 Thess. 5:21).

May the grace of our Lord Jesus Christ be with you. Amen.

Appendix A

A Closer Look at the Day of the Lord

Because God's wrath is part of the Day of the Lord, the starting point of this Day is crucial to determining the timing of the rapture. If the Church is not destined for wrath, the rapture must occur before the Day of the Lord begins. If the Day of the Lord begins with the opening of the seals, this requires the rapture to be pretribulational. If the Day starts after the opening of the seals, it does not.

What does the Bible say about the starting point of the Day of the Lord? "The sun shall be turned into darkness, and the moon into blood, before the great and terrible Day of the Lord" (Joel 2:31). This description is nearly identical to that of the sixth seal: "I looked when He opened the sixth seal, and behold, there was a great earthquake; and the sun became black as sackcloth of hair and the moon became like blood" (Rev. 6:12). If there is only one Day of the Lord, and if the events of Revelation are to be read literally, normatively, and consecutively, this places the start of the Day of the Lord after the cosmic disturbances of the sixth seal. Therefore, because the rapture occurs immediately before the Day of the Lord, this places the rapture after the sixth seal, as well. How do pretrib scholars answer this?

According to some scholars, the sixth seal takes place at the end of the 70th Week, concurrent with the last bowl judgment. This often relies on the "overview" interpretation of Revelation, in which the seals are seen as a condensed version of the entire 70th Week. I do not believe that this argument holds up, and the reasons for this are detailed in Chapter 18, "Is Revelation Consecutive?" Pretrib scholars who *do* see the judgments of Revelation as consecutive have to get around this post-sixth-seal Day of the Lord some other way. They often do this by suggesting that there are two days of the Lord: a broad "Day," which covers the entire 70th Week (supported by passages like Isaiah 13:6–13 and Zeph. 1:14–18); and a narrow "Day," which refers only to Armageddon (supported by passages like Joel 3:12–16).

Redefining Terms

This argument reminds me of the technique used by cults to redefine words to avoid the conclusions of the straightforward biblical text. The Jehovah's Witnesses, for example, redefine the Holy Spirit as a "force" like electricity rather than the third person of the Trinity, and redefine Jesus' holy title Son of Man to mean a created, perfected being rather than God incarnate. This enables them to use the same language as the Bible, while coming to entirely different conclusions. While I am *not* calling pretrib a cult, I do believe that these proponents fall prey to the same error of thinking by basing their method of interpretation on the need to reach a predetermined outcome. If the Day of the Lord has the same meaning in all end-times contexts, the Day of the Lord must begin with the return of Jesus after the sixth seal.

The precedent often used for the "two-stage" Day of the Lord interpretation is Moses' use of the word "day" in Genesis 1, which is sometimes used to describe a portion of the day, or that which produces light, and sometimes used to describe a longer creative period. In this view, this distinction is allowable because the Hebrew word for day, *yom*, can have multiple meanings, depending on the context. Because the same word, *yom*, is used in the phrase "Day of the Lord," the phrase can also have multiple meanings depending on the context.

Pretrib and Prewrath Approaches to "the Day of the Lord"

Day of the Lord Passage 1	Pretrib	Prewrath
"The great Day of the Lord is near, it is near, and hasteneth greatly, even the void of the Day of the Lord; the mighty man shall cry there bitterly. The day is a day of wrath, a day of trouble and distress, a day of waste and desolation..." (Zeph 1:14).	→ Broad Day of the Lord	Day of the Lord, starting after the opening of the sixth seal

Day of the Lord Passage 2	Pretrib	Prewrath
"The sun will turn dark, and the moon into blood, before the great and awesome Day of the Lord" (Joel 2:31).	→ Narrow Day of the Lord	Day of the Lord, starting after the opening of the sixth seal

284

This, in itself, should be enough for readers to question the validity of this argument. The Day of the Lord is one of the most frequently mentioned prophesied events in the Bible, both in the New and the Old Testaments. Like the Second Coming of Christ (which pretrib proponents also want to define as being two separate events), it had a unique and well-understood meaning for the audience for whom these prophets wrote. To suggest that there are actually two different Days, with the same name but covering different time periods, goes beyond the realm of credibility for divine inspiration (1 Cor. 14:33).

The Valley of Jehoshaphat

One of the few passages used as support for the "two days of the Lord" interpretation is Joel 3:12–16:

> Let the nations be wakened and come up to the Valley of Jehoshaphat; for there I will sit to judge all the surrounding nations. Put in the sickle, for the harvest is ripe. Come, go down; for the winepress is full, the vats overflow, for their wickedness is great. Multitudes, multitudes in the valley of decision! For the day of the Lord is near in the valley of decision. The sun and moon will grow dark, and the stars will diminish their brightness. The Lord also will roar from Zion.

From earlier in Joel 3, it is made clear that the gathering of the world's armies in the Valley of Jehoshaphat is a reference to Armageddon.[158] Therefore, some scholars reason, the valley of decision must also refer to Armageddon. Consequently, when the sun, moon, and stars go dark, this must be a different set of cosmic disturbances than those mentioned as part of the sixth seal, even though the wording is identical and no second set of these disturbances exists in the text. Because the pretrib position maintains that the broad Day of the Lord starts at the beginning of the 70th Week, the phrase "the day of the Lord *is*

---

[158] According to the *New Unger's Bible Dictionary*, "[S]ince no actual valley bore this name in pre-Christian antiquity, Joel's prophetic employment is figurative of the place where the judgment of the nations will take place prior to Christ's second advent and the setting up of the millennial kingdom." The entry in *The New Bible Dictionary* says, "Mentioned in Joel 3:14 as the place of God's judgment on the nations.... Second Chronicles 20 would explain the symbolism. In the valley of Beracah, 24 kilometers south of Jerusalem, King Jehoshaphat observed Yahweh's victory over heathen nations, a microcosm of the day of Yahweh."

near in the valley of decision" is seen as a second Day of the Lord that occurs at the end of the 70th Week.

Does this argument work? When interpreting a particular word or phrase, it is important to look for an antecedent, another use of that word or phrase earlier in the passage to help determine its context. On the surface, the antecedent to "valley of decision" appears to be "Valley of Jehoshaphat." However, the key word in this phrase is not "valley." It is "decision." There are many valleys described in the Bible. The fact that it is the valley of decision is what identifies it from all of the other valleys. So what is the valley of *decision*? We know that it cannot be the Valley of Jehoshaphat because this is not a valley of choosing. It is a valley where Jesus Christ sits in divine judgment at the end of the 70th Week. Although most Bible dictionaries equate the two, this is not necessarily the correct interpretation.

Multitudes in the Valley of Decision

If the valley of decision isn't the Valley of Jehoshaphat, what is it? The first place that immediately comes to mind is the valley of dry bones in Ezekiel 37. Here, Ezekiel is staring at a valley filled with dry bones, representing Israel. It is a valley of both spiritual and physical death:

> The hand of the Lord came upon me and brought me out in the Spirit of the Lord, and set me down in the midst of the valley; and it was full of bones. Then He caused me to pass by them all around, and behold, there were very many in the open valley, and indeed they were very dry. And He said to me, "son of man, can these bones live?" So I answered, "O Lord God, You know."

God tells Ezekiel to prophesy to the bones so that God will put flesh on them that they may live. And yet, even as the bones were covered with flesh, there was no breath in them—no spiritual life. These bones are symbolic of the nation of Israel, which in 1948 went from physical "death" to physical "life" but is still spiritually dead. Ezekiel then goes on to describe how, once the Lord causes breath to come from the four winds, the bones will be given life and God's Spirit will reside in them. How does one get God's Spirit and be raised to spiritual life? In the Old Testament, it is through faith in Jehovah. In the New Testament, it is through faith in Israel's Messiah, Jesus Christ. Ezekiel is telling us that, through a renewed faith in God (through Christ), the nation of Israel will go from being physically alive but spiritually dead, to being spiritually alive at some point in the future. This requires a *decision*—a decision to obey and submit to Christ.

This place of decision is reminiscent of another valley: the valley between the mountains of Ebal and Gerizim in which Moses pronounced the blessings and curses upon the nation of Israel (Deut. 27–30). Moses commanded half of the nation to stand on Mount Gerizim to bless the people and half to stand on Mount Ebal to curse them. The blessings were the promise of God that if the nation of Israel followed His voice and observed His commands, He would bless them with a great abundance of children, fruit of the field, rain, cattle and livestock, power over their enemies, and so on, and that in all they set their hand to do, they would be blessed.

Likewise, the curses were the promise of God that, if the nation did not follow His voice, "cursed shall you be when you come in, and cursed shall you be when you go out. The Lord will send on you cursing, confusion, and rebuke in all that you set your hand to do, until you are destroyed and until you perish quickly because of the wickedness of your doings in which you have forsaken Me" (Deut. 28:20).

After setting the blessings and the curses before the nation of Israel, Moses concluded by saying, "I call heaven and earth as witnesses today against you, that I have set before you life and death, blessing and cursing; therefore, *choose life, that both you and your descendants may live*" (Deut. 30:19). The importance of this event cannot be over-emphasized. The record of the event that occurred on the mountains of Gerizim and Ebal, which border the valley of Shechem, takes up four chapters in the book of Deuteronomy. This command, "choose life," became a central theme for the wayward nation of Israel throughout the Old Testament and continues today.

Many years later, Joshua took the nation of Israel back to this same spot between Gerizim and Ebal. He reminded them of this covenant and exhorted them to be faithful to the Lord their God:

> And if it seems evil to you to serve the Lord, *choose for yourselves this day* whom you will serve, whether the gods which your fathers served that were on the other side of the river, or the gods of the Amorites, in whose land you dwell. But as for me and my house, we will serve the Lord." (Joshua 24:15)

Thus, this valley at Shechem, the valley between the mountains of blessing and cursing, has great significance in the history of the nation of Israel. It is here that two of Israel's greatest leaders asked, "Whom will you serve?" It is also likely the figurative setting for the valley of dry bones. This spot, more than any other, can truly be called Israel's valley of decision.

Now, back to Joel 3. Could the figurative "Valley of Jehoshaphat" also be the valley of decision? Could it be the place where the Jews finally make their decision for Christ? No. The Bible tells us that the

Valley of Jehoshaphat is the place where God judges the unbelieving nations for their wickedness and their treatment of Israel: "Assemble and come, all you nations, and gather together all around. Cause Your mighty ones to go down there, O Lord. Let the nations be wakened, and come up to the Valley of Jehoshaphat; for there I will sit to judge all the surrounding nations" (Joel 3:11–12).

By the time Jesus comes at Armageddon, the decisions of earth's inhabitants for or against Christ will have already been made. They will have seen the Antichrist stand in the temple as if he were God. They will have seen Jesus coming on the clouds of heaven with power and great glory to rapture His Church. They will have heard the gospel preached by the witnesses, by post-rapture believers, and by the proclaiming angel (Rev. 14:6–7). They will have seen Jesus' power and fury during the Day of the Lord. Either they will choose life, or they will make a covenant with death in the form of submission to the Antichrist. There will be no middle ground, and their choice will be sealed for eternity:

All who dwell on the earth will worship him [the Antichrist], whose names have not been written in the Book of Life of the Lamb slain from the foundation of the world. (Rev. 13:8)

If anyone worships the beast and his image, and receives his mark on his forehead or on his hand, he himself shall also drink of the wine of the wrath of God, which is poured out full strength into the cup of His indignation. He shall be tormented with fire and brimstone in the presence of the holy angels and in the presence of the Lamb. And the smoke of their torment ascends forever and ever; and they have no rest day or night, who worship the beast and his image, and whoever receives the mark of his name. (Rev. 14:9–11)

The Valley of Jehoshaphat and the "valley of decision" should not be equated.

Thus, if these valleys should not be equated, there is no reason to require the "multitudes, multitudes in the valley of decision" to be part of the context of the battle of Armageddon, as proponents of the "two days of the Lord" position propose. When the prophet Joel cries, "Multitudes, multitudes in the valley of decision! For the day of the Lord is near in the valley of decision. The sun and moon will grow dark, and the stars will diminish their brightness. The Lord also will roar from Zion...," this takes us back, not to a physical valley at Armageddon but to *the spiritual condition of Israel before the return of the Messiah*. It is a warning to Israel, that although she is reborn as a nation, she is physically alive but spiritually dead. After having established the terrible final consequences, Joel asks Israel to make the decision for God *now*, before the Day arrives.

"Among the Remnant"

There is another indication that this is the proper reading. When Joel describes these same cosmic disturbances in Chapter 2, he says, "And it shall come to pass that whoever calls on the name of the Lord shall be saved. For in Mount Zion and in Jerusalem there shall be deliverance, as the Lord has said, among the remnant whom the Lord calls" (Joel 2:32). Notice that Joel wrote, "among the remnant." This is not the whole remnant, but only a portion of it.

Who are this remnant? Zechariah 13:8–9 tells us that, during the Day of the Lord, two-thirds of God's people will perish, but one-third He will bring through the fire and refine them as silver is refined and test them as gold is tested. "They will call on My name, and I will answer them. I will say, 'This is My people' and each one will say, 'The Lord is My God.'" This is the faithful remnant that the Lord promises to preserve for His name's sake (Eze. 36:20–28).

And yet, in Joel 2:32, the prophet says that in the day of deliverance following the great cosmic disturbances, there shall be deliverance "among the remnant." This can only be answered by the rapture. One portion of the remnant—those who are believers at the time of Christ's return—will go with the Church when He appears in the sky. The remainder will become believers either at His appearing or sometime afterwards and will remain on earth to evangelize the post-rapture world.

The Great Mystery

There are many references to the Day of the Lord in the Old Testament and many references to the cosmic disturbances in the sky. Some seem to imply that when Jesus comes on the clouds, He will immediately usher in His judgment of the nations and His eternal kingdom at Armageddon. While it is possible to discuss each instance, passage by passage, that would be beyond the scope of this book. But this does raise an interesting question. Why do so many of the Old Testament passages link Jesus' coming on the clouds following the cosmic disturbances with setting up His kingdom?

The Old Testament is silent about much of the second half of the 70th Week. It discusses in great detail the rise of the Antichrist, the persecution of God's people, the plagues and the famines, and the cosmic disturbances—all of the elements of the six seals—then skips right to Armageddon. This collapsing of two events into one is a common Old Testament technique called "telescoping," and it is the reason that so many Old Testament Jews were confused about the identity of Jesus. On one hand, the prophets described the Him as a Suffering Servant. On the other, they described Him as a Conquering King. Thus, Israel expected the Messiah to be both a Suffering Servant and a Conquering King at the same coming. They did not expect Him to be the Suffering Servant at one coming, then the Conquering King in the next.

This practice of telescoping would explain why there are so many passages in the Old Testament open to interpretation concerning the Second Coming. It also explains why Paul continually referred to the events of the rapture as "a mystery," since it is likely that he, himself, did not know the full content of the 70th Week. Nor was this revealed until the Revelation was given to John after Paul's death. This is also why it is dangerous to rely too heavily on the Old Testament prophets in determining the timing of the rapture. The prophets themselves often did not have a clear understanding of the events they were writing about (Dan. 12:8, 1 Pet. 1:10–12), and as the omission of the last half of the 70th Week indicates, they were operating on partial information.

Why would God hide the full picture of the latter half of the 70th Week from His people until close to the end of the age? Consider the context of Jesus' First Coming. The Jews were heavily oppressed by the Romans. The physical, financial, and emotional burden was excruciating. Enthusiasm in looking for the Messiah was driven by the people's desire for release from physical oppression, not from their desire to serve God. The nation of Israel didn't want the Suffering Servant who would free them from their burden of sin. They wanted the Conquering King who would free them from the burden of taxes. When the Messiah did not come in the form they desired—as a military leader—they rejected Him. Israel wanted the physical kingdom of God before the spiritual kingdom. But this is not what God had in mind.

Consider the parallel to the end times. Pretrib theology teaches that when Jesus comes at Armageddon to deliver Israel from her enemies, the unbelieving Jews will finally recognize Jesus as their Messiah and accept Him as their king. If this is the correct interpretation, they will have done *what Jesus rejected at His First Coming*: sought the physical kingdom before the spiritual one. If He didn't have this in mind the first time around, why would He do it the second time around? If, on the other hand, Jesus comes after the sixth seal, He will be giving the nation of Israel a chance to redeem themselves from their earlier sin. At His First Coming, He came in the midst of great tribulation and persecution, bringing the spiritual kingdom before the physical kingdom. At His Second Coming, He will once again offer the spiritual kingdom before the physical one.

Gleason Archer makes a similar point:

It is impossible to suppose that God would have so remarkably delivered the Jewish people if they persisted in rejecting Christ as Savior until the very end of the 70th Week. It was, after all, precisely because they rejected Jesus before

Pilate's judgment throne that the Lord condemned them to total defeat as a state and the destruction of Jerusalem as a city at the close of the First Revolt in 70 A.D. It is therefore inconceivable that the Lord would have put them back under His special protection and favor while they still persisted in rejecting Christ. The Apostle Paul himself affirms in Romans 11:23 concerning his own countrymen: "And they also, if they continue not in their unbelief, shall be grafted in; for God is able to graft them in again." In other words, unbelief in Jesus keeps the Jewish people from restoration to God's protection and favor.[159]

From day one, the story of Israel has been the story of God's people chasing after the things of this world rather than the things of heaven. The coming of Christ after the sixth seal, in the midst of their oppression, will be a true test for those who have a history of worshipping wood and stone. For God has said, "Bring charges against your mother, bring charges; for she is not My wife, nor am I her Husband! Let her put away her harlotries from her sight and her adulteries from between her breasts...For she said 'I will go after my lovers, who give me my bread and my water, my wool and my linen, my oil and my drink'" (Hosea 2:2,5).

God's Second Chances

It is wholly within the character of God to give His children a chance to redeem themselves from their prior sins. In the gospel of Luke, for example, Jesus told Peter that, the night of His arrest, Peter would deny Him three times. Despite Peter's repeated denials, he did exactly as Jesus foretold. Yet in His mercy, Jesus gave Peter the chance to redeem himself. After His resurrection, Jesus asked Peter, "Do you love me?" To which, Peter answered, "Yes, Lord." Then Jesus asked again, "Peter, do you love me?" To which, Peter answered, "Yes, Lord." Jesus asked yet again, "Peter, do you love me?" To which, Peter answered, "Yes, Lord" (John 21:15–17).

Peter denied Jesus three times, and three times Jesus gave him the opportunity to affirm his love. And just as Israel failed God's test to accept the Messiah on faith at His First Coming, so, too, will He give them an opportunity to accept Him on faith at His Second Coming—not as a deliverer out of physical bondage and oppression (although He will fulfill this function later, at the end of the 70th Week), but as the Messiah, whom they will love and serve in the midst of their circumstances, not after they have been delivered from them.

---

[159] *Three Views on the Rapture*, p. 111.

In Conclusion

In spite of pretrib scholars' attempts to create two days of the Lord, this simply does not fit with scripture. Not only is the prewrath view the preferred view for taking the text literally and normatively, but it is the preferred interpretation for Joel 3:12–16 and more accurately reflects the character of God as revealed through the patterns and examples set forth in scripture.

Response to *Maranatha! O Lord, Come!*

This book has been written to present a straightforward look at the prewrath rapture for a general church audience. I've offered few systematic refutations of the pretrib position because that was not my purpose in the text. However, I feel that it is appropriate to take at least one in-depth look at an academic treatment of this position for readers with a more in-depth interest in this subject. Understanding that scholarly defenses of this position can vary significantly in their approaches, I have selected *Maranatha! Our Lord, Come!*, by Dr. Renald Showers. I will not attempt to address every point, only the essential highlights that would be of interest and perhaps familiar to the general reader.

Before getting started, it is important to point out that I have the utmost respect for Dr. Showers and for his scholarship. This appendix should in no way be construed as a personal attack on Dr. Showers or on any other academic approach to biblical interpretation. Rather, I will present an examination of some of the over-arching theories and conclusions presented in his book. In an attempt to address the issues raised in *Maranatha!*, and not Dr. Showers personally, I will often address him simply as "the author" or cite the book itself.

In their refutations of the prewrath position, many scholars use Robert Van Kampen's views in *The Sign* as representative of all prewrath proponents. I am not comfortable with that comparison, since I differ from Van Kampen in some respects. It would be just as inaccurate to make Dr. Showers' beliefs representative of all pretrib scholars or vice versa. For this reason, I will also attempt to make distinctions when discussing Dr. Showers' individual position and when discussing the general precepts of pretribulationism as a whole.

Placing the Seals Within the Day of the Lord

Without dispute, the Day of the Lord is the period that contains God's wrath upon the earth. What *is* under dispute is when the Day of the Lord begins. If the Day of the Lord begins with the 70th Week, this lends support to the pretrib argument that the Church must be raptured prior to this terrible time. If the Day of the Lord does not begin with the 70th

Week, then the rapture can occur during the 70th Week as long as it is prior to God's wrath.

In order for the Day of the Lord to start at the beginning of the 70th Week, as pretribulationism maintains, the Day of the Lord must contain the seal judgments. One of the ways that *Maranatha!* attempts to show this is by creating two days of the Lord, an approach that is addressed in Appendix A. Suffice it to say that Paul invalidates this argument in 2 Thess. 2:1–3 when he writes: "Now, brethren, concerning the coming of our Lord Jesus Christ and our gathering together to Him, we ask, not to be soon shaken in mind or troubled, either by spirit or by word or by letter, as if from us, as though the day of Christ had come. Let no one deceive you by any means; for that Day will not come unless the falling away comes first, and the man of sin is revealed."

Here, Paul is making three very important points: (1) the physical return of the Lord Jesus and the gathering of believers to Him in the rapture occur in the same context; (2) both events precede the Day of the Lord (the *New American Standard* and *New International Version* both translate "day of Christ" as the Day of the Lord); and (3) the Day of the Lord is a singular event, not a two-stage event, that will not come until the falling away comes and the Antichrist is revealed. This makes it impossible for the Day of the Lord to start at the beginning of the 70th Week, with the seals, since the Antichrist does not reveal his true identity until the middle of the 70th Week (Matt. 24:15, 2 Thess. 2:3, Dan. 9:27).

The second way that *Maranatha!* attempts to show that the Day of the Lord must contain the seal judgments is by forcing that Day to include the Great Tribulation, also called the time of Jacob's Trouble. In order to do this, Dr. Showers uses a two-fold argument.

First, he relies heavily on comparisons, arguing that both periods

- are associated with tribulation;
- are periods of "unparalleled" trouble;
- have birth pangs associated with them;
- have Israel's future restoration associated with them;
- have the term "great" associated with them; and
- use the expression "that day."

Second, he argues that, since we know that the Great Tribulation starts at the midpoint of the 70th Week, the Great Tribulation must extend through the entire second half of the 70th Week, or a period of three-and-one-half years because

1. The Great Tribulation corresponds with the hiding place prepared by God for the Jews for 1,260 days, or three-and-one-half years.

2. When Daniel asks how long it will be until "the end of these wonders" and the ending of "the power of the holy people," he is told a "time, times, and half a time," or three-and-one-half years.

3. The Great Tribulation corresponds with the ending of the "overspreading of abominations" committed by the Antichrist for 42 months, or three-and-one-half years (pp. 44 –50).

While these arguments make a lot of intuitive sense, they work only by making correlations that are overly broad. For example, it is no surprise that the Great Tribulation and the Day of the Lord are both characterized by tribulation, since both occur during the 70th Week and tribulation is a characteristic of the entire 70th Week. However, not all tribulation is God's wrath. Some tribulation is designed for refining God's people (the six seals—Dan. 11:35, Rev. 3:10), some is designed as chastisement for unbelieving Israel (the Day of the Lord—Dan. 12:7; Rev. 12:6; Eze. 20:35–38), and some is designed as judgment on an unbelieving world (the Day of the Lord—Zeph 1:14–18, Isaiah 13:6–13; Joel 3:2). The question is, which kind of tribulation is it? *Maranatha* does not make a distinction.

The issue with the term "great" is similar. Just because the term "great" is associated with both the Day of the Lord and the Great Tribulation does not mean that one must include the other. Rather, they follow one another: the Great Tribulation after the fifth seal and the Day of the Lord after the sixth seal. The Hebrew and Greek words used for "great," *gadol* and *megas*, simply mean "exceedingly great" and their meaning is very broad. Since both the Day of the Lord and the Great Tribulation occur during the 70th Week, this use of "great" is appropriate, even if one does not include the other. These words are used in other end-times passages that are in no way associated with the Great Tribulation.

The author's use of "great" to equate the Day of the Lord with the Great Tribulation is further weakened by the fact that he dismisses the "great and terrible day of the Lord" in Joel 2:31 as *not* referring to the entire 70th Week (or the "broad" Day of the Lord—see Appendix A) but rather only to the return of Christ at Armageddon. Why does this use of the term "great" in the fifth seal correlate with the Day of the Lord, but in Joel 2:31 it does not? No answer to this problem is given. If the determination of whether a particular instance of "great" correlates with the Great Tribulation is based solely on its consistency with pretrib theology, it becomes a circular line of reasoning.

Another argument for equating the Day of the Lord with the Great Tribulation is that both periods are associated with birth pangs. The author uses scripture to divide these birth pangs into two distinct periods, the "lesser" (or Beginning of Sorrows) and the "greater" (the remainder of the 70th Week). These two periods are consecutive, and according to the author's own diagram, do not overlap. Thus the fact that the Great Tribulation and the Day of the Lord are both associated with birth pangs does not, by the author's own admission, require them to cover the same time period. Indeed, the Great Tribulation is associated with the lesser pangs, while the Day of the Lord is associated with the greater.

Maranatha! also draws great significance from the fact that both the Day of the Lord and the Great Tribulation have the judgment and the blessing of Israel associated with them. Thus, if they both contain divine blessing and divine judgment, the author reasons, they must overlap. This argument overlooks the fact that the blessings in these passages are of two different kinds. One refers to the *spiritual* blessings associated with the recognition of Jesus as the Messiah and the other to the *physical* blessings associated with the restoration of God's people to their homeland in peace and safety.

While the author concludes that these blessings will be poured out simultaneously, it is most likely that they will be consecutive: the blessings associated with the setting up of the *spiritual* kingdom will be felt during the 70th Week, after the physical return of Jesus at the end of the age; while the blessings associated with the setting up of the *physical* kingdom will be felt during the Millennium, after Jesus completes His judgment at Armageddon and is seated on His throne.

Why Grieve?

It is ironic that one of the passages Dr. Showers uses to illustrate the spiritual blessings bestowed upon Israel is actually a strong argument *against* the pretrib position. He cites Zech. 12:10–14:

> And I will pour on the house of David and on the inhabitants of Jerusalem the Spirit of grace and supplication; then they will look on Me whom they pierced. Yes, they will mourn for Him as one mourns for his only son and grieve for Him as one grieves for a firstborn. In that day, there shall be a great mourning in Jerusalem, like the mourning at Hadad Rimmon in the plain of Megiddo. And the land shall mourn, every family by itself: the family of the house of David by itself, and their wives by themselves; the family of the house of Nathan by itself, and their wives by themselves....

Most pretrib scholars believe that the day that Israel will look upon Him whom they pierced (also Rev. 1:7, Matt. 24:30), and therefore this grieving will occur, when the Jews see Jesus returning in the clouds at Armageddon. However, the intensity of this grieving doesn't make sense under these conditions. Jesus' return at Armageddon is associated with just about every blessing imaginable, including the restoration of

Israel's land to peace and bounty, the recognition of Jesus as the Messiah, the salvation of the believing remnant, the defeat of Israel's enemies, the punishment of the Gentile nations, and the ushering in of the Millennial kingdom. When will there be time to grieve? It does not make sense that Israel would grieve over her 2000-year rejection of the Messiah at this time. Judgment is over. Only joy is to come.

This grieving *does* make sense, however, in the context of the prewrath rapture, which places this grieving after the return of Christ when the Church (including believing Jews) will be raptured and the unbelieving Jews will watch in horror. This would allow for a period of grieving *and* account for the instant sealing and salvation of the 144,000 Jews that occurs at this time, leaving Jesus' return at Armageddon to bring nothing but joy.

Is the Great Tribulation 3 1/2 Years?

The association of the Great Tribulation with the entire latter part of the 70th Week is similarly false. One of the examples given in *Maranatha!* is Matt. 24:15–21, in which Jesus tells the Jews to flee to the wilderness when the Antichrist sets himself in the temple at the midpoint of the 70th Week. The author points out that this coincides with Rev. 12:6, in which God says that He has prepared a place for Israel to flee for three-and-one-half years.[160] According to this argument, the Great Tribulation must also last three-and-one-half years.

There are two things going on here.

First, at the beginning of the 70th Week, there are two different groups of Jews to be considered: the believing Jews, who have become part of the Church, and the unbelieving Jews, who are still part of unrepentant Israel. Jesus says that the Great Tribulation will be shortened for the sake of the elect. If this shortening is accomplished by the rapture, this does not preclude the unbelieving Jews from still being sheltered in the wilderness for the latter half of the 70th Week. God has made a promise to preserve a remnant for His name's sake, and that He will do. Second, Matt. 24:29 tells us that Jesus' return will be heralded by an unmistakable series of cosmic disturbances. We see those disturbances

---

[160] It is interesting that, in Eze. 20:34-38, God says that He will first gather His people out from among the nations, and during the time of His fury, "I will bring you into the wilderness of the people and there I will plead with you face to face. Like as in Egypt, so will I plead with you, saith the Lord God...and I will purge out from among you the rebels...." Although pretrib scholars like to place the gathering of Jews out of the nations at Armageddon, this clearly places this gathering *before the time of wrath*. This would coincide beautifully with the prewrath rapture after the sixth seal, followed by the Day of the Lord, and include the three-and-one-half years of shelter for the Jews during the 70th Week.

297

much earlier in the 70th Week, as part of the sixth seal, but there is no mention of this particular set of cosmic disturbances immediately prior to Armageddon.

The author gives another example from Dan. 12:6. After describing the reign of the Antichrist and the Great Tribulation, Daniel asks the angel, "How long until the end of these wonders?" The angel replies that it will be a time, times, and half a time, or three-and-one-half years. Thus, the author reasons, the Great Tribulation, or the time of Jacob's trouble, must last three-and-one-half years. This argument does not take into consideration that "these wonders" may refer to more than just the Great Tribulation. Daniel's vision includes additional details of the Antichrist's reign, as well. If the phrase "the end of these wonders" is more inclusive than the persecution of God's people, and if it is "the end of these wonders" that is to last three-and-one-half years, not the time of Jacob's Trouble itself, then this undermines the argument that the Great Tribulation and the Day of the Lord are one and the same.

Two More Reasons

There are two final arguments against placing the seals within the Day of the Lord. These are Joel 2:31 and Malachi 4:5.

First, Joel 2:31 tells us that the great cosmic disturbance (the sun turning dark and the moon turning to blood) will occur "before the great and terrible day of the Lord." This description is a nearly word-for-word correlation with the sixth seal. If the sixth seal must precede the Day of the Lord, it cannot be part of it.

Second, in Malachi 4:5, the Lord says, "I will send you Elijah the prophet before the great and dreadful Day of the Lord." Most scholars agree that Elijah is one of the two witnesses that begin their ministry during the 70th Week. Revelation 11:3 tells us that these witnesses will prophesy 1,260 days, or three-and-one-half years. This places the starting point of their ministry at the midpoint of the 70th Week. If the Lord will send Elijah prior to the Day of the Lord, and Elijah does not start his ministry until the midpoint of the 70th Week, the Day of the Lord cannot start until after the midpoint of the 70th Week.

The Shortening of the Great Tribulation

The shortening of the Great Tribulation is another evidence that the author uses to support the pretrib timing of the rapture. It is his contention that the shortening referred to in the phrase, "unless those days were shortened, no flesh would be saved" (Matt. 24:22), refers to Armageddon. The author suggests that the aorist tense of the Greek verb refers to an event determined by God in eternity past. In other words, it is an event that could have gone on indefinitely if it had not been foreordained by God to have a cut-off point, which occurs with the return of Christ at the end of the 70th Week. He compares this verse to Dan. 9:24 and 11:36, in which "70 weeks are determined for your people," and "what was determined [by God] shall be done." According to this argument, the Great Tribulation could have gone on indefinitely and resulted in the destruction of all flesh, but God in His love, faithfulness, and mercy preordained it to be shortened by Christ's return at Armageddon. While this is certainly a beautiful picture of God's faithfulness, this argument applies just as well to prewrath as it does to pretrib. The difference is that prewrath sees the cause of this shortening as the rapture. The word used in Matt. 24:22 is *koloboo*, which according to *Vine's Expository Dictionary of Greek and Hebrew Words*, denotes "to cut off, amputate; hence, to curtail, shorten, said of the shortening by God of the time of the great tribulation." This term is used only twice in the New Testament (Matt. 24:22, Mark 13:20), both in reference to this time of testing and trial.

In this context, the prewrath reading of "shortening" makes more sense than pretrib because the Bible tells us that the 70th Week will be complete once the power of the holy people is completely shattered (Dan. 12:7). In other words, through prolonged tribulation and distress, the holy people [Israel] will be worn down to a point at which they are finally ready to admit that they cannot continue in their state of rebellion. If this "cutting off" occurs at Armageddon, as Dr. Showers suggests, the power of the holy people will already have been broken through distress, and the concept of amputation would be completely lost.

The cutting off, or shortening, of the Great Tribulation is better described by God's amputation of the Antichrist's efforts at annihilating His people through the removal of millions of believers from the earth at the rapture. Although persecution will continue, the Great Tribulation itself will be ended. While millions of Jews will remain on earth, many will be protected in the hiding place prepared by God (Rev 12:6). The Antichrist will continue to persecute Jews and new believers, but he will be more interested in persecuting anyone—Jew, Christian, or not—who does not take his mark. When the global devastation brought by the sixth seal is compounded by the trumpet judgments that follow, his single-minded persecution of believers will likely be mitigated. What was once the Great Tribulation will get swallowed up in damage control. The remainder of the 70th Week, the Day of the Lord, will be characterized by God's judgment of the nations, not necessarily by the Antichrist's persecution of God's people.

The Start of the Day of the Lord

Another piece of evidence used by *Maranatha!* to support a pretrib rapture is that Jesus must rapture the Church prior to the start of the Day of the Lord, and that the Day of the Lord begins with the start of the 70th Week, because ...

1. *Paul said that the Day of the Lord would come as a thief in the night. Therefore, it must start prior to the opening of the first seal.*

According to Dr. Showers, this is because the seal judgments will be so clear, so unmistakable, that the world cannot fail to recognize them as the judgment of God (p. 60).

I disagree. As discussed in Chapter 5, there is nothing out of the realm of natural phenomena up to the sixth seal. Already, the world is rationalizing away bizarre diseases and the unusual severity of natural disasters as a matter of course. To say that the seals will cause a spiritually blind, rebellious world to see the judgment of God, I think, is to severely underestimate the power of human rationalization. Later in the book, the author himself acknowledges this point, saying: "Paul used two activities that normally take place in the dark of night to describe [the attitude of the unsaved]: sleeping and getting drunk. When people sleep or are drunk, they are not alert to reality and what is going on around them; thus, they do not respond with appropriate actions. Paul's point was that because of their sphere and nature of darkness and night, the unsaved are not alert to ultimate reality and the significance of what is going on around them" (p. 202).

Although Dr. Showers believes that the unsaved world will still be able to recognize the judgment of God in the seals, I do not. I see this passage as painting a picture of people who are perfectly capable of "sleeping" through the seals, which unlike the trumpets and the bowls, will not contain supernatural revelation of God's power until the end. After the sixth seal, the scriptures tell us that they will suddenly "wake up," and cry, "the wrath of the Lamb has come!" (Rev. 6:17).

2. 1 Thessalonians 5:3 tells us that the destruction of the Day of the Lord will come suddenly, "as labor pains upon a pregnant woman." According to Dr. Showers, the only way for this to happen is if there are no warning signs prior to its arrival.

We have already established that just because there are warning signs doesn't mean that people will recognize them. Furthermore, the beginning of the seals does not bring the sudden, destructive judgment his argument suggests. The 70th Week is set in motion with the confirming of the covenant by the Antichrist. This initiates the first seal, which is the horseman with the bow but no arrows, symbolizing the rise of false christs/the Antichrist. It is followed sometime later by world war (the second seal), famine (the third seal), and widespread death (the fourth seal), which by their very natures can be slow, cumulative processes.

Even John Walvoord sees the early stages of the birth pangs as relatively normal. He writes, "The opening hours of the day of the Lord do not contain great events. Gradually, the major events of the day of the

Lord unfold, climaxing in the terrible judgments with which the great tribulation is brought to conclusion."[161]

In contrast, the prewrath timing places the start of the Day of the Lord after Jesus has appeared in the sky with a shout, the blast of the trumpet, and the raising of the living and the dead to be with Him. Immediately after the sounding of the first trumpet, hail and fire are mingled with blood and thrown to the earth. This results in one-third of the trees and all of the green grass being burned up, then "something like a great mountain burning with fire [thrown] into the sea, and a third of the sea became blood. And a third of the living creatures in the sea died, and a third of the ships were destroyed" (Rev 8:8–9). If *Maranatha!* is going to use the "sudden and destructive" line of reasoning to determine the start of the Day of the Lord, the prewrath timing is a much closer fit.

3. *Maranatha! suggests that the Day of the Lord will begin once the world cries "peace and safety!", which can only be when the Antichrist confirms the seven-year covenant with Israel at the beginning of the 70th Week (p. 60).*

I disagree. Remember, the entire world will be undergoing the devastating plagues of famine, pestilence, and bloodshed of the first four seals, so the entire world will need a "savior." This makes this covenant the unlikely spark of such praise because it guarantees safety only for Israel. Thus, I believe this cry of "peace and safety!" will come, not when the Antichrist confirms the covenant, but when he stands in the temple, declaring himself to be God (or as God). His reign will be accompanied by many signs and wonders, including the apparent raising of himself from the dead. In the eyes of the unbelieving world, who better to bring relief from these worldwide disasters than "God" himself? But first, he must rid the world of any remaining opponents of world peace, namely the Christians and Jews who oppose his reign. Thus, the Great Tribulation will not be seen as a threat to world peace, but a promise of its coming.

Will there be tremendous upheaval in the world during this time? Certainly! There will be both war and natural disasters in addition to the persecution of God's people. But it must be remembered that "peace and safety!" is not the cry of believers but unbelievers. The natural disasters will be rationalized away, as they are today, and will likely increase the hope that the Antichrist will do as promised, especially if he is exhibiting supernatural powers. The war will be against those who oppose the Antichrist's rule—the orthodox Jews and Christians—who will become *de facto* enemies of world peace. The Great Tribulation will likely be met with approval as the world rids itself of the last remaining enemies of their new savior, the Antichrist. When Jesus arrives triumphantly in the

---

[161] *The Rapture Question*, p. 222.

midst of this chaos, raptures His Church, and initiates the devastating and supernatural trumpet judgments, truly this will be a terror and a shock to those who had been looking to the Antichrist for their hope.

4. *Maranatha! suggests that the Day of the Lord must start at the beginning of the 70th Week because the Day of the Lord is associated with birth pangs and the first birth pangs arrive at the beginning of the 70th Week, with the seals. Because the Day of the Lord comes suddenly, and birth pangs come suddenly, the Day of the Lord must begin with the 70th Week.*

The Day of the Lord is associated with birth pangs, but the author has already established that there are two periods of birth pangs: the lesser and the greater. As many women will tell you, the beginning of birth pangs may come suddenly, but they don't necessarily come decisively. Some even say that the beginning of this period can be mistaken for light cramping. The intense birth pangs that signal the beginning of hard labor, however, *do* come suddenly—like a shot in the stomach—as the body cries "Now! Now! Now!"

The Bible is very clear that the birth pangs associated with Day of the Lord come both suddenly *and* decisively. Thus, the greater birth pangs associated with the latter half of the 70th Week are a much better candidate for the start of the Day of the Lord. Because the author himself has identified these greater pangs as occurring after the seal judgments, beginning with the trumpets, this line of reasoning is once again better answered by the prewrath timing than pretrib.

What's Imminent?

Another evidence used to support the pretrib rapture is the doctrine of imminence. *Maranatha!* spends considerable time documenting the apostles' belief in the imminent return of Christ, citing such verses as Titus 2:13: "looking for the blessed hope and glorious appearing of our great God and Savior Jesus Christ," and James 5:7: "Be patient therefore, brethren, until the coming of the Lord." The conclusion is that, if Christ's return is imminent, nothing—not the rise of the Antichrist, not the seal judgments, not even the formation of the nation of Israel—must occur beforehand.

The word "imminent" is never used in the Bible. Nor does the Bible anywhere explicitly state that Jesus could come at any time, without warning. The term "imminence" is a descriptive term used by scholars to describe the apostles' expectant attitude toward the return of Christ. There are several recognized terms, such as the Trinity and the rapture of the Church, that also do not appear in the Bible, but their foundations are clearly grounded in scripture. The "any moment" rapture, however, is not. Expectancy, yes, but the "any moment" qualifier that has become synonymous with pretrib theology simply isn't there.

302

The main pretrib "proof" of this "any moment" reading comes from the belief that the New Testament writers thought Jesus could return at any time.[162] Thus, *Maranatha!* reasons, we must also believe that Jesus could return at any time. If the writers really did teach this, Dr. Showers would have a point. Unfortunately, they did not. The New Testament writers taught expectancy, but nowhere did they teach an "any moment" event. In fact, James taught that believers ought to be patient as they wait for the Lord, waiting with the same kind of patience with which a farmer waits for his crops (James 5:7–9), a description that hardly suggests an "any moment" event.

There is yet another difficulty here, one that the author recognizes, which is that Jesus did not return in the apostles' lifetimes. Thus, he notes that the term "imminent" cannot be interpreted to mean "soon." Even today, almost two thousand years later, Christ's return is still delayed. This illustrates the danger of turning a subject not explicitly stated in scripture into a biblical doctrine. As mentioned earlier, nowhere in scripture is it stated that Jesus could come at any time, without warning. On the contrary, there are many signs given to believers to watch for, including the great apostasy, the worldwide presentation of the gospel, and the revealing of the Antichrist, before this return can occur.

More Evidence Against an "Any Moment" Coming

Another justification for the "any moment" reading is that some of the first and second century church fathers felt that Jesus could come at any time. However, as I discuss in Chapter 6, this assessment is inaccurate. One can categorically state that writers such as Justin Martyr, Tertullian, Ireneaus, and other church fathers were overt in their expectation that the Church would endure the persecution of the Antichrist before the return of the Lord. Consider the following comments: "the man of apostasy, who...shall venture to do unlawful deeds on the earth against us the Christians" (Martyr); "Heresies, at the present time, will no less rend the church by their perversion of doctrine, than will Antichrist persecute her [the Church] at that day by the cruelty" (Tertullian), and "Now, concerning the tribulation of the persecution which is to fall upon the Church from the adversary ..." (Hyppolytus).

---

[162] John Walvoord makes this point, as well, writing, "In the light of this marvelous promise, Paul told the Thessalonians: 'therefore encourage each other with these words' (1 Thess. 4:18). It is obvious that the comfort offered by Paul had the prospect of immediate fulfillment, that the time of their separation from their loved ones could be short. Such a comfort would be impossible if they must first pass through the traumatic events of the Great Tribulation, which few would survive" (*Armageddon, Oil, and the Middle East Crisis* [Zondervan, 1990], p. 209).

But there is an even more important reason that the doctrine of imminence cannot be used to support an "any moment"—and therefore two-stage—pretrib rapture. The very verses that pretrib scholars use to support the imminent return of Christ also tell us that the rapture must occur at His bodily return. Take, for example, the two verses cited earlier: "looking for the blessed hope *and glorious appearing of our great God and Savior Jesus Christ*" (Titus 2:13), and "Be patient therefore, brethren, *until the coming of the Lord*" (Titus 5:7). And also "Now brethren, concerning *the coming of our Lord Jesus Christ* and our gathering together to Him..." (2 Thess. 2:1).

In these verses, Jesus' imminent return at the rapture and His bodily return are inextricably linked. The pretrib position places the rapture prior to the 70th Week but His physical return seven years later. This position is inconsistent with these verses, which state that His bodily return and the rapture occur together.

Prewrath, on the other hand, places Jesus' bodily return at the rapture, in accordance with scripture. This occurs after the opening of the sixth seal. Take the verse, "looking for the blessed hope and glorious appearing of our great God and Savior Jesus Christ." Where else in the Bible do we see the Lord coming in glory? After the cosmic disturbances of the sixth seal. "Then the sign of the Son of Man will appear in heaven, and then all the tribes of the earth will mourn, and they will see the Son of Man coming on the clouds of heaven with power and great glory" (Matt. 24:30–31). And yet, pretrib scholars, including the author of *Maranatha!*, claim that this passage refers to Armageddon.[163]

Am I trying to undermine the imminence of Christ's coming? No. The writings of the New Testament clearly emphasize the importance of continually looking for the Savior's return. It is our blessed hope and a catalyst for holy living. However, according to *Webster's Dictionary*, the word *imminence* simply means "ready to take place, especially hanging threateningly over one's head." I believe this is more true of Jesus' coming today than at any other time in history. Prewrath does not detract from a sense of imminence. It adds to it. When the full understanding of the timing of Christ's return arises, as it has today, during a time in which we can almost hear the hoofbeats of the four horsemen, it creates a new sense of urgency. Like the watchman on the tower, we cry, "Wake up!

---

[163] It is worth noting that, in the entire Revelation 19 passage, which is said to be the same as Jesus' coming in glory in Matt. 24:29-31, the word "glory" is conspicuously absent. And yet, the term "glory" *is* used in 1 Thess. 4:16, in reference to the rapture.

Wake up!" Far from breeding complacency, for the first time, we know what real imminence is like.[164]

Two of Everything

Like most pretrib scholars, the author of *Maranatha!* has gone to great lengths to avoid the plain meaning of the text. If Matt. 24:30–31 refers to the rapture, this puts the physical return of Christ after the sixth seal, which is unacceptable to the pretrib view. Thus, Christ's physical coming and His return at the rapture must be separated in the text. This is reminiscent of what pretrib has done with the Day of the Lord. Seeing the Day of the Lord as a single event also places the return of Christ after the opening of the sixth seal (Joel 2:31). Thus, scholars have created two days of the Lord, just as they have created two "comings in glory" (see Appendix A). Likewise, they have created two final trumpet blasts and two sets of cosmic disturbances of the sun, moon, and stars (see following arguments). It would seem that the need to create two of everything would cause these scholars to question the validity of the pretrib methodology. For some reason, it does not.

It is clear that the writers of the New Testament expected one return of the Lord Jesus, and that when He comes in the clouds, manifest in His glory, His return will have come.[165] There is only one glorious

---

[164] Although I do not agree with Matthew Henry's sometimes allegorical method of interpretation, he has an interesting insight into the language often used to describe end-times events: "It is usual in the prophetical style to speak of things great and certain as near and just at hand, only to express the greatness and certainty of them. (*Matthew Henry's Commentary in One Volume*, Zondervan Publishing House, Fourth Printing, 1964). This has implications for the doctrine of imminence. In discussing the "hour of trial," the author of *Maranatha!* makes this point, as well. He points out that, in a literal interpretation of this passage, it reads, "the one *about to come* upon all the inhabited earth." And yet, when this phrase was written, Jesus knew that the hour of trial was still at least 1,900 years hence (pp. 213-4); thus, the author points out, we know that this language is stylistic. What he does not point out, however, is that Jesus uses this same stylistic language in John 14:2-3, in which He used the present tense to describe His presence in His Father's house while He was yet still on earth. This creates a problem for the author's contention that John 14:2-3 must be read in a very rigid and literal sense.

[165] Earlier, I stated that the complete understanding of the end times was hidden from the apostles based on Daniel 12. How, then, can I use as proof that the apostles expected only one return of Christ? The doctrine of imminence is not explicitly stated in the text. The single coming of the Lord Jesus Christ, on the other hand, is an explicit, concrete teaching throughout the New Testament.

appearing of Christ. To suggest that Jesus makes this appearance twice—once to believers and once to the world—is an interpretation that is simply not warranted.

"I Will Prepare a Place" John 14:2–3

Another attempt to support the pretrib rapture is based on John 14:2–3: "In my Father's house are many mansions. If it were not so, I would have told you. I go to prepare a place for you. And if I go and prepare a place for you, I will come again and receive you to Myself; that where I am, there you may be also."

Scripture consistently refers to the relationship between the Church and the Lord Jesus Christ as being like a marriage covenant, with the Church as the Bride and Jesus as the Bridegroom. Based on this comparison, the author of *Maranatha!* looks at the timing of the rapture in comparison to the traditional Jewish marriage ceremony, which, he contends, would have been a familiar analogy to His audience.

According to Dr. Showers, the traditional Jewish wedding ceremony went like this: The bridegroom traveled to the home of the prospective bride, where he negotiated her purchase price. Once the price was paid, the two were considered to be husband and wife. As a symbol of their new covenant relationship, the bride and groom drank a cup of betrothal wine, after which the groom returned to his father's house to prepare a place for her. They remained separated for approximately 12 months. When the time came to fetch his bride, the bridegroom returned, usually at night, accompanied by male escorts in a torch-light procession. Because the bride did not know the time of the groom's coming, his arrival was proceeded by a shout, which gave her time to prepare. Once the groom arrived, the bride and her attendants returned with the procession to the groom's father's house, where the wedding guests were assembled. The couple then consummated their marriage and the wedding party spent the next seven days celebrating.[166]

The analogy to the relationship between Christ and the Church is lovely. Jesus, as the Bridegroom, pays the purchase price for His Bride with His own blood. As the traditional Jewish bride was declared to be sanctified (or set apart) after her betrothal, so, too, is the Church declared to be sanctified until Christ's return. Like the betrothal wine, Jesus gave

---

[166] There is dispute that the traditional Jewish wedding lasted seven days in any case. Gary Vaterlaus and Rev. Charles Cooper of Sola Scriptura report that despite repeated efforts, they have found no references in Jewish writings to support this analogy. Writes Vaterlaus, "In actuality, it seems that only the wealthy could afford a seven-day celebration. Most people only had a one or two-day party. Pretribulationists make it sound as if seven days were the customary length of the ceremony, when in fact this cannot be supported by historical documents."

us the communion cup. And just as the groom returned to his father's house to prepare a place for his bride, so, too, Jesus went to heaven to prepare a place for us. Now the Church, like the Jewish bride, awaits the shout. In like manner that the groom took his wife to live with him in his father's house, so, too, will Jesus take the Church to be with Him in His Father's house, where the heavenly angels and the saints will attend the marriage supper in a joyous celebration.

And here, in Dr. Showers' estimation, is the most critical aspect of the argument: Just as the bride and groom came out of hiding after seven days, so Christ and the Church will come out of hiding after the seven years of the 70th Week, when Jesus returns to earth with the Church at Armageddon. The author asks, "Which rapture view corresponds perfectly with this analogy? Only the pretrib view." In other words, only the pretribulation rapture teaches that Christ will rapture His Church to meet him in the air, where He will take her to heaven to live in His Father's house during the seven years of the "Tribulation." At the end of this time, Jesus will bring the Church with him to remain with Him on the earth throughout the Millennium.

Dr. Showers writes: "In contrast with the other rapture views, the pretribulation view corresponds fully with what has been observed in this chapter concerning Jesus' promised John 14 coming. In light of this, His promise in John 14:2–3 is a significant inference in favor of the pretribulation rapture" (p. 172).

Interpreting Parables

Because Dr. Showers interprets this as a parable, the basic rules for interpreting parables apply. According to *The New Unger's Bible Dictionary*, there are four restraints upon the interpretation of parables.

1. The analogies must be real, not arbitrary.
2. Parables are to be considered as parts of a whole and the interpretation of one is not to override or encroach upon the lessons taught by others.
3. The direct teaching of Christ presents the standard to which all interpretations are to be measured.
4. The parable may not be made the first source of doctrine. Doctrines otherwise and already grounded may be illustrated or further confirmed by them, but it is not allowable to constitute doctrine first by their aid.

The author's constructed analogy breaks all four of these rules.

First, many of the analogies are arbitrary. The author turns some aspects of this parable into a strict analogy, while rejecting others. Thus, when he makes this statement, "In contrast with the other rapture views, the pretribulation view corresponds fully with what has been observed in this chapter concerning Jesus' promised John 14 coming," what he really means is that the pretrib view is the only view that corresponds fully with *his* analogy, and of that, only with the details that support his position.

In fact, *no* rapture view corresponds perfectly with this parable. That is not the purpose of parables. If it were, Jesus would have negotiated with Satan for the purchase price of His Bride (since prior to the marriage covenant, man's father is Satan, not God), and there would be a period of waiting between the shout and the arrival of Jesus, giving the Church time to prepare. Furthermore, if the seven days of the wedding feast correspond with the seven years of the "Tribulation," then the period of separation between Jesus and the Church must also correspond to the 12 months of separation between the Jewish bride and the groom, which would have required Jesus to return for His Bride about the turn of the fourth century.[167]

There are other comparisons that could be made, but this would descend into the realm of the ridiculous. In fact, it is only one detail—the seven days of celebration—that the author attempts to turn into an exact analogy with the Second Coming. The other details are quite fuzzy, and understandably so.

Second, the strictness of this analogy creates contradictions with other parables that relate to the rapture if all are taken with equal strictness. Take, for example, the parable of the bridegroom and the wise and foolish virgins. When the bridegroom comes, it is at the *darkest* hour, not *before* the darkest hour as pretrib theology teaches. This parable also records a time period between the shout of the bridegroom and His arrival, not the "twinkling of an eye" as taught by scripture. It also records that when the foolish virgins cried out to the bridegroom, the door was shut, yet we know that many will be saved during the remainder of the 70th Week, including all of the remainder of Israel.

It is clear that this parable, like all parables, was meant to illustrate a point—preparedness—and if taken as a strict analogy in all details, the doctrine can quickly become distorted.

The third rule of interpretation is that Christ is the standard by which all of our interpretations are to be referenced. In this case, Jesus said only, "I go to prepare a place for you." The detailed analogy between the traditional Jewish marriage ceremony and the rapture, and all the implications that follow, are drawn solely by the author. Further, the direct teaching of Jesus, given to us in Matthew 24, is that His return is not prior to the 70th Week, but after the sixth seal. Instead of using

---

[167] This deduction comes from a simple math calculation. If seven days is to equal seven years (or 2,555 days), then 12 months equals 133,225 days, or 365 years. Since Jesus ascended about 33 A.D., according to this argument, this would make Jesus' return approximately 400 A.D.

Jesus' own words to interpret the parables, however, the author uses the parable to interpret Jesus. Thus, the author also breaks the fourth principle by making this parable a source of doctrine.

When we look at scripture as a whole, we see that the analogy between the rapture and the Jewish wedding ceremony is a beautiful one, but it was designed to make a general point, not to be used as a point-for-point analogy. In doing this, the author takes this comparison farther than it ought to be taken.

"Where I Am"

What about Jesus' statement, "that where I am, you may be also"? Doesn't this contradict the teaching that Jesus will rapture His Church, then remain on earth to administer His wrath? How can the Church and Jesus be together if the Church is in heaven and Jesus is on earth?

First, this suggestion begs for common sense. As I discussed in Chapter 17, when I pledged to my husband that I would be with him until our deaths, this did not mean that I would be with him physically every moment of every day. And yet, this is the conclusion that the author of *Maranatha!* requires: "Once the church meets the Lord in the air at the rapture, it will never be separated physically from Him again. From that time, wherever Christ goes, the church will go with Him" (p. 164). This creates a mental "Pied Piper" image that is at odds with the truth I read in scripture. The Bible tells us that we will rule and reign with Christ, that we will have responsibilities and jobs in heaven. How can we accomplish this if we are clumped about Him like a traveling entourage?

Second, this promise does not require an unbroken period of time. One of the most important covenants in the Bible, the Davidic covenant, is such an example. In 2 Samuel 7:16, God promised David that his kingdom would endure forever and that his seed would be on the throne for eternity. And yet, in 586 B.C., the last of the kings, Zedekiah, watched his two sons be executed, after which the kingdom of Judah followed her sister Israel into captivity. To this day, there has been no son of David on the throne of Israel. God's promise to David will not be fulfilled until Jesus returns in glory to claim His rightful throne. To require the phrase, "that where I am you may be also" to refer to an unbroken period of time is too narrow a view.

Besides, Jesus said, "Where I myself am." On this basis alone, the author justifies the assertion that the Church and Jesus *must* be together in heaven the entire time. However, Jesus made no restrictions on this phrase. He did not say, "Where I myself am during the 70th Week." The context was "for eternity." When eternity is involved, the Church will be with Christ in heaven. The author's requirement that the Church cannot be in heaven while Christ is on earth administering His judgments during the Day of the Lord is entirely too restrictive. Especially considering that

Jesus and the Father are one (John 10:30). Even if Jesus is on earth while we are with the Father, we are still with Jesus.

Lessons From the Parables

The author uses as additional evidence for the pretrib rapture the lessons taken from three famous parables: the wheat and the tares, the fisherman's dragnet, and the days of Noah. Because these parables occur in the context of Jesus' coming in glory in Matt. 24:30–31, the author re-interprets them to refer to Armageddon, not the rapture. By doing so, he gives support to the pretrib position. As he does in the previous example of the wedding feast, however, the author relies heavily upon selected details of the parables to prove his case. Therefore, the analogies he draws are false.

His line of reasoning is based on the order of events. In the parable of the wheat and the tares, the Son of Man sends His angels to "gather out of His kingdom all things that offend, and those who practice lawlessness, and will cast them into the furnace of fire" (Matt. 13:41–42). Once this judgment is accomplished, "the righteous will shine forth as the sun in the kingdom of their Father" (v. 43). Here, the wicked are judged (taken out) and the righteous are left. Because this order is reversed from the rapture, the author argues that the gathering of the wheat and the tares must take place at Armageddon, when Christ judges the earth by removing the wicked and leaving the righteous to enter the Millennium.

His second example is the fisherman's dragnet. The fishermen fill the dragnet with fish and throw it to shore, where the good fish are gathered into vessels and the bad are thrown away. "So it will be at the end of the age. The angels will come forth, separate the wicked from among the just" (Matt. 13:49). Because the wicked are separated out from among the just, the author reasons, this must refer to the judgment at Armageddon, leaving the just to enter the Millennium.

The third example is "as in the days of Noah." Once again, the author uses this to support the idea that the wicked will be removed from the earth in judgment, leaving the righteous to enter the Millennium. The flood sweeps the wicked away from the face of the earth, but leaves Noah and his family, the just.

In these parables, the message Jesus was delivering is clear—there will be a reckoning, and the wicked will be separated out for punishment while the just will be rewarded. But can the order be used to support the point the author is making? If, in all cases, the order truly were the same—the wicked are separated out from among the just—he might have a case. However, he does not.

In the parable of the wheat and the tares, the wicked are, in fact, separated out from among the just. But this is not the case with the fishermen and the dragnet. In this parable, the order is reversed.

Although Dr. Showers cites the verse, "The angels will come forth, separate the wicked from among the just," one verse earlier the parable reads, "They sat down and gathered the good into vessels, but threw the bad away." Here, the separating of the just occurs *prior to* the judgment of the wicked. If the author is using the order of events to prove his point, this is the opposite of what he intended. The fact that his argument ignores the earlier verse and focuses only on the latter reinforces the point that, if the author is going to make every detail significant, his choice of verses cannot be selective.

The same goes for the analogy to the days of Noah. The concept of separating the wicked out from among the just is not the image that is created by this analogy. Prior to the flood, God placed Noah and his family in a place of security, then lifted them high above the judgment that occurred below. It is the just who were removed, taken out of the way, before judgment fell. This would be a much better analogy for the rapture than the judgment at Armageddon. [168]

One Taken, One Left

Dr. Showers builds upon this "wicked taken from among the just" argument to re-interpret another parable, this time from Matthew 24. In this parable, two men are in the field; one will be taken and the other left; and two women are grinding at the mill, one will be taken and the other left (Matt. 24:41).

Once again, he sees this passage as the judgment at Armageddon, not the rapture. In this context, "taken" means destroyed, killed as a result of Christ's righteous judgment. This implies that, when Christ returns at Armageddon, He will not only destroy the Antichrist and the armies of the nations, but also unbelievers all over the globe. If they are walking in fields or milling grain thousands of miles away, they will be killed, leaving only the saved to enter the Millennium. Because this teaching occurs within the context of Jesus' coming in glory in Matt. 24:30–31, it is offered as further confirmation that there are two comings in glory—one prior to the 70th Week, at the rapture; and a second at the end of the 70th Week, at Armageddon.

I have three issues with this interpretation:

First, the example "one will be taken, one will be left" implies a relatively normal daily course of events. Jesus did not say, "one man cowering under a rock will be taken, one will be left; one woman hiding in the wilderness will be taken, the other left." He used normal, daily activities. If this judgment occurs at Armageddon, not after the sixth seal,

---

[168] John Walvoord also believes that the use of these parables, based on the order of events, is useless in determining the timing of the rapture. "If the order is a problem to pretribulationists, it is equally a problem to posttribulationists," *The Rapture Question*, p. 184.

these examples don't make sense. Immediately prior to Armageddon, as part of the seventh bowl, the earth will experience the greatest natural disaster it has ever seen—so great that the cities of all the nations will fall, the islands will disappear, and the mountains will "flee away":

> Then the seventh angel poured out his bowl into the air, and a loud voice came out of the temple of heaven, from the throne saying, 'It is done!' And there were noises and thunderings and lightnings; and there was a great earthquake, such a mighty and great earthquake as had not occurred since men were on the earth. Now the great city was divided into three parts, and the cities of the nations fell. And great Babylon was remembered before God, to give her the cup of the wine of the fierceness of His wrath. Then every island fled away and the mountains were not found. And great hail from heaven fell upon men, each hailstone about the weight of a talent. Men blasphemed God because of the plague of the hail, since that plague was exceedingly great. (Rev. 16:17–20)

Immediately after this, the Bible says that Jesus will descend from heaven, at which time the author suggests that one man in the field will be taken, one left, one woman grinding grain will be taken, another left. Will there be many women grinding at the mill immediately following the seventh bowl? I doubt it.

Second, Dr. Showers' interpretation requires the judgment at Armageddon to extend beyond the armies and touch the remainder of the world. This is the author's inference only. The Bible teaches that the judgment of the wicked will occur throughout the Day of the Lord, over a period of time. When Christ comes, it is for the purpose of destroying the Antichrist and the armies of the nations. If there is other judgment at this time, the Bible doesn't say. This is solely the author's inference.

Third, one of the foundational pillars of pretribulationism is that Jesus' return could occur at any moment and that no prophesied event or events must happen first. In large part, this belief comes from Jesus' warning in Matt. 24:36: "But of that day and hour no one knows, not even the angels of heaven, but My Father only." And yet, this warning is given in the context of the Matt. 24:30–31 coming, which Showers claims is Armageddon, not the rapture.

Kept From the Hour

Another evidence the author gives for the pretrib rapture is the promise given to the Church of Philadelphia that it will be "kept from the hour of trial" (Rev. 3:10). My assessment of this phrase and its meaning in relation to the timing of the rapture is given in Chapter 8. Once again, I do not agree with the author's interpretation, which relies heavily on the meaning of the Greek word used for "from," *ek*. In Dr. Showers' estimation, this means "to keep the church saints from the time or hour of testing by separating them from it." I think there is ample evidence to support a different reading: that it refers to keeping the saints safe, not from the trial, but in the midst of it.

Distinction Between Church and Israel

Another evidence the author uses for the pretrib rapture is Daniel's 70 Weeks prophecy. He bases his argument on these major points:

1. The nation of Israel and the Church are not the same.
2. The Church did not start until the 69th Week had ended.
3. God determined the 70 weeks for Israel.

Therefore...

4. Because God determined the 70 weeks for Israel, and because the Church was kept out of all 69 of the previous weeks, the Church will not be on earth for any part of the 70th Week either. For this reason, God will rapture the Church prior to Daniel's 70th Week (p. 243).

I agree with the first three major points made by Dr. Showers. However, scripture does not support the deductive leap that the Church must be kept out of all of the 70th Week. First, because this argument relies on the assumption that God uses a system of exclusivity that I do not see in the Bible. God has always had separate plans for the Jews and the Gentiles, but they have never operated independently (see my discussion on this subject in Chapter 5). While it is clear that the Church did not come into being until after the 69th Week, there is no explicit biblical reason to require the Church to be removed from the earth prior to the start of the 70th. And since God's purposes historically overlap, the use of a portion of the 70th Week to complete His plan for the Gentiles does not, in any way, preclude His use of the 70th Week to bring about His perfect plan for the nation of Israel.

This argument also ignores the fact that the Church has been grafted into the olive tree (Romans 11:17) and therefore will not be exempt from the persecution that comes upon her. It also requires the Antichrist's persecution of those who "keep the commandments of Jesus Christ" and "overcome by the blood of the Lamb" (Rev. 12:11, 17) to be against a new category of believers—"Tribulation saints" or "70th Week saints"—a complete fabrication of pretrib theologians for which there is not even a shred of scriptural support.

Where Is the Church in Revelation?

A final evidence offered in *Maranatha!* to support the pretrib rapture is the relative paucity of references to the Church in Revelation as compared to the numerous mentions of the nation of Israel. The author cites 24 references to the Church, 20 of which he attributes solely to "this church age" (p. 245). The remainder are in Revelation 19 and 20, two of which refer to the Church's return with Christ at Armageddon and two of which refer to the Church in her future state. He emphasizes that there are no references to the Church in Chapters 6 through 18.

Ironically, the author's argument is a strong case *against* a pretrib rapture and *for* a prewrath rapture. Revelation was written as an exposition on the 70th Week, so the letters to the churches in Revelation 2 and 3 must be also be in the context of the 70th Week. When Jesus tells these churches to repent and overcome, the natural question is "overcome what?" The most natural answer is the following trials and tribulations described by Jesus, which are the six seals. To suggest that these letters actually refer to "church ages," six of which are unrelated to the 70th Week, not only requires an arbitrary switch to allegory at this point, but it also ignores the context of the book. The fact that the reader must start with a normative reading, slip into an allegorical reading, then return to a normative reading without any textual indicators whatsoever ought to be a red flag for anyone evaluating this argument.

I would also disagree that the Church is not seen after Chapter 6. The Church can be seen in Chapter 7, in the multitude from all tribes, tongues, and nations. Prewrath sees the rapture taking place after the sixth seal, based on Jesus' answer to His disciples in Matthew 24. In Revelation 7, immediately after the sixth seal, we see the multitude from all tribes, tongues, and nations standing in white robes, singing, "salvation belongs to the Lamb," a perfect correlation to Paul's promise, "We are not destined for wrath but to salvation through Jesus Christ."

It is interesting that the author's discussion does not try to discredit the possibility that this could be the Church. He simply says, "The fact that the people of the great multitude of Revelation 7 were clothed in white robes and held palms in their hands does not require the conclusion that they are resurrected with literal, physical resurrection bodies" (p. 249). But it most certainly doesn't say that they aren't.

Most importantly, the fact that we do not see the Church after Chapter 7 of Revelation *is exactly what we would expect in the prewrath view*, since the rapture occurs between the sixth and seventh seals in Chapter 6.

A Question

I also have a question based on my reading of *Maranatha!* The author goes to great lengths in the beginning of the book to correlate the events in Matthew 24 with the first five seals. He correlates the wars and rumors of wars with the first and second seals, the famine and death with the third and fourth seals, and the Great Tribulation with the fifth seal. However, following these events, the text of Matthew 24 continues, "Immediately after the tribulation of those days, the sun will be darkened, and the moon will not give its light; the stars will fall from heaven, and the powers of the heavens will be shaken. Then the sign of the Son of Man will appear in heaven...." (v. 30).

Since the author correlates the earlier events of Matthew 24 with the first five seals, why does he correlate this passage, which is a nearly word-for-word description of the sixth seal, to Jesus' coming at Armageddon? Why would Jesus give so much detail on the first five seals, then jump over the sixth seal (along with the seven trumpet judgments and the seven bowls), and skip right to the end of the 70th Week? This is never addressed in *Maranatha!* And yet, if one accepts that Matt. 24:29–31 is what it appears to be—a description of the sixth seal—this would eliminate the need to go to the elaborate lengths to redefine other common sense readings of the text.

It would also avoid the need to:

• Make Jesus' coming on the clouds in power and great glory in Matt. 24:29–31 occur at Armageddon, not at the time of the sixth seal.
• Change the identity of the saints under the altar during the fifth seal into "70th Week saints," or "Tribulation saints."
• Explain away the great multitudes "from every tribe, tongue, and nation," in Chapter 7 as not being the Church.
• Redefine the multitudes in Chapter 7 who "came out of the great tribulation" as being a continual "coming out" over a period of seven years rather than the most natural reading, which is all at once (p. 250).

Common-Sense Interpretation

One of my greatest frustrations with the pretrib position is that, in order for the defense to work, events cannot be what they appear to be. Words cannot mean what they appear to mean. The common sense, natural reading of the text is not the message that God intends to convey—not just once or twice, but as a consistent pattern throughout the New Testament. The only way to create an in-depth defense of the pretrib position is to have advanced knowledge of the Greek and Hebrew lexicon that allows complex redefinitions of the text. This directly contradicts scriptures like, "You do not need that anyone teach you, but as the same anointing [of the Holy Spirit] teaches you concerning all things" (1 John 2:27); "Seek and you shall find; knock and it will be opened to you" (Matt. 7:7); and "God is not the author of confusion, but of peace" (1

315

Cor. 14:33). Not only is pretrib non-intuitive, but without an advanced degree, it is indefensible beyond the most superficial level of scripture.

Taking the most common sense reading of the scriptures, the repeated pattern throughout the New Testament is that the rapture occurs after the opening of the sixth seal and prior to the opening of the seventh. If you look at the scriptures this way, the timing of the rapture maintains the kind of elegant simplicity and consistency demanded by the Word of God. And it does this while taking the words, events, and passages in their normal, common sense meanings.

As I read through *Maranatha!* I searched for solid scriptural evidence for the pretribulation rapture. Despite the very thorough research by the author, I found none. The entire proof structure for the pretrib position is based on *reading between the lines*, on inference, supported by scholarly reinterpretations of the text.

Reassembling the Fragments

In order for the pretrib argument to work, a coherent biblical picture must be shattered into fragments and then pieced back together to fit the desired conclusion. This includes the need to...

- Interpret "the Day of the Lord" as being two separate events, rather than one, to avoid the conclusion that Jesus comes after the sixth seal.
- Interpret the coming of the Lord as being two separate events, rather than one, to avoid the conclusion that Jesus comes after the sixth seal.
- Interpret the Bible's references to the unique combination of cosmic disturbances in the sun, moon, and stars as occurring twice, rather than once, to avoid the conclusion that Jesus comes after the sixth seal.
- Interpret Jesus' coming in glory as occurring twice, rather than once, to avoid the conclusion that Jesus comes after the sixth seal.

With so much energy expended to avoid the same conclusion, could it be that the conclusion is, in fact, what the Bible teaches?

Maranatha!'s approach also requires dissecting the parables, treating some aspects as strict analogies and others as generalities. It requires readers to accept that the lesser and greater birth pangs of the Messiah, the hour of trial, the Day of the Lord, the 70th Week, the "Tribulation," and the Great Tribulation, are one and the same, covering the same time period, rather than representing different time frames and different purposes of God. In order to make these interpretations work, *Maranatha!*, in the tradition of other scholarly pretrib works, requires very technical treatments of words to be used to explain away the common sense, normative reading of passages.

In contrast, the prewrath timing allows the passages to mean just what they appear to mean. It also allows Jesus to come once, not twice; for there to be only one Day of the Lord, not two; one set of cosmic disturbances, not two; and one coming in glory, not two. The prewrath timing takes the text at face value. Although deeper word study is always profitable, it is not required. Prewrath stands on straightforward reading of scripture alone—the kind of reading that allows the timing of the rapture to be evaluated by all Spirit-led believers with a sincere desire to study out the truth.

A More Detailed Look at "Amad"

In determining the timing of the rapture, there is much controversy surrounding the phrase "And at that time Michael shall stand up, the great prince who stands watch over the sons of your people; and there shall be a time of trouble, such as never was since there was a nation, even to that same time" (Dan. 12:1). Having a correct understanding of this phrase is important because it relates directly to the controversy surrounding Paul's statement in 2 Thess. 2:6–8:

> And now you know what is restraining, that he may be revealed in his own time. For the mystery of lawlessness is already at work; only he who now restrains will do so until he is taken out of the way. And then the lawless one will be revealed....

If the restrainer is the Holy Spirit, this gives strong support to the pretrib interpretation that the Holy Spirit is removed from the earth at the rapture. Once this restraint is removed, the Antichrist is allowed to arise to power during the 70th Week. If the restrainer is not the Holy Spirit, however, one of the strongest supports for the pretrib position is eliminated. But if the restrainer is not the Holy Spirit, who is it? Most likely, it is the archangel Michael, who is identified as the historical protector of Israel. In the passage under discussion, Dan. 12:1, however, Michael, who has been contending for the nation of Israel all these years, does something unusual: he stands up. This standing up immediately precedes the Great Tribulation.

Michael "stands up." What does this mean? What significance does it have for the discussion regarding the restrainer?

Marvin Rosenthal, who heads the Jewish Messianic organization Zion's Hope and is the author of *The Pre-Wrath Rapture of the Church*, has done a thorough analysis of this issue, so it is one I will not try to duplicate. Rather, I will reproduce a portion of his article, "Daniel Chapter Twelve: A Deeper Look," from the July/August, 1999, issue of his magazine, *Zion's Fire*:

Daniel was told that at the beginning of the Great Tribulation Michael would "stand up." But what is meant by "stand up"? Major prophetic portions of scripture like 2 Thessalonians 2 and Revelation 12 and 13 are greatly impacted by the answer given. The overwhelming majority of commentators suggest that "stand up" means that Michael in "standing up" will come to Israel's defense. It is usually understood that the one against whom this defense will be made is the Antichrist, who oppresses Israel during the Great Tribulation.

A highly respected prophetic scholar, commenting on Daniel 12:1, states the view this way: "In their distress, the children of Israel are especially aided by Michael, the archangel (Jude 9). As the head of the holy angels, Michael is given the special responsibility of protecting the children of Israel. (See *Daniel: the Key to Prophetic Revelation*, by John Walvoord, p. 283.) According to this widely held view, then, to "stand up" means that Michael will come to Israel's defense while she is experiencing the Great Tribulation.

With respect for those who champion this position, I nonetheless strongly suggest that the text is teaching precisely the exact opposite. Michael does not "stand up" to help Daniel's people during the Great Tribulation. He "stands still" or "desists" from his normal role as defender of Israel, thus permitting the Great Tribulation to occur. In other words, the Great Tribulation is not the cause for Michael to come to Israel's defense. Rather, it is because he desists from defending her that the Great Tribulation occurs.

The expression "stand up" is the translation of the Hebrew word *amad*. *Amad* simply means to "stand." It does not mean to "stand up," and it does not mean to "stand still." It simply means to "stand." If a man seated and inactive were said to *amad*, he would "stand up." However, if a man already standing and active were said to *amad*, he would "stand still," or desist, in his activity.

Daniel had just been told by the angel who was sharing this prophetic vision with him that Michael was actively involved in the defense of Daniel's people. The angel said to Daniel, "But the prince [a fallen angel] of the kingdom of Persia withstood me one and twenty days: but, lo, Michael, one of

319

the chief princes, came to help me" (Dan. 10:13). Michael was actively engaged in helping Israel. And once again the angel said to Daniel, "But I will shew thee that which is noted in the scripture of truth: and there is none that holdeth with me in these things, but Michael your prince" (Dan. 10:21).

What does the word "holdeth" (Hebrew, *chazaq*) mean? According to the *Strong's Exhaustive Concordance of the Bible*, "holdeth" can mean "to bind" or "restrain." That means, in context, that the archangel Michael already had a hindering or restraining ministry against the forces of Satan on Israel's behalf. So when it is said that Michael will "stand," it means he will "stand still," "desist," or "cease" from defending Israel.

This, of course, would be in dramatic contrast to Michael's normal activity described in the words "which standeth [a present, continuous action] for the children of thy people" (Dan. 12:1). In other words, just prior to the Great Tribulation, the archangel Michael will cease or desist from what was his historically ongoing responsibility of defending Israel. It would make little sense to tell Daniel that Michael was defending his people in Chapter 12 when he had already clearly told him that fact, not once but twice, in Daniel, Chapter 10.

Rashi, one of Israel's greatest teachers, and a man whose Hebrew scholarship is unexcelled, understood "stand up" (Hebrew, *amad*) to literally mean "stand still" in Daniel 12:1. He wrote: "The Holy One [a Jewish designation for God], Blessed be He, said to Michael, 'You are silent? You do not defend my children.'"

Young's Analytical Concordance to the Bible says that *amad* means "to stand, stand still, or fast." And *Strong's Concordance* cites one of the root meanings of *amad* as "cease," and one of its definitions as "stand still." A biblical illustration of *amad* meaning "to be still" or "desist" is, "they...stood still [desisted], and answered no more" (Job 32:16).

Response to John Walvoord's
The Rapture Question

Inevitably, my challenge to the pretrib rapture will be followed by a challenge of its own: Have I read John Walvoord, who is one of the most respected scholars in this debate? This appendix is to assure potential critics that I have. For this, I have selected Walvoord's *The Rapture Question: Revised and Enlarged Edition.*[169] Because I have covered most of Walvoord's points in the text already, I will not attempt a full-blown discussion on each. Rather, I will keep my comments concise, discussing only those arguments that have not already been covered elsewhere in this book.

Walvoord takes the position that the Great Tribulation covers the entire length of the 70th Week (p. 12), placing its inception earlier than the abomination of desolation at the midpoint of this seven-year time period. I hold to the position that the Great Tribulation does not start until after the midpoint of the 70th Week, based on Matt. 24:21, and see no justification for placing it earlier. Moreover, a Great Tribulation that covers seven years, as Walvoord teaches, requires Jesus' coming in glory in Matt. 24:29–31 to coincide with Armageddon, which creates many scriptural problems covered elsewhere in this book.

On page 62, Walvoord uses what he calls "the extended treatment of the great tribulation" in Revelation 4–18 to "prove" that the Church cannot be on earth during any of that time. Considering the strong parallels between the events in the Olivet Discourse and the first six seals, however, I believe these events to be one and the same. Thus, as Jesus indicates in Matt. 24:29, the Great Tribulation ends prior to the sun turning dark, the moon turning to blood, and the stars falling from the sky—a nearly word-for-word description of the sixth seal. I see the 70th Week as a period of God's judgment, of which the Great Tribulation is a

---

[169] John Walvoord, *The Rapture Question: Revised and Enlarged Edition* (Zondervan Publishing House, 1979).

short, intense period coinciding with the fifth seal and ending prior to the sixth seal, just before the Day of the Lord.

When it comes to the identification of the restrainer in 2 Thessalonians, Walvoord takes the standard dispensationalist position that this is the Holy Spirit. I fall into the camp of those such as Marvin Rosenthal and Robert Van Kampen, who see the restrainer as Michael the Archangel (see Chapter 7, Appendix C).

Walvoord repeatedly dismisses the idea that God's wrath could start anywhere other than the seal judgments. His entire argument, with the exception of the commonly cited Rev. 6:17 ("For the great day of wrath has come; and who can stand?"), seems to be based on his judgment of the severity of the seals. I believe that a scriptural definition of God's wrath places its beginning later, as part of the Day of the Lord.

Regarding Rev. 6:17, I believe that, based on the context and the aorist tense of this verb, this statement refers to an imminent *but future* coming of wrath, not one that has already occurred. Not even pretrib proponents uniformly agree that this phrase can be used to prove the point Walvoord is trying to make. He has the same problem when he makes the sweeping statement about "kept from the hour of trial," when he writes that "translators have made clear, the thought of the Greek is to 'keep from,' not to 'keep in.'" In fact, a brief survey of various scholars shows that their opinions are quite diverse.

Is There *Really* a Pretrib Consensus?

Indeed, throughout *The Rapture Question*, Walvoord appeals to the consensus of pretrib scholars as a selling point for pretrib theology, especially in contrast to posttrib theologians, whom he categorizes as "[varying] greatly in their explanation of the exegetical and theological problems." He then refers to pretrib theology as "popular with premillenarians who have specialized in prophetic study" (pp. 18–19), as if pretrib scholars are not only more educated on the subject but their "proper" interpretation of the scriptures unites them in exegesis.

This is an argument that is made forcefully and repeatedly, but is, unfortunately, unsupported. For example, in his discussion on the identity of the restrainer, Walvoord emphatically states, "The chief proof text concerning the return of the Holy Spirit to heaven is found in 2 Thess. 2:6–8, in connection with the lawless one..." (p. 78). Several sentences later, he admits, "Expositors of all classes have had a field day in attempting to identify this restrainer." Then, one page later, he further admits that the exegesis of key words in the passage are "themselves indecisive." On page 84, he calls the identification of the 24 elders of Rev. 5:8 with the Church (an often cited proof text for the pretrib rapture) "a disputed point."

In fact, Walvoord repeatedly admits that there are a wide variety of pretrib interpretations of key passages, many of which contradict one another. These include interpretations of such foundational issues as the nature of the Day of the Lord; the start of the Day of the Lord; the length of the Great Tribulation; the definition of "to keep from the hour of trial" (Rev. 3:10); the implications of "God's wrath has come" in Rev. 6:17; the identity of the elect in Matt. 24:31; the identity of the restrainer in 2 Thess. 2:6–8; the exegesis of Luke 21:36; and even whether Christ's coming in John 14:1–3, 2 Timothy 4:1, and Titus 2:13 refer to His coming at the rapture or at Armageddon (pp. 59, 78, 79, 102, 173, 178, 212, 213). Another issue hotly debated among pretribulationists, but not mentioned by Walvoord, is whether the seals are an overview of the 70th Week or whether they are part of a consecutive series of events.

For a group of scholars that Walvoord characterizes as being in consensus due to their "correct" exegesis, these men of God are certainly at odds on the most fundamental issues regarding the 70th Week.

Reliance on Inference

I take a particularly strong stand against Walvoord's contention that the pretrib rapture, if correct, does not have to be found in direct scriptural references but can be wholly supported by the "proper use of inductive logic" (p. 14). On page 18, he calls pretribulationism "an induction based on scriptural facts rather than an explicit statement of the Bible." Ironically, in the same breath, Walvoord impresses upon the reader the practical importance of the timing of the rapture, calling it "an issue with great practical and doctrinal implications."

This begs the following question: Are we to believe that an event of such monumental importance is not directly addressed in scripture? That it must be *inferred*, and then only by academic theologians? This is one of my strongest criticisms of the pretrib rapture position. Indeed, I believe the apostle Paul would criticize such a position based on his encouragement to the Corinthians "not to think beyond what is written" (1 Cor. 4:6). Ironically, later in his book, Walvoord criticizes Marcus Dods for his "novel" interpretation of John 14:3, that Jesus comes in bodily form each time a believer dies, as "a teaching that is never found explicitly in the scriptures" (p. 72).

Issue of Imminence

I also disagree with Walvoord's contention that only the pretrib timing of the rapture is consistent with the imminent return of Christ. I agree that the pretrib rapture is consistent only with pretrib's "any moment" *definition* of imminence, but this is not the imminence we find in scripture. When Walvoord says, "If the church is destined to endure the persecutions of the Tribulation, it is futile to proclaim the coming of the Lord as an imminent hope" (p. 15), I believe he is missing one of the most important messages given to us regarding the Great Tribulation: preparedness. Repeatedly, believers are admonished to prepare, not for God's wrath, but for the fiery trials that will precede it. Unlike Walvoord,

I believe that the seals—the judgments prior to the Day of the Lord—are for the refinement of the Church.

One of the most repeated proofs for pretribulationists, including Walvoord, is that the early church fathers held strictly to the doctrine of imminence. And yet, this is one of Walvoord's many examples that disintegrate upon his own examination. On pages 51–53, he gives a sampling of early church writings that reflect a great diversity of opinions. At the end of this section, he writes, "While the teachings of the Fathers are not clear on details, some at least seem to have regarded the coming of the Lord as a matter of daily expectancy." This is a far cry from the implication that *all* church fathers held to this belief.

(For a sampling of the church fathers' own writings on this subject, in context, see Appendix F.)

Like his overstatement about the church fathers, Walvoord uses a definition of imminence that is neither accurate nor realistic. It is a narrow, academic definition derived from a specific agenda that, if correct, would discredit all but the pretrib position. This definition, however, cannot be found in scripture; in fact, scripture supports a sense of imminence far different from the "any moment" definition most pretribulationists espouse.

"Imminence," according to *Webster's Dictionary*, means only "hanging threateningly over one's head" and does not necessarily exclude the occurrence of prior events. Once I have finished my dinner and am preparing for bed, my getting up for work the next morning is imminent, yet there are certain things that must happen before I do. For a woman whose husband has been at sea for months, his return becomes imminent weeks ahead of time. And for someone diagnosed with a terminal illness, death can seem imminent even though it may be months or years away. Still, pretrib proponents, including Walvoord, redefine imminence as including an "any moment" component that is neither found in the dictionary nor in the scriptures. Unfortunately, this misdefinition has become nearly synonymous with pretrib theology.

Walvoord creates a similarly narrow definition for concepts such as "eagerly wait" or "wait patiently": "Most of the immediate significance of this hope would be lost if, as a matter of fact, the coming of Christ was impossible until the Thessalonians had passed through the tribulation period. In 1 Thess. 5:6, they are exhorted to be 'alert and self-controlled,' hardly a realistic command if the coming of Christ was greatly removed from their expectation. In 1 Cor. 1:7, Paul exhorted the Corinthians to 'eagerly wait for our Lord Jesus Christ to be revealed.'"

I disagree. People eagerly await things every day, even though they know that they will not come to pass right away. As mentioned in Chapter 6, children eagerly await summer vacations starting right after Christmas. They eagerly await events like birthdays months in advance.

Adults eagerly await events that are even further ahead, like meeting their future mate, marriage, retirement, or answers to prayer—all of which may be seen as imminent, as well. Does the fact that many things must intervene take away from their expectancy? Absolutely not. Nowhere in scripture does it say that earnest expectation requires an "any moment" rapture. In fact, when God describes to Habakkuk His plan for the end times, He says, "For the vision is yet for an appointed time; but at the end it will speak, and it will not lie. *Though it tarries, wait for it;* because it will surely come" (Hab. 2:3). Although the fulfillment of this promise is clearly in the future, Habakkuk is still told to wait.

"I Will Come Again"

Another proof text that is extremely important to Walvoord is John 14:3, "And if I go and prepare a place for you, I will come again and receive you to Myself; that where I am, there you may be also." Ironically, Walvoord uses this as a proof, not for the rapture (see Renald Showers' use of the same verse to support the opposite position in Appendix B), but for the literalness of Christ's physical and bodily return at Armageddon: "It is rather strange that the literal interpretation of this passage should be even questioned," he writes. "It is perfectly obvious that Christ's departure from earth to heaven represented in the expression 'if I go' was a literal departure. He went bodily from earth to heaven. By the same token, 'I will come back' should be taken as a literal and bodily return" (p. 70).

If Walvoord is correct that this verse refers to Christ's bodily return, this puts many other pretrib scholars who identify John 14:3 as referring to the rapture in an uncomfortable position. Walvoord's interpretation that this refers to Armageddon is therefore not only in conflict with a common sense reading of the passage, but it also undermines one of the fundamental arguments of many of his pretrib counterparts. Once again, this goes against his contention that there is a united front in this camp.

The Day of the Lord

I remain confused by Walvoord's interpretation of the Day of the Lord as comprising the Great Tribulation (p. 175). Joel 2:31 clearly states that that Day will not arrive until after the sun turns dark and the moon into blood, a clear reference to the sixth seal. If the sixth seal is *part of* the Day of the Lord, as Walvoord contends, how can the sixth seal occur *before* the Day of the Lord? Walvoord evades this issue by saying, "What is meant here is not that the day of the Lord will begin after these wonders in heaven, but that it will come to its climax when the judgment is actually executed." Why the use of the word "before" does not mean "before," he gives no explanation (p. 218).

Walvoord's chapter on the necessity of intervening events poses no conflicts with the prewrath rapture (although it does pose a problem

325

for posttribulationists) since prewrath agrees that there is an intervening time period between the removal of believers from nonbelievers and the judgment at Armageddon. Walvoord writes, "In the judgment of the Gentiles and the judgment of Israel, the mass of detail points to the fact that the separation of saved from unsaved is accomplished by a series of judgments occurring chronologically after the Second Advent," which he places at Armageddon (p. 91). I agree that the separation of the saved from the unsaved occurs after the Second Advent, but I see the Second Advent occurring after the sixth seal, with the judgment taking place during the trumpets and the bowls. Armageddon is reserved for the Antichrist, the false prophet, and the nations gathered to fight him. Further judgments require reading beyond the text.

Many of the issues raised by Walvoord contrasting the bodily translation at the rapture and the Second Coming relate to the fact that he sees the Second Advent occurring at Armageddon, not after the sixth seal. If the Second Advent and the translation occur at the same time, as prewrath contends, all of these differences disappear while still allowing for time to elapse between the translation of the saints and the judgment of the nations, which Walvoord discusses in the earlier chapter.

Israel and the Church

Walvoord also makes the assumption that making a distinction between the Church and Israel *necessarily* leads to a pretrib rapture. This assumes a degree of exclusivity in God's dealings with Israel and the gentile nations that I do not see (see Chapter 5). As I have said several times throughout this book, I believe that God's plan for the Church is different from His plan for Israel, but this does not require the Church to be taken prior to the start of the 70th Week. On page 56, Walvoord states: "One of the major factors of confusion in eschatology in the history of the church has been to confuse the program of God for Israel with the program of God for the church." I would counter that one of the major factors of confusion in eschatology in the history of pretribulationism has been to mistake God's programs for Israel and the Church as being mutually exclusive. It is a false leap of logic to assume that, just because God has different programs for Israel and the Church, this requires them to be at two entirely different times.

Walvoord also places great importance on the fact that in none of the passages dealing with the Great Tribulation is the Church clearly seen (pp. 41–45). Ironically, he undermines his own argument on page 186 when he writes, "The answer, of course, is that up to this time the rapture had not even been revealed and the subject matter did not concern itself with the rapture.... At this point in their spiritual education, the disciples would not have understood the subject of the rapture any more than they understood the subject of the death and resurrection of Christ" (p. 186). In his own statement, Walvoord takes care of two of the three explicit references to the Great Tribulation, leaving him with only one reference without specific reference to the Church, a poor basis for an argument.

The third reference is in Rev. 7:9–14 (which I have used as evidence *for* the fact that the Church will go through the Great Tribulation). This passage comprises only three verses, and since the context refers to the letters to the churches—in which many were told to repent and overcome—the fact that the Church is in view seems clear.

As part of his defense for the removal of the Church prior to the 70th Week, Walvoord makes the statement that the corporate church body can be equated with the Church of Philadelphia. He writes, "That all in the assembly are not necessarily true believers is clear from messages to the seven churches of Asia (Rev. 2–3)" (p. 22). However, as I discuss in Chapter 18, based on Jesus' praise of many of these churches for their faithfulness, patience, and good works, there is strong reason to believe that many in these assemblies *are* believers.

Not only this, but Walvoord's belief that all believers are in the Church of Philadelphia creates a false picture of the Church today. Can we really say that the *entire* Church body is sanctified, spotless, and ready to be taken to heaven? I agree with Walvoord that there is no condemnation for those in Christ Jesus, but this is a far cry from being "without blemish."

Defining "Saints" and "Elect"

Walvoord also goes to great lengths to prove that Old Testament saints are not part of the Church, a fact with which I agree. However, he takes this a step further, suggesting that because Old Testament saints are not part of the Church, the 70th Week saints cannot be part of the Church either. Again, this is a leap of logic that is not supported by the text. It *is* supported by the dispensational approach to interpretation, which is a man-made framework often used to (wrongly) interpret the biblical text. In his earlier work, *The Return of the Lord*, Walvoord writes, "One of the reasons for confusion concerning future events is the failure to analyze correctly the purpose of God in this present age. Some have come to the Bible without the proper method of interpretation."[170] In *The Rapture Question*, he makes this leap of logic in several areas, including the separation of the Jew and Gentile in the kingdom age.

Walvoord also uses the common pretrib argument that the term "elect" in Matt. 24:31 does not refer to the Church because this verse relates to Christ's coming at Armageddon. He writes, "The fact is that the church is not mentioned at all in this passage by any distinctive title such as the word church or the term body of Christ or any other term peculiarly a reference to the church" (p. 61). Why would it? Jesus had not yet died, risen, ascended, and sent His Spirit to the believers at Pentecost.

---

[170] *Return of the Lord* (Zondervan Publishing House, 1974), p. 19.

The mystery of the Church had not yet been revealed, nor had the mystery of the translation (answering Walvoord's point on p. 62). Why would Jesus use a term to describe a body of believers that had not yet been formed? And yet, these believers to whom Jesus spoke would be the same ones present at Pentecost—members of the future Church.

And what of Walvoord's point that the Church is not mentioned in Revelation after Chapter 5 (p. 37)? Why should it be, if believers are raptured at the end of Chapter 6? From this point on, Revelation describes the Day of the Lord, which is focused on Israel and the Gentile nations. It discusses some issues relating to believers, but this is not the main focus of the text. Also keep in mind that the book of Revelation was written by the Apostle John, who did not use the word "church" in the Gospel of John or in 1 and 2 John either. The absence of this term in Revelation is consistent with his other writings.

Spiritualizing the Great Tribulation

Walvoord repeatedly suggests that, in order to believe that the Church will endure the Great Tribulation, one must spiritualize it to some degree (p. 39). As one can see from the arguments presented in this book, I do not spiritualize the Great Tribulation to any degree. I also believe this is why Jesus' emphasis on preparedness was so strong. On page 50, Walvoord makes this implication again, only stronger, suggesting that only those who are amillennial or postmillennial in their interpretations— approaches that regularly spiritualize the text—could dispute the pretrib position. For premillennarians who take the scriptures literally, Walvoord implies that pretrib is the only possible option. Needless to say, I disagree.

At the conclusion of his section on the Great Tribulation, Walvoord writes, "This survey of the major portions of scripture dealing with the tribulation has served to confirm that the church is in no way involved in this time of future trouble" (p. 46). What Walvoord sees as confirmation, I see as a shaky foundation.

Undermining Foundations

Just as Walvoord makes sweeping statements that seem to support a cohesive pretrib exegesis on the surface but that dissolve upon his own examination, he regularly asks questions, such as the one above, that appear to undermine all but the pretrib position; but later sabotage his own arguments. He does this again in his discussion on Matt. 24:31, in which he attempts to prove that this is not a reference to the rapture. He writes, "The major objection to making this equivalent to the rapture is that there is no mention of either translation or resurrection, the two major features of the rapture of the gathering of all the elect" (p. 187). Yet, only one page earlier, he writes, "It is not unusual in presenting prophetic events for only select events to be included," which is followed

328

by his point that, at the time this discourse was given, the rapture had not yet been revealed.

On page 49, Walvoord, in my opinion, reasserts pretrib's shaky foundation when he writes, "The seven years of Daniel, bringing to a close the program of Israel prior to the Second Advent, will, therefore, be fulfilled between the translation of the church and the Second Advent of Christ to establish His kingdom on earth." What does Walvoord do with verses like 2 Thess 2:1, "Now brethren, concerning the coming of our Lord Jesus Christ and our gathering together to Him," in which the rapture of the Church is tied to the bodily (not spiritual) return of Christ? Or the dozens of verses such as "waiting for that blessed hope" that support, not only the imminence of His return but also His bodily return? Or the pretrib claim that there are two returns of Christ when the New Testament clearly refers to only one?

Are There Two Comings?

Walvoord handles these issues by making no systematic distinction in the terminology between the "coming" of Jesus at the rapture and His "coming" at Armageddon. They seem to be identified only by which references conflict with the pretrib position and which do not. On page 109, for example, referring to the rapture, "In the sense used in this passage, all true Christians are waiting for Christ in *His second coming.*" Then, on page 103, referring to Armageddon, "They [those who get saved after the rapture and survive during the 70th Week] will watch, for *His coming* is their only hope." On page 12, in defining the word "rapture," he notes that the scriptures predict that the Church will be raptured "*at the coming of the Lord* for them." Three sentences later, he writes that the rapture "is part of the larger truth of *a literal second coming* of the Lord Jesus Christ," referring to Armageddon. On page 70, Walvoord spends much time attempting to prove that Jesus' promise to "come again" in John 14:3 refers to His bodily return at the end of the 70th Week, at Armageddon, but on page 15, he flip-flops again: "On the other hand, if Christ will come for His church before the predicted time of trouble, Christians can regard *His coming* [at the rapture] as an imminent daily expectation."

This semantic flip-flopping is, understandably, necessary, since the scriptures use "the coming of the Lord" (including the Greek terms *parousia, apokalypsis,* and *epiphaneia)* to refer both to the rapture and Jesus' bodily return. But rather than seeing these as one and the same event, Walvoord must go to great lengths to create two comings and therefore much confusion in the process.

Poor Handling of Terminology

I find his discussion on pages 172–3, in which he addresses his handling of this terminology, particularly frustrating. He writes, "A simple concordance study will demonstrate that these are general rather than specific terms and that all three of them are used of the coming of Christ at the translation and may also refer to His coming at the Second Advent." This, despite the fact that a plain reading of the text tells us that there is only one coming, hence "*the* coming of the Lord," and "*the* Second Advent." Is this the same man who, on page 113, complains that posttribulationists "ignore plain teaching [of the text]"?

Walvoord follows by citing various uses of the term *parousia*, including the coming of Stephanas, Fortunatus, and Achaicus (1 Cor. 16:17), the coming of Titus (2 Cor. 7:6), the coming of Paul (Phil. 1:26), and the coming of the day of God (2 Peter 3:12). His point is that just because they use the term *parousia* does not mean that they are the same event—hence, the coming of Christ at the rapture and His coming at Armageddon could be different events. What Walvoord ignores is that, in each instance, although *parousia* is used to describe the coming of different people, each use looks forward to a *singular* event—one coming of Paul, one coming of Stephanas, one coming of Titus. Each of these events was a clearly identifiable occurrence. I believe Walvoord's argument does much to disprove, rather than prove, his point. Not only this, but he goes so far as to try to prove that all three terms used of the coming of the Lord—*parousia, apokalypsis*, and *epiphaneia*—are used of both the rapture and the Second Advent. Rather than see these as one and the same event, he prefers to divide them into two separate events.

I think of the character of Paul, who wrote many of the epistles in which these terms appear. Paul was a very detail-oriented writer who often went to great lengths to alleviate misconceptions and explain fine points of theology. In 1 Corinthians 14, he spent an entire chapter on the proper use of tongues, which he called *the least* of the gifts, simply because it was being misused. If there were really two comings of Christ, two bodily appearances, wouldn't Paul have said so? Wouldn't there be some clear reference in the text? Why would Paul have used the same three words to describe both the return of Christ at the rapture and the return of Christ at Armageddon, without textual indicators, unless they were not the same event? It is true that, in the Old Testament, the prophets did not make a distinction between the First and Second comings of Christ, the Suffering Servant and the Lion of Judah. However, the Old Testament contained many mysteries. The New Testament is a place for mysteries to be revealed.

On page 173, Walvoord adds to this confusion by piling the word "glorious" onto his list of interchangeable terms related to the Second Coming: "In Titus 2:13 the expression 'the glorious appearing' has been taken to refer to the coming of Christ to establish His kingdom because of the reference to the word glorious. However, the church will see the glory of Christ at the coming of the Lord for His church before the

Tribulation, and there is no valid reason the term glorious appearing should not be a reference to the rapture."

I agree. Therefore, I must ask this question: If Jesus' glorious [*doxa*] appearing in Titus 2:13 refers to the rapture, why is Christ's glorious [*doxa*] appearing in Matt. 24:30 *not* a reference to the rapture? Walvoord has already argued that the various Greek terms used for the coming of Christ can refer both to the rapture and to Armageddon. Thus, if context is used to determine which is which, wouldn't the combination of this phrase with the term "glory" or "glorious"—which Walvoord has just tied to the rapture—be proof that these are the same event? Why is one "glorious appearing" the rapture and another "glorious appearing" Armageddon?

In Conclusion

Pretrib rapturists could go to great lengths to explain away each of the questions I have raised. Or they could concede that the rapture and the Second Coming occur at the same time, after the opening of the sixth seal. This would allow all of the verses to fit together harmoniously in the plain reading of the text.

Ironically, in Walvoord's discussions of other rapture theories, such as partial rapturism and posttribulationism, he criticizes these proponents for the very thing that he, himself, is doing. For example, he criticizes Dods for proposing a reading "that is never found explicitly in the scriptures" (p. 72—compare this to his own justification of pretrib theology based on "inductive logic"); and chastises partial rapturists for the fact that this theology can only be found by "reading into the passage a preconceived doctrine" (p. 108). Again, on page 113, he complains that "these proponents ignore plain teaching [of the text]." Ironically, he holds up his belief in a pretrib translation as "a natural and literal interpretation" (p. 87).

I believe that Walvoord, like the many pretrib scholars who ardently defend this doctrine, is a sincere man of God who desires to bring to light the truth of God's Word. However, I believe it is possible to get too close to any subject and not see the forest for the trees. If many of these scholars could stand back from their arguments and view the forest, I believe that they might be surprised at what they see.

The pretrib argument is not a unified front, nor is it the plain meaning of the scriptures. It is an attempt, passage by passage, scripture by scripture, to defend a doctrine that cannot be naturally found; and the end result is a fragmented patchwork that does not hold together well. Prewrath, on the other hand, is tightly woven, with each passage fitting perfectly and consistently into the whole. Nowhere does it need to "be harmonized," as Walvoord frequently requires for the pretrib theology, but it is the natural and expected reading in every context.

331

Appendix E

Do *Parousia, Apocalypse, Epiphany* Require
Different Comings?

One of the arguments made by pretribulationists to support a two-stage return of Christ is that the variety of words used in the New Testament to describe Christ's return indicate that there are actually two separate comings: a spiritual coming at the rapture and a bodily coming at Armageddon. Dr. Oswald T. Allis, an acknowledged authority in the field of linguistics, has given the following analysis of these terms, showing that the distinctions made by pretribulationists are not tenable:

> (a) "Coming" (*parousia*) is used by Paul 14 times, eight of which refer to the coming of Christ. 1 Thessalonians 4:15, which speaks of the catching up of believers, clearly refers to the rapture; likewise 2 Thess. 2:1, which speaks of our "gathering together with Him." On the other hand, 1 Thess. 3:13 speaks of the "coming of our Lord Jesus with all his saints." If "saints" means or includes the Church, as all dispensationalists believe, this verse speaks quite as plainly of the appearing. In 2 Thess. 2:8, which clearly refers to the appearing, since it speaks of the slaying of Antichrist, the expression used is "the manifestation" (or "brightness," *epiphany*) of His "coming" (*parousia*).

> Consequently, we must recognize that Paul uses "coming" both of the rapture and of the appearing and even combines the two expressions in 2 Thess. 2:8 to describe what is apparently one and the same event.

> (b) "Revelation" (*apocalypse*) is used 13 times by Paul. In 1 Cor. 1:7, it is used of the rapture. It is what the Christian waits for. In 2 Thess. 1:7, the reference is as plainly to the appearing, the coming in glory.

332

(c) "Appearing" (*epiphany*). This word is used only by Paul. In 1 Tim. 6:14, the reference to the rapture seems unmistakable. In 2 Tim. 4:1, 8, the allusions to judgment, as in Titus 2:13 to glory, favor the reference to the appearing.

Paul uses all three words and he uses them ambiguously. Particularly clear is the fact that he uses *parousia* both of the rapture and of the appearing.... How is this to be explained, if he had been told by the Lord that there was an important difference between these two events?

The question which confronts us is this: If the distinction between the rapture and the appearing is of as great a moment as dispensationalists assert, how are we to explain Paul's failure to distinguish clearly between them? And the failure of other writers, Peter, James, and John, to do the same? Paul was a logician. He was able to draw sharp distinctions. If he had wanted, or regarded it important, to distinguish between these events, he could have done so very easily. Why did he use language which dispensationalists must admit to be confusing?

Feinberg recently made the following surprising statement regarding the three words we have been discussing: "We conclude, then, that from a study of the Greek words themselves the distinction between the coming of the Lord for His saints and with His saints is not to be gleaned" (*Premillennialism or Amillennialism?*, p. 207). Such an admission raises the question whether the distinction itself is valid. If the distinction is of importance, Paul's ambiguous language is — [if] we may say it reverently — inexcusable.

If the distinction is negligible, accuracy of statement would be quite unnecessary. We conclude, therefore, that the language of the New Testament and especially of Paul not merely fails to prove the distinction insisted on by dispensationalists but rather by its very ambiguity indicates clearly and unmistakably that no such distinction exists.[171]

---

[171] Oswald T. Allis, *Prophecy and the Church* (Presbyterian and Reformed Publishing Company, 1945), pp. 181–185.

Appendix F

What the Church Fathers Taught About the Church and the Coming of the Antichrist

by Gary Vaterlaus

Many claims have been made by pretribulationists that the early Church believed that Christ would come before the events of the 70th Week of Daniel begin — that is, before the period commonly called "the Tribulation." Dwight D. Pentecost in his book *Things to Come* uses selected quotes from some of the early church fathers to try to show that they believed in the imminent return of Christ (pp. 168-169). More recently, Grant R. Jeffrey in his book *Apocalypse: The Coming Judgement of the Nations* devotes the entire Appendix to references to early church writings, some which he claims show that they held to an "any moment," imminent coming of the Lord.

I believe that we should let the Church fathers speak for themselves. Below are lengthy quotes from 12 documents of the early Church fathers from the first four centuries showing that they believed that the Church would be present on the earth during the Great Tribulation of the Antichrist. From a review of the early Church writings, I would have to agree with Robert Gundry's conclusion that "...the early Church did *not* hold to the doctrine of imminence. The very passages cited for imminence [by the pretribulationists] reveal a belief that the Church will pass through the tribulation" (Robert Gundry, *The Church and the Tribulation*, p. 179). In fact, in this same book, Gundry shows convincingly that the pretribulation theory of the rapture was not known nor widely held until the mid-nineteenth century (pp. 185-188).

Our sole rule for faith and practice must be scripture. The teachings of the early Church do not "prove" that pretribulationism is incorrect; only scripture can do that (and it does). However, as Robert Gundry states, "...the antiquity of a view weighs in its favor, especially when that antiquity reaches back to the apostolic age. For those who received their doctrine first-hand from the apostles and from those who heard them stood in a better position to judge what was apostolic doctrine

334

than we who are many centuries removed" (*The Church and the Tribulation*, p. 172).

The prewrath rapture position has its roots in historical premillennialism, the belief that the Church will be persecuted by the Antichrist, delivered at Christ's coming, and then God's wrath will be poured out on the wicked who remain. As can be seen from the quotes below, this is precisely what the early Church fathers wrote:[172]

It therefore behooves us, who inquire much concerning events at hand, to search diligently into those things which are able to save us. Let us then utterly flee from all the works of iniquity, lest these should take hold of us; and let us hate the error of the present time, that we may set our love on the world to come: let us not give loose reins to our soul, that it should have power to run with sinners and the wicked, lest we become like them. The final stumbling block (or source of danger) approaches.... We take earnest heed in these last days; for the whole [past] time of your faith will profit you nothing, unless now in this wicked time we also withstand coming sources of danger, as becometh the sons of God. That the Black One may find no means of entrance, let us flee from every vanity, let us utterly hate the works of the way of wickedness. Take heed, lest resting at our ease, as those who are the called [of God], we should fall asleep in our sins, and the wicked prince, acquiring power over us, should thrust us away from the kingdom of the Lord.

—*The Epistle of Barnabas* [100-120 AD]

Watch for your life's sake. Let not your lamps be quenched, nor your loins unloosed; but be ye ready, for ye know not the hour in which our Lord cometh. But often shall ye come together, seeking the things which are befitting to your souls: for the whole time of your faith will not profit you, if ye be not made perfect in the last time. For in the last days false prophets and corrupters shall be multiplied, and the sheep shall be turned into wolves, and love shall be turned into hate; for when lawlessness increaseth, they shall hate and persecute and betray one another, and then shall appear the world-deceiver as Son of God, and shall do signs and wonders, and the earth shall be delivered into his hands, and he shall do iniquitous things which have never yet come to pass since the beginning. Then shall the creation of men come into the fire of trial, and many shall be made to stumble and shall perish; but they that endure in their faith shall be saved from under the curse itself. And then shall appear the signs of the truth; first, the sign of an out-spreading in heaven; then the sign of the sound of the trumpet; and the third, the

---

[172] All quotes taken from *The Ante-Nicene Fathers*, edited by A. Roberts and J. Donaldson, Master Christian Library CD, Ages Software (c) 1999.

resurrection of the dead; yet not of all, but as it is said: The Lord shall come and all His saints with Him. Then shall the world see the Lord coming upon the clouds of heaven.

—*The Didache (The Teaching of the Twelve Apostles)* [100-120 AD]

O unreasoning men! understanding not what has been proved by all these passages, that two advents of Christ have been announced: the one, in which He is set forth as suffering, inglorious, dishonored, and crucified; but the other, in which He shall come from heaven with glory, when the man of apostasy, who speaks strange things against the Most High, shall venture to do unlawful deeds on the earth against us the Christians, who, having learned the true worship of God from the law, and the word which went forth from Jerusalem by means of the apostles of Jesus, have fled for safety to the God of Jacob and God of Israel....

—Justin Martyr, *Dialogue with Trypho* [150-165 AD]

Those, therefore, who continue steadfast, and are put through the fire, will be purified by means of it. For as gold casts away its dross, so also will ye cast away all sadness and straitness, and will be made pure so as to fit into the building of the tower. But the white part is the age that is to come, in which the elect of God will dwell, since those elected by God to eternal life will be spotless and pure. Wherefore cease not speaking these things into the ears of the saints. This then is the type of the great tribulation that is to come.

—*The Pastor of Hermas* [160 AD]

Who are the ravening wolves but those deceitful senses and spirits which are lurking within to waste the flock of Christ? Who are the false prophets but deceptive predictors of the future? Who are the false apostles but the preachers of a spurious gospel? Who also are the Antichrists, both now and evermore, but the men who rebel against Christ? Heresies, at the present time, will no less rend the church by their perversion of doctrine, than will Antichrist persecute her at that day by the cruelty of his attacks, except that persecution makes even martyrs, [but] heresy only apostates.

—Tertullian, *The Prescription Against Heretics* [190-210 AD]

And therefore throughout all time, man, having been molded at the beginning by the hands of God, that is, of the Son and of the Spirit, is made after the image and likeness of God: the chaff, indeed, which is the apostasy, being cast away; but the wheat, that is, those who bring forth fruit to God in faith, being gathered into the barn. And for this cause tribulation is necessary for those who are saved, that having been after a manner broken up, and rendered fine, and sprinkled over by the patience of the Word of God, and set on fire [for purification], they may be fitted for the royal banquet. As a certain man of ours said, when he was condemned to the wild beasts because of his testimony with respect to God: "I am the wheat of Christ, and am ground by the teeth of the wild beasts, that I may be found the pure bread of God." Moreover, another danger, by no means trifling, shall overtake those who falsely presume that they know the name of Antichrist. For if these men assume one [number], when this [Antichrist] shall come having another, they will be easily led away by him, as supposing him not to be the expected one, who must be guarded against.... It is therefore more certain, and less hazardous, to await the fulfillment of the prophecy, than to be making surmises, and casting about for any names that may present themselves, inasmuch as many names can be found possessing the number mentioned; and the same question will, after all, remain unsolved.... But he indicates the number of the name now, that when this man comes we may avoid him, being aware who he is.

— Ireneaus, *Against Heresies* (Book 5) [182-188 AD]

✤ Being questioned by His disciples when those things were to come to pass which He had just been uttering about the destruction of the temple, He discourses to them first of the order of Jewish events until the overthrow of Jerusalem, and then of such as concerned all nations up to the very end of the world. For after He had declared that "Jerusalem was to be trodden down of the Gentiles, until the times of the Gentiles should be fulfilled"—meaning, of course, those which were to be chosen of God, and gathered in with the remnant of Israel—He then goes on to proclaim, against this world and dispensation (even as Joel had done, and Daniel, and all the prophets with one consent), that "there should be signs in the sun, and in the moon, and in the stars, distress of nations with perplexity, the sea and the waves roaring, men's hearts failing them for fear, and for looking after those things which are coming on the earth." "For," says He, "the powers of heaven shall be shaken; and then shall they see the Son of man coming in the clouds, with power and great glory. And when these things begin to come to pass, then look up, and lift up your heads, for your redemption draweth nigh." He spake of its "drawing nigh," not of its being present already; and of "those things beginning to come to pass," not of their having happened: because when they have come to pass, then our redemption shall be at hand, which is said to be approaching up to that time, raising and exciting our minds to what is then the proximate harvest of our hope.

He immediately annexes a parable of this in "the trees which are tenderly sprouting into a flower-stalk, and then developing the flower, which is the precursor of the fruit." "So likewise ye," (He adds), "when

337

ye shall see all these things come to pass, know ye that the kingdom of heaven is nigh at hand. Watch ye, therefore, and pray always, that ye may be accounted worthy to escape all those things, and to stand before the Son of man;" that is, no doubt, at the resurrection, after all these things have been previously transacted. Therefore, although there is a sprouting in the acknowledgment of all this mystery, yet it is only in the actual presence of the Lord that the flower is developed and the fruit borne. Who is it then, that has aroused the Lord, now at God's right hand, so unseasonably and with such severity to "shake terribly" (as Isaiah expresses it ("that earth," which, I suppose, is as yet unshattered? Who has thus early put "Christ's enemies beneath His feet" (to use the language of David), making Him more hurried than the Father, whilst every crowd in our popular assemblies is still with shouts consigning "the Christians to the lions?" Who has yet beheld Jesus descending from heaven in like manner as the apostles saw Him ascend, according to the appointment of the two angels? Up to the present moment they have not, tribe by tribe, smitten their breasts, looking on Him whom they pierced. No one has as yet fallen in with Elias; no one has as yet escaped from Antichrist....

In the Revelation of John, again, the order of these times is spread out to view, which "the souls of the martyrs" are taught to wait for beneath the altar, whilst they earnestly pray to be avenged and judged: (taught, I say, to wait) ... and that the beast Antichrist with his false prophet may wage war on the Church of God ... Since, then, the Scriptures both indicate the stages of the last times, and concentrate the harvest of the Christian hope in the very end of the world....

—Tertullian, *On the Resurrection of the Flesh* [190-210 AD]

Wherefore we ought neither to give it out as if this were certainly his [Antichrist's] name, nor again ignore the fact that he may not be otherwise designated. But having the mystery of God in our heart, we ought in fear to keep faithfully what has been told us by the blessed prophets, in order that when those things come to pass, we may be prepared for them, and not deceived. For when the times advance, he too, of whom these thing are said, will be manifested....

Now, concerning the tribulation of the persecution which is to fall upon the Church from the adversary, John also speaks thus: "And I saw a great and wondrous sign in heaven; a woman clothed with the sun, and the moon under her feet, and upon her head a crown of twelve stars... And the dragon was wroth with the woman, and went to make war with the saints of her seed, which keep the commandments of God, and have the testimony of Jesus."

"...And to the woman were given two wings of the great eagle, that she might fly into the wilderness, where she is nourished for a time, and times, and half a time, from the face of the serpent." That refers to the one thousand two hundred and threescore days (the half of the week) during which the tyrant is to reign and persecute the Church....

These things, then, I have set shortly before thee, O Theophilus, drawing them from Scripture itself, in order that, maintaining in faith what is written, and anticipating the things that are to be, thou mayest keep thyself void of offense both toward God and toward men, "looking for that blessed hope and appearing of our God and Savior," when, having raised the saints among us, He will rejoice with them, glorifying the Father. To Him be the glory unto the endless ages of the ages. Amen.

—Hyppolytus, *On Christ and Antichrist* [220 AD]

After this, then, what remains, beloved, but the toes of the feet of the image, in which "part shall be of iron and part of clay mixed together?" By the toes of the feet he meant, mystically, the ten kings that rise out of that kingdom. As Daniel says, "I considered the beast; and, lo, [there were] ten horns behind, among which shall come up another little horn springing from them;" by which none other is meant than the Antichrist that is to rise; and he shall set up the kingdom of Judah. And in saying that "three horns" were "plucked up by the roots" by this one, he indicates the three kings of Egypt, Libya, and Ethiopia, whom this one will slay in the array of war. And when he has conquered all, he will prove himself a terrible and savage tyrant, and will cause tribulation and persecution to the saints, exalting himself against them....

When the times are fulfilled, and the ten horns spring from the beast in the last [times], then Antichrist will appear among them. When he makes war against the saints, and persecutes them, then may we expect the manifestation of the Lord from heaven.

—Hyppolytus, *On Daniel* [220 AD]

Notwithstanding, not even then will the merciful and benignant God leave the race of men without all comfort; but He will shorten even those days and the period of three years and a half, and He will curtail those times on account of the remnant of those who hide themselves in the mountains and caves, that the phalanx of all those saints fail not utterly. But these days shall run their course rapidly; and the kingdom of the deceiver and Antichrist shall be speedily removed. And then, in fine, in the glance of an eye shall the fashion of this world pass away, and the power of men shall be brought to nought, and all these visible things shall be destroyed....

As these things, therefore, of which we have spoken before are in the future, beloved, when the one week is divided into parts, and the abomination of desolation has arisen then, and the forerunners of the Lord have finished their proper course, and the whole world, in fine, comes to the consummation, what remains but the manifestation of our Lord and Savior Jesus Christ, the Son of God, from heaven, for whom we have hoped; who shall bring forth fire and all just judgment against those who have refused to believe in Him?

—Hyppolytus, *Elucidation* [220 AD]

For as, by the condescension of the Lord instructing me, I am very often instigated and warned, I ought to bring unto your conscience also the anxiety of my warning. For you ought to know and to believe, and hold it for certain, that the day of affliction has begun to hang over our heads, and the end of the world and the time of Antichrist to draw near, so that we must all stand prepared for the battle; nor consider anything but the glory of life eternal, and the crown of the confession of the Lord; and not regard those things which are coming as being such as were those which have passed away. A severer and a fiercer fight is now threatening, for which the soldiers of Christ ought to prepare themselves with uncorrupted faith and robust courage, considering that they drink the cup of Christ's blood daily, for the reason that they themselves also may be able to shed their blood for Christ....

Nor let any one of you, beloved brethren, be so terrified by the fear of future persecution, or the coming of the threatening Antichrist, as not to be found armed for all things by the evangelical exhortations and precepts, and by the heavenly warnings. Antichrist is coming, but above him comes Christ also. The enemy goeth about and rageth, but immediately the Lord follows to avenge our sufferings and our wounds. The adversary is enraged and threatens, but there is One who can deliver us from his hands. He is to be feared whose anger no one can escape, as He Himself forewarns, and says: "Fear not them which kill the body, but are not able to kill the soul; but rather fear Him which is able to destroy both body and soul in hell." And again: "He that loveth his life, shall lose it; and he that hateth his life in this world, shall keep it unto life eternal." And in the Apocalypse He instructs and forewarns, saying, "If any man worship the beast and his image, and receive his mark in his forehead or in his hand, the same also shall drink of the wine of the wrath of God, mixed in the cup of His indignation, and he shall be tormented with fire and brimstone in the presence of the holy angels, and in the presence of the Lamb; and the smoke of their torments shall ascend up for ever and ever; and they shall have no rest day nor night, who worship the beast and his image."

—Cyprian, *Epistle 55 of Cyprian* [252 AD]

The Apostle also himself says, "Let no one deceive you by any means, for that day shall not come except there come a falling away first, and that man of sin be revealed, the Son of Perdition, who opposeth and

340

exalteth himself above everything that is called God, or that is worshipped, so that he sitteth in the temple of God, shewing himself as though himself were God." And soon afterwards, "Then shall that wicked one be revealed, whom the Lord Jesus shall slay with the breath of His mouth, and shall destroy with the brightness of His coming: whose coming is after the working of Satan with all power and signs and lying wonders." And again, shortly afterwards, "And therefore the Lord shall send unto them strong delusion, that they may believe a lie, that all may be judged who have not believed the truth."' For this reason, therefore, is this "delusion" foretold unto us by the words of Prophets, Evangelists, and Apostles, lest any one should mistake the coming of Antichrist for the coming of Christ. But as the Lord Himself says, "When they shall say unto you, lo, here is Christ, or lo, He is there, believe it not. For many false Christs and false prophets shall come and shall seduce many." But let us see how He hath pointed out the judgment of the true Christ: "As the lightning shineth from the east unto the west, so shall the coming of the Son of Man be."

— Rufinus, *A Commentary on the Apostle's Creed* [307-309 AD]

The little season signifies three years and six months, in which with all his power the devil will avenge himself trader Antichrist against the Church.

— Victorinus, *Commentary On Apocalypse* [300-400AD]

Oh! my dearly beloved, if we shall gain comfort from afflictions, if rest from labors, if health after sickness, if from death immortality, it is not right to be distressed by the temporal ills that lay hold on mankind. It does not become us to be agitated because of the trials which befall us. It is not right to fear if the gang that contended with Christ, should conspire against godliness; but we should the more please God through these things, and should consider such matters as the probation and exercise of a virtuous life. For how shall patience be looked for, if there be not previously labors and sorrows? Or how can fortitude be tested with no assault from enemies? Or how shall magnanimity be exhibited, unless after contumely and injustice? Or how can long-suffering be proved, unless there has first been the calumny of Antichrist? And, finally, how can a man behold virtue with his eyes, unless the iniquity of the very wicked has previously appeared?

— Athanasius, Festal Letters, Letter 10 [338 AD]

The things then which are seen shall pass away, and there shall come the things which are looked for, things fairer than the present; but as to the time let no one be curious. For it is not for you, He says, to know times or seasons, which the Father hath put in His own power. And venture not thou to declare when these things shall be, nor on the other hand supinely slumber. For he saith, Watch, for in such an hour as ye expect not the Son of Man cometh. But since it was needful for us to know the signs of the end, and since we are looking for Christ, therefore, that we may not die deceived and be led astray by that false Antichrist, the Apostles, moved by the divine will, address themselves by a providential arrangement to the True Teacher, and say, Tell us, when shall these things be, and what shall be the sign of Thy coming, and of the end of the world? We look for Thee to come again, but Satan transforms himself into an Angel of light; put us therefore on our guard, that we may not worship another instead of Thee.... Look therefore to thyself, O man, and make safe thy soul. The Church now charges thee before the Living God; she declares to thee the things concerning Antichrist before they arrive. Whether they will happen in thy time we know not, or whether they will happen after thee we know not; but it is well that, knowing these things, thou shouldest make thyself secure beforehand. The true Christ, the Only-begotten Son of God, comes no more from the earth. If any come making false shows in the wilderness, go not forth; if they say, Lo, here is the Christ, Lo, there, believe it not. Look no longer downwards and to the earth; for the Lord descends from heaven; not alone as before, but with many, escorted by tens of thousands of Angels; nor secretly as the dew on the fleece; but shining forth openly as the lightning. For He hath said Himself, As the lightning cometh out of the east, and shineth even unto the west, so shall also the coming of the Son of Man be; and again, And they shall see the Son of Man coming upon the clouds with power and great glory, and He shall send forth His Angels with a great trumpet; and the rest.... But this aforesaid Antichrist is to come.... At first indeed he will put on a show of mildness (as though he were a learned and discreet person), and of soberness and benevolence: and by the lying signs and wonders of his magical deceit a having beguiled the Jews, as though he were the expected Christ, he shall afterwards be characterized by all kinds of crimes of inhumanity and lawlessness, so as to outdo all unrighteous and ungodly men who have gone before him displaying against all men, but especially against us Christians, a spirit murderous and most cruel, merciless and crafty....

For this cause the Lord knowing the greatness of the adversary grants indulgence to the godly, saying, 'Then let them which be in Judaea flee to the mountains.' But if any man is conscious that he is very stout-hearted, to encounter Satan, let him stand (for I do not despair of the Church's nerves), and let him say, Who shall separate us from the love of Christ and the rest? But, let those of us who are fearful provide for our own safety; and those who are of a good courage, stand fast: for then shall be great tribulation, such as hath not been from the beginning of the world until now, no, nor ever shall be. But thanks be to God who hath confined the greatness of that tribulation to a few days; for He says, But for the elect's sake those days shall be shortened....

But as in the persecutions which happen from time to time, so also then God will permit these things, not because He wants power to hinder them, but because according to His wont He will through patience crown His own champions like as He did His Prophets and Apostles; to the end that having toiled for a little while they may inherit the eternal kingdom of heaven.... Guard thyself then, O man; thou hast the signs of Antichrist; and remember them not only thyself, but impart them also freely to all. If thou hast a child according to the flesh, admonish him of this now; if thou hast begotten one through catechizing, put him also on his guard, lest he receive the false one as the True. For the mystery of iniquity doth already work. I fear these wars of the nations; I fear the schisms of the Churches; I fear the mutual hatred of the brethren. But enough on this subject; only God forbid that it should be fulfilled in our days; nevertheless, let us be on our guard...

And may the God of the whole world keep you all in safety, bearing in mind the signs of the end, and remaining unsubdued by Antichrist. Thou hast received the tokens of the Deceiver who is to come; thou hast received the proofs of the true Christ, who shall openly come down from heaven. Flee therefore the one, the False one; and look for the other, the True.

—Saint Cyril, Archbishop of Jerusalem, Lecture 15 [326 AD]

About the Author

H. L. Nigro was born in Springfield, OH, in 1967, earned a Bachelor of Science degree from the University of Michigan, Ann Arbor, and has worked as a professional writer, researcher and analyst, and book and magazine editor for 15 years.

She currently runs an independent writing and editing business, and, as an evangelical Christian, serves as an active witness for the gospel of Jesus Christ by using her business as a ministry to reach those who might not otherwise hear the gospel.

In addition to her years as a professional author and editor, Nigro runs Strong Tower Publishing, which publishes niche books for the Christian marketplace. Her own titles include *Before God's Wrath: The Bible's Answer to the Timing of the Rapture, The Everyday Evangelist,* and *Do You Really Want to Self-Publish Your Book?* Other Strong Tower Publishing titles include the prewrath primer *Who Will Be Left Behind and When?*, by Dave Bussard, and an upcoming reprint of the classic *The Hope of Christ's Second Coming*, by Samuel Tregelles, a critique of the budding pretribulation rapture view, first published in 1863.

Since 2001, Nigro has been the co-moderator of the Yahoo! Prewrath Only discussion group on the Internet devoted to Christ-centered discussion of the prewrath view.

Nigro lives in Bellefonte, PA, with her husband, Tom, and her daughter, Megan, and is a worship leader in her local congregation.

QUICK ORDER FORM

Before God's Wrath: Revised and Expanded Edition
by H. L. Nigro

A detailed look at the rapture of the Church from a
prewrath perspective and an analysis of the prewrath rapture in
comparison to pretribulational rapture view.

348 pages. $14.00.

 # Copies _____
Total Merchandise: $ _____
UPS Shipping ($5.50 for one book, $7.50 for 2–5 books; contact
Strong Tower Publishing for shipping on larger orders):
$ _____
Total Order $ _____

Please send check or money order to:

Strong Tower Publishing
P.O. Box 973
Milesburg, PA 16853

For credit card orders:

Strong Tower Publishing will accept credit card orders through
PayPal. Send payment to: strongtowerpubs@aol.com.

Pricing good through 2004.
For updated shipping and pricing information, visit our Web site at
www.strongtowerpublishing.com.

CPSIA information can be obtained at www.ICGtesting.com
Printed in the USA
LVOW080746120412

277308LV00001B/104/A

9 780970 433077